Inequality a

Inequality and Poverty Re-Examined

edited by
Stephen P. Jenkins and John Micklewright

OXFORD
UNIVERSITY PRESS

OXFORD
UNIVERSITY PRESS

Great Clarendon Street, Oxford OX2 6DP

Oxford University Press is a department of the University of Oxford.
It furthers the University's objective of excellence in research, scholarship, and education by publishing worldwide in

Oxford New York

Auckland Cape Town Dar es Salaam Hong Kong Karachi
Kuala Lumpur Madrid Melbourne Mexico City Nairobi
New Delhi Shanghai Taipei Toronto

With offices in

Argentina Austria Brazil Chile Czech Republic France Greece
Guatemala Hungary Italy Japan Poland Portugal Singapore
South Korea Switzerland Thailand Turkey Ukraine Vietnam

Published in the United States
by Oxford University Press Inc., New York

First published 2007

British Library Cataloguing in Publication Data

Data available

Library of Congress Cataloging in Publication Data

Data available

Typeset by SPI Publisher Services, Pondicherry, India
Printed in Great Britain
on acid-free paper by
Biddles Ltd., King's Lynn, Norfolk

ISBN 978–0–19–921811–0 (Hbk.) 978–0–19–921812–7 (Pbk.)

1 3 5 7 9 10 8 6 4 2

To Tony Atkinson

Contents

Part III Public Policy

List of Figures

List of Tables

Acknowledgements

The idea for this book first arose during a walk on the Apennine hills approximately five years ago. Turning our scheme into reality required the assistance of a number of people and institutions. First, we thank the contributors, whose whole-hearted commitment to the project made the editors' job substantially easier. Sarah Caro and her colleagues at Oxford University Press were enthusiastic supporters of the book from the time we initially approached them. In addition to their work on the book's production, the Press generously contributed to the costs of holding a workshop at Nuffield College, Oxford, in September 2006, at which the chapters were presented. Nuffield College is thanked for its warm hospitality, for helping to arrange the workshop, and for its financial support of the event. We thank Tina Gericke and Lucinda Platt for their forbearance throughout the preparation of the volume. Last, and above all, we thank Tony Atkinson, whose work has inspired several generations of researchers, including all of the contributors to this project. We dedicate the book to him.

Stephen P. Jenkins
John Micklewright
December 2006

Notes on the contributors

Steve Bazen is a Professor of Economics at the Université de Savoie, Annecy-le-Vieux, France, and a member of the Low Wage Employment Research Network (LoWER). His research focuses on the impact of minimum wages in a number of countries and on factors that influence the distribution of earnings.

Alison L. Booth is a Professor of Economics at the University of Essex, UK, and at the Australian National University. She is a Research Associate of the Institute for Social and Economic Research, University of Essex, and Research Fellow of the Centre for Economic Policy Research, London, and of IZA, Bonn. She is also a Fellow of the Royal Society of Arts, and of the Academy of Social Sciences in Australia, and is currently President of the European Association of Labour Economists.

Andrea Brandolini is Deputy Director of the Real Economy Division of the Economic Research Department of the Bank of Italy, Rome. He is a member of the Italian Commission of Inquiry into Social Exclusion. His current research focuses on long-run changes in income inequality and wealth distribution from a comparative perspective. He is co-director of the Luxembourg Wealth Study, a project that is constructing a cross-national database on household wealth.

Mark L. Bryan is a Chief Research Officer at the Institute for Social and Economic Research, University of Essex, UK. His research interests include the economics of training, the dynamics of low-paid labour markets and applied microeconometrics. Recent work focuses on the determinants of working hours, paid holiday entitlements and variation in the gender pay gap over the wage distribution.

Peter Burton is a Professor in the Department of Economics, Dalhousie University, Halifax, Canada. His research interests are in applied microeconomic theory, natural resource and environmental economics, and the economics of the family.

Lorenzo Cappellari is an Associate Professor in the Istituto di Economia dell'Impresa e del Lavoro, Università Cattolica di Milano, Italy, and a Research Associate of the Institute for Social and Economic Research, University of Essex, UK. His research interests are in the field of empirical labour economics, in particular earnings and income dynamics, labour market transitions, job satisfaction, education and training, and applied microeconometrics.

Jean-Yves Duclos is Professor in the Département d'économique and Director of the Centre interuniversitaire sur le risque, les politiques économiques et l'emploi (CIRPÉE), Université Laval, Québec, Canada. His current research focuses on public and distributive analysis as well as on the use of statistical techniques to assess poverty and equity.

Ann Harding is Director of the National Centre for Social and Economic Modelling and Professor of Applied Economics and Social Policy at the University of Canberra, Australia. She is currently President of the International Microsimulation Association and her key research interests lie in using microsimulation models to provide policymakers with reliable estimates of the distributional impacts of proposed policy changes.

Stephen P. Jenkins is Professor of Economics and Director of the Institute for Social and Economic Research, University of Essex, UK, Chair of the Council of the International Association for Research on Income and Wealth, Research Professor of DIW Berlin, and Research Fellow of IZA, Bonn. His current research focuses on income dynamics, labour market transitions, and survival analysis.

Horacio Levy is a Research Affiliate at the European Centre for Social Welfare Policy and Research, Vienna, Austria, and formerly a Senior Research Officer at the Institute for Social and Economic Research, University of Essex. His current research interests are the development and application of microsimulation methods to analyse and evaluate the effects of social and fiscal policies in developed and developing countries.

Christine Lietz is a researcher at the Institute for Advanced Studies (IHS), Vienna, Austria. She also works as part of the team that develops and uses EUROMOD, the multi-country Europe-wide tax-benefit model. Her current research interests focus on building and using tax-benefit microsimulation models and distributional effects of taxes and social policies.

Rachel Lloyd works at The Australian Treasury. When this research was conducted, she was a Principal Research Fellow at the National Centre for Social and Economic Modelling at the University of Canberra, where she undertook a wide range of projects including modelling the tax and social security system, regional modelling and research into poverty and the socio-economic factors affecting the use of information technology.

John Micklewright is Professor of Social Statistics in the School of Social Sciences and Southampton Statistical Sciences Research Institute, University of Southampton, UK. He is a Research Fellow of the Centre for Economic Policy Research, London, and of IZA, Bonn. His current research focuses on labour market flows, education, and charitable donations.

Brian Nolan is Professor of Public Policy in the School of Applied Social Science, University College Dublin, Ireland. He has published widely on income inequality, poverty, public economics, social policy, health economics and health inequalities.

Shelley Phipps is at Dalhousie University, Halifax, Canada, where she holds the Maxwell Chair in Economics and is a Fellow of the Canadian Institute for Advanced Research. Her current research interests include the economic vulnerability of Canadian families with children in terms of time as well as money, and the implications of child disability for parental health and labour market participation.

Martin Ravallion is Senior Research Manager in the World Bank, Washington DC. His main research interests are poverty in developing countries and policies for fighting it. He has published extensively on these topics, as well as advising numerous governments and international agencies. He serves on the editorial boards of several economics journals and is a Senior Fellow of the Bureau for Research in Economic Analysis of Development.

David Sahn is a professor of economics at Cornell University. He has published widely on issues of poverty, inequality, education, and health, and he also devoted considerable effort to capacity building in Africa, particularly through his years of collaboration with the African Economic Research Consortium. His recent publications include work on risk behaviours for HIV/AIDS, the determinants of cognitive achievement, and methods for analysing the multiple dimensions of inequality and poverty.

Sylke V. Schnepf is a Research Fellow in the Southampton Statistical Sciences Research Institute, University of Southampton, UK. She is a Research Fellow of the HWWI, Hamburg, and of IZA, Bonn. Her main research interests are educational achievement and inequalities, social segregation in schools, gender inequality in Central and Eastern Europe, and charitable donations.

Bernd Süssmuth is an Assistant Professor of Economics at the Technische Universität München, Germany. He is also a Faculty Member at Munich Intellectual Property Law Center at the Max Planck Institute for Intellectual Property, Competition and Tax Law. His current research focuses on fiscal and monetary policy and the distribution of income and wealth. He also has research interests in the economics of education.

Holly Sutherland is a Research Professor in the Institute for Social and Economic Research, University of Essex, UK, and a Research Professor of DIW Berlin. She coordinates research and other activities related to EUROMOD, the EU-wide tax-benefit model. Her main research interests are in developing microsimulation as a tool for international comparative research, the gender effects of re-distribution policies, and child poverty measurement and analysis.

Neil Warren is a Professor of Taxation and Head of School at the Australian School of Taxation, University of New South Wales, Sydney. His current research focuses on tax gap, tax reform and fiscal federalism issues.

Robert K. von Weizsäcker is Professor of Economics, Finance, and Industrial Organization at the Technische Universität München, Germany, a member of the Munich Intellectual Property Law Center at the Max Planck Institute for Intellectual Property, Competition and Tax Law, Research Fellow of the Centre for Economic Policy Research, London, the Ifo-Institute, Munich, and the IZA, Bonn. He has published widely in the fields of public finance, corporate finance, population economics, the economics of education and industrial organization.

Christopher T. Whelan is a Research Professor at Economic and Social Research Institute, Dublin, Ireland, and Chairperson of the Governing Council of the EU EQUALSOC network. His current research interests include the causes and consequences of poverty and inequality, measurement and monitoring of poverty and social exclusion, cumulative disadvantage and vicious circle processes and social mobility and inequality of opportunity.

Frances Woolley is a Professor in the Department of Economics, Carleton University, Ottawa, Canada, and Secretary-Treasurer of the Canadian Economics Association. Her research focuses on household decision-making and public policy towards families. She serves on the editorial boards of several journals.

Stephen D. Younger is Associate Director of the Cornell Food and Nutrition Policy Program at Cornell University, Ithaca, USA, and Adjunct Professor of Economics at the Facultad Latinoamericana de Ciencias Sociales in Quito, Ecuador. His current research concerns public policy and poverty in developing countries, particularly Africa.

Introduction

1

New directions in the analysis of inequality and poverty

*Stephen P. Jenkins and John Micklewright**

Over the last four decades, academic and wider public interest in inequality and poverty has grown substantially. This book aims to contribute to debates about the analysis of inequality and poverty and to provide new empirical evidence from around the world. Papers written by an international cast list of authors form the remaining twelve chapters. An overview of these chapters follows in the second part of this Introduction. First, however, we place them in a wider context, relating them to previous research, by addressing the question: what have been the major new directions in the analysis of inequality and poverty over the last thirty to forty years?

This time period coincides with a marked upsurge in interest in income distribution and related topics. If we go back thirty to forty years, a number of landmark publications about the personal income distribution had recently become available. *The Economics of Inequality* by Tony Atkinson appeared in 1975, a comprehensive and wide-ranging textbook on the subject of the title, referring to the 'relative neglect of the distribution of income and wealth' in mainstream economics (1975: 1). Many of the same topics were also covered by Jan Pen's (1971, 1974) engaging monograph on *Income Distribution* directed at students, fellow economists and the general public. Amartya Sen's conceptual tour de force *On Economic Inequality* was published in 1973. Harold Lydall (1968) combined data on more than 500 distributions of earnings covering 36 countries from 1890 onwards with a review of theories to explain the wage structures observed.

Much of the evidence about the income distribution that existed in the 1960s and 1970s was based upon statistics published by national statistical offices or similar agencies. Distributions were typically summarized in terms of the numbers of workers, persons or households falling within various earnings,

* We thank Tony Atkinson, Andrea Brandolini, Mark Bryan, Brian Nolan, and Lucinda Platt for their comments on an earlier draft of this chapter.

income, or (less frequently) wealth ranges, or the shares of the same held by different quantile groups. A diversity of summary indices was employed, the most common of which was the Gini coefficient, and the extent of poverty was typically summarized in terms of the proportion of a population that was poor. The inadequacies of data were commonly remarked upon, though there were also major initiatives to improve the nature of evidence. In Britain, to take one example, these were led by the 1975–79 Royal Commission on the Distribution of Income and Wealth.

This was a period when it was perceived that the income distribution was not changing much in Britain. The Royal Commission's seventh report stated that 'if the decline in the share of the top 1 per cent is ignored, the shape of the distribution is not greatly different in 1976–77 from what it was in 1949. . . . The income distribution shows a remarkable stability from year to year' (1979: 17). International comparative studies involving many countries were uncommon, with the studies by Sawyer (1976) and Stark (1977) relatively rare exceptions. The studies cited, and virtually all income distribution research and official statistics, were based on cross-sectional evidence, but some new evidence on income dynamics was beginning to emerge from the recently established (1968) US Panel Study of Income Dynamics: see for example Morgan *et al.* (1974).

Models of the distribution of earnings, income and wealth took various forms. There was a long tradition of modelling based on stochastic processes that aimed to explain the distinctive skewed shape of empirical income distributions (for example Champernowne 1973). Another approach was regression modelling, especially of labour earnings, drawing on human capital theory developed by Mincer (1974) and others. The use of multivariate regression models to decompose differences in average earnings between population sub-groups, and hence assess the extent of discrimination, was pioneered by Blinder (1973) and Oaxaca (1973), and followed pioneering theoretical work on the same topic by Becker (1971). There were a number of contributions that had sought to provide a fully fledged theory for the distribution of income, such as the classic paper by Stiglitz (1969) extending the Solow growth model, and the analysis by Meade (1964). See also Conlisk's (1969) three-equation recursive model. In addition, there was a growing literature on the impact on the income distribution of macroeconomic phenomena such as unemployment and inflation, represented by for example Metcalf (1969), Thurow (1970), and Blinder and Esaki (1978).

How then has the analysis of inequality and poverty changed in recent decades? We draw attention to developments under seven headings: changes in the extent of inequality and poverty, changes in the policy environment, increased scrutiny of the concepts of 'poverty' and inequality' and the rise of multidimensional approaches, the use of longitudinal perspectives, an increase in availability of and access to data, developments in analytical methods of measurement, and developments in modelling.

1.1 New directions and developments

Changes in inequality and poverty

Analysis has changed because the context has changed. The picture of inequality and poverty in different parts of the world is not the same as it was in the 1970s. There were notable changes in the shape of the income distribution in many, but not all, western developed nations. By contrast with the Royal Commission's description of stability cited earlier, a second major inquiry into the income distribution, reporting in 1995, stated that

> inequality in the UK grew rapidly between 1977 and 1990, reaching a higher level than recorded since the war. ... [T]he pace at which inequality increased in the UK was faster than in any other [country], with the exception of New Zealand. (Barclay, 1995: 6)

Atkinson also drew attention to the 'unparalleled rise in United Kingdom income inequality during the 1980s' (1997: 300), but took pains to stress that the rise was better described as a series of distinct episodes than a single secular trend and, moreover, that the particular British pattern of change was not shared by most other OECD countries. Atkinson's (2003*a*) study of the experience of nine OECD countries (Canada, the UK and the USA, Italy, the Netherlands, West Germany, Norway, Finland and Sweden) pointed not only to major changes in income distribution (with the exception of Canada), but also a great heterogeneity in the patterns and timing of change. Changes in real income levels were also heterogeneous across countries, though a notable feature of the US and UK experience was that the real income of the poorest groups remained almost unchanged over the 1980s; virtually all the income growth was experienced by middle-income and especially the richest groups (Danziger and Gottschalk 1995, Fig. 3.3; Jenkins 2000*a*, Fig. 3). In both the USA and UK, absolute poverty rates rose in the early 1980s, and then levelled off or fell (Danziger and Gottschalk 1995, Fig. 3.8; Jenkins 2000*a*, Fig. 5).[1]

Much of the responsibility for the distributional changes in household income in the UK and the USA during the 1980s has been attributed to widening dispersion in the distribution of wages, and it is this distribution—or, rather, the wage distribution for men—that has received by far the greatest attention from economists. The predominant explanations refer to increases in the relative demand for higher-skilled workers arising because of either skill-biased technological change or globalization. However, as the survey by Katz and Autor (1999) points out, the relative importance of these factors compared to labour supply or institutions is likely to look different when considered from a longer-term perspective. Katz and Autor also point to the heterogeneity of experience across

[1] The US estimates are based on the official US poverty line. The UK estimates cited use a low income cut-off of 60% of median 1991 income.

OECD countries: 'patterns of changes ... in overall wage inequality are much more divergent in the 1980s and 1990s than in the 1970s' (1999: 1502).

Atkinson (2003*b*) also reminds us of the 'several steps between relative factor prices ... and the distribution of disposable income among households' (2003*b*: 23), an argument developed in Atkinson (2003*c*). Household income depends on all income sources, not only wages, and the incomes of all household members, and the taxes paid and social transfers received. Atkinson (2003*a*) points to the impact of a rise in the net rate of return on capital, especially among those at the top of the distribution. There have been notable disequalizing changes in the distribution of self-employment income in Britain (Jenkins 1995). Johnson and Webb (1993) draw attention to the disequalizing impact of the cuts in UK income taxes during the 1980s. Daly and Valletta (2006) find that the rising inequality in US family income between 1969 and 1989 was driven most by the changes in the distribution of men's earnings, but the rising proportion of lone parent families also had a significant disequalizing impact. (The increasing female labour force participation rate had an offsetting impact.) These patterns contrast with Britain, where family structure changes had little impact on the rise in inequality over the 1980s (Jenkins 1995).

The end of communism in Eastern Europe and Central Asia has been accompanied by large increases in the dispersion of earnings and household income. This is particularly true in former Soviet republics. Inequality in per capita household income in Russia was well above the top of the OECD range by the mid-1990s (Flemming and Micklewright 2000: 903). When taken with the sharp falls in mean incomes in the early 1990s, again especially in the former Soviet Union, the result has been substantial rises in levels of absolute poverty (see, for example, Milanovic 1998).

Distributional changes in industrialized countries over the last few decades have occurred alongside widespread poverty and some marked changes in income inequality in developing nations. Chen and Ravallion's (2000) authoritative World Bank study found that, in 1998, 24 per cent of the population of the developing world were living on less than $1 per day, some four percentage points lower than 1987. Over this period, the total number of people who were poor according to this criterion changed little, about 1.2 billion. The authors emphasize that these global numbers hide differences in experiences across countries and regions and within subperiods. For example, growing affluence in China during the mid-1990s reduced the number of $1-a-day-poor people substantially, despite large increases in income inequality. (There is now a large literature on income distribution in China: see for example the survey in Benjamin *et al.* 2005.) In regions such as Latin America, there was no clear trend in the poverty rate. Chen and Ravallion suggest that there were

> two proximate causes of the low overall rate of poverty reduction in the 1990s, despite aggregate economic growth in the developing world. Firstly, too little of that economic

growth was in the poorest countries. Secondly, persistent inequalities (in both income and non-income dimensions) within those countries and elsewhere prevented the poor from participating fully in the growth that did occur. (2000: 21)

Given the disparities in income between rich and poor countries, it is no surprise that the degree of inequality in the world as a whole is very substantial, with a Gini coefficient of between about 0.63 and 0.68 in the 1990s (Milanovic 2006: 14), almost twice the figure for Britain. These estimates relate to the 'world distribution', that is the distribution of income among all people in the world, taking account of the differences both within as well as between countries. The literature on this subject has grown considerably. However, there is little consensus about the trend in the world distribution between the 1980s and 1990s. Milanovic's own estimates point to a small increase between 1988 and 1993, followed by a small decline in the next five years, and then another small increase between 1998 and 2002 (2006: 15). Sala-i-Martín (2006) concluded that global inequality fell during the 1980s and 1990s, though Dowrick and Akmal (2005) obtained divergent trends using different indices of purchasing power parities. For an analysis of changes over the very long term (1820–1992), see Bourguignon and Morrisson (1992).

Changes in the policy environment

A second and related development over the last few decades has been major changes in the policy environment in both industrialized and developing countries.

In the OECD countries, the 1990s saw national policy initiatives such as the UK Labour Government's pledge to eradicate child poverty and the Irish National Anti-Poverty Strategy, to take just two examples. The story has not necessarily been one of a steady growth in concern for distributional equity. In the case of the UK, the Conservative government that took power in 1979 abruptly discontinued the Royal Commission referred to earlier and pursued policies that contributed to widening the distribution of income. Similar changes, one way and then the other, can be seen in other countries, notably the USA. Policy shifts may be one of the causes of the episodic changes in income inequality noted by Atkinson (1997).

In Europe, the expansion of the European Union (EU) has had a major influence on concepts, statistics, and social monitoring, all of which have had direct or indirect effects on policy. The concept of poverty has been defined in terms of social exclusion, and encompasses more than conventional income-based measures of poverty and inequality (of which more later). The 2001 Laeken Council adopted a set of indicators to monitor progress in reducing social exclusion (see Atkinson, Cantillon *et al.* 2002 for details and discussion). The Statistical Office of the European Communities ('Eurostat') has also had a powerful influence on analysis by its adoption of particular practices, for example adjusting incomes for differences in needs using the 'modified OECD' equivalence scale and using 60 per cent of national median income as the principal low-income cut-off.[2] There have also been major coordinated data initiatives, for example the European Community Household Panel (ECHP) for 15 EU countries, and its replacement, the Statistics on Income and Living Conditions (EU-SILC) covering the EU-25.

There have also been global initiatives. The UN's Millennium Development Goals, endorsed by 189 countries at the 2000 Millennium Summit, include the aim to 'reduce by half the proportion of people living on less than a dollar a day' by 2015. The national Poverty Reduction Strategies fostered by the World Bank are tools to further this aim in developing countries.

The World Bank has a major influence on the policy environment in developing countries. The Bank's stance on distributional issues over the last three decades has changed notably. As with national governments, the changes have not always been in one direction. Jolly (2005) cites Karpur, Lewis, and Webb (1997) as recording Robert McNamara's persistent highlighting of income and wealth disparities in the early 1970s when he was World Bank President—and the Bank's subsequent shift in emphasis away from concern with inequality towards a concern for absolute poverty. The *World Development Report 1990: Poverty* marked the Bank's commitment to the goal of poverty reduction. But, perhaps inevitably, this in turn has led in time to more interest in inequality as one driver of poverty. As a result, the *World Development Report 2006: Equity and Development* is another landmark. The emphasis is on equality of opportunity (starting at birth) rather than on inequalities in outcomes in terms of income or consumption.[3] The former is viewed as unambiguously bad (or at least something to be reduced), in contrast to the latter. That emphasis, with its concern for education, health, gender, race and other determinants of economic outcomes, reflects in part the issues discussed under our next heading.

Scrutiny of 'inequality' and 'poverty' and the rise of multidimensional approaches

The concepts of inequality and poverty have themselves come under scrutiny. Dissatisfaction has been expressed with conventional approaches to inequality and poverty, and this has led to multidimensional approaches to measurement, in both rich and poor countries alike. In part, these developments reflect the

[2] Britain, for instance, is changing the equivalence scale used to produce its official income distribution series (*Households Below Average Income*) from the 'McClements' scale to the 'modified OECD' scale. And it has switched from using 50% of mean income to 60% of median income as the main low income cut-off.

[3] The Report draws intellectual inspiration from work of John Roemer and others. Roemer (2006) offers a critique of the logical consistency of goals expounded in the Report, while supporting enthusiastically its general thrust.

view that poverty is not only about not having enough money, and that inequality is not just about differences in money income.

In the European context in particular—and, interestingly, largely only in Europe rather than elsewhere in the OECD—there has been much discussion of 'social exclusion'.[4] Related to this, and building on Townsend's (1979) pioneering work, there has been a growing body of research that has examined poverty in terms of lack of access to a number of goods or services, rather than a lack of income *per se*. This has led to social monitoring based on summaries of a collection of indicators rather than simply income.

Multidimensional approaches have also been prompted by the fundamental reconsideration of the concepts of poverty and inequality that was stimulated by the work of Nobel Prizewinner, Amartya Sen. In short, a person's ability to participate in society and to live a decent life (to be nourished, healthy, etc.) is summarized in terms of a number of key 'functionings', and poverty is conceptualized as a lack of various capabilities to achieve these functionings. In Sen's words,

> Concern with positive freedoms leads directly to valuing people's capabilities and instrumentally to valuing things that enhance these capabilities. The notion of capabilities relates closely to the functioning of a person. This has to be contrasted with the ownership of goods, the characteristics of the goods owned, and the utilities generated. (Sen 1984: 324)

A thoughtful assessment of the operational content of this approach is provided by Brandolini and D'Alessio (1998). The UNDP Human Development Index, first published in 1990, is perhaps the most well-known measure that follows the spirit of Sen's approach. It combines indicators of longevity (measured by life expectancy at birth), knowledge (a weighted average of the adult literacy rate and school enrolment rates), and living standards (GDP per capita converted to US$ using PPPs). A recent development of this type of index is the Index of Economic Well-Being (Osberg and Sharpe 2005) that takes into account assessments of consumption, accumulation, distribution and security.

More fundamentally, an approach based on capabilities and functionings may also be viewed as a move away from the individual-based welfarist approach that has underpinned most of the measurement literature to date. That is, conventionally the welfare of individuals is related to their income (or consumption), and social welfare is assumed to be the sum of those individual welfares. Implicitly or explicitly, there is some money-metric utility function employed that maps the income (or expenditure) of an individual to his or her well-being. Atkinson has distinguished one approach to poverty measurement as being concerned with an 'individual's right to a minimum level of resources' rather than 'standards

[4] Micklewright (2002) discusses the possible penetration of the social exclusion concept in the USA.

of living' (Atkinson 1989: 7), and has also suggested that meeting those rights may imply a concern about particular income sources. Similarly, although most welfare measures for an individual are based on the total income of the household or family within which that individual lives, a rights-based approach would emphasize the importance of knowing about the within-household distribution of that income (Jenkins 1991). The rights-based approach might also be used to interpret the US Census Bureau decision in 1980 to eliminate any distinction between male- and female-headed households (of the same size and composition) when defining poverty thresholds—such differences had been criticized as contrary to sex discrimination legislation (Fisher 1997).[5]

Multidimensional approaches to distributional issues draw on non-monetary measures. Each of these measures has also come to be used extensively in its own right, with researchers employing a unidimensional perspective but applying the analytical methods typically applied to a monetary measure of well-being. There is a large literature in health economics examining equity issues built on borrowings of this kind: see *inter alia* Kakwani, Wagstaff, and van Doorslaer (1997) and Allison and Foster (2004). The measurement of the prevalence of literacy has also benefited from the approach in economics to inequality and poverty measurement: see for example Basu and Foster (1998).

There has also been continuing interest in measures of economic resources that complement the conventional money income measures. We refer, for instance, to studies of the distributional impacts of non-cash benefits of education and health services provided by governments in addition to cash benefits (for example Smeeding *et al.* 1993). One issue in the former communist economies in transition is how changes in non-cash benefits have altered the picture obtained from cash incomes alone (Flemming and Micklewright 2000: 905–9). Similarly, the accumulation of wealth, and other assets more generally, have recently started to receive growing attention alongside income. One factor has been the increases in investment income experienced by the very rich. Another has been the various initiatives around the world to try and increase the accumulation of financial resources for retirement. We return to analyses of the distribution of wealth below.

Even where it is agreed to use some monetary measure of resources to measure economic well-being, there remains disagreement about whether resources should be measured in terms of consumption expenditure or income. As an illustration of continuing differences in approach, we note the European Union emphasis on income rather than expenditure among financial indicators of poverty. This may be justified on a minimum rights basis (Atkinson, Cantillon *et al.* 2002: 82–3). By contrast, most analysis of developing countries emphasizes the attraction of consumption expenditure, on the grounds that it is consumption rather than income that is the argument that

[5] We owe this example to Tony Atkinson.

enters the individual's utility function according to the conventional welfarist approach. Consumption expenditure is also less affected by transitory variation than income (Ravallion 1994: 15). Deaton states that 'all the difficulties of measuring consumption [in developing countries] ... apply with greater force to the measurement of income, and a host of additional issues arise' (1997: 29). The problems of income measurement in poorer countries are an issue for EU-SILC, given the inclusion in the database of Accession countries where there is significant agricultural production for home consumption.

Longitudinal as well as cross-sectional perspectives

Forty years ago, most perspectives on the income distribution were derived from cross-sectional data—whether a series of snapshots over time for a particular country or snapshots for a number of countries. But today this approach has been supplemented in a major way by longitudinal perspectives. (This reflects the growing availability of panel data on incomes: see below.) There is now much more information not only about how many people are poor at a given time, but also about how long individuals remain poor, and about the repetition of poverty spells.

Taking a longitudinal perspective has also become an essential ingredient in policy formulation and leads to different anti-poverty strategies. See the case made by Ellwood (1998) or the statements by the UK's HM Treasury (1999). In the USA, the longitudinal perspective led to a diverse set of programmes designed to help get welfare benefit recipients (mostly lone mothers) into jobs; it also led to the introduction of time limits on welfare benefit receipt. The dynamic perspective has been embraced elsewhere too. The 'New Deal' policies for the unemployed and lone parents introduced in the UK by the Labour government are an example of this change in focus. The official UK publication on income distribution, *Households Below Average Income* (Department for Work and Pensions 2006), now includes a chapter on income dynamics. International comparisons of income and poverty dynamics in industrialized countries have begun to appear: see for example Duncan *et al.* (1993), Bradbury, Jenkins, and Micklewright (2001) and Valletta (2006). Analyses of dynamics in developing countries have also started to be carried out: see the reviews by Baulch and Hoddinott (2000) and Fields (2001).

As for cross-sectional analysis of inequality, a good part of the work on dynamics has tended to be focused on men's earnings (although the references above are all to analyses of household income or consumption). Lillard and Willis's (1978) paper estimating the permanent and transitory components of earnings variability was an important early contribution. Atkinson, Bourguignon, and Morrisson (1992) survey some of the subsequent literature.

Interest in the longitudinal perspective has also extended to the association in incomes between parents and their children. In the extensive programme of research on 'transmitted deprivation' sponsored by the UK Economic and Social Research Council in the late-1970s and early 1980s, there was only one study of the inheritance of income (Atkinson, Maynard, and Trinder 1983). Even in the mid-1980s, the number of empirical studies cited by Becker and Tomes's (1986) influential study was fewer than ten. By the end of the 1990s, however, the number of studies in industrialized countries had expanded tremendously, illustrated for example by the collection of papers in Corak (2004).

Increases in the quantity and quality of data

A further development since the early 1970s, and one that underpins the developments cited so far, concerns data. The quantity and quality of data to analyse distributional issues have both increased substantially. So too has researchers' access to unit-record data on earnings, incomes and wealth. For example, in Britain in the 1970s, researchers had no access to the main income survey, the Family Expenditure Survey (FES), having to rely on grouped data from published reports. Today, researchers can download unit-record data from every FES for over thirty years within minutes. At the same time, historical series of tabulated data have been uncovered and used to shed much more light on long-term trends. Examples are the work on the income of the very rich across the twentieth century carried out by Atkinson and Piketty (2007) and colleagues for a range of industrialized countries, and the analysis of earnings and household incomes in the communist period in Eastern Europe by, for example, Atkinson and Micklewright (1992).

In the 1970s, cross-national comparisons of income distribution required skilful manipulation of the scanty and often non-comparable data available for a limited number of countries. Nowadays, there are the data contained in the Luxembourg Income Study (LIS, http://www.lisproject.org). Founded in 1983, the LIS currently encompasses unit-record data on income from more than 30 industrialized countries, and from up to five time points for each country over three decades. From each national survey, the LIS project produces a dataset containing a common set of harmonized and standard variables on incomes and related concepts. It provided the data used in major international comparative studies of income distribution such as Atkinson, Rainwater, and Smeeding (1995), and Gottschalk and Smeeding (1997). LIS project developments are discussed by Smeeding (2004) and Atkinson (2004).

The availability of data on wealth has lagged well behind that on household incomes, with consequent effects on the empirical analysis of wealth distributions. The new Luxembourg Wealth Study, modelled on the LIS, therefore represents an important advance. The project brings together data for an initial nine countries (Sierminska, Brandolini, and Smeeding 2006).

The growth in data availability has also occurred in the developing world, notably through the World Bank's sponsorship of Living Standards

Measurement Surveys (LSMS). These have been carried out in over 40 countries since 1980. Much of the LSMS microdata can be downloaded from the Bank's website (http://www.worldbank.org/lsms) and tabulated summaries from these and other surveys together with software to analyse them are also available (http://iresearch.worldbank.org/povcalnet). The LSMS surveys are described in Angus Deaton's (1997) book, *The Analysis of Household Surveys*, an influential guide to research on distributional issues in developing countries. Mention should also be made of the Demographic and Health Surveys (DHS), which have been carried out in more than 70 developing countries since the mid-1980s with funding from USAID. As with the LSMS, DHS microdata are readily available through the internet (http://www.measuredhs.com). Although the surveys typically do not contain information about income or earnings, important work on distributional issues has been done with the data by constructing indices of household physical assets in the form of durable goods and housing amenities (Filmer and Pritchett 1999; Montgomery *et al.* 2000).

The physical assets data in the DHS represent one form of wealth measurement in developing countries. There are also household survey data on financial assets, and these have been collected in the three most populous countries, China, India and Indonesia. Financial asset data, from survey and other sources, for both developing and industrialized countries, have been used by Davies *et al.* (2006) to estimate the world distribution of wealth, thereby complementing the estimates for the world distribution of income referred to earlier.

Besides the greater availability of microdata, compendia of summary statistics of income inequality (typically Gini coefficients and quantile shares) for a range of countries and time periods have been produced and made available by a number of authors and organizations. These 'secondary' datasets include the World Income Inequality Database (WIID) database at UNU-WIDER (http://www.wider.unu.edu/wiid/wiid.htm), which builds on an earlier World Bank initiative (Deininger and Squire 1996). The country panel data provided by these summary statistics have been heavily used in analyses of the relationship between inequality and growth (see below). However, there are significant issues of quality and comparability that arise in the construction and use of the data, as Atkinson and Brandolini (2001) have demonstrated with data on OECD countries in the Deininger-Squire dataset.

That caveat made, we need to recognize major initiatives aimed at improving the quality of data on income distribution. Just as there is a long-standing development of a consistent conceptual framework for the measurement of macro-economic activity in market economies (the System of National Accounts, sponsored by the United Nations), there have been developments directed specifically at income and expenditure surveys. An important role has been played by organizations such as the LIS, the World Bank, and Eurostat, together with the group of international experts known as the Canberra Group: see, for example, Canberra Group (2001).

Studies of income dynamics have also been facilitated by the increase in the number of household panel surveys around the world. Since the advent of the PSID, there have been panel studies started in Sweden, the Netherlands, Germany, Britain, Russia and, more recently Australia and New Zealand, as well as the EU-wide ECHP referred to earlier. Several of the LSMS datasets on developing countries have panel elements. There have also been initiatives providing cross-nationally harmonized data such as the Cross National Equivalent File which covers the USA, Canada, Germany, and Britain (Burkhauser *et al.* 2001).

Developments in analytical methods of measurement

Atkinson's (1970) paper 'On the measurement of inequality' was a pioneer of what became two major developments in analytical approaches to measurement. First, Atkinson, and also Kolm (1969), drew attention to the relationship between the non-intersection of Lorenz curves and clear cut orderings of income distributions according to complete classes of social evaluation functions. This is an example of the stochastic dominance approach to analysis of income distributions that is now ubiquitous, and that has been developed in many directions. The second major contribution of Atkinson's (1970) paper was to characterize a particular class of inequality indices, now known as the Atkinson family. This assumed that the increasing concave social welfare function took a particular parametric functional form, with the key parameter representing how income differences in different ranges of the income distribution were treated (the degree of 'inequality aversion'). The key message was that the choice of a summary inequality index was not innocuous, but incorporated a particular set of normative assumptions. On this issue, see also Sen (1973) and Blackorby and Donaldson (1978).

Subsequent research extended these two aspects in a number of directions, and there has been immense cross-fertilization between inequality measurement and the measurement of social welfare, poverty and mobility. For example, Shorrocks (1983*a*) considered comparisons of social welfare, and showed the correspondence between non-intersection of the generalized Lorenz curve (the Lorenz curve scaled up by mean income) and increasing concave social welfare functions. This has proved an important tool for distributional assessments that take account of real income levels as well as inequality. Generalized Lorenz dominance corresponds to second-order dominance of distributions. Other research showed the links between first-order dominance and non-crossing cumulative distribution functions (Saposnik 1981)—thus giving normative content to Pen's (1971) evocative Parade of Dwarves and a few Giants—and derived dominance results for the case in which Lorenz (and generalized Lorenz) curves intersect: see for example Dardanoni and Lambert (1988), Davies and Hoy (1995), and Foster and Shorrocks (1987).

In applications to poverty, graphical devices analogous to the Lorenz curve have been developed, including the normalized poverty deficit curve (Atkinson 1987) and the Three 'I's of Poverty curve (Jenkins and Lambert 1997). The choice of summary poverty measure is not the only aspect over which judgements may differ: there is also the choice of the poverty line itself. This has led to concepts of 'restricted' dominance in which the range of incomes over which comparisons are made becomes crucial: see for example Atkinson (1987) and Foster and Shorrocks (1988). Consideration of dominance for mobility extends dominance results from one dimension to two and potentially more dimensions. Many of the key results in multidimensional applications were developed by Atkinson and Bourguignon (1982), with the implications for comparisons of social mobility specifically drawn out by Atkinson (1983). The same multidimensional methods have also proved useful for welfare and poverty comparisons that allow for variations in social judgements concerning the treatment of differences in 'needs' between households: see for example Atkinson and Bourguignon (1987), Atkinson (1992), and Jenkins and Lambert (1993).

In parallel, the characterization of classes of inequality indices and the drawing out of their normative properties has undergone substantial development. By contrast with Atkinson's approach to index derivation that involved placing of assumptions on the social welfare functions, indices were also characterized using axioms placed on the inequality measure itself. Consideration of the property of decomposability by population subgroup has proved particularly fruitful and led to the generalized entropy class of inequality measures (Bourguignon 1979; Cowell 1980; Shorrocks 1980, 1984), with sensitivity to differences in income shares captured by a single parameter. Particularly useful for empirical work has been the property that total inequality can be expressed as the weighted sum of the inequality within each population subgroup plus the inequality between subgroups (the inequality arising were there no inequality within each group). This literature has also illuminated the properties of other inequality indices such as the Gini coefficient, now known not to be additively decomposable in the same sense. Research has also shown how the decomposition of inequality by factor sources is an issue that is largely independent of the choice of inequality measure: see Shorrocks (1982, 1983*b*). For an extensive survey of recent developments in inequality measurement: see Cowell (2000).

The characterization of poverty indices has also benefited much from axiomatic approaches. Sen's (1976) paper was a pioneer in this respect, leading to a measure taking into account not only the proportion of poor—the conventional summary measure—but also the depth of poverty and the inequality of income among the poor. The properties of the Sen index and related 'rank'-based measures are reviewed by Osberg and Xu (2002). Similar motivations, but with attention given in addition to decomposability by population subgroup, led to the class of poverty indices that is most widely used in empirical work nowadays, the Foster, Greer, and Thorbecke (1984) class. A single parameter characterizes differences in aversion to poverty—the extent to which attention is focused on those with the very lowest incomes—and total poverty may be expressed as a population-weighted sum of the poverty within each population subgroup, thereby facilitating production of poverty 'profiles'. For extensive surveys of recent developments, including a large number of other poverty indices, see Seidl (1988) and Zheng (1997).

Development of mobility indices has not proceeded at the same pace as for inequality and poverty indices, in part because there are a multiplicity of 'mobility' concepts, illustrated by differing choices about whether to treat mobility as related to a lack of association between incomes in two periods ('origin independence'), or as related to the degree of change between incomes ('income movement'). For a review of these issues and existing mobility measures, see for example Fields and Ok (1999).

Another major development in analytical methods concerns the treatment of sampling variability when estimating measures. Forty years ago, relatively little attention was given to these issues. In part, this was because non-sampling issues were viewed as more important. We referred, for instance, to issues of data quality and access earlier. Another example is the choice of particular equivalence scale with which to adjust household incomes to take account of differences in household size and composition, and there is now much greater awareness of the potential sensitivity of measures to different choices: see for example Buhmann *et al.* (1988) and Coulter, Cowell, and Jenkins (1992). Another reason for the neglect of sampling variability was the (often implicit) claim that sample sizes were sufficiently large to ensure that standard errors for estimates would be relatively trivial. This was typically an untested assertion, however, and overlooked the fact that many population subgroups of particular interest (for example lone parents) were to be found in only small numbers in sample surveys. A third constraint was that methods for deriving variance estimates were not well-developed and that, in any case, suitable software was not easily available to calculate them.

The situation has changed substantially in the last few decades. Beach and Davidson (1983) was a pioneering paper, establishing distribution-free variance formulae for Lorenz and generalized Lorenz curves. Davidson and Duclos (2000) provide an overview of developments, and derive general results for variance estimators of poverty and inequality measures and thence stochastic dominance. For applications, see *inter alia* Bishop, Formby, and Smith (1991*a*, 1991*b*). In parallel, analytical formulae have been developed for distribution-free variance estimates of inequality and poverty indices, also taking account of the impact of complex survey design features such as clustering and stratification. See, *inter alia*, Binder and Kovačević (1995) and Biewen and Jenkins (2006) for inequality indices and, for poverty indices, Berger and Skinner (2003) and Howes and Lanjouw (1998). All the papers cited develop analytical formulae for the sampling variances of estimates. A parallel stream of work has shown how variance estimates may be derived using computationally intensive resampling methods such as the bootstrap: see for example Biewen (2002) and references therein.

Access to software for computing estimates and their sampling variances is now much less of a constraint. There are stand-alone packages that are free to researchers, of which the leading example is DAD (Duclos and Araar 2006). There are also freely available suites of programmes that can be used with general purpose statistical software packages such as Stata® (Jenkins 2006).

Developments in modelling

At the start of the chapter we mentioned several approaches to modelling the income distribution that were in use in the 1970s. Of these, models based on stochastic processes have become less favoured. (Champernowne and Cowell 1999 provide a good overview of this area.) On the other hand, regression modelling as a route to explanation of empirical distributions of earnings and household income has developed considerably. The technique of quantile regression has provided a flexible approach for this. The Oaxaca-Blinder decomposition of differences in means has been extended to account for differences at different parts of the distribution and for changes in unobserved differences (Juhn, Murphy, and Pierce 1993). There are a number of other regression-based decomposition methods: see for example Bourguignon, Fournier, and Gurgand (2001), Fields (2003), and Morduch and Sicular (2002). Developments in the modelling of poverty dynamics using household panel data are discussed by Jenkins (2000*a*).

There has also been a range of new developments in theoretical modelling. Atkinson and Bourguignon (2000: 3) note that new models of imperfect competition and informational asymmetries have helped explain why identical workers get paid different amounts and, in addition, call into question a crude view of an efficiency–equity trade-off. This idea is developed in the survey by Neal and Rosen (2000) of theories of the distribution of earnings. In addition to reviewing stochastic process models, selection models building on the original Roy (1951) paper, and human capital models, much of their chapter is given over to discussion of new models of sorting and agency and tournaments. They also point out how different models may be more appropriate for different parts of the distribution. An example of a model for the upper tail is Rosen's (1981), referring to 'superstars'.

Models that attempt to explain the capital market as well as the labour market, and thus provide an explanation of non-labour income as well as earnings, are less common. Atkinson (1997) outlines such a model, as well as referring to research since the Stiglitz (1969) paper cited earlier. Atkinson (1999, 2000) draws attention to the importance of labour market institutions and the role of social norms in shaping income distributions. A recent example of a model in the Stiglitz tradition is Caselli and Ventura (2000), who introduce heterogeneity in consumers' tastes, skills, and initial wealth. Atkinson and Bourguignon (2000) review the various building blocks of a theory of income distribution, and emphasize that no unified theory yet exists.

There has been enormous interest in the relationship between economic growth and inequality, bringing greater links between macroeconomics, political economy and income distribution. On the one hand, this had led to the development of theoretical models to address the issues of whether income inequality helps or hinders economic growth. On the other hand, and in tandem, a large literature has addressed these issues empirically using aggregate-level regressions of growth, estimated with panels of growth rates and inequality indices. Examples include Persson and Tabellini (1994), Brandolini and Rossi (1998), Forbes (2000), and Bannerjee and Duflo (2003). There remains no consensus on whether inequality has an adverse impact on a country's growth rate, but this literature has increased interest in income distribution data and the measurement of income inequality. For overviews, see Bénabou (1996), Kanbur (2000), and Perotti (1996).

One area of modelling, microsimulation, is almost a complete newcomer to the scene since the early 1970s, and was made possible by a combination of better access to data and the significant advances in computer hardware and software. Microsimulation involves the characterization of the rules of a country's tax and state benefit rules within a computer program, enabling assessment of the tax liabilities and social security benefit entitlements for each household in a household sample survey. The impact on the distribution of household incomes of changes in tax and benefit rules can then be simulated. The use of microsimulation vastly increases the scope of analysis of tax and benefit systems from what was possible 40 years ago, as represented by the then innovative work of Atkinson (1969) on potential reforms to Britain's social security system. Microsimulation models are tools that enable policy-makers, journalists and the public to understand the distributive effects of different tax-benefits schedules.

The growth of, and future prospects for, microsimulation are discussed by Bourguignon and Spadaro (2006). Microsimulation models now exist for many OECD countries and in a growing number of other countries. (For example, models for five African nations are available via http://models.wider.unu.edu/africa_web/.) International comparisons are enabled by the EUROMOD project that has created a model for the EU-15 (see Atkinson, Bourguignon *et al.* 2002).

Forty years of progress

The overview of developments indicates substantial progress in concepts, methods, models and data. There are a number of other indicators of the maturing of research on these topics. There are now three extensive 'handbooks' on income distribution, with expert authors surveying a range of topics.[6] See Atkinson and Bourguignon (2000), Silber (1999) and Salverda, Nolan, and Smeeding (forthcoming). There is also a 71-article two-volume compendium of landmark papers (Cowell 2003). A second edition of Atkinson's text, *The Economics of Inequality*, appeared in 1983, and has been joined by others, including Cowell (1995), Duclos and Araar (2006), Kakwani (1984), Lambert (three editions: 1989, 1993, 2001), and Ravallion (1994). Sen's 1973 monograph has been substantially extended by Sen (1997) in collaboration with Foster. The growth in research on income inequality and poverty is also illustrated by the increasing role of topics concerning the personal income distribution in long-standing scientific associations such as the International Association for Research in Income and Wealth (http://www.iariw.org). It is also reflected in the establishment of a new association, the Society for the Study of Economic Inequality (http://www.ecineq.org/).

Research on income distribution over the last few decades has of course been much more extensive than we have been able to communicate here. And the refinement of concepts, methods and models, and the availability of new data, is a continuing process. But what are the challenges for the future?

Perhaps the greatest challenge is to develop more comprehensive models of the household income distribution, incorporating not only models of labour market earnings but also reflecting income from other sources including social benefits and investment income, and the demographic factors affecting who lives with whom. The demand for such models persists if only because policy-makers continue to be interested in the poverty and affluence of individuals and these depend on the household context in which individuals live. And yet, at the same time, perhaps we should recognize that development of such comprehensive models may be an unattainable Holy Grail. Each building block—for example individual earnings or household demography—itself reflects a complex set of determinants, and may well differ for rich and poor people. We therefore conclude that modelling income distribution will continue to be a very heterogeneous research exercise, ranging from relatively abstract theoretical models to very empirical models that are inevitably less structural. Each has a role to play.

At the same time, we seek greater mainstreaming of income distribution topics within the discipline of economics, echoing the call by Atkinson (1997) to bring the study of the income distribution 'in from the cold'. As Atkinson and Bourguignon have pointed out, this is not a new idea. David Ricardo himself stated that '[t]o determine the laws which regulate this distribution is the principal problem in Political Economy' (cited by Atkinson and Bourguignon 2000: 2). We note, for

[6] We have said nothing about taxation and related public finance aspects of the income distribution, for example. See e.g. Atkinson and Stiglitz (1980).

example, that the large literature about the 'measurement' of inequality has remained rather separate from theoretical modelling of income determinants. And the substantial increase in the analysis of wage inequality in the 1980s by labour economists made little reference to the substantial literature on the measurement of household income inequality.

The literature on inequality and growth cited earlier is an example of the mainstreaming that we suggest should be the norm, and perhaps arose because of the development of theoretical models and empirical applications side by side. Another example is the Mincer-Becker tradition of human capital modelling and the huge empirical literature about determinants of earnings that it spawned in empirical labour economics. Perhaps the best contemporary example of integration has been in the study of income distribution in developing countries, well illustrated by the 2006 World Development Report (World Bank 2005). The report's subtitle is 'Equity and Development', indicating how distributional issues in various forms are central to economic development. Its contents reflect the interplay of analysis of key concepts, modelling, empirical applications and data, and their policy applications.

1.2 The organization of the book and the topics addressed

The three- to four-decade window used to frame the discussion so far was chosen deliberately. We believe that there was a marked increase in interest in income distribution matters from around the start of the 1970s, and we have described the main developments thereafter. At the same time, and not unrelated, the beginning of the period broadly coincides with the start of Tony Atkinson's professional career—a career that continues to flourish.

Atkinson's direct impact on the analysis of inequality and poverty, right across the subject, has been enormous. This is reflected by the large number of references to his work in the review in the preceding section, even though we have not attempted to be comprehensive in our coverage of his research, which of course has spanned several areas in economics alongside income distribution.[7] His research programme is an enviable model of how to integrate theoretical analysis of models and measurement, empirical analysis, and policy relevance. Tony Atkinson has also had indirect impacts through the research of the many people who have been influenced by him, in particular his research students and their collaborators. This book illustrates this impact: every chapter is authored or co-authored by one of his former doctoral students.[8]

[7] Atkinson's publications up to December 2004 are listed at http://www.nuff.ox.ac.uk/economics/people/atkinson.htm.

[8] These students all did their doctoral research in the 1980s, reflecting just one period in Atkinson's career. As of October 2006, he had supervised some 40 completed doctoral theses.

Atkinson has worked on most of the issues that the chapters address. Two very different examples serve as illustrations. The world income distribution, the most extreme case of the supranational entities of Chapter 2, was the subject of a whole chapter in the first edition (1975) of *The Economics of Inequality*. Close attention was paid in the same book to issues of low pay and minimum wage policy, the subject of Chapters 11 and 12. Other examples are indicated by the references to his work in our review or in the chapters that follow.

The rest of the book is divided into three Parts, each with four chapters. Part I deals with major conceptual issues that arise in analyses that are based on money-metric measures of inequality and poverty. Part II is also concerned to an extent with conceptual issues but its focus is on the consideration of concepts of inequality and poverty that include dimensions other than income (or expenditure). Part III considers selected examples of the impact of public policy on income distribution. The book therefore connects with many of the developments that we highlighted in the previous section, the main exceptions being theoretical modelling of the determinants of the income distribution, and the use of longitudinal data.

Part I: Conceptual Issues

Chapter 2, by Martin Ravallion, considers the major issue of why we should care about inequality at all if our main goal is reduction of absolute poverty. The view that inequality is unimportant in this sense has underlined parts of the World Bank's thinking following its commitment to poverty eradication in the early 1980s. It has also been prominent among many academic economists working on development, who have seen growth as all-important. Ravallion dissects the various arguments that have been made concerning this issue. In doing so, he draws on data on growth and inequality for some 80 developing countries before turning to analyse the important case of China's experience since 1980. He concludes that high inequality does indeed obstruct the reduction of poverty and discusses the implications that follow for policy-makers.

In Chapter 3, Andrea Brandolini tackles the measurement of inequality and poverty in the supranational context. His empirical setting is the EU, where the paucity of estimates for the distribution of income in the Union as a whole contrasts with the burgeoning literature on the world distribution. This is despite distributional issues being central to the EU's declared goals. Brandolini discusses the issues involved in measurement at the level of supranational entities, and for the enlarged 25-country EU in particular, before producing EU-level estimates of income inequality and the incidence of poverty. He concludes that inequality in the EU-25 is not yet as high as in the USA. One issue that he notes is the extent to which EU citizens in one member state do actually care about living standards in other member states, illustrated by his demonstration of how EU-25 poverty estimates differ depending on whether one uses a poverty line that is a fraction of EU median income or a fraction of a national median, or a weighted average of these.

Chapter 4, by Ann Harding, Neil Warren, and Rachel Lloyd, considers the definition of 'income'. The impacts of non-cash benefits in kind, such as education and health, and of indirect taxation have long concerned analysts of income distribution but studies that move beyond measures of cash income net of direct taxation are still comparatively rare. Harding, Warren, and Lloyd note the Canberra Group's support for such a move when assessing governments' redistributive impact and then discuss the difficulties, both in principle and in practice, of making the move. Their empirical evidence allows them to compare the UK and Australia on very similar bases. Despite the two countries having rather different tax and benefit systems, the similarity in impact of the in-kind benefits (progressive) and indirect taxes (regressive) across the net cash income distributions is striking. The authors note that, in general, comparisons across countries or over time that are restricted to cash income net of direct taxation may mislead as to differences or changes in governments' redistributive stance.

Chapter 5, by Peter Burton, Shelley Phipps, and Frances Woolley, addresses the issue of inequality within the household. This is a subject about which very little was known in the 1970s and the authors note the greatly increased literatures for both industrialized and developing countries that have subsequently appeared. The first part of the chapter reviews this research. The authors consider the variety of approaches to the issue—both theoretical and empirical—that have been adopted. The second part of the chapter provides new empirical evidence with a quasi-experimental analysis of how expenditure patterns of Canadian couples change when the wife becomes eligible for additional social security income at a particular age. These data relate to elderly couples and stimulate discussion of how inequality within the household and its impacts may change over the life cycle.

Part II: Multiple dimensions

Interest in 'life chances' and inequality of opportunity has focused greater attention on inequalities in education, the topic of Chapter 6 by John Micklewright and Sylke Schnepf. The authors compare the dispersion of educational achievement recorded in standardized test score data for children of compulsory school age in 21 industrialized countries. In contrast to earlier studies that have focused on a single data source, Micklewright and Schnepf draw on three different surveys in order to establish a picture of cross-national differences that does not depend on the choice of one particular survey. They urge caution with the application of inequality measurement tools to test score data, which certainly do not share all the properties of data on incomes.

A reasonable degree of agreement between the surveys is found, allowing conclusions to be drawn about where inequality in learning is greatest and about the association between inequality in learning and average learning across countries.

Chapters 7, 8 and 9 all consider multidimensional approaches to inequality and poverty. In Chapter 7, Brian Nolan and Chris Whelan point out that, although multidimensionality is a concept that is embraced by many, its precise meaning and implications are less well appreciated. Nolan and Whelan argue that a clear distinction needs to be maintained between conceptualizing, measuring, understanding, and responding to poverty, and show that the nature and role of a multidimensional approach may differ in each case. Their arguments are illustrated using household survey data about non-monetary indicators of whether households have particular items or participate in a number of activities. The authors show that such information has two important and complementary advantages for the analysis of poverty and social exclusion. First, because income is not an error-free measure of living standards, the indicators provide useful additional information for identifying the individuals who are genuinely poor. Second, a battery of non-monetary indicators can be used to distinguish different dimensions of deprivation and exclusion, and hence go a long way towards capturing the multifaceted nature of social exclusion that is often referred to. Nolan and Whelan also illustrate how latent class analysis provides a particular means of using multidimensional information to identify the individuals who may be categorized as poor.

Statistical methods for aggregating information from non-monetary indicators are also employed in Chapter 8, by Lorenzo Cappellari and Stephen Jenkins. By contrast with Nolan and Whelan, the authors consider the use of such indicators for deriving a metric scale that differentiates households in terms of their 'deprivation' levels, from highest to lowest, but not the additional issue of where to draw a line between the most deprived (the 'poor') and those who are less deprived. Chapter 8 assesses the ubiquitous practice of constructing a deprivation scale as the sum of a relatively small set of dichotomous indicators. Cappellari and Jenkins argue that the theoretical foundations of these 'sum-score' scales are relatively weak, and they suggest that 'item response' modelling provides a more promising way to summarize multiple deprivation indicators. (These techniques were also used to produce the test score data in Chapter 6.) In their illustrative application based on British Household Panel Survey data, both the item response modelling and the sum-score approaches provide very similar pictures of basic lifestyle deprivation and their determinants. How this result might be interpreted, together with further discussion of the relative merits of the two approaches, forms the remainder of the chapter.

Chapter 9, by Jean-Yves Duclos, David Sahn, and Stephen Younger, links the topic of multidimensionality with methods for stochastic dominance, thereby bringing together two of the developments discussed earlier. The authors derive the conditions for ordering multivariate distributions in terms of their poverty in the case where one of the dimensions is a conventional measure of income (a continuous variable), and the other dimensions are intrinsically discrete or recorded in that way, examples of which include household size (as a measure of needs) or level of educational achievement. The authors also derive expressions for the sampling distributions for the statistics required for their multivariate poverty comparisons, so that researchers can also assess whether any differences found are statistically significant or attributable to sampling variation. Four applications illustrate the methods using data from countries at different stages of development. In each case, the authors combine a measure of income (or consumption expenditure) with information on another one or more dimensions. For Romania, that dimension is household size; for Peru, it is a measure of literacy; for Ecuador, it is a measure of residential location; and for Britain, there are measures of educational achievement and health status.

Part III: Public policy

Part III considers selected examples of the impact of public policy on income distribution. (Chapter 4 also contributes to this, although its focus is more on concepts and issues of measurement.) There are four chapters, three of which focus on the bottom end of the distribution reflecting a concern with poverty, whereas the final chapter considers the very wealthy.

Chapter 10, by Horacio Levy, Christine Lietz, and Holly Sutherland, considers a minimum income guarantee for children. The position of children has attracted considerable attention in several governments' domestic policy agendas in recent years but this chapter considers an EU-wide policy, and in particular its effect on child poverty. The authors first examine the extent to which existing levels of financial support for children in each country fall short of a series of illustrative minimum levels of income. They then estimate the cost of bringing support up to those levels, and the impact on poverty among children of doing so. The effect of financing this cost of a guaranteed minimum income using a European flat tax is explored. The analysis uses EUROMOD, the European tax-benefit microsimulation model, and illustrates the choices that must be made when designing such a scheme for redistribution between countries and towards children.

Chapters 11 and 12 address minimum wage policy. A minimum wage has a direct impact on the lower end of the earnings distribution, reducing earnings inequality, but there may be accompanying indirect effects. In particular, any negative impact on employment that arises as employers respond to the increased cost of labour, will tend to increase household income inequality and hence poverty.

Chapter 11, by Stephen Bazen, considers both the first round impact on earnings and the second round behavioural responses, focusing on empirical evidence about the USA, where the debate about the impact of minimum wages has been vociferous. Bazen first discusses the variety of impacts that the minimum wage can have on earnings, documenting shifts in the distribution of hourly wages. He then undertakes a careful review of work over the last 15 years that has considered the employment effects of minimum wages. This includes both state-level quasi-experimental analyses and aggregate time-series studies, where, as Bazen notes, techniques have changed enormously since the start of the 1980s, a period when the literature had reached a consensus on employment effects. He concludes that there has been a clear impact on the lower end of the earnings distribution of both federal and state level increases in the minimum during the 1980s and 1990s, but only the sporadic federal level changes have had a significant impact on employment, and this only for teenagers.

In Chapter 12, Alison Booth and Mark Bryan take a longer-term perspective on effects of minimum wages on the distribution of income. They address the impact that the minimum wage has on training undertaken by low wage workers, and hence on increasing their earning power. If labour markets are imperfectly competitive, any compression of the earnings distribution through minimum wages may induce firms to provide general training because they can keep some of the surplus generated. Using household panel data for Britain, Booth and Bryan show that lower paid workers are less likely than higher paid workers to receive training and that training significantly increases longer-term earnings. They then use a difference-in-differences estimator to show that the introduction of a national minimum wage in Britain in 1999 had a small but significant positive impact on the prevalence of training for affected workers.

Chapter 13, by Bernd Süssmuth and Robert von Weizsäcker, examines the opposite end of the distribution, the very rich, and focuses on unearned rather than earned income. The chapter considers the relationships between the types of debt policy that a government may pursue, and differences in the risk aversion of different groups within a society, especially those between the poor and the rich. This is relevant to the question of whether governments can roll over their debt and interest without ever increasing taxes (a 'Ponzi debt game'). Süssmuth and von Weizsäcker analyse whether such debt games are sub-optimal, starting from the observation that some European governments apparently issue excessive amounts of safe debt that are disproportionately held by the rich. By using a different set of assumptions from previous research, notably that risk aversion may be greater for the rich than the poor, they show that, although it is possible to identify a scenario in which a perpetual rollover of public debt improves intergenerational risk sharing, such a scenario is not very probable. The chapter provides an example of how theoretical models informed by stylized facts may be used to illuminate issues of public policy.

References

Allison, R. A. and Foster, J. E. (2004). 'Measuring Health Inequality using Qualitative Data'. *Journal of Health Economics*, 23: 505–24.

Atkinson, A. B. (1969). *Poverty in Britain and the Reform of Social Security*. Cambridge: Cambridge University Press.

—— (1970). 'On the Measurement of Inequality'. *Journal of Economic Theory*, 2: 244–63.

—— (1975). *The Economics of Inequality*. (2nd edn, 1983.) Oxford: Clarendon Press.

—— (1983). 'The Measurement of Economic Mobility', in A. B. Atkinson, *Social Mobility and Public Policy*. Hemel Hempstead: Harvester-Wheatsheaf, 61–76.

—— (1987). 'On the Measurement of Poverty'. *Econometrica*, 55: 759–64.

—— (1989). 'How Should We Measure Poverty? Some Conceptual Issues', in A. B. Atkinson, *Poverty and Social Security*. Hemel Hempstead: Harvester-Wheatsheaf, 7–24.

—— (1992). 'Measuring Poverty and Differences in Family Composition'. *Economica*, 59: 1–16.

—— (1997). 'Bringing Income Distribution in from The Cold'. *Economic Journal*, 107: 297–321.

—— (1999). 'Is Rising Inequality Inevitable? A Critique of The Transatlantic Consensus'. WIDER Annual Lectures No. 3. Helsinki: World Institute for Development Economics Research. http://www.wider.unu.edu/publications/annual-lectures/annual-lecture-1999.pdf.

—— (2000). 'The Changing Distribution of Income: Evidence and Explanations'. *German Economic Review*, 1: 3–18.

—— (2003*a*). 'Income Inequality in OECD Countries: Data and Explanations'. *CESifo Economic Studies*, 49: 479–513.

—— (2003*b*). 'Income Inequality in OECD Countries: Data and Explanations'. CESifo Working Paper No. 881. Munich: CESifo. http://www.cesifo.de/DocCIDL/881.pdf.

—— (2003*c*). 'Ungleichheit, Armut und der Wohlfahrtsstaat: eine europäische Perspektive zur Globalisierungsdiskussion', in W. Müller and S. Scherer (eds), *Mehr Risiken-Mehr Ungleichheit?* Frankfurt: Campus Verlag, 63–82.

—— (2004). 'The Luxembourg Income Study (LIS): Past, Present and Future'. *Socio-Economic Review*, 2: 165–90.

—— and Bourguignon, F. (1982). 'The Comparison of Multi-Dimensional Distributions of Economic Status'. *Review of Economic Studies*, 49: 183–201.

—— and —— (1987). 'Income Distribution and Differences in Needs', in G. Feiwel (ed.), *Arrow and the Foundations of the Theory of Economic Policy*. London: Macmillan, 350–70.

—— and —— (2000). 'Introduction: Income Distribution and Economics', in A. B. Atkinson and F. Bourguignon (eds), *Handbook of Income Distribution Volume 1*. Amsterdam: North-Holland, 1–58.

——, ——, and Morrisson, C. (1992). *Empirical Studies of Earnings Mobility*. Fundamentals of Pure and Applied Economics, Volume 52. Chur, CH: Harwood Academic Publishers.

——, ——, O'Donoghue, C., Sutherland, H., and Utili, F. (2002). 'Microsimulation of Social Policy in the European Union: Case Study of a European Minimum Pension'. *Economica*, 69: 229–43.

—— and Brandolini, A. (2001). 'Promise and Pitfalls in the Use of "Secondary" Data-sets: Income Inequality in OECD Countries'. *Journal of Economic Literature*, 39: 771–99.

——, Cantillon, B., Marlier, E., and Nolan, B. (2002). *Social Indicators: The EU and Social Inclusion*. Oxford: Oxford University Press.
——, Maynard, A. K., and Trinder, C. G. (1983). *Parents and Children: Incomes in Two Generations*. London: Heinemann.
—— and Micklewright, J. (1992). *Economic Transformation in Eastern Europe and the Distribution of Income*. Cambridge: Cambridge University Press.
—— and Piketty, T. (eds) (2007). *Top Incomes Over the Twentieth Century. A Contrast Between European and English-Speaking Countries*. Oxford: Oxford University Press.
——, Rainwater, L., and Smeeding, T. M. (1995). *Income Distribution in OECD Countries: Evidence from the Luxembourg Income Study (LIS)*. Social Policy Studies No. 18. Paris: Organisation for Economic Cooperation and Development.
—— and Stiglitz, J. E. (1980). *Lectures on Public Economics*. New York: McGraw-Hill.
Banerjee, A. V. and Duflo, E. (2003). 'Inequality and Growth: What Can the Data Say?' *Journal of Economic Growth*, 8: 267–99.
Barclay, P. (chair) (1995). *Income and Wealth, Volume I: Report of the Enquiry Group*. York: Joseph Rowntree Foundation.
Basu, K. and Foster, J. E. (1998). 'On Measuring Literacy'. *Economic Journal*, 108: 1733–49.
Baulch, B. and Hoddinott, J. (2000). 'Economic Mobility and Poverty Dynamics in Developing Countries'. *Journal of Development Studies*, 36: 1–24.
Beach, C. M. and Davidson, R. (1983). 'Distribution-free Statistical Inference with Lorenz Curves and Income Shares'. *Review of Economic Studies*, 50: 723–35.
Becker, G. S. (1971). *The Economics of Discrimination* (2nd edn). Chicago, IL: Chicago University Press.
—— and Tomes, N. (1986). 'Human Capital and the Rise and Fall of Families'. *Journal of Labor Economics*, 4: S1–S39.
Bénabou, R. (1996). 'Inequality and Growth', in B. Bernanke and J. Rotemberg (eds), *NBER Macroeconomics Annual 1996*. Cambridge, MA: MIT Press, 11–74.
Benjamin, D., Brandt, L., Giles, J., and Wang, S. (2005). 'Income Inequality during China's Economic Transition'. Department of Economics Working Paper 238. Toronto: University of Toronto. http://www.msu.edu/gilesj/BBGW.pdf.
Berger, Y. G. and Skinner, C. J. (2003). 'Variance Estimation of a Low-Income Proportion'. *Journal of the Royal Statistical Society Series C (Applied Statistics)*, 52: 457–68.
Biewen, M. (2002). 'Bootstrap Inference for Inequality, Mobility and Poverty Measurement'. *Journal of Econometrics*, 108: 317–42.
—— and Jenkins, S. P. (2006). 'Variance Estimation for Generalized Entropy and Atkinson Inequality Indices: the Complex Survey Data Case'. *Oxford Bulletin of Economics and Statistics*, 68: 371–83.
Binder, D. A. and Kovačević, M. S. (1995). 'Estimating Some Measures of Income Inequality from Survey Data: an Application of the Estimating Equations Approach'. *Survey Methodology*, 21: 137–45.
Bishop, J. A., Formby, J. P., and Smith, W. J. (1991*a*). 'Lorenz Dominance and Welfare: Changes in the U.S. Distribution of Income, 1967–1986'. *Review of Economics and Statistics*, 73: 134–9.
——, ——, —— (1991*b*). 'International Comparisons of Income Inequality: Tests for Lorenz Dominance across Nine Countries'. *Economica*, 58: 461–77.
Blackorby, C. and Donaldson, D. (1978). 'Measures of Relative Inequality and their Meaning in Terms of Social Welfare'. *Journal of Economic Theory*, 18: 58–90.

Blinder, A. S. (1973). 'Wage Discrimination: Reduced Form and Structural Estimates'. *Journal of Human Resources*, 8: 436–55.

—— and Esaki, H. (1978). 'Macroeconomic Activity and Income Distribution in the Postwar United States'. *Review of Economics and Statistics*, 60: 604–9.

Bourguignon, F. (1979). 'Decomposable Income Inequality Measures'. *Econometrica*, 47: 901–20.

—— and Morrisson, C. (1992). 'Inequality Among World Citizens: 1820–1992'. *American Economic Review*, 92: 727–44.

—— and Spadaro, A. (2006). 'Microsimulation as a Tool for Evaluating Redistribution Policies'. *Journal of Economic Inequality*, 4: 77–106.

——, Fournier M., and Gurgand M. (2001). 'Fast Development with a Stable Income'. *Review of Income and Wealth*, 47: 139–63.

Bradbury, B., Jenkins, S. P., and Micklewright J. (eds) (2001). *The Dynamics of Child Poverty in Industrialised Countries*. Cambridge: Cambridge University Press.

Brandolini, A. and D'Alessio, G. (1998). 'Measuring Well-Being in the Functioning Space'. Unpublished paper. Rome: Banca D'Italia. Presented at 26th General Conference of The International Association for Research in Income and Wealth, Cracow, Poland. http://www.iariw.org/papers/2000/brandolini.pdf.

—— and Rossi, R. (1998). 'Income Distribution and Growth in Industrial Countries' in V. Tanzi and K.-Y. Chu (eds), *Income Distribution and High-Quality Growth*. Cambridge, MA: MIT Press, 69–105.

Buhmann, B., Rainwater, L., Schmauss, G., and Smeeding, T. (1988). 'Equivalence Scales, Well-Being, Inequality and Poverty: Sensitivity Estimates across Ten Countries using the Luxembourg Income Study (LIS) Database'. *Review of Income and Wealth*, 43: 319–34.

Burkhauser, R. V., Butrica, B. A, Daly, M. C., and Lillard, D. R. (2001). 'The Cross-National Equivalent File: A Product of Cross-National Research', in I. Becker, N. Ott, and G. Rolf (eds), *Soziale Sicherung in Einer Dynamischen Gesellschaft*. Frankfurt: Campus Verlag, 354–76.

Canberra Group (Expert Group on Household Income Statistics) (2001). *Final Report and Recommendations*. Ottawa: Statistics Canada. http://www.lisproject.org/links/canberra/finalreport.pdf.

Caselli, F. and Ventura, J. (2000). 'A Representative Consumer Theory of Distribution'. *American Economic Review*, 90: 909–26.

Champernowne, D. G. (1973). *The Distribution of Income Between Persons*. Cambridge: University Press.

—— and Cowell, F. A. (1999). *Economic Inequality and Income Distribution*. Cambridge: Cambridge University Press.

Chen, S. and Ravallion, M. (2000). 'How did the World's Poorest Fare in the 1990s?' Policy Research Working Paper No. 2409. Washington, DC: World Bank.

Conlisk, J. (1969). 'An Approach to the Theory of Inequality in the Size Distribution of Income'. *Western Economic Journal*, 7: 180–6.

—— (1974). 'Can Equalization of Opportunity Reduce Social Mobility? *American Economic Review*, 64: 80–90.

Corak, M. (ed.) (2004). *Generational Income Mobility in North America and Europe*. Cambridge: Cambridge University Press.

Coulter, F. A., Cowell, F. A., and Jenkins, S. P. (1992). 'Equivalence Scale Relativities and the Extent of Inequality and Poverty'. *Economic Journal*, 102: 1067–82.

Cowell, F. A. (1980). 'On The Structure of Additive Inequality Measures'. *Review of Economic Studies*, 47: 521–31.

—— (1995). *Measuring Inequality* (2nd edn). Hemel Hempstead: Harvester-Wheatsheaf.

—— (2000). 'Measurement of Inequality', in A. B. Atkinson and F. Bourguignon (eds), *Handbook of Income Distribution Volume 1*. Amsterdam: North-Holland, 87–166.

—— (ed.) (2003). *The Economics of Poverty and Inequality*. International Library of Critical Writings in Economics, volume 158. Cheltenham: Edward Elgar.

Daly, M. C. and Valletta, R. G. (2006). 'Inequality and Poverty in the United States: the Effects of Rising Dispersion on Men's Earnings and Changing Family Behavior'. *Economica*, 73: 75–98.

Danziger, S. and Gottschalk, P. (1995). *America Unequal*. Cambridge, MA: Harvard University Press.

Dardanoni, V. and Lambert, P. J. (1988). 'Welfare Rankings of Income Distributions: a Role for the Variance and Some Insights for Tax Reform'. *Social Choice and Welfare*, 5: 1–17.

Davidson, R. and Duclos, J.-Y. (2000). 'Statistical Inference for Stochastic Dominance and for the Measurement of Poverty and Inequality'. *Econometrica*, 68: 1435–64.

Davies, J. B. and Hoy, M. (1995). 'Making Inequality Comparisons When Lorenz Curves Intersect'. *American Economic Review*, 85: 980–6.

——, Sandstrom, S., Shorrocks, A., and Wolff, E. N (2006). 'Estimating the World Distribution of Household Wealth' paper presented at the 29th General Conference of The International Association for Research in Income and Wealth, Joensuu, Finland. http://www.iariw.org/papers/2006/davies.pdf.

Deaton, A. (1997). *The Analysis of Household Surveys*. Baltimore, MD: The Johns Hopkins University Press for the World Bank.

Deininger, K. and Squire, L. (1996). 'A New Dataset Measuring Income Inequality'. *World Bank Economic Review*, 10: 565–91.

Department for Work and Pensions (2006). *Households Below Average Income. An Analysis of the Income Distribution 1994/5–2004/5*. Leeds: Corporate Document Services.

Dowrick, S. and M. Akmal (2005). 'Contradictory Trends in Global Income Inequality: A Tale of Two Biases'. *Review of Income and Wealth*, 51: 201–29.

Duclos, J.-Y. and Araar, A. (2006). *Poverty and Equity: Measurement, Policy and Estimation with DAD*. New York: Springer, and Ottawa: International Development Research Centre. http://www.idrc.ca/openebooks/229-5/.

Duncan, G., Gustafsson, B., Hauser, R., Schmauss, G., Messinger, H., Muffels, R., Nolan, B., and Ray, J.-C. (1993). 'Poverty Dynamics in Eight Countries'. *Journal of Population Economics*, 6: 295–334.

Ellwood, D. (1998). 'Dynamic Policy Making: an Insider's Account of Reforming US Welfare', in L. Leisering and R. Walker (eds), *The Dynamics of Modern Society: Policy, Poverty and Welfare*. Bristol: The Policy Press, 49–62.

Fields, G. S. (2001). *Distribution and Development*. New York: Russell Sage Foundation and Cambridge, MA: MIT Press.

—— (2003). 'Accounting for Income Inequality and its Change: a New Method, with Application to the Distribution of Earnings in the United States'. *Research in Labor Economics*, 22: 1–38.

—— and Ok, E. (1999). 'The Measurement of Income Mobility: an Introduction to the Literature', in J. Silber (ed.), *Handbook on Income Inequality Measurement*. Dordrecht and New York: Kluwer Academic Publishers, 557–96.

Filmer, D. and Pritchett, L. (1999). 'The Effect of Household Wealth on Educational Attainment: Evidence from 35 Countries'. *Population and Development Review*, 25: 85–120.

Fisher, G. M. (1997). 'The Development of the Orshansky Poverty Thresholds and their Subsequent History as the Official U.S. Poverty Measure'. Poverty Measurement Working Paper. Washington, DC: US Bureau of the Census. http://www.census.gov/hhes/poverty/povmeas/papers/orshansky.html.

Flemming, J. and Micklewright, J. (2000). 'Income Distribution, Economic Systems and Transition', in A. B. Atkinson and F. Bourguignon (eds), *Handbook of Income Distribution Volume 1*. Amsterdam: North-Holland, 843–918.

Forbes, K. J. (2000). 'A Reassessment of the Relationship between Inequality and Growth'. *American Economic Review*, 90: 869–87.

Foster, J. E. and Shorrocks, A. F. (1987). 'Transfer Sensitive Inequality Measures'. *Review of Economic Studies*, 54: 485–97.

—— and —— (1988). 'Poverty Orderings'. *Econometrica*, 56: 173–7.

——, Greer, J., and Thorbecke, E. (1984). 'A Class of Decomposable Poverty Indices'. *Econometrica*, 52: 761–6.

Gottschalk, P. and Smeeding, T. M. (1997). 'Cross-National Comparisons of Earnings and Income Inequality'. *Journal of Economic Literature*, 35: 633–87.

Howes, S. and Lanjouw, P. (1998). 'Does Sample Design Matter for Poverty Rate Comparisons?' *Review of Income and Wealth*, 44: 99–109.

Jenkins, S. P. (1991). 'Poverty Measurement and the Within-Household Distribution: Agenda for Action'. *Journal of Social Policy*, 20: 457–83.

—— (1995). 'Accounting for Inequality Trends: Decomposition Analyses for the UK, 1971–86'. *Economica*, 62: 29–63.

—— (2000*a*). 'Trends in the UK Income Distribution', in R. Hauser and I. Becker (eds), *The Personal Distribution of Income in an International Perspective*. Berlin: Springer Verlag, 129–57.

—— (2000*b*). 'Modelling Household Income Dynamics'. *Journal of Population Economics*, 13: 529–67.

—— (2006). 'Estimation and Interpretation of Measures of Inequality, Poverty, and Social Welfare using Stata'. Presentation at North American Stata Users' Group Meeting 2006, Boston. MA. http://econpapers.repec.org/paper/bocasug06/16.htm.

—— and Lambert, P. J. (1993). 'Ranking Income Distributions when Needs Differ'. *Review of Income and Wealth*, 39: 337–56.

—— and —— (1997). 'Three "I's of Poverty" Curves, with an Analysis of U.K. Poverty Trends'. *Oxford Economic Papers*, 49: 317–27.

Johnson, P. and Webb, S. (1993). 'Explaining the Growth in UK Income Inequality'. *Economic Journal*, 103: 429–35.

Jolly, R. (2005). 'Global Inequality in Historical Perspective'. Paper presented at UNU-WIDER Jubilee Conference: 'WIDER Thinking Ahead: The Future of Development Economics', Helsinki. http://www.wider.unu.edu/conference/conference-2005-3/conference-2005-3-papers/Jolly.pdf.

Juhn, C., Murphy, K. M., and Pierce, B. (1993). 'Wage Inequality and the Rise in Returns to Skill'. *Journal of Political Economy*, 101: 410–42.

Kakwani, N. C. (1984). *Income Inequality and Poverty. Methods of Estimation and Policy Applications*. Oxford: Oxford University Press for the World Bank.

——, Wagstaff, A., and van Doorslaer, E., (1997). 'Socioeconomic Inequality in Health: Measurement, Computation and Statistical Inference'. *Journal of Econometrics*, 77: 87–104.

Kanbur, R. (2000). 'Income Distribution and Development', in A. B. Atkinson and F. Bourguignon (eds), *Handbook of Income Distribution Volume 1*. Amsterdam: North-Holland, 791–841.

Karpur, D., Lewis, J. P., and Webb, R. (1997). *The World Bank: its First Half Century, Volume 1 History*. Washington, DC: The Brookings Institution.

Katz, L. F. and Autor, D. H. (1999). 'Changes in the Wage structure and Earnings Inequality', in O. C. Ashenfelter and D. Card (eds), *Handbook of Labor Economics Volume 3A*. Amsterdam: North-Holland, 1464–1555.

Kolm, S. C. (1969). 'The Optimal Production of Social Justice', in J. Margolis and H. Guitton (eds), *Public Economics*. London: Macmillan, 145–200.

Lambert, P. J. (1989). *The Distribution and Redistribution of Income*. Manchester: Manchester University Press (2nd edn 1993; 3rd edn 2001).

Lillard, L. A. and Willis, R. J. (1978). 'Dynamic Aspects of Earnings Mobility'. *Econometrica*, 46: 985–1012.

Lydall, H. (1968). *The Structure of Earnings*. Oxford: Clarendon Press.

Meade, J. E. (1964). *Efficiency, Equality and the Ownership of Property*. London: George Allen and Unwin.

Metcalf, C. E. (1969). 'The Size Distribution of Personal Income during the Business Cycle'. *American Economic Review*, 59: 657–68.

Micklewright, J. (2002). 'Social Exclusion and Children: a European View for a US Debate', in A. J. Kahn and S. B. Kamerman (eds), *Beyond Child Poverty: The Social Exclusion of Children*. New York: The Institute for Child and Family Policy, Columbia University, 89–130.

Milanovic, B. (1998). *Income, Inequality and Poverty during the Transition from Planned to Market Economy*. Washington, DC: The World Bank.

—— (2006). 'Global Income Inequality: What it is and Why it Matters'. Policy Research Working Paper No. 3865. Washington, DC: World Bank.

Mincer, J. (1974). *Schooling, Experience and Earnings*. New York: Columbia University Press for National Bureau of Economic Research.

Montgomery, M., Gragnolati, M., Burke, K., and Paredes, E. (2000). 'Measuring Living Standards with Proxy Variables'. *Demography*, 37: 155–74.

Morduch, J. and Sicular, T. (2002). 'Rethinking Inequality Decomposition, with Evidence from Rural China'. *Economic Journal*, 112: 93–106.

Morgan, J., Dickinson, K., Dickinson, J., Benus, J., and Duncan, G. (1974). *Five Thousand American Families—Patterns of Economic Progress. Volume I*. Ann Arbor, MI: ISR, University of Michigan.

Neal, D. and Rosen, S. (2000). 'Theories of the Distribution of Earnings', in A. B. Atkinson and F. Bourguignon (eds), *Handbook of Income Distribution Volume 1*. Amsterdam: North-Holland, 379–427.

Oaxaca, R. L. (1973). 'Male–Female Wage Differentials in Urban Labor Markets'. *International Economic Review*, 14: 693–709.

Osberg, L. and Sharpe, A. (2005). 'How Should We Measure the "Economic" Aspects of Well-being?' *Review of Income and Wealth*, 51: 311–36.

—— and Xu, K. (2002). 'The Social Welfare Implications, Decomposability and Geometry of the Sen family of Poverty Indices'. *Canadian Journal of Economics*, 35: 138–52.

Pen, J. (1971). *Income Distribution*. Harmondsworth, Mx.: Penguin Books. Pelican edition, 1974.

Perotti, R. (1996). 'Growth, Income Distribution, and Democracy'. *Journal of Economic Growth*, 1: 149–87.

Persson, T. and Tabellini, G. (1994). 'Is Inequality Harmful for Growth?' *American Economic Review*, 84: 600–21.

Ravallion, M. (1994). *Poverty Comparisons*. Fundamentals of Pure and Applied Economics, Volume 56. Chur, CH: Harwood Academic Publishers.

Roemer, J. E. (2006). 'Review Essay, "2006 World Development Report: Equity and development"'. *Journal of Economic Inequality*, 4: 233–44.

Rosen, S. (1981). 'The Economics of Superstars'. *American Economic Review*, 71: 845–58.

Roy, A. D. (1951). 'Some Thoughts on the Distribution of Earnings'. *Oxford Economic Papers*, 3: 135–46.

Royal Commission on the Distribution of Income and Wealth (1979). *Report no. 7. Fourth Report on the Standing Reference*. London: HMSO.

Sala-i-Martín, X. (2006). 'The World Distribution of Income: Falling Poverty and ... Convergence, Period'. *Quarterly Journal of Economics*, 121: 351–97.

Salverda, W., Nolan, B., and Smeeding, T. M. (eds) (forthcoming). *Oxford Handbook on Economic Inequality*. Oxford: Oxford University Press.

Saposnik, R. (1981). 'Rank Dominance in Income Distribution'. *Public Choice*, 36: 147–51.

Sawyer, M. C. (1976). *Income Distribution in OECD Countries*. OECD Occasional Studies. Paris: Organisation for Economic Cooperation and Development.

Seidl, C. (1988). 'Poverty Measurement: a Survey', in D. Bös, M. Rose, and C. Seidl (eds), *Welfare and Efficiency in Public Economics*. London: Springer-Verlag, 71–147.

Sen, A. K. (1973). *On Economic Inequality*. Oxford: Clarendon Press.

—— (1976). 'Poverty: an Ordinal Approach to Measurement'. *Econometrica*, 44: 219–31.

—— (1984). 'Rights and Capabilities', in A. K. Sen, *Resources, Values and Development*. Oxford: Basil Blackwell, 307–24.

—— (1997). *On Economic Inequality. Expanded Edition with a Substantial Annexe by J. E. Foster and A. K. Sen*. Oxford: Clarendon Press.

Shorrocks, A. F. (1980). 'The Class of Additively Decomposable Inequality Measures'. *Econometrica*, 48: 613–26.

—— (1982). 'The Impact of Income Components on the Distribution of Family Incomes'. *Quarterly Journal of Economics*, 98: 311–26.

—— (1983*a*). 'Ranking Income Distributions'. *Economica*, 50: 3–17.

—— (1983*b*). 'Inequality Decomposition by Factor Components'. *Econometrica*, 50: 193–212.

—— (1984). 'Inequality Decomposition by Population Subgroup'. *Econometrica*, 52: 1369–85.

Sierminska, E., Brandolini, A., and Smeeding T. (2006). 'The Luxembourg Wealth Study—a Cross-Country Comparable Database for Household Wealth Research'. *Journal of Economic Inequality*, 4: 375–83.

Silber, J. (ed.) (1999). *Handbook on Inequality Measurement*. Boston: Kluwer Academic Publishers.

Smeeding, T. M. (2004). 'Twenty Years of Research on Income Inequality, Poverty, and Redistribution in the Developed World: Introduction and Overview'. *Socio-Economic Review*, 2: 149–63.

——, Saunders, P., Coder, J., Jenkins, S., Fritzell, J., Hagenaars, A. J. M., Hauser, R., and Wolfson, M. (1993). 'Poverty, Inequality and Family Living Standards Impacts across Seven Nations: the Effect of Non-Cash Subsidies for Health, Education and Housing'. *Review of Income and Wealth*, 39: 229–56.

Stark, T. (1997). *The Distribution of Income in Eight Countries*. Background Paper to Report 5, Royal Commission on the Distribution of Income and Wealth. London: HMSO.

Stiglitz, J. (1969). 'The Distribution of Income and Wealth among Individuals'. *Econometrica*, 37: 382–97.

Thurow, L. C. (1970) 'Analyzing the American Income Distribution'. *American Economic Review, Papers and Proceedings*. 60: 261–9.

Townsend, P. (1979) *Poverty in the United Kingdom: a Survey of Household Resources and Standards of Living*. Harmondsworth, Mx.: Penguin.

HM Treasury (1999). 'Tackling Poverty and Extending Opportunity'. The Modernisation of Britain's Tax and Benefit System Paper No. 4. London: HM Treasury.

Valletta, R. (2006). 'The Ins and Outs of Poverty in Advanced Economies: Government Policy and Poverty Dynamics in Canada, Germany, Great Britain, and the United States'. *Review of Income and Wealth*, 52: 261–84.

World Bank (2005). *World Development Report 2006: Equity and Development*. Washington, DC: World Bank.

Zheng, B. (1997). 'Aggregate Poverty Measures'. *Journal of Economic Surveys*, 11: 123–63.

Part I

Conceptual Issues

2

Inequality *is* bad for the poor

*Martin Ravallion**

It has long been argued that high inequality should be of little concern in poor countries on the grounds that: (i) absolute poverty in terms of consumption (or income) is the overriding issue, and (ii) the only thing that really matters to the reduction of absolute poverty is the rate of economic growth. Some observers have gone a step further to argue that (iii) higher inequality is the unavoidable by-product of the economic growth needed to reduce poverty. The message for policy is that developing countries—including their poor—need not worry about inequality.

This chapter takes (i) as given but takes issue with (ii) and (iii) on the basis of empirical evidence for developing countries. The following section looks at the empirical relationship across countries between inequality and growth, while section 2.2 turns to the relationship between inequality and poverty reduction. Section 2.3 examines whether the evidence from the experiences of developing countries supports the view that there is an aggregate trade-off between growth and reducing inequality. China is discussed in some detail since this country is widely seen to exemplify the idea of a growth–equity trade off. Finally, section 2.4 tries to draw out some lessons for policy and for policy-relevant research.

2.1 Inequality and growth revisited

The classic argument for believing that inequality will rise, more or less inevitably, as poor economies grow, is based on the Kuznets Hypothesis (KH)

* For their comments on this chapter, I am grateful to the editors and to participants at the authors' workshop held at Nuffield College, Oxford, September 2006. For expert assistance with the data used here, my thanks go to Shaohua Chen and Prem Sangraula. In writing this chapter, I have also benefited from discussions with many colleagues at the World Bank although the mandatory disclaimer applies: these are the views of the author, and should not be attributed to the World Bank or any affiliated organization. Last but not least, a special acknowledgement goes to Tony Atkinson, to whom this volume is dedicated. Tony's special ability in combining relevance with rigour in the study of inequality has long served as a model for us all.

(Kuznets 1955). This states that relative inequality increases in the early stages of growth in a developing country but begins to fall after some point, that is, the relationship between inequality (on the vertical axis) and average income (horizontal) is predicted to trace out an inverted U. As typically formalized, the KH assumes that the economy comprises a low-inequality and poor (low-mean) rural sector, and a richer urban sector with higher inequality.[1] Growth occurs by rural labour shifting to the urban sector. In the classic formulation of the KH, this is assumed to happen in a rather special way, such that a representative slice of the rural distribution is transformed into a representative slice of the urban distribution. Thus distribution is assumed to be unchanged *within* each sector. Starting with all the population in the rural sector, when the first worker moves to the urban sector, inequality must increase even though the incidence of poverty has fallen. And when the last rural worker leaves, inequality must clearly fall again. Between these extremes, the relationship between inequality and average income traces out an inverted U.

Kuznets was writing in the 1950s and he had very few survey data for developing countries to draw on. Since then, and notably since around 1980, there has been a huge expansion in the collection of nationally-representative household surveys for developing countries. These data do not suggest that most growing developing countries have seen the trend increase in inequality predicted by the KH; indeed, very few developing economies have seen a trend increase (or decrease) in overall inequality (Bruno, Ravallion, and Squire 1998). Yes, many countries have seen periods of rising inequality, but this has only rarely been sustained, with periods of falling inequality following. (Later we examine one of the commonly identified exceptions, namely China, although even there we will see that the reality is more complicated.) Studies of specific developing countries have suggested a number of reasons why the KH does not hold, but in practice an important role appears to be played by distributional shifts *within* both rural and urban areas, including distributional non-neutralities of the migration process itself.

Simple generalizations of developing country experiences—such as the claim that rising inequality is more or less inevitable—do not fit easily with the accumulated data. A number of papers have found that changes in inequality at the country level have virtually zero correlation with rates of economic growth: see, for example, Ravallion and Chen (1997), Ravallion (2001), and Dollar and Kraay (2002). Among growing economies, inequality tends to fall about as often as it rises, that is, growth tends to be 'distribution neutral' on average. If all levels of real income grow at roughly the same rate then absolute poverty must fall. This makes it unsurprising that the literature has also found

[1] For a more precise formulation of the KH, and necessary and sufficient conditions for the inverted U for various inequality measures, see Anand and Kanbur (1993).

that measures of absolute poverty tend to fall with growth—that 'growth *is* good for the poor' (to quote the title of an influential paper by Dollar and Kraay 2002). Supportive evidence for the view that absolute poverty tends to fall with growth can be found in Ravallion (1995, 2001), World Bank (2000), Fields (2001) and Kraay (2006).

There are a number of reasons for caution in interpreting this lack of correlation between changes in inequality and growth, and in drawing implications for policy. First, there can be considerable 'churning' under the surface, with gainers and losers at all levels of living and re-ranking, even when there is little or no change in overall inequality. The churning cannot be seen in cross-sectional surveys, but it is revealed in the (more limited) panel data sets available.[2] Simulations of the impacts of specific policy changes intended to promote growth also point to 'horizontal inequality' in the impacts of reform.[3] An aggregate measure of inequality will (implicitly) attach some weight to such horizontal inequalities, but one can question whether that weight is sufficient, given their import for social stability and social policies.[4]

Second, the measures of 'inequality' in this literature are typically measures of *relative* inequality, whereby multiplying all incomes by a constant leaves the measure unchanged. Finding that a relative inequality measure is unchanged during an aggregate economic expansion is perfectly consistent with large increases in *absolute* income disparities. Growth in average income tends to come with higher absolute inequality between the 'rich' and the 'poor'; in marked contrast to Figure 2.1 (discussed below), a strong positive relationship (a correlation coefficient of 0.64) is found between changes in the absolute Gini index and growth rates (Ravallion 2004). Arguably, it is the absolute changes that are more obvious to people living in a growing developing economy than the proportionate changes.[5] It may well be the case that much of the debate

[2] A useful compilation of studies using panel data can be found in the August 2000 special issue of the *Journal of Development Studies*; see the introduction by Baulch and Hoddinott (2000). The churning also stems in part from time-varying measurement errors, though plausible covariates have been evident in the studies that tested for this (see, for example, Jalan and Ravallion 2000).

[3] For example, in the context of trade reform, Ravallion (2006) reviews evidence on the extent of horizontal inequality, as indicated by the dispersion in welfare impacts at any given level of pre-intervention income. This reflects differences in variables such as household demographics and location that influence the net trading positions in relevant markets and (hence) the welfare impacts of reform.

[4] There have been efforts to address this concern. In the context of tax reform policies, Auerbach and Hassett (2002) show how an Atkinson (1970) index of social welfare can be decomposed into vertical and horizontal components in which the inequality aversion parameters can be different between the two. In the context of poverty measurement also see Bibi and Duclos (2007), who allow differential weights on the horizontal versus vertical components of the impacts of targeted transfers.

[5] In surveys of university students, Amiel and Cowell (1999) found that 40% or so thought about inequality in absolute terms rather than relative terms. For further discussion, see Atkinson and Brandolini (2004) and Ravallion (2004).

about what is happening to inequality in the world is actually a debate about the meaning of 'inequality' (Ravallion 2004; Atkinson and Brandolini 2006).

Third, there are also signs that the growth processes seen in many reforming economies in the 1990s have been putting more upward pressure on (relative) inequality. Lopez (2006) reports evidence to support this view (though based on a smaller, selected, sample of countries than will be studied in this chapter). To re-examine the relationship between growth and changes in inequality, I created 290 observations of the change between two successive household surveys for a given country with more than one observation for most countries; there are about 80 countries represented, spanning 1980–2000.[6] I then compared the changes in the Gini index with the changes in the survey mean (in real terms, using local CPIs). Figure 2.1 gives a scatter plot of changes in the log Gini index against changes in the log real survey mean between successive household surveys. The correlation coefficient is –0.13 and is not statistically significant (at the 10 per cent level). Among growing economies, inequality increased about as often as it fell, and similarly among contracting economies. If one focuses solely on the period after 1992, one finds a mild positive correlation coefficient of 0.26, which is significant at the 5 per cent level.[7]

Fourth, it must be acknowledged that there is likely to be considerable measurement error in the changes in inequality and the survey means. The errors can come from a variety of sources, including sampling errors (probably a minor concern in most cases for the surveys used here), errors arising from selective compliance (whereby certain types of households participate in surveys with lower probability than others), under-reporting of incomes and comparability problems between surveys arising from differences in questionnaires, interviewing procedures or processing methods. These errors can greatly weaken the power of the tests found in the literature for detecting the true relationship. This is obvious enough for tests that regress changes in inequality on growth. But the problem is no less severe when one regresses growth rates of the poorest quintile (say) on the overall growth rate (as in Dollar and Kraay 2002); time-varying measurement errors in inequality will bias the regression coefficient toward unity.

There are a couple of things we can do to test robustness to time-varying measurement errors. One is to use data over longer periods. Figure 2.1 uses whatever time periods are available between successive surveys. If instead one uses changes over three surveys (taking the log difference between the survey

[6] The data are drawn from *PovcalNet* and the *World Development Indicators*. *PovcalNet* is a new interactive tool that provides the distributional data from about 500 surveys for 100 developing countries, drawing on the World Bank's data base; see http://iresearch.worldbank.org/povcalnet.

[7] All significance tests in this paper are based on White standard errors (corrected for heteroscedasticity, which is clearly present).

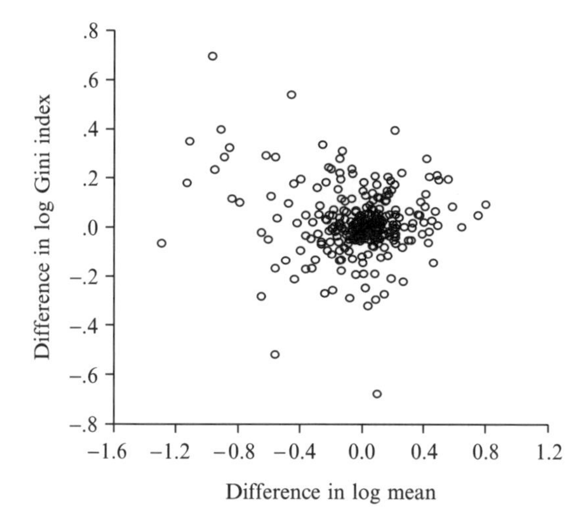

Figure 2.1 Changes in inequality and growth in the mean between successive surveys, 1980–2000

for date t and $t{-}2$) the correlation over the whole period becomes significantly negative ($r = -0.24$, $n = 206$), and that remains true for the data points after 1992. Alternatively, one can use the longest spell for each country; again there is no significant correlation ($r = 0.10$, $n = 80$).

Another test is to use growth rates in consumption from national accounts (NAS) as the instrumental variable for the growth rates based on the survey means (following Ravallion 2001). This assumes that the measurement errors in the two data sets are uncorrelated. While in practice there are sometimes overlaps in the underlying data sources used (such as when specific consumption items in the national accounts are benchmarked from household survey data), by and large the assumption is probably defensible for the purpose of testing robustness. By this test, one finds no significant correlation (in either direction) between changes in inequality and (instrumented) growth in survey means for either the 1990s, or the period as a whole since the early 1980s. Using all available observations, the IV estimate of the regression coefficient of the change in log Gini index on change in log survey mean using the change in log private consumption per capita from the NAS as the instrument is 0.04 with a standard error of 0.26. Confining the estimation to the post-1992 period, the IV regression coefficient rises substantially to 0.15, but this is only significantly different from zero at the 15 per cent level (White standard error of 0.11). So the claim that growth has been inequality-increasing in the 1990s is not particularly robust to allowing for time-varying measurement errors.

While acknowledging these data issues and caveats, the lack of a robust correlation between changes in relative inequality and growth does not imply that policy-makers aiming to fight poverty in any given country can safely focus on growth alone. Putting measurement problems to one side, all this empirical finding tells us is that, on average, there was little effective redistribution in favour of the poor. It does not tell us that redistribution rarely happens or that distribution is unimportant to the outcomes for poor people from economic growth or that social protection policies are unnecessary. The rest of this chapter takes up these issues.

2.2 Inequality and the pace of poverty reduction

While it can be agreed that economies in which household income per person is growing tend to see falling measures of absolute poverty, there is still wide variation around the trend. Consider the rate of poverty reduction in a country with a 2 per cent rate of growth in per capita income (roughly the mean rate for the developing world in 1980–2000). The 95 per cent confidence interval of the regression coefficient of the proportionate rate of poverty reduction (log difference in headcount index) on the rate of growth (log difference in mean) found in Ravallion (2001) implies that a 2 per cent rate of growth will bring anything from a modest drop in the poverty rate of about 1 per cent to a more dramatic 7 per cent annual decline. For a country with a headcount index of 40 per cent (the mean '$1-a-day' poverty rate for the developing world around 1980), we have 95 per cent confidence that the index will fall in the first year by somewhere between slightly less than one half of a percentage point and a far more impressive three points.

Why do we find that the same rate of growth can bring such different rates of poverty reduction? In answering this question it is convenient to start with the identity that the proportionate rate of poverty reduction is the product of the 'growth elasticity of poverty reduction' and the rate of growth. Note that this is not the same as the elasticity of poverty with respect to the mean holding distribution constant. The latter can be thought of as the *partial* elasticity with inequality held constant, as distinct from the total elasticity given by the proportionate rate of poverty reduction divided by the rate of growth. The partial elasticity is negative by construction; the total elasticity can have either sign. Of course, if growth is distribution-neutral on average then the two elasticities will be similar on average, although they may differ greatly in specific countries and time periods. If growth tends to come with higher (lower) inequality then (minus one times) the partial elasticity will tend to be higher (lower) than the total elasticity.

Two factors can be identified as the main proximate causes of the differing total elasticities of poverty reduction found in practice: the initial level of inequality and how inequality changes over time. I consider these in turn.

Initial inequality

It is intuitive that the higher the initial inequality in a country, the less the poor will share in the gains from growth; unless there is sufficient change in distribution, a larger (smaller) initial share of the pie will tend to come with a larger (smaller) share in the pie's expansion. While this intuition is compelling, it is in fact theoretically ambiguous as to how differences in initial inequality will affect the growth elasticity of poverty reduction. Consider two countries, one with a Lorenz curve that unambiguously dominates the other, that is, inequality is higher in one country for all inequality measures with the standard properties (Atkinson 1970). Suppose first that the Lorenz curves remain unchanged over time. It can be readily shown that the proportion of the population below any given level of income will then be homogeneous of degree zero in the mean and the level of income considered.[8] Then it is plain that the growth elasticity of poverty reduction for the headcount index (H) is (minus one times) the elasticity of the cumulative distribution function evaluated at the poverty line.[9] Next note that there can be no presumption that the country with higher inequality will have a higher H; depending on the specific properties of the Lorenz curve at H, the higher inequality country could have either a higher or lower headcount index.[10] The implications for the growth elasticity are then also ambiguous. Non-neutralities in the growth process add a further source of ambiguity in the implications of initial differences in inequality for the elasticity of the headcount index to the mean (allowing the Lorenz curve to change). Even when the initial share held by the poor is low, their gains from growth can be sizeable if growth is accompanied by sufficient pro-poor redistribution.

Some special cases yield unambiguous results, which are achieved by collapsing the potential differences in initial distribution into just one parameter. Analytic results obtained under the assumption that household income or consumption is log-normally distributed predict that the partial growth elasticity of poverty reduction holding distribution constant will fall (in absolute value) as inequality rises (Bourguignon 2003). Son and Kakwani (2004) invoke the Kakwani (1993) assumption that the Lorenz curves across countries only differ in a rather special way, namely that the entire curve shifts by a constant proportion of the difference between the actual value on the Lorenz curve and the line of equality. They also assume that the growth process is distribution-neutral and that the poverty line is less than the mean. Under

[8] This follows from the fact that $L'(p) = y/\mu$ where $L(p)$ is the Lorenz curve and $p = F(y)$ is the cumulative distribution function.

[9] In other words, the growth elasticity is $-zf(z)/H$ where $H = F(z)$ is the headcount index at the poverty line z and $f(.)$ is the density function. (Kakwani 1993 provides formulae for the partial elasticity for many other poverty measures.)

[10] This ambiguity stems from the fact that H is found at the tangency of the Lorenz curve at z/μ where μ is the mean (i.e. $L'(H) = z/\mu$).

these assumptions, Son and Kakwani show that the partial growth elasticity of poverty reduction (for the Foster-Greer-Thorbecke class of poverty measures) is monotonically decreasing in the initial value of the Gini index, which essentially becomes the sole parameter locating the Lorenz curve.

These theoretical results are for special cases but they are still instructive, and consistent with intuition. In practice, however, distributions vary by more than one parameter and growth processes are only (roughly) distribution-neutral *on average*. In fact, growth in specific countries and time periods is rarely distribution-neutral, so that assumption can be quite deceptive in predicting outcomes of specific growth episodes. For example, consider the growth process in Brazil in the 1980s. Datt and Ravallion (1992) show that if one had assumed at the outset of the decade that growth would be distribution neutral then one would have predicted a 4.5 per cent point decline in the headcount index of poverty. In fact, there was no change over the decade, with the headcount index staying at 26.5 per cent. Distributional shifts working against the poor exactly offset the gains from growth.

What does the empirical evidence suggest about the relationship between initial inequality and the growth elasticity of poverty reduction? Support for the intuition that higher inequality countries tend to have lower (absolute) elasticities was first presented in Ravallion (1997) and subsequently verified by Ravallion (2001) and Kraay (2006). These papers have used (parametric) regression-based methods (in which rates of change in poverty are regressed on rates of growth both on its own and interacted with initial inequality). We will return to this approach presently, but first it is instructive to look again at the empirical relationship in a more flexible way.

A simpler non-parametric test is to calculate the total elasticity as the log difference in the headcount index divided by the log difference in the mean, both based on successive household surveys. There is clearly a lot of noise in such a measure (as already discussed). To help reduce the noise, I smoothed the period-specific elasticities by taking the simple average of two-period elasticities (across three surveys). I also trimmed 15 extreme elasticities (below −20 or above 20). Figure 2.2 gives the results for the '$1-a-day' poverty rate. The elasticity is negative in 80 per cent of cases. We see a rather weak tendency for the elasticity to rise (become less negative) as inequality rises, from an average of about −4 at the lowest Gini index to roughly zero at the highest. The correlation coefficient is 0.26, which is significant at the 1 per cent level. The two high positive elasticities in Figure 2.2 are almost certainly measured with large errors, and this is exaggerating the slope of the line of best fit. Dropping these two observations, the correlation is still significant at the 1 per cent level, and the line of best fit still passes through an elasticity of zero at a Gini index of about 60 per cent. Among the highest inequality countries, poverty incidence is quite unresponsive (on average) to economic growth.

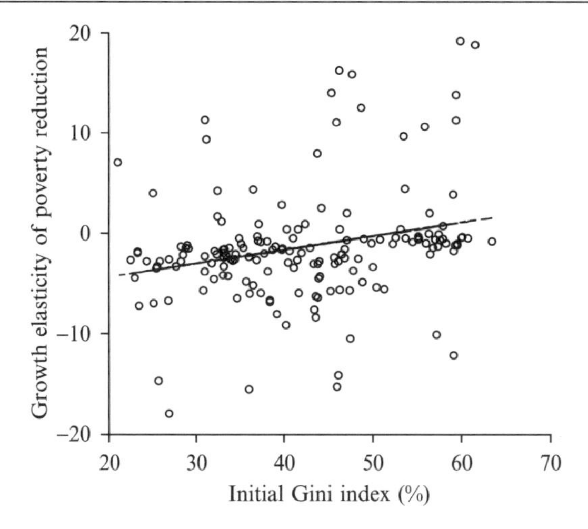

Figure 2.2 Empirical growth elasticities of poverty reduction against initial Gini index
Source: Author's calculations (see text).

In modelling the relationship between poverty reduction and growth, Ravallion (1997) postulated that the rate of poverty reduction (measured as the difference in the log of the measure of poverty) is directly proportional to the 'distribution-corrected rate of growth' where the latter is given by the ordinary rate of growth (log difference in mean consumption or income) times a distributional term. In Ravallion (1997), the distributional correction used is one minus the initial Gini index. This model can be improved (in terms of fit with data on actual spells of changes in poverty matched with growth) by using instead an adjustment for nonlinearity in the relationship between the growth elasticity of poverty and the initial inequality, giving a simple model of the expected proportionate rate of change in poverty over any period:

$$\text{Rate of change in poverty} =$$
$$[\text{Constant} \times (1-\text{Inequality index})^{\theta}] \times \text{Ordinary growth rate}$$

The constant term is negative and θ is a parameter not less than one. The total growth elasticity of poverty reduction is the term in square brackets.

To interpret this formula, note first that at high levels of inequality the poor will gain little or nothing from growth; at the extreme in which the inequality index is one, the richest person has all the income and so all the gains from growth will go to that person; the elasticity will be zero. For values of θ strictly greater than one, higher levels of initial inequality will have progressively smaller impacts on the elasticity as inequality rises. This is what one would expect intuitively as long as the poverty rate is sufficiently less than unity; growth will have no impact on poverty when the richest person has all the income, but equally well it would have no effect when the richest two people share all the income. The above model can be augmented by adding one or more terms for changes in distribution, to isolate the partial elasticity. This raises the R^2 but does not affect the results of interest here, given that (as we have already seen) changes in distribution tend to be uncorrelated with growth rates.

Quite a good fit with data on actual rates of poverty reduction across developing countries can be obtained using the initial Gini index as the measure of inequality and using $\theta = 2$.[11] The total elasticity of poverty reduction is directly proportional to the squared 'equality index' $(1-G)$. I find that the constant of proportionality is -6.07, with a standard error of 0.48 and $R^2 = 0.65$ ($n = 89$).[12]

To help interpret this empirical model, consider again the rate of poverty reduction with a 2 per cent rate of growth and a headcount index of 40 per cent. In a low-inequality country, with a Gini index of 0.30 (say) the elasticity will be about -3 and the headcount index will fall by about 6 per cent per year (or 2.4 percentage points in the first year); the headcount index will be halved in 11 years. By contrast, consider a high-inequality country with a Gini index of 0.60 growing at the same rate and with the same initial headcount index. The growth elasticity of poverty reduction will be about -1. This is higher (in absolute value) than suggested by Figure 2.2. But, even so, it will take about 35 years to halve the initial poverty rate. Poverty responds more slowly to growth in high inequality countries; or (to put the same point slightly differently) high inequality countries will need unusually high growth rates to achieve rapid poverty reduction.

The argument works in reverse too; high inequality will help protect the poor from the adverse impact of aggregate economic contraction. Low inequality can thus be a mixed blessing for poor people living in an unstable macroeconomic environment; it helps them share in the benefits of growth, but it also exposes them to the costs of contraction (Ravallion 1997). There is evidence

[11] The nonlinear least squares estimate of θ on a sample of estimates of the changes in the log of the '$1/day' poverty rates for the longest available spells between surveys for 90 countries gave 3.73 with a standard error of 0.93. However, on deleting one outlier this dropped to 2.10 (0.73). I constructed this data set from *PovcalNet*; see note 6.

[12] Measurement errors in surveys will now generate two sources of bias: the rate of poverty reduction and the growth rate are measured from the same surveys and there will be an extra bias from measurement error in the initial Gini index. Under plausible conditions (essentially classical measurement errors) these two sources of bias will work in opposite directions. As a check for net bias, I used a constructed variable based on a lagged value of the Gini index and the growth rate of private consumption from the national accounts as an IV. The net effect was a slightly higher (more negative) regression coefficient, which remained highly significant. However, this estimator requires that one must use shorter time periods (to retain the lagged Gini index for use in the IV) and one loses country observations as well (countries with only two surveys). So I rely on the OLS estimate in the following discussion.

that this also happens at the local level during an economy-wide crisis; high inequality districts of Indonesia experienced less dramatic rates of increase in poverty during the 1998 financial crisis than did low inequality districts (Ravallion and Lokshin 2004).

So far we have focused on how initial inequality affects the growth elasticity of poverty reduction. What about the initial mean? The theoretical relationship between the partial growth elasticity of the headcount index and the mean is ambiguous although, in the special case of a log-normal distribution of income, the partial elasticity is strictly decreasing in the mean (Bourguignon 2003) and this also holds for the poverty gap index and other 'higher order' poverty measures in the Foster-Greer-Thorbecke class under quite general conditions (Son and Kakwani 2004). However, the empirical evidence does not offer much support for this theoretical prediction. There is little or no robust evidence of a significant correlation between the growth elasticity of poverty reduction and the initial mean (either on its own, or controlling for initial inequality).

None of this is inconsistent with the findings in the literature indicating that a large share of the variance in rates of poverty reduction can be attributed to differences in ordinary rates of growth (Ravallion 1995; Ravallion and Chen 1997; Fields 2001; Kraay 2006). In a recent contribution, Kraay (2006) presents Datt-Ravallion decompositions of changes in '$1-a-day' poverty measures into growth and redistribution components for as many countries as possible. Kraay's growth component is the product of the growth rate and the partial elasticity.[13] Kraay finds that the variance in the growth component is largely attributable to the growth rate, rather than the partial elasticity or its covariance with growth. For example, he attributes 81 per cent of the variance in the log absolute value of the growth component of changes in the headcount index to the variance in the log absolute growth rate.

This is perfectly consistent with finding that poverty responds little to growth in specific countries. Kraay's results are based on averages formed from cross-country comparisons.[14] For a country with average inequality, which does not increase with growth, Kraay's results offer some support for his policy conclusion that for reducing poverty the main thing to worry about is achieving a higher rate of growth. However, that does not mean that growth is sufficient even when inequality is low. If growth in a low inequality country comes with a sufficient increase in inequality then it will by-pass the poor. And, as already noted, the empirical finding that growth is roughly distribution-neutral on average is consistent with the fact that it increases roughly half the time during growth

[13] Recall that it is a partial elasticity because it holds distribution constant; by contrast the 'total elasticity' lets distribution vary consistently with the data; the elasticity in square brackets in the above equation is a total elasticity. The analytic elasticities of poverty measures discussed in Kakwani (1993) and Bourguignon (2001) are partial elasticities.

[14] A variance is an average too, namely the mean of the squared deviations from the ordinary mean.

spells (Ravallion 2001). Policy efforts to keep inequality low may then be crucial to achieving pro-poor growth in many low-inequality countries.

Furthermore, as we have seen, for high inequality countries, growth can be quite a blunt instrument against poverty unless that growth comes with falling inequality. Here the heterogeneity in country circumstances cannot be ignored. Averages formed across countries can be quite uninformative about how best to achieve pro-poor growth in specific countries.

The preceding discussion has pointed to the role of initial income inequality as a proximate determinant of differing rates of poverty reduction at a given rate of growth. However, to help inform policy we need to probe more deeply into the relevant sources of inequality. There are inequalities in a number of dimensions that are likely to matter, including access to both private (human and physical) assets and public goods. Inequalities in access to infrastructure and social services naturally make it harder for poor people to take up the opportunities afforded by aggregate economic growth. For example, although India has relatively low overall inequality (of consumption, which tends to have somewhat lower inequality than income, given consumption smoothing), the country has high inequalities in some specific and important dimensions, including human resource development and access to markets (as influenced in part by rural infrastructure). These inequalities have interacted powerfully with the sectoral composition of economic growth in influencing India's progress against poverty, which has been disappointing in the 1990s, particularly given the (relatively high) growth rates.[15]

Changing income distribution

A second factor influencing the rate of poverty reduction at a given rate of growth is changing income distribution. As I have emphasized, finding that growth tends to be distribution neutral on average does not mean that distribution is unchanging. Whether inequality is rising or not can make a big difference to the rate of poverty reduction. Among growing economies, the median rate of decline in the '$1-a-day' headcount index is 10 per cent per year among countries that combined growth with falling inequality, while it is only 1 per cent per year for those countries for which growth came with rising inequality (Ravallion 2001). Either way, poverty tends to fall, but at very different rates. (And similarly among contracting economies; poverty rises on average, but much more rapidly when inequality is rising than falling.) As one would expect, changes in distribution matter even more for higher-order poverty measures (such as the squared poverty gap), which can respond quite elastically to even small changes in overall inequality.

[15] On the interaction effects referred to here for India, see Ravallion and Datt (2002); on the implications for India's progress against poverty in the 1990s, see Datt and Ravallion (2002).

What underlies the changes in distribution, as they affect poverty? There are a great many country-specific idiosyncratic factors, such as shocks to agricultural incomes, changes in trade regime, shifts in relative prices, tax reforms, welfare-policy reforms and changes in demographics. Generalizations across country experience are never easy, but one factor that is likely to matter in many developing countries is the geographic *and* sectoral pattern of growth. The greater availability of nationally-representative household surveys has revealed marked and persistent concentrations of poor people in specific regions and/or sectors. The evidence from such poverty profiles points to the importance of the pattern of growth to overall poverty reduction and this is consistent with cross-country evidence on how rates of poverty reduction vary with the sectoral composition of economic growth (Loayza and Raddatz 2006). The extent to which growth favours the rural sector is often key to its impact on poverty. The geographic incidence of both rural and urban economic growth is also important. Of course, there is country specificity here too. The extent to which the pattern of growth (rather than simply the overall growth rate) matters to the rate of poverty reduction is likely to vary from country to country depending on, *inter alia*, how unbalanced the growth process has been in the past and, hence, how much difference one currently finds between sectors or regions in levels of poverty.

While it still appears to be the case that (relative) inequality falls about as often as it increases during spells of aggregate economic expansion, there are also signs that higher growth in a number of developing countries has come with widening regional disparities and little or no growth in some lagging poor areas. The two most populous countries, China and India, are examples (Chaudhuri and Ravallion 2006). We shall return to the case of China.

2.3 A growth–equity trade-off?

High inequalities in specific dimensions not only generate higher poverty now but can also impede future growth and poverty reduction.[16] A plausible way this can happen stems from credit market failures, such that some people are unable to exploit opportunities for investment. It will tend to be the asset poor for whom these constraints are most likely to be binding. With declining marginal products of capital, the output loss from the market failure will be greater for the poor. The higher the proportion of people who are poor, the lower the aggregate growth rate; poverty is then self-perpetuating. There are other ways this can

[16] There is now a sizeable theoretical literature on the various ways in which inequality can impede growth. Contributions include Galor and Zeira (1993), Banerjee and Newman (1993), Benabou (1996), Aghion, Caroli, and Garcia-Penalosa (1999), and Bardhan, Bowles, and Gintis (1999).

happen. Even without credit market failures, high inequality can also foster social and macroeconomic instability and impede efficiency-promoting reforms that require cooperation and trust.[17]

These arguments do not justify the claim that higher income inequality will necessarily imply lower growth. Exceptions arise when the higher inequality is the result of removing a control regime that kept inequality low by compressing the labour-market returns to schooling or the returns to other forms of investment. In certain circumstances, inequality can be inefficiently low, bringing costs to the poor. Rising inequality can then play a positive role in facilitating rapid poverty reduction, such as when the rising inequality is the by-product of pro-poor institutional changes.[18]

However, economic theory does lead one to question any presumption that high inequality is good for growth, or even that a trade-off can be expected in general. That will depend on the specific sources of high inequality. When it comes from social exclusion, restrictions on migration, inequalities in human capital and in access to credit and insurance, corruption and uneven influence, then the inequality can entail that certain segments of the population are unable to escape poverty. There will almost certainly be more poverty and lower mean income than in the absence of these specific inequalities.

What does the evidence suggest? There is supportive evidence for the view that inequality is bad for growth from cross-country comparisons of growth rates, suggesting that countries with higher initial inequality experienced lower rates of growth controlling for other factors such as initial average income, openness to trade and the rate of inflation.[19] When combined with the findings reported earlier in this chapter, we see that poor people in high inequality countries face a double handicap: such countries will tend to experience lower growth rates and the growth that does occur will have less impact on poverty.[20] This is not to say that there are many countries for which inequality is too high to allow growth and poverty reduction; the available data and parameter estimates from the literature imply that the level of inequality needed to stall future poverty reduction is around the upper bound of the range found in the data (Ravallion 1997). Rather, the point is that the observed pace of poverty reduction will tend to be appreciably lower in high inequality countries, even if that inequality does not rise further.

[17] Aghion *et al.* (1998) and Bardhan *et al.* (1999) review these and related arguments.

[18] For example, rising rural landlessness in the wake of an equitable land reform in Vietnam has proved to be a poverty reducing force (Ravallion and van de Walle 2006).

[19] See Persson and Tabellini (1994), Alesina and Rodrik (1994), Clarke (1995), Birdsall, Ross, and Sabot (1995), Perotti (1996), Deininger and Squire (1998), and Easterly (2002).

[20] Inequality convergence (whereby inequality tends to fall in high inequality countries and rise in low inequality countries) will help compensate for these tendencies; the evidence on the extent and pace of such convergence is still somewhat unclear, but it does appear to be happening (Ravallion 2003).

Not surprisingly, and despite the explosion of new data and analysis, there are still a number of concerns about the data and methods underlying these findings based on cross-country comparative analysis (Ravallion 2001). The data problems do not all suggest the same direction of bias. For example, the aggregation biases in cross-country growth empirics can actually hide the true costs to the poor of high inequality (Ravallion 1998). More geographically disaggregated (including micro) data have shown more robust evidence that inequality is bad for growth.[21] A continuing limitation of past work is that the empirical literature using cross-country growth regressions has generally failed to identify the relevant sources of inequality, recognizing that some inequalities are likely to be more inefficient than others (as I have already discussed). Future research will hopefully throw more light on the magnitude of the efficiency costs of specific dimensions of inequality.

China is often cited as an example of the idea of an aggregate growth–equity trade off. Probably no other country has had the steep rise in both mean income *and* income inequality that China has seen since the early 1980s. There can be no doubt that absolute poverty in China has fallen greatly since around 1980. While China's poverty rate today is probably slightly lower than the average for the world as a whole,[22] it was a very different story around 1980, when the incidence of extreme poverty in China was one of the highest in the world.[23] I estimate that only four countries (Cambodia, Burkina Faso, Mali and Uganda) had a higher poverty rate than in China around 1980.[24] Income inequality has also been rising, though not continuously, and more so in some periods and provinces. Figure 2.3 gives the estimates of the Gini index, which rose from 28 per cent in 1981 to 39 per cent in 2001.[25] Also notice that (in contrast to every other developing country I am aware of) inequality is higher in rural China than urban China, although there is a clear indication of convergence.

The Gini index is only one possible measure of inequality, and it need not reflect well the normative judgements one makes about how different levels of living should be weighted when measuring 'inequality' (Atkinson 1970). A more revealing way of representing the distributional impacts of China's

[21] See Ravallion (1998), Ravallion and Chen (2007) and Benjamin, Brandt, and Giles (2006), all using data for China.

[22] See Chen and Ravallion (2004) who estimate that in 2001, 17% of China's population live below $1 a day at 1993 Purchasing Power Parity; the corresponding figure for the world as a whole is 18% (21% for developing countries alone).

[23] The proportion of China's population living below $1 a day in 1981 is estimated to have been 64% (from *Povcalnet*, see note 6).

[24] Based on the '$1-a-day' poverty rates for 1981 from *Povcalnet*.

[25] Note that the latter figure is somewhat lower than past estimates for China; this is because the estimates in Figure 2.3 include corrections for urban–rural cost-of-living differences, which have tended to rise over time because of higher inflation in urban areas. Without these corrections the Gini index for 2001 rises to 45%.

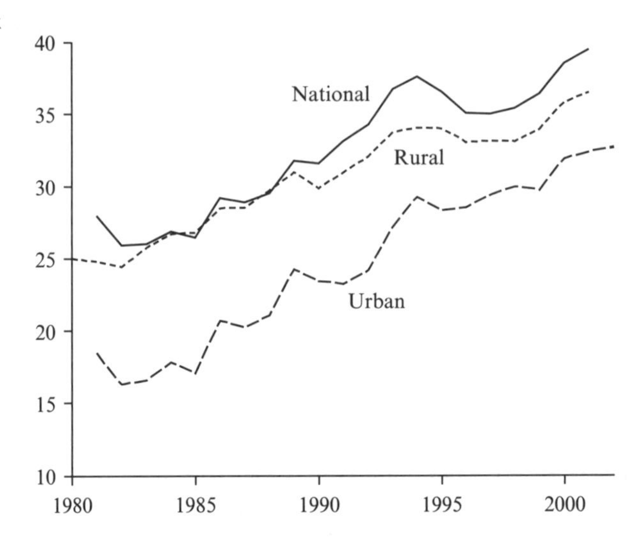

Figure 2.3 China: income inequality in rural and urban areas and nationally, Gini index (%)

growth is the growth incidence curve (GIC), as given in Figure 2.4 for the 1990s. The GIC gives the rate of growth at each percentile of the distribution (ranked by income per person).[26] We see that growth rates in China in the 1990s tend to rise as we move up the distribution; the annual rate of growth in the 1990s varies from about 3 per cent for the poorest percentile to nine per cent for the richest. While the growth rate in the overall mean was 6.2 per cent, the mean growth rate for the poorest 20 per cent (roughly according with China's '$1-a-day' poverty rate in 1990) was 4.0 per cent.[27]

Has China faced a growth–equity trade-off? It is undoubtedly the case that some of the rise in inequality was the result of efficiency-promoting economic reforms. From a pre-reform legacy of wage compression and low labour mobility, China moved gradually to a market-based system featuring a dynamic non-state sector and an increasingly open labour market. Wage dispersion within skill and

[26] The GIC is obtained by calculating growth rates on the date-specific quantile functions (obtained by inverting the cumulative distribution function); see Ravallion and Chen (2003). If the GIC is normalized by the growth rate in the mean then one obtains a curve giving the (total) elasticity to growth at each level of income; for further discussion see Essama-Nssah and Lambert (2006).

[27] This is the Ravallion–Chen (2003) 'rate of pro-poor growth', namely the mean growth rate of the poor. This gives the change in the Watts index per unit time divided by the initial headcount index. Notice that the mean growth rate of the poor is not the same thing as the growth rate in the mean for the poor, which will not in general be consistent with even the direction of change in any sensible measure of the level of poverty.

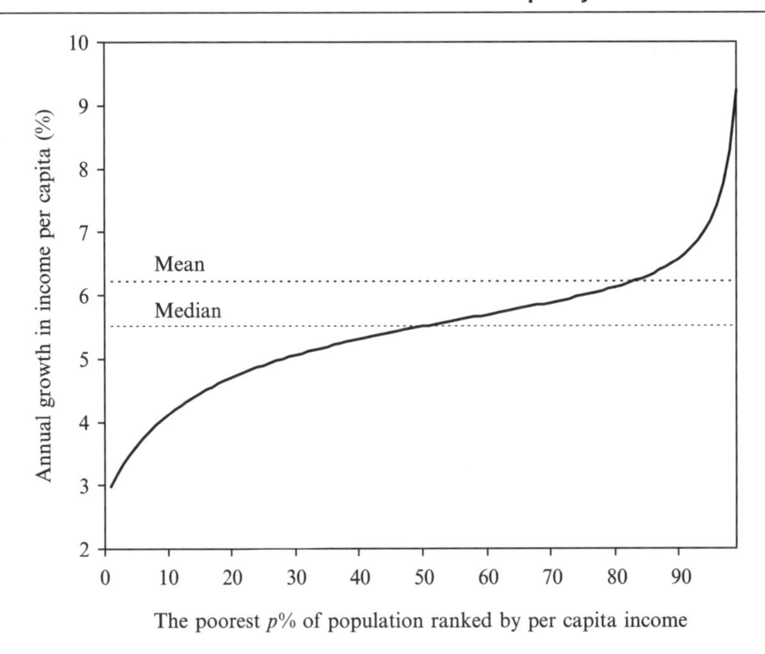

Figure 2.4 Growth incidence curve for China, 1990–99

experience categories has increased considerably and returns to schooling have also risen (Park *et al.* 2004; Heckman and Li 2004). In rural areas, the Household Responsibility System (HRS) (introduced in around 1980) assigned land to households who became the residual claimants on output. This policy reform restored incentives for work. The reform naturally put upward pressure on inequality within rural areas, as some farmers were more able than others, although the HRS clearly put downward pressure on inequality in the country as a whole by reducing the gap in living standards between urban and rural areas.

While some of the policy reforms and institutional changes in China's economic transition simultaneously increased inequality and reduced poverty, other economic and political forces have also been at work to generate less benign inequalities. These include geographic poverty traps (whereby prospects of escaping poverty depend causally on where one lives), emerging inequalities in opportunities for enhancing human capital, obtaining credit and insurance, protecting one's rights under the law and influencing public affairs.[28] These 'bad inequalities'—rooted in market failures, coordination failures and governance failures—limit people's opportunities to take actions that will help them escape poverty.

[28] Chaudhuri and Ravallion (2006) review the evidence on these specific inequalities in China. For a more general discussion and review of the evidence on these sources of inequality of opportunity in developing countries see World Bank (2005).

Strikingly, the evidence for China does not suggest an aggregate growth–equity trade off. We have seen that inequality in China has shown a tendency to rise over time just as GDP rose. The regression coefficient of the Gini index on GDP per capita has a t-ratio of 9.22 (a correlation coefficient of 0.90). However, this could well be spurious; the Durbin-Watson statistic is 0.45, indicating strong residual auto-correlation. This is not surprising since both inequality and mean income have strong trends, possibly associated with different causative factors.

A better test is to compare the growth rates with changes in inequality over time.[29] Then it becomes far less clear that higher inequality has been the price of China's growth. The correlation between the growth rate of GDP and log difference in the Gini index is −0.05. Now the regression coefficient has a t-ratio of only 0.22 (and a Durbin-Watson of 1.75). This test does not suggest that higher growth *per se* meant a steeper rise in inequality.

The periods of more rapid growth did not bring more rapid increases in inequality; indeed, the periods of falling inequality (1981–85 and 1995–98) had the highest growth in average household income (Ravallion and Chen 2007). Also, the sub-periods of highest growth in the primary sector (1983–84 1987–88 and 1994–96) did not come with lower growth in other sectors. Nor does one find that the provinces of China with more rapid rural income growth experienced a steeper increase in inequality; if anything it was the opposite.

To consider one of these periods more closely, Figure 2.5 gives the GIC for China in 1993–96, which (in marked contrast to Figure 2.4) took on an inverted U shape, with highest growth rates observed at around the 25th percentile. The growth rate for the poorest quintile for this sub-period was 10.1 per cent per annum—above the ordinary growth rate of 8.2 per cent, indicating the extent to which the distributional shift in this sub-period favoured the poor. (Note also that the overall rate of growth was higher in this sub-period than for the 1990s as a whole.) Ravallion and Chen (2007) argue that the main reason for this change in the mid-1990s was a sharp reduction in the taxation of farmers, associated with a rise in the government's procurement price of foodgrains. (China had a long-term policy of taxing farmers this way to provide cheap food to urban areas; naturally this was inequality increasing.)

The diverse post-reform growth experiences of China's provinces are also consistent with the evidence from cross-country comparisons in suggesting that high inequality impedes growth and poverty reduction. China's provinces did not all start out at the beginning of the reform period with very low inequality. The Gini index around the mid-1980s varied from 18 per cent to 33 per cent. These differences are correlated with the subsequent growth rates. Provinces starting with relatively high inequality saw slower progress against

[29] There is still positive first-order serial correlation of 0.48 in the first difference of log GDP although there is no sign of serial correlation in the residuals from the regression of the first difference of log Gini on log GDP. So the (first-order) differenced specification is appropriate.

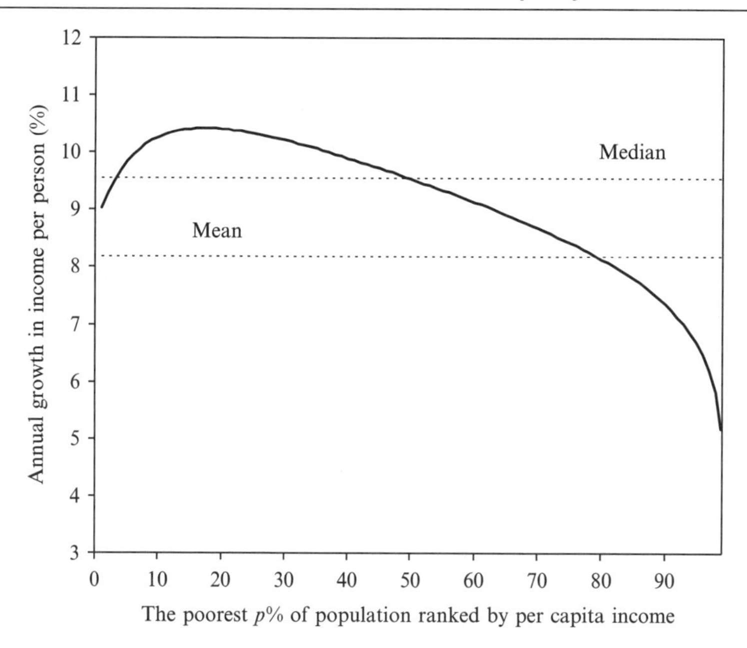

Figure 2.5 Growth incidence curve for China, 1993–96

poverty, due both to lower growth and a lower growth elasticity of poverty reduction (Ravallion and Chen 2007). Similarly, Benjamin, Brandt, and Giles (2006) find that Chinese villages with higher initial inequality (near the beginning of the reform period) tended to see lower subsequent growth rates through the 1990s. In explaining this finding, Benjamin *et al.* point to the adverse consequences of high inequality for the collective action within village economies that is needed for efficiency-enhancing reforms and public investments.

This lack of any evident aggregate trade-off has important implications. On the one hand, it means that growth will tend to reduce absolute poverty. Naturally, with the same growth rate and no rise in inequality, the number of poor in China would be lower; indeed, it would be less than one-quarter of its actual value (a poverty rate in 2001 of less than 1.5% rather than 8%). This calculation would clearly be deceptive if inequality rises with economic growth, as the 'price' of that growth. However, as we have seen, the evidence does not support that view. On the other hand, the absence of such a trade-off also means that rising inequality put a serious brake on China's pace of poverty reduction. That is also borne out by the finding reported by Ravallion (2005*c*) that the provinces that saw a more rapid rise in rural inequality saw *less* progress against poverty, not more.

As China's policy-makers now realize, it will be harder for China to maintain its past rate of progress against poverty without addressing the problem of rising inequality. To the extent that recent history is any guide to the future, we can expect that the historically high levels of inequality found in many provinces today will inhibit future prospects of poverty reduction—just as we find that the provinces that started the reform period with relatively high inequality faced a double handicap in future poverty reduction: they had lower subsequent growth *and* the poor shared less in the gains from that growth.

Other factors point to the same conclusion. It appears that aggregate economic growth in China is increasingly coming from sources that bring more limited gains to the poorest. The low-lying fruit of efficiency-enhancing pro-poor reforms are possibly getting scarce. Inequality is continuing to rise *and* poverty measures are becoming more responsive to rising inequality. At the outset of China's current transition period to a market economy, levels of poverty were so high that inequality was not an important concern. That has changed.

2.4 Lessons for development policy

Accepting that high inequality impedes poverty reduction, what should policy-makers do about inequality? First we must be clear on the objective. If we agree that poverty reduction is the overall goal for development policy rather than reducing inequality *per se*, then we should not accept redistributive policies that come at the cost of lower longer-term living standards for poor people. To accept that there is no aggregate trade-off between mean income and inequality does not imply that there are no trade-offs at the level of specific policies. Reducing inequality by adding further distortions to an economy will have ambiguous effects on growth and poverty reduction. But it should not be presumed either that there will be such a trade-off with all redistributive policies. The potential for 'win–win' policies stems from the fact that some of the things that impede growth also entail that the poor share less in the opportunities unleashed by growth.

More rapid poverty reduction requires a combination of more growth, a more pro-poor pattern of growth and success in reducing the antecedent inequalities that limit the economic opportunities of poor people. Even a distribution-neutral growth process—which is hardly a high standard for 'equitable growth' in high-inequality countries—can leave many poor people behind. The challenge is to better understand the specific factors that constrain some poor people from participating in the benefits of a growing economy, and to draw out the lessons for the types of policies that are needed for rapid poverty reduction.

A majority of the world's poor still live in rural areas and this is likely to remain true for some time to come (Ravallion 2002). It can be expected that agriculture and non-farm rural development will remain a high priority in setting sectoral policies for poverty reduction. Higher agricultural productivity promotes growth in other sectors; in developing economies, the evidence suggests that agricultural growth tends to (Granger-)cause overall economic growth (Tiffin and Irz 2006). Higher farm productivity can be expected to reduce overall inequality within a typical developing economy (where food producers tend to be poor and poor consumers have high budget shares devoted to food). Achieving higher farm yields in rain-fed, drought-prone, settings will require both more research on appropriate farm technologies (including appropriate to labour-abundant settings) and policy reforms and public investments to help assure successful adoption of those technologies.

Spatial concentrations of extreme poverty remain even in the more rapidly growing developing economies. A recurrent issue is striking the right balance between investing in poor areas and reducing costs of out-migration from those areas. Does it make more sense to move jobs to people, or people to jobs? Is there a trade-off between achieving greater regional equity—such as by focusing on areas with high poverty rates but low poverty densities—and poverty reduction in the aggregate? There is fertile ground here for future research. However, here too the trade-offs may not be as acute as some observers think; the right sorts of investments in poor areas (such as in education and managing risks) may well be necessary conditions for out-migration to begin.

Recognizing that it is typically the poor rather than the rich who are locked out of profitable opportunities for self-advancement by the failures of markets and governments, interventions that make these institutions work better can help promote pro-poor growth. Successful policies can focus on either correcting the underlying market and governmental failures or on directly intervening to redress the inequalities, notably by fostering the accumulation of (physical and human) assets by poor people. Here one can point to the potential importance of a wide range of policies including sound public investments in rural infrastructure, better policies for delivering quality health and education services to poor people, and policies that allow key product and factor markets (for land, labour and credit) to work better from the point of view of poor people. The right combination of interventions will naturally depend on country and regional circumstances.

There is still much we do not know about the most appropriate policy combinations in specific circumstances, although some pointers have emerged from research. Making the provision of health and education services more responsive to the needs of poor people is likely to be crucial to achieving pro-poor growth in most settings (World Bank 2004*a*). In rural economies, security of access to land through tenancy reform and titling programmes is arguably no less important (World Bank 2004*b*). In some circumstances, rural infrastructure development can also play a decisive role; for example, research has revealed the importance of rural roads to achieving more pro-poor growth processes in rural China (Jalan and Ravallion 2002). Better instruments for credit and insurance can also help, in both smoothing consumption and underpinning otherwise risky growth-promoting strategies. Removing biases against the poor in taxation, spending and regulatory (including migration) policies can also play an important role. Again taking an example from China, reducing the government's taxation of farmers through its under-priced foodgrain procurement quotas has been a powerful instrument against poverty (Ravallion and Chen 2007).

The challenge for policy is to combine growth-promoting policies with the right policies for assuring that the poor can participate fully in the opportunities unleashed, and so contribute to that growth. If a country gets the combination of policies right, then both growth and poverty reduction can be rapid. Get it wrong, and both may well be stalled.

References

Aghion, P., Caroli, E., and Garcia-Penalosa, C. (1999). 'Inequality and Economic Growth: The Perspectives of the New Growth Theories'. *Journal of Economic Literature*, 37: 1615–60.

Alesina, A. and Rodrik, D. (1994). 'Distributive Politics and Economic Growth'. *Quarterly Journal of Economics*, 108: 465–90.

Amiel, Y. and Cowell, F. (1999). *Thinking about Inequality: Personal Judgment and Income Distributions*. Cambridge: Cambridge University Press.

Anand, S. and Kanbur, R. (1993). 'The Kuznets Process and the Inequality–Development Relationship'. *Journal of Development Economics*, 40: 25–52.

Atkinson, A. B. (1970). 'On the Measurement of Inequality'. *Journal of Economic Theory*, 2: 244–63.

—— (1987). 'On the Measurement of Poverty'. *Econometrica*, 55: 749–64.

Atkinson, A. B. and Brandolini, A. (2006). 'On the World Distribution of Income'. Unpublished paper. Oxford: Nuffield College, Oxford University.

Auerbach, A. J. and Hassett, K. A. (2002). 'A New Measure of Horizontal Equity'. *American Economic Review*, 92: 1116–25.

Banerjee, A. V. and Newman, A. F. (1993). 'Occupational Choice and the Process of Development'. *Journal of Political Economy*, 101: 274–98.

Bardhan, P., Bowles, S., and Gintis, H. (1999). 'Wealth Inequality, Wealth Constraints and Economic Performance', in A. B. Atkinson and F. Bourguignon (eds), *Handbook of Income Distribution, Volume 1*. Amsterdam: North-Holland, 541–604.

Baulch, R. and Hoddinott, J. (2000). 'Economic Mobility and Poverty Dynamics in Developing Countries'. *Journal of Development Studies*, 36: 1–24.

Benabou, R. (1996). 'Inequality and Growth', in B. Bernanke and J. Rotemberg (eds), *National Bureau of Economic Research Macroeconomics Annual*. Cambridge: MIT Press, 11–74.

Benjamin, D., Brandt, L., and Giles, J. (2006). 'Inequality and Growth in Rural China: Does Higher inequality Impede Growth?' Unpublished paper. Toronto: Department of Economics, University of Toronto.

Bibi, S. and Duclos, J.-Y. (2007). 'Equity and Policy Effectiveness with Imperfect Targeting'. *Journal of Development Economics*, 83: 109–40.

Birdsall, N., Ross, D., and Sabot, R. (1995). 'Inequality and Growth Reconsidered: Lessons from East Asia'. *World Bank Economic Review*, 9: 477–508.

Bourguignon, F. (2001). 'The Pace of Economic Growth and Poverty Reduction'. Paper presented at LACEA 2001 Conference, Montevideo.

—— (2003). 'The Growth Elasticity of Poverty Reduction: Explaining Heterogeneity across Countries and Time-periods', in T. Eichler and S. Turnovsky (eds), *Growth and Inequality*. Cambridge, MA: MIT Press, 3–26.

Bruno, M., Ravallion, M., and Squire, L. (1998). 'Equity and Growth in Developing Countries: Old and New Perspectives on the Policy Issues', in V. Tanzi and K.-Y. Chu (eds), *Income Distribution and High-Quality Growth*. Cambridge, MA: MIT Press, 117–46.

Chaudhuri, S. and Ravallion, M. (2006). 'Partially Awakened Giants: Uneven Growth in China and India'. Policy Research Working Paper, The World Bank.

Chen, S. and Ravallion, M. (2001). 'How Did the World's Poorest Fare in the 1990s?' *Review of Income and Wealth*, 47: 283–300.

—— and —— (2004). 'How Have the World's Poorest Fared Since the Early 1980s?' *World Bank Research Observer*, 19: 141–70.

Clarke, G. (1995). 'More Evidence on Income Distribution and Growth'. *Journal of Development Economics*, 47: 403–28.

Datt, G. and Ravallion, M. (1992). 'Growth and Redistribution Components of Changes in Poverty Measures: A Decomposition with Applications to Brazil and India in the 1980s'. *Journal of Development Economics*, 38: 275–95.

—— and —— (1996). 'India's Checkered History in the Fight Against Poverty: Are There Lessons for the Future?' *Economic and Political Weekly*, 31: 2479–86.

—— and —— (2002). 'Has India's Post-Reform Economic Growth Left the Poor Behind'. *Journal of Economic Perspectives*, 16: 89–108.

Deininger, K. and Squire, L. (1998). 'New Ways of Looking at Old Issues: Inequality and Growth'. *Journal of Development Economics*, 57: 259–87.

Dollar, D. and Kraay, A. (2002), 'Growth Is Good for the Poor'. *Journal of Economic Growth*, 7: 195–225.

Easterly, W. (2002). 'Inequality does Cause Underdevelopment: New Evidence'. Working Paper 1, Washington, DC: Center for Global Development.

Essama-Nssah, B. and Lambert, P. J. (2006). 'Measuring the Pro-Poorness of Income Growth Within an Elasticity Framework'. Unpublished paper. Eugene, OR: University of Oregon.

Fields, G. S. (2001). *Distribution and Development*. New York: Russell Sage Foundation.

Fleisher, B. and Xiaojun, W. (2004). 'Skill Differentials, Return to Schooling and Market Segmentation in a Transition Economy: The Case of Mainland China'. *Journal of Development Economics*, 73: 315–28.

Foster, J. Greer, J., and Thorbecke, E. (1984). 'A Class of Decomposable Poverty Measures'. *Econometrica*, 52: 761–5.

Galor, O. and Zeira, J. (1993). 'Income Distribution and Macroeconomics'. *Review of Economic Studies*, 60: 35–52.

Heckman, J. and Li, X. (2004). 'Selection Bias, Comparative Advantage and Heterogeneous Returns to Education: Evidence from China in 2000'. *Pacific Economic Review*, 9: 155–71.

Jalan, J. and Ravallion, M. (2000), 'Is Transient Poverty Different? Evidence for Rural China'. *Journal of Development Studies*, 36: 82–99.
—— and —— (2002). 'Geographic Poverty Traps? A Micro Model of Consumption Growth in Rural China?' *Journal of Applied Econometrics*, 17: 329–46.
Kakwani, N. (1993). 'Poverty and Economic Growth with Application to Côte D'Ivoire'. *Review of Income and Wealth*, 39: 121–39.
Kraay, A. (2006). 'When is Growth Pro-Poor? Evidence from a Panel of Countries'. *Journal of Development Economics*, 80: 198–227.
Kuznets, S. (1955). 'Economic Growth and Income Inequality'. *American Economic Review*, 45: 1–28.
Loayza, N. and Raddatz, C. (2006). 'The Composition of Growth matters to Poverty Reduction'. Unpublished paper, Development Research Group. Washington, DC: The World Bank.
Lopez, H. (2006). 'Did Growth become Less Pro-Poor in the 1990s?' Policy Research Working Paper 3931. Washington, DC: The World Bank.
Park, A., Song, X., Zhang, J., and Zhao, Y. (2004). 'The Growth of Wage Inequality in Urban China 1988 to 1999'. Unpublished paper. Ann Arbor, MI: Department of Economics, University of Michigan.
Perotti, R. (1996). 'Growth, Income Distribution and Democracy: What the Data Say'. *Journal of Economic Growth*, 1: 149–87.
Persson, T. and Tabellini, G. (1994) 'Is Inequality Harmful for Growth?' *American Economic Review*, 84: 600–21.
Ravallion, M. (1995). 'Growth and Poverty: Evidence for Developing Countries in the 1980s'. *Economics Letters*, 48: 411–17.
—— (1997). 'Can High Inequality Developing Countries Escape Absolute Poverty?', *Economics Letters*, 56: 51–7.
—— (1998). 'Does Aggregation Hide the Harmful Effects of Inequality on Growth?' *Economics Letters*, 61: 73–7.
—— (2001). 'Growth, Inequality and Poverty: Looking Beyond Averages'. *World Development*, 29: 1803–15.
—— (2002*a*). 'On the Urbanization of Poverty'. *Journal of Development Economics*, 68: 435–42.
—— (2002*b*). 'Inequality Convergence'. *Economics Letters*, 80: 351–6.
—— (2004). 'Competing Concepts of Inequality in the Globalization Debate'. *Brookings Trade Forum 2004*, 1–38.
—— (2005*a*). 'Looking Beyond Averages in the Trade and Poverty Debate'. Policy Research Working Paper 3461. Washington, DC: The World Bank.
—— (2005*b*). 'Externalities in Rural Development: Evidence for China', in R. Kanbur and T. Venables (eds), *Spatial Inequality and Development*. Oxford: Oxford University Press, 137–61.
—— (2005*c*). 'A Poverty–Inequality Trade-Off?' *Journal of Economic Inequality*, 3: 169–82.
—— and Chen, S. (1997). 'What Can New Survey Data Tell Us about Recent Changes in Distribution and Poverty?' *World Bank Economic Review*, 11: 357–82.
—— and —— (2003). 'Measuring Pro-Poor Growth'. *Economics Letters*, 78: 93–9.
—— and —— (2007). 'China's (Uneven) Progress Against Poverty'. *Journal of Development Economics*, 82: 1–42.
—— and Datt, G . (1996). 'How Important to India's Poor is the Sectoral Composition of Economic Growth?' *World Bank Economic Review*, 10: 1–26.

—— and —— (2002). 'Why Has Economic Growth Been More Pro-Poor in Some States of India than Others?' *Journal of Development Economics*, 68: 381–400.

—— and Huppi, M. (1991). 'Measuring Changes in Poverty: A Methodological Case Study of Indonesia During an Adjustment Period'. *World Bank Economic Review*, 5: 57–82.

—— and Lokshin, M. (2004). 'Lasting Local Level Impacts of a Crisis'. Policy Research Working Paper 3503, Washington, DC: The World Bank.

—— and van de Walle, D. (2006). 'Does Rising Landlessness Signal Success or Failure for Vietnam's Agrarian Transition?' Policy Research Working Paper 3871. Washington, DC: The World Bank.

Son, H. and Kakwani, N. (2004), 'Economic Growth and Poverty Reduction: Initial Conditions Matter'. Working Paper 2, International Poverty Center, UNDP.

Sundaram, K. and Tendulkar, S. D. (2003). 'Poverty in India in the 1990s: Revised Results for All-India and 15 Major States for 1993–94'. *Economic and Political Weekly*, 38: 4865–73.

Tiffin, R. and Irz, X. (2006). 'Is Agriculture the Engine of Growth?' *Agricultural Economics*, 35: 79–89.

World Bank (2000). *World Development Report: Attacking Poverty*. New York: Oxford University Press.

—— (2004*a*). *World Development Report: Making Services Work for Poor People*. New York: Oxford University Press.

—— (2004*b*). *Land Policies for Growth and Poverty Reduction*. Washington, DC: The World Bank.

—— (2005). *World Development Report: Equity and Development*. New York: Oxford University Press.

3

Measurement of income distribution in supranational entities: the case of the European Union

*Andrea Brandolini**

The rapidly growing literature on world income inequality has drawn attention to the measurement of income distribution in supranational entities. This exercise raises some new problems, like the conversion to a common currency standard, but mainly forces us to see in a different light questions that are encountered in studying income distribution at the national level. Developing these issues is one aim of this chapter. However, I shall not take the entire world, but the European Union (EU) as my case study. The first reason for doing so is that the abundance and quality of available data and statistics for the EU allow me to examine in depth the questions involved in deriving the distribution of income in a supranational entity. The second reason is that EU member countries are engaged in a process of economic and political unification which has no parallel at the global level. This gives EU-wide indices of poverty and inequality a significance that goes well beyond intellectual curiosity.

Economic objectives—the single market and the monetary union—have long obscured the social dimension of the European unification process. As observed by Sen (1996: 33), it is surprising how these instrumental objectives overshadowed the underlying '. . . bigger objectives that involve social commitment to the well-being and basic freedoms of the involved

* I thank participants at the authors' workshop held at Nuffield College, Oxford, September 2006 and, in particular, Stephen Jenkins and John Micklewright, for very useful comments on a first draft of the chapter. I also thank for very helpful comments Giorgio Gobbi and Luisa Minghetti. I am grateful to Paul Alkemade for his precious help with LIS data, and to Sarah Bruch, Janet Gornick, Kathleen Short, and Tim Smeeding for their advice on the cost-of-living indices for the US states. The views expressed here are solely those of the author; in particular, they do not necessarily reflect those of the Bank of Italy.

population'. The Lisbon European Council of 2000 marked a change of perspective in recognizing the strategic goal of 'greater social cohesion' and committing to taking steps 'to make a decisive impact on the eradication of poverty' (Council of the European Union 2000). The 'Lisbon strategy' led to the adoption in 2001 of the Laeken social indicators, which in a sense parallel the Maastricht criteria of economic convergence (Atkinson *et al.* 2002; Daly 2006). These indicators, which include income poverty and inequality indices, are deemed to monitor and compare the social performance of each EU member state. The picture of the Union emerges only by aggregation of the national evidence, and no attempt is made to directly estimate EU-wide values: these are typically computed as 'population-weighted averages of available national values' (European Commission 2006: 77). Yet the level and evolution of inequality and poverty measured for the EU as if it was a single country can be regarded as basic information in evaluating the progress of the Union towards greater social cohesion. This very same point was made by Atkinson, in a different context, as early as 1989 (but published in 1995):

> If the Community continues to assess poverty purely in national terms, taking 50 per cent of national average income, then the impact of growth on poverty in the Community will depend solely on what happens within each country. However, a central question concerns the possibility of moving to a Community-wide poverty line, with the same standard applied in all countries. In that case, the effect of growth on the extent of low income is affected by the relative growth rates of different member countries. (Atkinson 1995: 71)

Statistical and conceptual difficulties so far may have prevented Eurostat and the European Commission from producing official Community-wide estimates (except for European Commission 2000: 20). Somewhat surprisingly, however, academic research has also lagged behind. The only attempts of which I am aware to estimate income inequality in the EU have been made by Atkinson (1996), Beblo and Knaus (2001), and Boix (2004), while Atkinson (1995, 1998), de Vos and Zaidi (1998), Förster (2005), and Fahey, Whelan, and Maître (2005) examine the implications of adopting area-wide poverty lines. This state of affairs contrasts with the large number of studies and the passionate debate on world income inequality—the measurement of which is certainly no less arduous than that for the EU. Thus, the second aim of this chapter is to provide new estimates of income distribution in the enlarged EU as a whole.

The methodological issues involved in deriving the personal distribution of income in a supranational entity are examined in section 3.1. After a description of data sources, section 3.2 presents the estimates of inequality and poverty in the EU around 2000 and compares them with the corresponding values for the USA. Section 3.3 concludes.

3.1 Conceptual problems in measurement

In this chapter, I am interested in the distribution of real income, which I take as an indicator of (material) standard of living. Nominal incomes are adjusted to take into account that households differ in their composition, needs vary with age, and cohabitation generates economies of scale in consumption: the income necessary for a single person to achieve a certain living standard is quite different from the income necessary for a couple with two young children. Moreover, households face different price vectors which influence their actual command over resources: for instance, housing tends to be far more expensive in large cities than in rural areas. Thus, if x_{ijk} denotes income of type i (e.g. property income) received by household j in country k, real income is defined as

$$y_{jk} \equiv \frac{\Sigma_i c_{ijk} x_{ijk}}{e_k p_{jk} m_k (h_{jk})}, \qquad [1]$$

where m is some function, possibly country-specific, of household characteristics h_{jk} relative to the reference household (for which $m_k = 1$); p_{jk} is the index of prices faced by the household; e_k is the conversion rate from country k's currency to the common unit of account; and the c_{ijk} is a correction factor which adjusts survey data to benchmarks derived from national accounts to allow for under-reporting or simply the misalignment between micro and macro sources.

Definition [1] helps to put the analysis of income distribution in a supranational entity in the more general context of research on income distribution. In studies of national distributions, where the conversion rate plays no role, the p_{jk} and c_{ijk} are generally ignored and real income is simply defined as $\Sigma_i x_{ijk}/m_k(h_{jk})$. However, this is not always the case: differences in the cost of living are receiving growing attention, as I discuss later, and there is a tradition of studies which adjust survey data to national accounts. For instance, van Ginneken and Park (1984) produced adjusted income distributions in nine countries by applying proportional correction factors to labour and transfer incomes while attributing the entire difference between national accounts and aggregated survey data to the top fifth of the unadjusted income distribution. In the literature on the world income distribution, comparisons are usually made in terms of per capita income, adjusted to gross national income and expressed in some common international standard: real income is defined as $c_k \Sigma_i x_{ijk} / e_k s_{jk}$, where s_{jk} is the household size and c_k is a correction factor equal across all households and income types in country k.[1]

[1] To my knowledge, Whalley (1979) was the first to estimate world income inequality. A non-exhaustive list of subsequent contributions include Berry, Bourguignon, and Morrisson (1983*a*, *b*), Grosh and Nafziger (1986), Chotikapanich, Rao, and Valenzuela (1997), Schultz (1998), Bhalla (2002), Bourguignon and Morrisson (2002), Milanovic (2002), Dowrick and Akmal (2005), and Sala-i-Martín (2006). Svedberg (2004) and Milanovic (2006) are recent surveys of this literature.

Four conceptual questions in the estimation of income distribution in a supranational entity are examined in the rest of this section. The background is provided by the research on world income inequality, but the discussion is extended to embody aspects relevant to the EU context. The important issue of the comparability of the data used to estimate the world income distribution is not addressed here; on this, see Atkinson and Brandolini (2001).

Conversion to a common currency standard

Conversion of incomes measured in different units of account to a common standard could be straightforwardly achieved by using market exchange rates. However, these rates are influenced by many factors, such as the flows of international trade or speculative capital movements, and need not reflect the price structures that prevail in the various countries. In poor countries labour-intensive non-tradable services are typically cheaper than in richer countries: since market exchange rates are unlikely to account for these price differences, their use would lead to understatement of real incomes in poor countries. Purchasing Power Parities (PPPs) have been developed to obviate these problems. They are the relative values, in national currencies, of a fixed bundle of goods and services, and provide the conversion rates from national currencies to an artificial common currency, such as Purchasing Power Standard (PPS) in Eurostat statistics and international dollars in the Penn World Table. Note that PPPs embody both the conversion to a common standard, e_k, and the adjustment for price level differences, p_{jk}, where p_{jk} is supposed to be the same for all households within a country. Although widely followed, this approach is not exempt from problems.

First, there is a multiplicity of sources. The real GDP estimates by Maddison (2001) and the Penn World Table constructed by Summers and Heston (1991) are two sources frequently used in the literature on world income distribution, but PPPs are routinely computed by international organizations such as the World Bank or the Organization for Economic Co-operation and Development. Here, I use the annual estimates by Eurostat that cover all European countries and the USA (Stapel, Pasanen, and Reinecke 2004).

Second, methods to estimate PPPs differ. The methodology applied by Maddison and the Penn World Table multiplies quantities of goods (or services) by average international prices which are obtained, for each good, by weighting the national price with the country's share in the total world consumption. This implies that the structure of international prices tends to approximate that prevailing in relatively richer, and more populous, nations, as prices in countries with a bigger share of world consumption get higher weights. As stressed by Dowrick and Akmal (2005), the use of average international prices leads to a bias that is opposite in sign to the 'traded sector bias' implicit in market exchange rates: the real income of people living in poor countries is bound to be overstated if the goods and services that are consumed there in greater quantity, because they are cheaper, are valued at the prices prevailing in richer countries. Dowrick and Akmal (2005) show that adopting a PPP index which corrects for this bias affects the conclusion on the trend in global income inequality.

Third, PPP indices are estimated for various national accounts aggregates. In the case of European countries, Eurostat makes available not only the index for gross domestic product (GDP) but also specific indices for a number of expenditure components of GDP. Results may vary considerably. Were nominal incomes deflated by the PPP index for household final consumption expenditure (HFCE) rather than the PPP index for GDP, in 2000 real incomes would be 8 to 12 per cent lower in Finland, Latvia, Lithuania, Malta, and Poland, but 6 and 11 per cent higher in Germany and Luxembourg, respectively. As these differences are positively correlated with the level of per capita gross national income (GNI) in PPS, the use of the PPP index for GDP tends to narrow international differences in real incomes relative to the PPP index for HFCE. In order to derive the EU distribution of real incomes, it might be preferable to employ the latter because it measures purchasing power in terms of consumption goods and services and because GDP covers items such as in-kind transfers for education and health care, which are generally not included in the household disposable income measured in surveys (Smeeding and Rainwater 2004). On the other hand, Eurostat currently applies the index for GDP to derive all national accounts variables expressed in PPS (see methodological notes in Eurostat 2006). For this reason, in the following I present figures obtained with both types of PPP index.

Differences in price levels

One objection that can be raised against using PPP indices is that it is mistaken to apply the same conversion factor for the poor and the rich, when we know that expenditure composition varies across the income distribution. This question, however, does not arise only in relation to PPPs. It is part of the more general issue of whether we should use group-specific price indices to transform nominal incomes into real incomes. A related question is, for example, the extent to which inflation affects differently people at diverse positions in the income distribution (see Atkinson 1983: 91–4). It is beyond the scope of this chapter to investigate these issues, but one question needs to be briefly addressed here: is it not inconsistent to correct only for cost-of-living differences across nations, ignoring differences across geographical areas within the same nation? Such a differential treatment could be justified if the latter were less important than the former. However, even interpreting these differences in the broadest sense as reflecting the direct provision of public services or the structure of product markets, it is not obvious that this is the case. The fact is that we have little information about territorial variations in the price level. Hence, the choice of correcting only for cross-national differences is basically made out of ignorance.

This problem is recognized by statistical offices, which are especially concerned with the cost of housing. In the USA, the National Research Council of the National Academy of Sciences Panel on Poverty and Family Assistance recommended that poverty thresholds be adjusted for differences in the cost of housing across geographical areas of the country (Citro and Michael 1995). This recommendation was applied by Short *et al.* (1999) and Short (2001). Insee (1997) and Mogstad, Langørgen, and Aaberge (2007) used, instead, an indirect approach and accounted for regional price-level differences in France and Norway, respectively, by setting region-specific relative poverty lines. The shortcoming of this procedure, however, is that it mixes up the differences in the cost of living with those in the level of economic development. To the extent that price levels only partially compensate for geographical differentials in development, using region-specific relative poverty lines amounts to setting a lower real standard for poorer regions.

Accounting for geographical differences in price levels, across regions and between urban and rural areas, is important in the evaluation of the material standard of living, but is at present prevented by the lack of data. In this chapter, I provide both PPP-adjusted estimates to correct for cross-national differences in the cost of living, and unadjusted figures. Note that using unadjusted figures parallels the standard practice in national reports of ignoring territorial differences in price levels, and is a perfectly sensible exercise in analyses of income distribution in the Euro area (and, to a large extent, in the entire EU, given the relative stability of the exchange rates vis-à-vis the euro).

Sample surveys vs. national accounts

In the first edition of *The Economics of Inequality*, Atkinson distinguished between the 'international' distribution of income, 'the differences between countries in terms of average *per capita* incomes', and the 'world' distribution of income, 'the distribution of income among all people of the world' (1975: 237). To show that the former is less concentrated than the latter, he graphed the 40th and 95th percentiles of national income distributions together with the average per capita income for the USA, the UK, Brazil, and India (1975: 246, Fig. 12–2). This graph anticipated the practice of merging survey data on income distribution with mean incomes from national accounts, which is now standard in the literature on world income inequality.

This method is a natural extension of the analysis of international differences in mean incomes: it accounts for within-country distributions, without altering the country ranking provided by the national accounts. On the other hand, it tends to obscure the fact that national accounts are intrinsically different from survey data. As recently put by Deaton:

the differences in coverage and definition between [National Accounts] and surveys mean that, even if everything were perfectly measured, it would be incorrect to apply inequality or distributional measures which are defined from surveys, which measure one thing, to means that are derived from the national accounts, which measure another. (2005: 17)

The same view is taken in research conducted at the World Bank. The estimates of world poverty by Chen and Ravallion (2001) and world inequality by Milanovic (2002) do not use national accounts means and are only based on survey data (except for PPP indices).

What are the implications for the estimation of the EU-wide income distribution? Several income concepts in national accounts can provide a benchmark for survey data. Table 3.1 reports three aggregates: gross national income (GNI), household gross disposable income (HGDI) and household net disposable income (HNDI). (These aggregates, expressed in PPS and per capita terms, refer to the year for which survey data are available.) The GNI concept, which is the most common in the literature on the world income distribution, sums the incomes received by all residents (net of incomes paid out), including the government, financial, and non-financial sectors. Excluding the incomes of these sectors reduces considerably the reference aggregate income: on average, in the countries for which data are reported in Table 3.1, HGDI is 64 per cent of GNI, a figure that falls to 61 per cent after deducting the depreciation on the capital stock owned by households (HNDI). By focusing on the household sector, HGDI and HNDI are somewhat closer to the incomes recorded in household surveys. Yet, except in Denmark, survey means (TNHI) fall considerably short of them. As is well known from studies reconciling micro and macro sources (e.g. Atkinson and Micklewright 1983, for the UK; Brandolini 1999, for Italy), only part of these discrepancies can be attributed to under-reporting and sampling errors in surveys; in some part, they are due to the many conceptual differences.[2]

What matters here is the change in international differences in mean incomes. The per capita income of Estonia, for instance, falls from 35 per cent of the UK value using GNI to 26 per cent using TNHI. This is a large variation that could influence estimates of the EU-wide distribution. As the ratio of survey means to national accounts aggregates is positively correlated with the level of per capita GNI expressed in PPS, the alignment of household-level data to aggregate statistics is likely to reduce measured income inequality.[3]

[2] For instance, since separate accounts for non-profit institutions serving households are only available in some countries, HGDI and HNDI include the disposable income of these institutions; they also include the disposable income of persons living permanently in institutions (hostels, nursing homes for the elderly, military bases, etc.), who are generally excluded from sample surveys. Moreover, HGDI and HNDI incorporate, as GNI, the imputed rents on owner-occupied houses, whose amount is significant in many EU countries.

[3] This evidence runs counter to that for world countries presented by Milanovic (2002: 64, Figure 1).

Table 3.1 Per capita income in EU countries around 2000 in PPS (GDP)

Country	Gross national income (GNI)	Household gross disposable income (HGDI)	HGDI to GNI ratio	Household net disposable income (HNDI)	HNDI to GNI ratio	ECHP-LIS total net household income (TNHI)	TNHI to GNI ratio	TNHI to HNDI ratio
Austria	24,778	16,393	0.662	15,618	0.630	10,685	0.431	0.684
Belgium	23,979	14,800	0.617	14,047	0.586	11,172	0.466	0.795
Cyprus	15,824	–	–	–	–	–	–	–
Czech Republic	11,316	6,595	0.583	6,258	0.553	4,331	0.383	0.692
Denmark	24,819	11,790	0.475	10,951	0.441	11,233	0.453	1.026
Estonia	7,916	5,103	0.645	4,775	0.603	3,145	0.397	0.659
Finland	22,724	12,195	0.537	11,268	0.496	9,882	0.435	0.877
France	23,125	14,939	0.646	14,433	0.624	10,507	0.454	0.728
Germany	22,272	15,423	0.693	14,412	0.647	11,071	0.497	0.768
Greece	14,749	11,028	0.748	10,342	0.701	6,835	0.463	0.661
Hungary	9,156	5,768	0.630	–	–	3,318	0.362	–
Ireland	21,807	–	–	16,783	0.770	8,784	0.403	0.523
Italy	22,600	15,671	0.693	14,721	0.651	8,064	0.357	0.548
Latvia	7,090	4,588	0.647	4,277	0.603	–	–	–
Lithuania	7,530	5,213	0.692	4,947	0.657	–	–	–
Luxembourg	38,889	–	–	–	–	15,957	0.410	–
Malta	15,325	–	–	–	–	–	–	–
Netherlands	25,506	13,263	0.520	12,460	0.489	10,284	0.403	0.825
Poland	8,579	6,228	0.726	6,064	0.707	3,438	0.401	0.567
Portugal	15,757	11,362	0.721	10,594	0.672	6,477	0.411	0.611
Slovak Republic	7,546	4,464	0.592	4,317	0.572	2,511	0.333	0.582
Slovenia	13,905	9,061	0.652	8,402	0.604	5,551	0.399	0.661
Spain	18,390	12,410	0.675	11,711	0.637	7,927	0.431	0.677
Sweden	23,701	11,817	0.499	11,408	0.481	10,156	0.428	0.890
UK	22,521	15,251	0.677	14,542	0.646	11,894	0.528	0.818

Notes: Data refer to 2000 except for Czech Republic and Slovak Republic (1996), and Hungary, Poland, and Slovenia (1999). Except for Hungary, the household sector includes non-profit institutions serving households. For Slovenia, the series for household gross and net disposable income are available only since 2000: the figures for 1999 have been extrapolated by using the rate of growth of gross national income.
Source: Author's estimates from aggregate data (national accounts, population and conversion rates) drawn from Eurostat (2006) and national sources for Ireland and Hungary, and household-level data from ECHP (Waves 1–8, December 2003) and LIS (as of 28 September 2006).

To sum up, Deaton and the World Bank researchers correctly warn against unwarily merging national accounts and survey data. On the other hand, the twofold need to correct for deficiencies in household-level data and to re-establish the cross-country income ratios known from national accounts—whose rationale can be found in the role played by regional GDP per capita in the allocation of EU structural funds—may justify a controlled use of the adjustment to aggregate statistics. These considerations bring me to examine both unadjusted and adjusted incomes (either to GNI or to HNDI).

Using a common income equivalization procedure?

As already mentioned, the literature on world income inequality tends to focus on per capita incomes, at least in theory. (In practice, several studies mix up statistics computed on per capita, equivalent and household bases, drawn from international compilations of income distribution statistics.) This choice amounts to assume away economies of scale in consumption, and is at variance with the practice followed in developed countries. Atkinson, Rainwater and Smeeding (1995: 18–21) describe a wide range of equivalence scales in use in OECD countries, which explains why the function m in (1) is indexed by k. In the UK, for example, estimates of households below average income are derived using the McClements equivalence scale, although as noted in Chapter 1 this scale is soon to be replaced with the modified OECD scale recommended by Eurostat (DWP 2006: 207). This scale assigns value 1 to the first adult, 0.5 to any other person aged 14 or older, and 0.3 to each child younger than 14.

The Eurostat recommendation enhances cross-country comparability, as it is well known that income distribution figures are very sensitive to the choice of the equivalence scale (e.g. Buhmann *et al.* 1988). On the other hand, the modified OECD equivalence scale may be too rigid. For instance, the assumption that economies of scale in consumption are the same everywhere has been questioned by researchers from Eastern Europe. According to Szulc, the original OECD scale (which assigns weights 0.7 to any adult member beyond the first and 0.5 to children) is more appropriate than the modified OECD scale for Poland and 'less developed countries' since they have 'relatively high expenditures on food (characterized by low economy of scale) and relatively low expenditures on housing (characterized by high economy of scale)' (2006: 427). Éltetõ and Havasi (2002: 137) argue along similar lines against the use of the modified OECD scale for Hungary, and reject the appropriateness of any 'generally applicable' equivalence scale that does not reflect a country's special circumstances. In the past, the standard practice of Eastern European statistical agencies was to calculate income per capita (Atkinson and Micklewright 1992: 69–71).

The adoption of a single equivalization procedure across EU countries is required by international comparability, but it does not imply the strict formulation of the modified OECD scale. The scale could be made dependent on the income level of the household, or of the country or region where the household lives. In my empirical analysis, I present results based on a per capita adjustment, the original and the modified OECD scales, and a 'mixed OECD' scale combining the original OECD scale for Eastern European countries with the modified OECD scale for the EU-15. The issue is worth further investigation, but it must be borne in mind that assuming lower economies of scale in less developed countries would associate a lower real income to a given nominal income, amplifying the distance between rich and poor countries within the EU.

3.2 Income distribution in the enlarged EU

Data sources

Data for the 15 countries which were members of the EU in 2000 are drawn from the European Community Household Panel (ECHP), the official source used by the European Commission to compare income poverty and inequality in the 1990s. The ECHP was a fully harmonized annual longitudinal survey conducted by national agencies from 1994 to 2001 under Eurostat coordination in order to collect detailed information on income, standard of living, demographic characteristics and labour market behaviour.[4] Here, I use information on incomes earned in 2000 drawn from the last wave. Total household disposable income is obtained by aggregation of all income sources net of direct taxes and social contributions (variable HI100). All observations are weighted by cross-sectional weights (variable HG004).

Data for six of the ten countries that joined the EU in 2004 (Czech Republic, Estonia, Hungary, Poland, Slovak Republic, Slovenia) and for the USA are drawn from the Luxembourg Income Study (LIS). (See Chapter 1 for information on the LIS project.) Unlike the ECHP, variables in the LIS database are derived from independent surveys which are harmonized *ex post*. The LIS total household disposable income is also obtained by aggregation (variable DPI). As incomes for Hungary, Poland, and Slovenia refer to 1999, and for the Czech and Slovak Republics to 1996, I raise the LIS values by the cumulative increase of per capita GNI (at current prices) between the available year and 2000; no such adjustment is necessary for Estonia.

Distribution is measured among individuals, attributing to each person the equivalent or per capita income of the household to which he or she belongs. For each country, sample weights are rescaled so that they add up to the total

[4] All EU countries participated for the whole period, except Austria and Finland, which joined in 1995 and 1996 respectively, and Sweden, which later added data from the Swedish Survey of Living Condition. In 1996 the ECHP was discontinued in Germany, Luxembourg, and the UK and replaced with existing national panel surveys.

population. This amounts to an assumption that income distribution is the same among persons living permanently in institutions (nursing homes, residential schools, prisons, military bases, etc.) as it is among those living in households. Nationality is defined on the basis of residence: Estonians living in France are regarded as part of the French population. (As for other private transfers, there could be a problem of double-counting with remittances, if they are not subtracted from the sender's income.) In computing the OECD equivalence scales, it is assumed that all members are adult whenever information on the age of household members is missing. Unfortunately, this is the case for all Slovakian data; since the equivalence coefficient is higher for adults than for children, this hypothesis means that equivalent incomes are understated for all Slovakian households with children younger than 14. Non-positive incomes are dropped.

The estimates I shall now discuss for the Euro area and the EU-15 are based on the ECHP data, while those for the EU-25 are obtained after merging the ECHP data with the LIS data. The label EU-25 is used throughout the chapter, although Cyprus, Latvia, Lithuania, and Malta are not included because of lack of data; the 21 countries for which data are available account for 98.5 per cent of the total EU population in 2000. Results must be taken with some caution, especially for the EU-25. Comparability is supposedly higher for the ECHP data, which are from surveys harmonized *ex ante* (at least in eleven countries), than for the LIS data, which derive from an *ex post* standardization. Moreover, the LIS and ECHP income definitions are broadly consistent but no adjustment is made for the remaining discrepancies. Finally, the representativeness of the last ECHP wave used here may have been reduced by the significant sample attrition recorded in most countries (Lehmann and Wirtz 2003: 2–3).

Inequality

Figure 3.1 summarizes the distribution of real incomes in 2000 in the 21 EU member countries for which household-level data are available. The graph shows for each country the median value (the thick horizontal mark), the distance between the 20th and the 80th percentiles (the thick vertical bar), and the 5th and 95th percentiles (the two extremes of the thin vertical bar). All values are unadjusted equivalized survey statistics in thousands of PPS (GDP). The country ranking by median real income follows a known pattern, with Eastern European nations preceding Southern European countries, and then the remaining EU countries rather close to each other except for Luxembourg which is clearly leading. Income differences in the Union are sizeable, both across and within countries. The Estonian median is only 18 per cent of the Luxembourger median, and this figure falls to 14 per cent if the comparison is made at the 5th percentile. For 80 per cent of Eastern Europeans, incomes are below, or at most comparable to, the incomes of the poorest 20 per cent of Europeans living in Central and Nordic countries. The variable lengths of the vertical bars reveal some noticeable differences in within-country income dispersion, such as that between Denmark and the UK. It should be noted that these bars show *absolute* and not *relative* differences. If percentiles were expressed as percentages of national medians, as customary in cross-national inequality comparisons, income differences in Eastern European countries would not look so small compared to those in the EU-15. Indeed, Estonia would exhibit the second largest value of relative inequality after Portugal.

These cross-national income differences impinge on measured inequality in the EU as a whole. Table 3.2 reports several statistics on the distribution of real incomes in the Euro area, the EU as of 2000 (EU-15) and the enlarged EU (EU-25). (The corresponding figures for the USA are discussed later.) Eight values are reported for each statistic: seven of them differ either for the unit of account (euros vs. PPS), or for the type of adjustment to national accounts (none, to GNI, and to HNDI); the last is the population-weighted average of national values, which corresponds to the concept used in Eurostat publications. Table 3.3 shows the impact of different equivalence scales on the same statistics.

Four results can be noted with regards to the various methodological hypotheses.

- Measured inequality is higher when incomes are expressed in euros than in either of the two PPS measures. The difference is modest for the Euro area

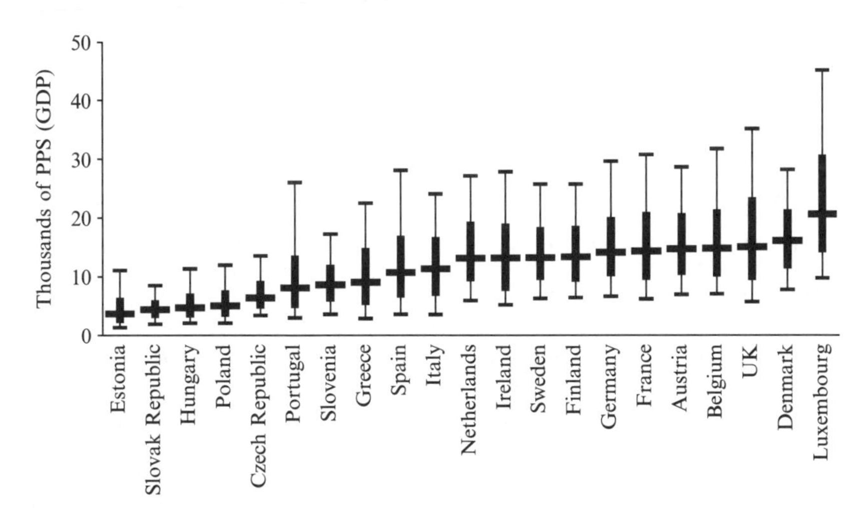

Figure 3.1 Income distribution in EU countries, 2000

Source: Author's estimates from household-level data from ECHP (Waves 1–8, December 2003) and LIS (as of 28 September 2006). Incomes are equivalized by the modified OECD equivalence scale, are not adjusted to national accounts, and are in PPS (GDP).

Table 3.2 Inequality and poverty measures by income definition, 2000

Income definition	Atkinson index: $\varepsilon = 1$	Atkinson index: $\varepsilon = 2$	Gini index	Percentiles to median ratios (%)				Head-count ratios (%)		
				P10	P20	P80	P90	$\theta = 0.0$	$\theta = 0.5$	$\theta = 1.0$
				European Union 25						
Income in euros										
Unadjusted	0.258	0.815	0.378	22	43	161	206	15.2	23.5	27.9
Adjusted to GNI	0.234	0.802	0.361	26	46	157	198	15.2	22.4	26.7
Adjusted to HNDI	0.231	0.799	0.359	26	47	157	199	15.2	21.9	26.0
Income in PPS (GDP)										
Unadjusted	0.182	0.770	0.328	39	55	154	195	15.2	18.4	23.0
Adjusted to GNI	0.168	0.761	0.316	43	59	154	192	15.2	17.2	20.9
Adjusted to HNDI	0.168	0.758	0.317	44	59	154	194	15.2	16.9	20.4
Income in PPS (HFCE)										
Unadjusted	0.189	0.773	0.334	37	54	155	196	15.2	18.8	23.7
Population-weighted national values	0.138	0.395	0.284	–	–	–	–	15.2	–	–
				European Union 15						
Income in euros										
Unadjusted	0.168	0.830	0.313	44	60	152	192	15.5	17.1	19.9
Adjusted to GNI	0.155	0.821	0.300	46	62	149	185	15.5	16.7	18.6
Adjusted to HNDI	0.153	0.818	0.298	47	63	149	187	15.5	16.4	18.0
Income in PPS (GDP)										
Unadjusted	0.148	0.799	0.294	48	64	148	185	15.5	16.2	17.3
Adjusted to GNI	0.143	0.791	0.289	49	65	149	184	15.5	15.8	16.4
Adjusted to HNDI	0.143	0.789	0.291	50	65	150	186	15.5	15.6	16.1
Income in PPS (HFCE)										
Unadjusted	0.150	0.801	0.296	48	63	148	186	15.5	16.3	17.7
Population-weighted national values	0.138	0.417	0.284	–	–	–	–	15.5	–	–
				Euro area						
Income in euros										
Unadjusted	0.164	0.846	0.307	44	60	150	187	15.4	17.2	20.3
Adjusted to GNI	0.154	0.843	0.298	45	62	148	184	15.4	16.8	18.8
Adjusted to HNDI	0.152	0.841	0.296	46	62	148	184	15.4	16.5	18.4
Income in PPS (GDP)										
Unadjusted	0.146	0.823	0.290	48	63	146	183	15.4	16.3	17.5
Adjusted to GNI	0.142	0.820	0.288	49	65	149	184	15.4	15.7	16.3
Adjusted to HNDI	0.142	0.818	0.288	50	65	150	185	15.4	15.5	16.1
Income in PPS (HFCE)										
Unadjusted	0.149	0.825	0.293	47	63	147	183	15.4	16.4	18.1
Population-weighted national values	0.137	0.430	0.282	–	–	–	–	15.4	–	–
				United States of America						
Income in US dollars	0.225	0.966	0.369	39	55	163	213	22.8	23.0	23.4
Income in PPS	0.224	0.966	0.368	39	55	162	212	22.8	22.9	23.2

Source: Author's estimates from household-level data from ECHP (Waves 1–8, December 2003) and LIS (as of 28 September 2006). Incomes are equivalized by the modified OECD equivalence scale.

and the EU-15, but is significant for the EU-25. Inequality is slightly lower with the PPP index for GDP than with the index for HFCE.

- Adjusting to national accounts decreases measured inequality, but whether GNI or HNDI is chosen makes little difference.

Table 3.3 Inequality and poverty measures by equivalence scale, 2000

Equivalence scale	Atkinson index: $\varepsilon = 1$	Atkinson index: $\varepsilon = 2$	Gini index	Percentiles to median ratios (%)				Head-count ratios (%)		
				P10	P20	P80	P90	$\theta = 0.0$	$\theta = 0.5$	$\theta = 1.0$
				European Union 25						
Modified OECD	0.182	0.770	0.328	39	55	154	195	15.2	18.4	23.0
OECD	0.189	0.764	0.336	38	55	157	199	15.5	18.5	23.0
Per capita	0.209	0.759	0.357	37	54	164	211	17.2	19.8	24.0
Mixed OECD	0.197	0.773	0.338	34	53	154	196	15.3	19.6	24.3
				European Union 15						
Modified OECD	0.148	0.799	0.294	48	64	148	185	15.5	16.2	17.3
OECD	0.154	0.792	0.301	48	64	151	189	15.7	16.4	17.5
Per capita	0.174	0.786	0.324	46	62	158	201	17.2	17.7	18.6
				Euro area						
Modified OECD	0.146	0.823	0.290	48	63	146	183	15.4	16.3	17.5
OECD	0.152	0.816	0.298	48	63	149	187	15.7	16.3	17.8
Per capita	0.171	0.810	0.320	46	62	157	199	17.0	17.8	18.9
				United States of America						
Modified OECD	0.224	0.966	0.368	39	55	162	212	22.8	22.9	23.2
OECD	0.232	0.968	0.377	39	55	166	221	22.9	23.1	23.4
Per capita	0.255	0.973	0.399	37	54	176	242	23.9	24.0	24.1

Source: Author's estimates from household-level data from ECHP (Waves 1–8, December 2003) and LIS (as of 28 September 2006). Incomes are not adjusted to national accounts and are in PPS GDP for EU countries. In the 'Mixed OECD' results, the modified OECD equivalence scale is used for countries in EU-15 and the original OECD scale for new member countries.

- The highest inequality is found for per capita incomes; inequality is lower with the modified OECD scale than with the original OECD scale. In the EU-25, incomes are more concentrated when deflated by the mixed OECD scale than by any of the other two OECD scales, essentially because people at the bottom of the distribution are poorer (see the values of P10 and P20).
- The degree of inequality measured for the EU as a whole is always higher than the population-weighted average of national values. The difference is particularly large for the enlarged EU. This is a warning against using a population-weighted average as a proxy whenever real income differences are large. More generally, this exposes the weak theoretical justification of such a measure: it is unclear what the average of within-country relative inequality indices tells us about the distribution of income in the EU.

Focusing on unadjusted real incomes in PPS, in 2000 the degree of inequality was very similar in the Euro area and in the EU-15. The Gini index was just below 30 per cent, about the same value found in Italy, and midway between the minimum 22 per cent of Denmark and the maximum 37 per cent of Portugal. The richest 10 per cent earned at least 85 per cent more than the median person, while the real income of the poorest 10 per cent did not reach half the median, a situation fairly close to that of the UK. The enlargement to Eastern Europe has perceptibly increased the EU-wide concentration of incomes, as measured in 2000. The Gini index has grown by over three percentage points to 33 per cent, the 10th percentile has fallen below 40 per cent of the median, and the 90th percentile has risen to almost twice the median.

Poverty

When the EU is analysed as a single country, the replacement of national poverty lines with a single Community-wide line is the main departure from Eurostat methodology for the measurement of poverty. As observed by Atkinson, if the poverty line is regarded as the minimum level of resources that a European citizen should have in order to fully participate in the life of society, which of these lines is chosen is a 'political judgement': the EU-wide line would represent 'a significant move towards viewing the European Union as a social entity' (1998: 29).[5] Atkinson (1995, 1998) suggests that we may want to take an intermediate position and proposes a weighted geometric average of national and EU poverty lines. Following his lead, I consider the family of poverty lines for country *k*

$$z_\theta \equiv 0.6(\bar{y}_{EU})^\theta(\bar{y}_k)^{1-\theta}, \qquad [2]$$

where $\bar{y}_{EU}$ and $\bar{y}_k$ are the median real incomes for the EU and country *k*, respectively. The parameter θ ranges from 0 to 1: $\theta = 0$ corresponds to Eurostat methodology of setting lines at the national level, while $\theta = 1$ implies a move towards treating the EU as a single country.

Table 3.2 reports the head-count poverty ratios for three values of θ and various real income definitions. Looking at $\theta = 0$ first, about 15 per cent of Europeans were in poverty in 2000, regardless of the boundaries of the Union. This figure corresponded to 47 million persons in the euro area, 59 million in the EU-15, and 68 million in the EU-25. As the computation is fully relative, the income adjustment and the account unit do not evidently make any difference. Results are quite different when $\theta = 1$: adopting an EU-wide line raises the incidence of poverty. It is more so when incomes are not adjusted to national accounts, and when they are expressed in euros at the market conversion rates rather than in PPS (either HFCE or GDP). The head-count rates change monotonically as θ varies from 0 to 1. Table 3.3 shows that poverty figures are very similar using either of the OECD equivalence scales, but are

[5] The adoption of an EU-wide standard does not require that people feel members of the European society more than they do of their national or regional community. Fahey, Whelan, and Maître (2005) rest their case for adding an EU-wide measure of poverty to the existing national measures on the observation that the reference frame used by people to determine their sense of deprivation includes the European context as well as the national context. Using a wide range of objective and subjective indicators of the quality of life, they show that even people in the upper middle classes in the poorest countries are and feel worse off than low or middle income groups in the wealthy EU countries. On the related issue of the choice between local and national poverty standards, see also Jesuit, Rainwater, and Smeeding (2003).

uniformly higher when it is assumed that there are no economies of scale in consumption. In the EU-25, the closer the threshold to the EU-wide line, the more the estimates based on the mixed OECD scale exceed those based on the other OECD scales.

Considering unadjusted incomes in PPS (GDP), poverty rates increase from 15.4 to 17.5 per cent in the Euro area and from 15.5 to 17.3 in the EU-15, as the area-wide line replaces the national lines. In the enlarged European Union, the incidence of poverty goes up by a half, from 15.2 to 23.0 per cent, and the absolute number of poor people increases from 68 to 103 millions. An even more dramatic change takes place in the geography of poverty. As the line changes from national to area-wide, half or more of the Eastern European population 'moves' into poverty, with a peak of 79 per cent in the Slovak Republic; a significant fraction of the population is also re-classified as poor in Southern Europe; the opposite occurs in the rest of the EU countries, with poverty virtually disappearing in Luxembourg (Figure 3.2). These numbers are roughly halved when an intermediate stance is taken ($\theta = 0.5$). Figure 3.3 illustrates the 'easternization' of poverty as we move away from the national lines toward the Community-wide line: whereas the share of poor living in Eastern Europe rises from 13.6 to 49.5 per cent, all other shares fall slightly in Southern Europe (from 33.8 to 30.2), more sharply in Continental Europe (from 33.4 to 12.8), in the Nordic countries (from 3.1 to 1.2), and in the UK and Ireland (from 16.1 to 6.3).

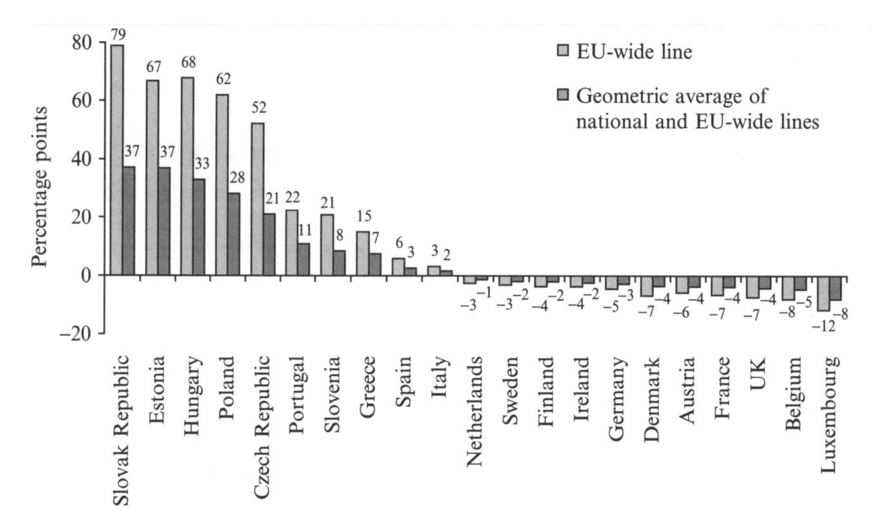

Figure 3.2 Share of people moving into poverty as the line is changed from national to EU-wide or to their geometric mean, 2000 (%).

Source: Author's estimates from household-level data from ECHP (Waves 1–8, December 2003) and LIS (as of 28 September 2006). Incomes are equivalized by the modified OECD equivalence scale, are not adjusted to national accounts, and are in PPS (GDP).

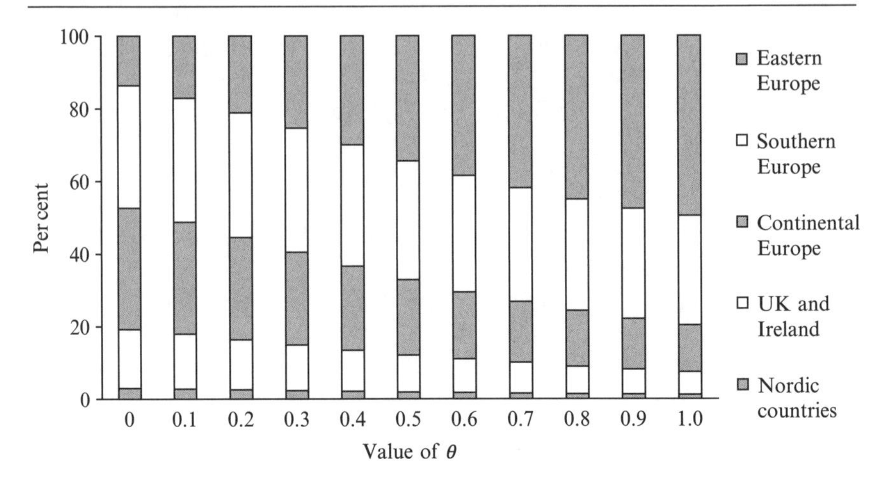

Figure 3.3 Poverty composition in EU-25 by alternative values of θ, 2000.

Source: Author's estimates from household-level data from ECHP (Waves 1–8, December 2003) and LIS (as of 28 September 2006). Incomes are equivalized by the modified OECD equivalence scale, are not adjusted to national accounts, and are in PPS (GDP).

Are inequality and poverty higher in the EU-25 than in the USA?

Available estimates suggest that income distribution is less unequal in the EU than in the USA. This is the case of the EU-15 in the 1980s, according to Atkinson's (1996: 25–6) LIS-based 'prototype' estimates, and of the Euro area in 1995, as assessed by Beblo and Knaus (2001: 308) on the basis of the ECHP data plus the LIS data for Finland and the USA. The calculations by Boix (2004: 7, Table 3) on data assembled by Milanovic for his 2002 article indicate that per capita income inequality in the USA is not only higher than in the EU-15 but also the EU-25: the Gini indices were 39.4 per cent in the USA, 34.2 per cent in the EU-15, and 38.0 per cent in the EU-25 in 1993.

My own calculations confirm this conclusion, in so far as the comparison is made in PPP terms. Earlier exercises compared PPP-adjusted incomes for the EU with dollar incomes for the USA, thus ignoring the variation in price levels within the USA. However, this variation is not negligible: for instance, according to the cost-of-living indices estimated by Berry, Fording, and Hanson (2000, as revised in 2004), in 2000 one dollar was worth a third more in Mississippi than in Massachusetts. To control for this source of inconsistency, I supplement the customary statistics in US dollars with novel estimates adjusting for price level differences across the American states with the indices calculated by Berry, Fording, and Hanson.[6] Note, however, that these indices are estimated

[6] The original values are rescaled so that the weighted index for the entire country (with weights given by the state income shares in the LIS database) equals the PPP value provided by Eurostat for the US dollar in 2000. The country mean is used for Alaska, Hawaii, and the District of Columbia, which are not included in Berry, Fording, and Hanson's calculations.

by means of econometric techniques and are only partially comparable to those calculated by Eurostat. They are used here as a first approximation in the absence of official state-level PPP series. Unlike in the EU, the adjustment for the cross-state variation in price levels makes virtually no difference to measured US inequality and poverty (see bottom two lines in Table 3.2).

Income distribution in the USA is consistently wider than in the EU-15 and the Euro area; it is wider than in the EU-25 provided that incomes are adjusted for differences in purchasing power. When survey unadjusted incomes in PPS are considered, the Gini index is 33 per cent in the EU-25 against 37 per cent in the USA. Differences appear to lie not at the bottom, as P10 and P20 look rather similar, but at the top: the 80th and 90th American percentiles are further away from the median than their European counterparts. The difference is stark when inequality is measured by the Atkinson index with $\varepsilon = 2$, a value which suggests substantial aversion to inequality. The head-count poverty ratio is more or less the same on both sides of the Atlantic, around 23 per cent, when the area-wide lines are adopted; it is, however, 50 per cent higher in the USA than in the EU-25 when poverty lines are country- or state-specific. Note the tiny effect on US poverty rates of shifting the line from the national to the state level.

The ratio of the highest to the lowest median equivalent income in PPS is 1.5 in the USA vis-à-vis 5.6 in the EU-25, or 4.3 if the outlier Luxembourg is excluded. Given the much more pronounced internal disparities, it is notable that income is less unequally distributed in the EU-25 than in the USA. This result must be read against the background of a substantially higher mean real income in the USA (about 75 per cent).

3.3 Conclusions

Drawing on the extensive research on world income inequality, in this chapter I have analysed the conceptual issues in the measurement of income distribution in supranational entities. By taking the EU as a case study and the USA as a basis for comparison, I have shown how the conclusions are affected by the methodological choices on the currency conversion rate, the PPP index, the adjustment of survey data to national accounts, and the equivalence scale. In doing so, I have provided the first systematic picture of inequality and poverty in the enlarged EU as if it were a single country.

There are at least two reasons for investigating the distribution of income in the EU as a whole. The first is instrumental. Inequality and poverty are important measures of the heterogeneity of EU society, and it could be argued that the higher this heterogeneity, the more fragile is the process of European integration. Thus, Boix has suggested that 'unless the trade and security gains of any new enlargement wave are considerable, the European Union will be forced to delay any plans for tighter institutional integration' (2004: 8). The evidence discussed in this chapter does not seem worrisome on this account. The enlargement of May 2004 has indeed coincided with a noticeable rise of both inequality and poverty in the EU as a whole, as could have been predicted on the basis of the different level of economic development of the new member countries.[7] Yet the worsening does not look large on a comparative basis, nor by national historical records. As seen, when the comparison is properly made in PPP terms, the EU-25 shows lower inequality and poverty than the USA, with poverty rates becoming similar only when area-wide lines are adopted. By taking the British historical experience as a reference, the increase by 3 percentage points of the Gini index associated with the EU enlargement compares to a rise in the UK by 7 points between 1985 and 1990, or a fall by 4 points between 2001–02 and 2004–05 (Jones 2006: 39, Table 27).

The second reason of interest is substantive. 'Greater social cohesion', the goal set out by the Lisbon summit, is an elusive concept. It is a basic tenet of this chapter that the degree of inequality and the extent of poverty measured for the EU as a whole give it a clear and significant operational content, even if admittedly not the only one. The specific merit of considering the personal distribution of income in the EU as a whole is that it provides a unitary framework to jointly assess within-country relative income inequalities (the concern of EU social policy) and cross-country income disparities (the concern of EU regional policies). (For a similar argument, see Fahey, Whelan, and Maître 2005.) A fall in inequality in all countries may not be progress towards greater social cohesion if incomes grow much more rapidly in the richest countries: it is easy to construct examples where the Gini index, or any other inequality measure, decreases in all countries but rises in the EU as a whole. The EU-wide perspective leads naturally to look at these contrasting trends together, and supplies fundamental information to integrate the analysis at the national level.

As pointed out by Atkinson, the EU-wide perspective can be seen as a significant move towards viewing the EU as a social entity. Does it require a strong sense of European identity? Not necessarily. The adoption of the EU-wide perspective would enrich our knowledge of the characteristics of a unification process that is going on anyway, and would help to bring to the fore what Sen called its underlying 'bigger objectives'.

[7] The expansion of the EU population to include a considerable number of households with much lower real incomes leads to a fall of the EU median income, and hence of any poverty line which is based on it ($\theta > 0$). Thus, in comparing the poverty rates for the EU-15 and the EU-25, it should be taken into account that the EU-wide poverty line decreases by 9% as a result of the enlargement; as a fifth of the people that were classified as poor using the EU-15 line are no longer poor according to the lower EU-25 line, the head-count poverty rate in the EU-15 countries falls from 17.3% to 13.7%.

References

Atkinson, A. B. (1975). *The Economics of Inequality* (1st edn). Oxford: Clarendon Press.

—— (1983). *The Economics of Inequality* (2nd edn). Oxford: Clarendon Press.

—— (1995). 'Poverty, Statistics and Progress in Europe', in A. B. Atkinson, *Income and the Welfare State. Essays on Britain and Europe*. Cambridge: Cambridge University Press, 64–77.

—— (1996). 'Income Distribution in Europe and the United States'. *Oxford Review of Economic Policy*, 12: 15–28.

—— (1998). *Poverty in Europe*. Oxford: Basil Blackwell.

—— and Brandolini, A. (2001). 'Promises and Pitfalls in the Use of "Secondary" Data-Sets: Income Inequality in OECD Countries as a Case Study'. *Journal of Economic Literature*, 39: 771–800.

—— and Micklewright, J. (1983). 'On the Reliability of Income Data in the Family Expenditure Survey 1970–1977'. *Journal of the Royal Statistical Society*, Series A, 146, Part 1: 33–53.

—— and —— (1992). *Economic Transformation in Eastern Europe and the Distribution of Income*. Cambridge: Cambridge University Press.

—— Rainwater, L., and Smeeding, T. M. (1995). *Income Distribution in OECD Countries: The Evidence from the Luxembourg Income Study (LIS)*. Paris: Organization for Economic Cooperation and Development.

Atkinson, T., Cantillon, B., Marlier, E., and Nolan, B. (2002). *Social Indicators: The EU and Social Inclusion*. Oxford: Oxford University Press.

Beblo, M. and Knaus, T. (2001). 'Measuring Income Inequality in Euroland'. *Review of Income and Wealth*, 47: 301–20.

Berry, A., Bourguignon, F., and Morrisson, C. (1983*a*). 'The Level of World Inequality: How Much Can One Say?' *Review of Income and Wealth*, 29: 217–41.

——, ——, and —— (1983*b*). 'Changes in the World Distribution of Income between 1950 and 1977'. *Economic Journal*, 93: 331–50.

Berry, W., Fording, R., and Hanson, R. (2000). 'An Annual Cost of Living Index for the American States, 1960–1995'. *Journal of Politics*, 62: 550–67. Revised and updated data (2004) available at: http://webapp.icpsr.umich.edu/cocoon/ICPSR-STUDY/01275.xml.

Bhalla, S. S. (2002). *Imagine There's No Country. Poverty, Inequality, and Growth in the Era of Globalization*. Washington, DC: Institute for International Economics.

Boix, C. (2004). 'The Institutional Accommodation of an Enlarged Europe'. *Friedrich Ebert Stiftung, Europäische Politik*, 6: 1–9.

Bourguignon, F. and Morrisson, C. (2002). 'Inequality Among World Citizens: 1820–1992'. *American Economic Review*, 92: 727–44.

Brandolini, A. (1999). 'The Distribution of Personal Income in Post-War Italy: Source Description, Data Quality, and the Time Pattern of Income Inequality'. *Giornale degli economisti e Annali di economia*, 58 (new series): 183–239.

Buhmann, B., Rainwater, L., Schmaus, G., and Smeeding, T. M. (1988). 'Equivalence Scales, Well-Being, Inequality, and Poverty: Sensitivity Estimates across Ten Countries using the Luxembourg Income Study (LIS) Database'. *Review of Income and Wealth*, 34: 115–42.

Chen, S. and Ravallion, M. (2001). 'How Did the World's Poorest Fare in the 1990s?' *Review of Income and Wealth*, 47: 283–300.

Chotikapanich, D., Rao, D. S. P., and Valenzuela, R. (1997). 'Global and Regional Inequality in the Distribution of Income: Estimation with Limited and Incomplete Data'. *Empirical Economics*, 22: 533–46.

Citro, C. F. and Michael R. T. (eds) (1995). *Measuring Poverty: A New Approach*. Washington, DC: National Academy Press.

Council of the European Union (2000). 'Presidency Conclusions. Lisbon European Council 23–24 March 2000'. Available at: http://ue.eu.int/ueDocs/cms_Data/docs/pressData/en/ec/00100-r1.en0.htm.

Daly, M. (2006). 'EU Social Policy after Lisbon'. *Journal of Common Market Studies*, 44: 461–81.

de Vos, K. and Zaidi, M. A. (1998). 'Poverty Measurement in the European Union: Country-specific or Union-specific Poverty Lines?' *Journal of Income Distribution*, 8: 77–92.

Deaton, A. (2005). 'Measuring Poverty in a Growing World (Or Measuring Growth in a Poor World)'. *Review of Economics and Statistics*, 87: 1–19.

DWP (Department for Work and Pensions) (2006). *Households Below Average Income (HBAI) 1994/95–2004/05*. Available at: http://www.dwp.gov.uk/asd/hbai/hbai2005/contents.asp.

Dowrick, S. and Akmal, M. (2005). 'Contradictory Trends in Global Income Inequality: A Tale of Two Biases'. *Review of Income and Wealth*, 51: 201–29.

Éltetõ, Ö. and Havasi, É. (2002). 'Impact of Choice of Equivalence Scale on Income Inequality and on Poverty Measures'. *Review of Sociology of the Hungarian Sociological Association*, 8: 137–48.

European Commission (2000). *European Social Statistics—Income, Poverty and Social Exclusion*. Luxembourg: Office for Official Publications of the European Communities.

—— (2006). *Joint Report on Social Protection and Social Inclusion 2006*. Luxembourg: Office for Official Publications of the European Communities.

Eurostat (2006). 'National accounts (including GDP)'. Data downloaded on 14 August 2006 from: http://epp.eurostat.ec.europa.eu/portal/page?_pageid=1996,45323734&_dad=portal&_schema=PORTAL&screen=welcomeref&open=/nation/aggs&language=en&product=EU_MASTER_national_accounts&root=EU_MASTER_national_accounts&scrollto=0.

Fahey, T., Whelan, C. T., and Maître, B. (2005). *First European Quality of Life Survey: Income inequalities and deprivation*. European Foundation for the Improvement of Living and Working Conditions. Luxembourg: Office for Official Publications of the European Communities.

Förster, M. F. (2005). 'The European Social Space Revisited: Comparing Poverty in the Enlarged European Union'. *Journal of Comparative Policy Analysis*, 7: 29–48.

Grosh, M. E. and Nafziger, E. W. (1986). 'The Computation of World Income Distribution'. *Economic Development and Cultural Change*, 34: 347–59.

INSEE (1997). *Revenus et Patrimoine des Ménages. Édition 1997*. Syntheses, 11. Paris: INSEE.

Jesuit, D., Rainwater, L., and Smeeding, T. M. (2003). 'Regional Poverty within the Rich Countries', in Y. Amiel and J. A. Bishop (eds), *Inequality, Welfare and Poverty: Theory and Measurement, Volume 9*. Oxford: Elsevier Science: 345–77.

Jones, F. (2006). 'The Effects of Taxes and Benefits on Household Income, 2004/05'. Office for National Statistics. Available at: http://www.statistics.gov.uk/articles/nojournal/taxesbenefits200405/Taxesbenefits200405.pdf.

Lehmann, P. and Wirtz, C. (2003). 'The EC Household Panel "Newsletter" (01/02)'. *Eurostat. Methods and Nomenclatures. Theme 3: Population and Social Conditions*. Luxembourg: Office for Official Publications of the European Communities.

Maddison, A. (2001). *The World Economy. A Millennial Perspective*. Paris: Organisation for Economic Co-operation and Development.

Milanovic, B. (2002). 'True World Income Distribution, 1988 and 1993: First Calculation based on Household Surveys Alone'. *Economic Journal*, 112: 51–92.

—— (2006). 'Global Income Inequality: What It Is and Why It Matters'. Policy Research Working Paper, 3865. Washington, DC: The World Bank,

Mogstad, M., Langørgen, A., and Aaberge, R. (2007). 'Region-Specific versus Country-Specific Poverty Lines in Analysis of Poverty'. *Journal of Economic Inequality*, 5: 115–22.

Sala-i-Martín, X. (2006). 'The World Distribution of Income: Falling Poverty and... Convergence, Period'. *Quarterly Journal of Economics*, 121: 351–97.

Schultz, T. P. (1998). 'Inequality in the Distribution of Personal Income in the World: How It Is Changing and Why'. *Journal of Population Economics*, 11: 307–44.

Sen, A. K. (1996). 'Social Commitment and Democracy: The Demands of Equity and Financial Conservatism', in P. Barker (ed.), *Living as Equals*. Oxford: Oxford University Press: 9–38.

Short, K. (2001). 'Where We Live: Geographic Differences in Poverty Thresholds'. Poverty Measurement Working Paper, January. Washington, DC: US Census Bureau.

——, Garner, T., Johnson, D. and Doyle, P. (1999). *Experimental Poverty Measures: 1990 to 1997*. US Census Bureau, Current Population Reports, P60-205. Washington, DC: US Government Printing Office.

Smeeding, T. M. and Rainwater, L. (2004). 'Comparing Living Standards across Nations: Real Incomes at the Top, the Bottom, and the Middle' in E. N. Wolff (ed.), *What Has Happened to the Quality of Life in the Advanced Industrialized Nations?* Northampton, MA: Edward Elgar: 153–83.

Stapel, S., Pasanen, J., and Reinecke, S. (2004). 'Purchasing Power Parities and related economic indicators for EU, Candidate Countries and EFTA. Data 1991 to 2003, including final results of the revision 1995–2000'. *Eurostat. Statistics in Focus. Economy and Finance*, 37.

Summers, R. and Heston, A. (1991). 'The Penn World Table (Mark 5): An Expanded Set of International Comparisons, 1950–1988'. *Quarterly Journal of Economics*, 106: 327–68.

Svedberg, P. (2004). 'World Income Distribution: Which Way?' *Journal of Development Studies*, 40: 1–32.

Szulc, A. (2006). 'Poverty in Poland during the 1990s: Are the Results Robust?' *Review of Income and Wealth*, 52: 423–48.

van Ginneken, W. and Park, J. (1984). *Generating Internationally Comparable Income Distribution Estimates*. Geneva: International Labour Office.

Whalley, J. (1979). 'The Worldwide Income Distribution: Some Speculative Calculations'. *Review of Income and Wealth*, 25: 261–76.

4

Beyond conventional measures of income: including indirect benefits and taxes

Ann Harding, Neil Warren, and Rachel Lloyd

The size of the income gap between rich and poor, how the gap is changing, and how government programmes redistribute income are all topics of major concern to policy-makers, researchers, and the public. Huge progress has been made in developing comparable and accessible household microdata through initiatives such as the Luxembourg Income Study. These developments have facilitated many cross-national studies of the distribution of income.

Most such studies, however, have used cash income (adjusted in various ways) as their measure of economic well-being. Researchers typically focus on the distribution of 'equivalent disposable income', derived by taking the private income of households, adding any cash transfers received from the state, subtracting any income taxes and social security contributions paid, and then adjusting by an equivalence scale to take account of the number of people supported by that income. This measure has been used in studies in Australia (Australian Bureau of Statistics 2005; Saunders 2001), in the UK (Brewer *et al.* 2004), in Germany (Biewen 2000), in the USA and Canada (Wolfson and Murphy 1998), and in a series of OECD reports providing comparative data for member countries (Förster and d'Ercole 2005; Atkinson *et al.* 1995). Such studies often also examine the redistributive impact of the income tax and cash transfer programmes captured within their ambit, by comparing the distributions of disposable and private income.

Equivalent disposable income can now usually be readily calculated from the income and expenditure survey microdata released by national statistical offices—and this is one reason for the popularity of this measure. However, equivalent disposable income provides only a partial picture of economic well-being and of the degree of income redistribution achieved by government programmes.

On the expenditure side of the ledger, this traditional measure ignores the benefits of publicly provided goods and services (also called 'non-cash benefits' or 'social transfers in kind'), particularly those which provide a personal benefit to individuals such as public health and education and which would otherwise have to be purchased out of cash income. On the taxation side of the ledger, it usually ignores the impact of all sources of taxation apart from income tax and social security contributions. In countries that are heavily reliant on indirect taxes, this may mean that the majority of government taxation is not taken into account in the redistributive picture.

Many researchers have attempted to estimate who pays specific taxes (tax incidence studies), while others have tried to allocate the benefits derived from particular government outlays (expenditure incidence studies). Those studies that seek to put both the tax and outlay side together are often called 'fiscal incidence studies', and their history is described in more detail in section 4.1.

Part of the reason why non-cash benefits and taxes apart from income tax are less often included in studies of income distribution is the complexity of the calculations required to estimate their incidence. If surveys do not record the number of household members attending public educational institutions, for example, then it is difficult to impute the benefits arising to households from public education spending. Similarly, attempts to impute the incidence of indirect taxes, such as Value Added Taxes, require details of the expenditure patterns of households. This complexity often defeats attempts to estimate broader measures of economic well-being.

But these additional difficulties do not mean that we should not try to calculate more comprehensive measures of economic well-being. Where the magnitude or direction of the excluded taxes and transfers has been changing over time within a particular country, then an exclusive concentration upon equivalent disposable income may bias our assessment of whether inequality has increased or decreased. Equally, where the excluded taxes and benefits are not spread evenly among the population but concentrated among particular subgroups, then our judgements about the relative well-being of different types of families will be inaccurate. This can be particularly important for the aged and families with children.

Similarly, as the distribution of the missing outlays and taxes can vary systematically by country, as well as over time within countries, international comparisons of economic well-being can be erroneous. As Smeeding *et al.* observe,

> governments may seek to achieve their redistributive goals through programs which provide non-cash benefits rather than just through tax-transfer mechanisms. This means that measures of economic well-being based on disposable cash income are subject to the vagaries of the overall fiscal structure within countries and that comparisons of both the level and distribution of well-being between countries are dependent upon the existing fiscal structures. (1993: 232)

Having acknowledged these issues, the authoritative international Canberra Group concluded that adjusted disposable income (that is, adjusted by including the value of social transfers in kind) should be 'the preferred measure for analyzing the total redistributive effect of government intervention in the form of benefits and taxes on income distribution' (2001: 24). The Group added that 'in such studies it may also be desirable to impute the value of indirect taxes embodied in consumption expenditure to complete the picture'. Despite this strong support, there are considerable difficulties in moving from concept to implementation, as section 4.1 explains. Section 4.2 provides some initial comparisons of the redistributive impact of government tax and benefit programmes in the UK and Australia—while in addition highlighting some of the difficulties involved in making such comparisons. It also demonstrates the extent to which an exclusive focus on equivalent disposable income understates the redistribution undertaken by government. Finally, section 4.3 summarizes the findings of the chapter and points to directions for future research.

4.1 Theory and practice

While there has always been intense interest in how the welfare state redistributes income, the theoretical and practical difficulties involved in measuring the net effect of government expenditures and taxation on the distribution of household economic well-being are substantial. Fiscal incidence studies attempt to compare the distribution of economic well-being before and after specified government actions. Such studies typically adopt the 'zero government counterfactual' (Reynolds and Smolensky 1977: 11–26), assuming that the difference between 'post-fisc' income and the original 'pre-fisc' private or market income represents the redistributive impact of government. While there is no doubt that public expenditures and taxes change household income—via employment and output changes and by affecting the location and scale of private sector activity—such factors are excluded from the scope of most fiscal incidence studies (Wolff and Zacharias 2006).

Further challenges are created because there is still no clear consensus about exactly where the economic burden of taxes falls (Entin 2004). For example, does the burden of corporation tax rest largely upon consumers (via higher prices) or upon shareholders (via lower dividends)? Such apparently technical assumptions drive the conclusions reached. For example, if the burden is assumed to fall upon consumers, corporation tax appears regressive whereas, if it is assumed to fall upon shareholders, then it appears progressive. Most tax incidence studies also tend to assume that the cost of a tax is the same as the revenue generated—that is, there is no allowance for compliance and administration costs or for deadweight loss or welfare losses to households (Fullerton and Metcalf 2003). In addition, generally, all of the tax burden is allocated within the time period being examined (typically a year) even though, in the real world, effects may spread over years or lifetimes.

On the expenditure side, two key categories of outlays can be distinguished. Divisible public goods and services (such as public education) are those which can be seen as conferring a personal benefit upon users and the benefits from such outlays are generally distributed among the users of the relevant good or service. Typically, the monetary value of the benefit is assumed to be the cost to government of its provision (thus ignoring, for example, the positive externalities to society often assumed to be associated with public education). The 'cost to government of provision' measure is not entirely uncontroversial, with the Canberra Group observing that 'the beneficiary may have no idea of the value of the benefit and if offered a comparable cash sum might spend it very differently' (2001: 15). Indivisible expenditures are those for which it is very hard to identify particular beneficiaries, with outlays on defence, the environment, and roads falling within this category. When they are allocated within fiscal incidence studies, the benefits of such indivisible or 'pure public goods' outlays are generally distributed either equally between all income units (or persons) or in line with cash income shares.

The pioneering fiscal incidence studies in the UK, the USA and Canada in the 1950s, 1960s and 1970s tended to try to allocate the incidence of all taxes and all outlays, thus including within their scope the 'difficult' corporation and other taxes as well as pure public goods expenditures (Dodge 1975; Gillespie 1965; Musgrave, Case, and Leonard 1974; Peacock and Browning 1954). Comparably broad later studies include those for the USA in 1970 (Ruggles and O'Higgins 1981) and in 2000 (Wolff and Zacharias 2006); for the UK for 1971 (O'Higgins and Ruggles 1981); for the Philippines (Devarajan and Hossain 1995), and for New Zealand in 1982 (Snively 1987).

In contrast, the UK Office for National Statistics, which began its annual reports on the impact of taxes and outlays many years ago (with the most recent being ONS 2006), has excluded from its ambit corporation tax, 'because it would be too difficult', and indivisible public goods such as defence and law and order, 'for which there is no clear conceptual basis for allocation or for which we do not have sufficient information to make an allocation' (ONS 2003: 40). It has excluded in addition those indirect taxes which are incident on non-household final consumers. The same approach has also been adopted by the Australian Bureau of Statistics (ABS), which reports every five years on the distributional impact of taxes and benefits but similarly excludes corporate taxes and capital gains taxes from its scope, as well as those benefits 'for which there [is] no clear conceptual basis for allocation', such as defence (2001: 46).

Table 4.1 summarizes some of the key methodological issues outlined above and adds some others, providing a checklist for the important distinguishing features of the various fiscal incidence studies. Many of the methodological issues have not yet been conclusively resolved. For example, the most appropriate way to measure the benefits of public health services is still a contested issue (as discussed further in section 4.2).

Notwithstanding the studies cited above, progress internationally in including the missing taxes and benefits within the definition of economic well-being has been relatively slow in the 1990s and the first half of this decade. Within Europe, the EUROMOD microsimulation model has generated highly comparable estimates for the EU countries of the redistributive impact of income taxes and cash transfers (Immervoll *et al.* 2005). EUROMOD is now being extended to include estimates of non-cash benefits, some non-cash private incomes and indirect taxes, and in the future this development should greatly enhance information about how these currently excluded items affect the distribution of economic well-being across Europe.

4.2 Redistributive impact of taxes and benefits in Australia and the UK

This section provides a case study of the importance of broadening our definition of economic well-being and our assessment of the redistributive impact of government, through taking account of additional taxes and non-cash benefits—using Australia and the UK in 2001–02 as an example. The original Australian study is described in more detail in Harding, Lloyd, and Warren (2006), while the original UK study for the same year is described in more detail in ONS (2003). The

Table 4.1 Methodological issues in fiscal incidence studies

Issue	Main points
Coverage of taxes and expenditures	Taxes: are corporation taxes or indirect taxes that are not incident on households included? Are capital and wealth taxes or tax expenditures included? Expenditures: are 'pure public goods' included?
Incidence assumptions	Who bears the burden of taxes or receives the benefits of outlays? Are formal tax burdens assumed to be shifted to others, e.g. corporation taxes? Are benefits from health and education assumed to be incident upon users or potential users of the services?
Valuation	What is the assumed value of taxes paid and benefits received? Benefits: cost of provision by government? Taxes: dollar value of taxes collected, value to consumers of the service, or some other social welfare measure? Health services: value based on insurance premia approach or actual usage recorded in microdata?
Time period	What is the time period analysed? (e.g. a year, the lifetime)
Unit of analysis	Person, family, or household?
Inter-unit comparisons	What equivalence scales are used to compare income units of different size and composition? Is the same metric applied to both cash and non-cash benefits?
Redistributive impact of government	What measures are used? Vertical equity measures such as Gini, horizontal equity measures concerned with re-ranking, concentration curves or concentration coefficients?

two studies did not include exactly the same taxes and transfers, so some adjustments have been made (as will now be described) to improve comparability.

Methodology

On the tax side, both studies included income tax and excises/duties on such items as tobacco, alcohol, oil, and liquid petroleum gas. Both also included the central government broad-based consumption taxes, known as the Value Added Tax (VAT) in the UK and the Goods and Services Tax (GST) in Australia. Both studies assumed that the burden of income taxes was fully incident upon the taxpayer and that, for all taxes paid, the value of the burden equalled the dollar value of the tax collected.

Both studies used the expenditure patterns of households as shown in sample surveys in the two countries to allocate the relevant consumption taxes to final consumers within households. The Australian study did not consider State and local government taxes and so some taxes included in the UK study were removed so as to improve comparability with the Australian results.[1] Both studies excluded corporation tax and capital taxes.

On the outlays side, in addition to the standard inclusion of cash transfers, the Australian study added the estimated value of health, housing, and education non-cash benefits consumed by households. In addition to cash transfers, the UK study also included the estimated value of education, the National Health Service, subsidies for housing, rail travel and bus travel, and school meals and welfare milk. While there are issues about possible differences in the scope of the minor non-cash benefits allocated, in both countries the key non-cash benefits were health and education. In Australia, education non-cash benefits amounted to 43 per cent and health benefits a further 55 per cent of all non-cash benefits allocated to households. In the UK the comparable figures were 38 and 58 per cent respectively (Table 4.2).

Generally speaking, both studies identified the households and individuals who used each publicly provided or subsidized service, estimated the likely cost to government of that use, and then attributed that cost as a non-cash benefit to the household. In the case of primary education, for example, in both countries the microdata contained information about the number of

[1] The taxes removed from the UK study were council tax, betting duties, Camelot payments to NLDF, stamp duty on house purchase, television licences, customs duties NEC, insurance premium tax, air passenger duty, 'other' taxes on final goods and services, employers' National Insurance contributions, commercial and industrial rates, vehicle excise duty and 50.4% of 'other' taxes on intermediate goods and services. The remaining 49.6% of 'other taxes on intermediate goods and services' represented 'VAT on intermediate goods and services', and, as this item was conceptually included within the Australian results, we assumed that its burden was distributed in the same way as for 'other taxes on intermediate goods and services'. Out of the £10,296 tax per household allocated in the original ONS study, £7,744 remained within scope for the comparative analysis.

Table 4.2 Effects of taxes and benefits by quintile group of equivalent household disposable income, UK and Australia, 2001–02

	Quintile Group of Equivalent Household Disposable Income					
	1st (bottom)	2nd	3rd	4th	5th (top)	All
United Kingdom (£ per year)						
Original income	3,415	9,137	19,244	31,999	62,084	25,176
Direct benefits	5,494	5,686	4,014	2,234	1,146	3,715
Gross income	8,909	14,824	23,258	34,233	63,230	28,891
Direct tax	389	1,383	3,316	6,281	14,073	5,089
Disposable income	8,520	13,441	19,942	27,952	49,157	23,802
Indirect tax	1,852	2,004	2,909	3,647	4,633	3,009
Post-tax income	6,668	11,437	17,033	24,305	44,524	20,793
Indirect benefits	5,244	4,526	4,086	3,638	2,650	4,029
Health	2,775	2,736	2,332	2,148	1,790	2,356
Education	2,253	1,630	1,653	1,409	770	1,543
Other	216	160	101	81	90	130
Final income	11,912	15,963	21,119	27,943	47,174	24,822
Share of total disposable income (%)	7.2	11.3	16.8	23.5	41.3	100.0
Share of total disposable income + indirect benefits (%)	9.9	12.9	17.3	22.7	37.2	100.0
Share of total final income (%)	9.6	12.9	17.0	22.5	38.0	100.0
Australia ($ per year)						
Original income	1,486	15,682	40,439	65,709	108,959	46,461
Direct benefits	12,199	13,354	6,506	2,602	578	7,047
Gross income	13,685	29,036	46,946	68,310	109,537	53,509
Direct tax	132	2,013	7,226	13,732	28,751	10,372
Disposable income	13,553	27,023	39,719	54,579	80,786	43,137
Indirect tax	3,053	4,186	5,812	6,985	9,764	5,960
Post-tax income	10,500	22,837	33,907	47,594	71,023	37,176
Indirect benefits	9,970	12,325	11,496	9,573	6,686	10,011
Health	6,172	6,648	5,688	4,815	3,997	5,464
Education	3,063	5,481	5,721	4,734	2,677	4,336
Other	736	196	86	24	12	211
Final income	20,471	35,162	45,403	57,167	77,708	47,187
Share of total disposable income (%)	6.3	12.5	18.4	25.3	37.5	100.0
Share of total disposable income + indirect benefits (%)	8.9	14.8	19.3	24.1	32.9	100.0
Share of total final income (%)	8.7	4.9	19.2	24.2	32.9	100.0

Note: The distributions are of households, ranked by their equivalent disposable income (see text for equivalence scale). The £ and $ figures show averages per household within each quintile group.

primary school students within each household, so that the imputation of this non-cash benefit was based on information about actual usage.

However, how to best impute the value of publicly provided health services has always been a vexed issue for fiscal incidence studies. If the value of health non-cash benefits is based on the actual usage shown in a microdata source, then the very sick are allocated the highest benefits and thus, ultimately, much higher 'final' incomes. Consequently, most fiscal incidence studies adopt an 'insurance premia' approach, where typically the population is first divided into age/gender sub-groups; all members within each sub-group are next imputed the average utilization rates of the relevant health service by their sub-group; and the cost to government of the provision of such services is then calculated.[2]

The UK study followed this standard methodology, while the Australian study also adopted the insurance premia approach but with some additional refinements to take account of the greater importance of private health services in Australia. For hospitals, the Australian study first divided the population into those who did and did not hold private health insurance and then, given this, estimated the number of days that would be spent as a public patient, a private patient in a public hospital and a private patient in a private hospital, by each age/gender/State population sub-group. For doctor visits, the likely number of visits was estimated for each age/gender/State/income quintile sub-group, based on earlier research showing that the less affluent were more likely to visit the doctor than the more affluent.

On the UK side, £193 billion of cash benefits and benefits in kind have been allocated to households, representing 50 per cent of general government expenditure of around £384 billion in 2001–02. On the tax side, £202 billion of total taxes and employee social security contributions have been allocated and included within this comparative study, representing 53 per cent of general government expenditure.[3] On the Australian side, $126 billion of direct and indirect benefits have been allocated, representing 48 per cent of total spending of $262 billion by all levels of government in 2001–02. On the tax front, $124 billion of taxes have been allocated, representing 47 per cent of total government spending. In both countries, therefore, the benefits of roughly half of total government outlays have been allocated directly to households and the total quantum of taxes attributed directly to households is reasonably comparable although in the UK case slightly more taxes than outlays are allocated, and in the Australian case slightly more outlays than taxes.

As noted earlier, still excluded from this broader 'fiscal incidence' balance sheet are corporation tax, capital taxes and the various State and local government taxes. On the outlays side, neither study has made any attempt to allocate the benefits of such pure public goods as defence or law and order—or those other government services such as roads or transport which some other researchers have included within their fiscal incidence balance sheet as having private benefits to households (Wolff and Zacharias 2006).

In both studies, households were ranked by their equivalent disposable income into quintile groups. The equivalence scales used were slightly different,

[2] Atkinson and Micklewright (1992: 153) cite results from a Hungarian study where health benefits were dependent upon actual usage.

[3] We were unable to reconcile the aggregate estimates presented on page 19 of ONS (2003) with the household averages presented on page 21. To derive the above estimates, we multiplied the relevant household averages by the number of households (both shown on page 21) and then compared the summed totals with the ONS estimate that total government expenditure in the UK was £384bn in 2001 (2003: 3).

with the UK study using the McClements Before Housing Costs equivalence scale and the Australian study using the modified OECD scale. However, a comparison of the two scales suggests that they are not dissimilar for the key household types—and thus that these differences in the equivalence scale used would be unlikely to change the broad conclusions that follow.[4]

Outcomes for the average household

The overall outcomes for the average household in the UK and Australia are compared in Figure 4.1. At first glance, the most striking result is how similar the outcomes of the two tax and benefit systems are, despite their different structures. In both the UK and Australia, the original (or market) income of the average household represents 87 per cent of the gross income of the average household. As government direct benefits (or cash transfers) are added to original income to derive the gross income measure, this necessarily means that direct benefits account for 13 per cent of the gross income of the average household in both countries. In the UK direct taxes take an 18 per cent slice out of the average household's gross income while, in Australia, the comparable figure is 19 per cent. The indirect taxes allocated in both studies take a further 10 per cent from gross income in the UK and 11 per cent in Australia. The value ascribed to the usage of publicly funded health, education and housing services amounts to 14 per cent of average household income in the

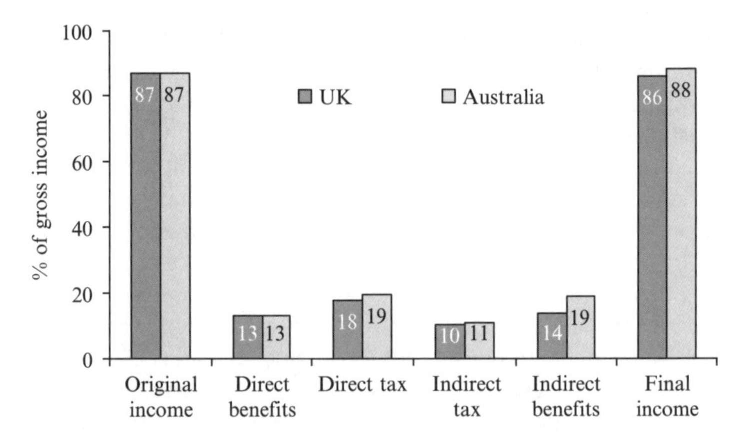

Figure 4.1 Taxes, benefits and income as a percentage of gross income for the average household, UK and Australia, 2001–02

[4] For example, using a couple without children to represent the base value of 1, the equivalence scale values for a couple with one child aged 8 to 10 years are 1.2 and 1.23, for two children 1.4 and 1.46, for three children 1.6 and 1.69, for a sole parent with one child aged 8 to 10 years 0.87 and 0.84, and for a single person household 0.67 and 0.61 (with the Australian equivalence scale values being shown first in each case and the UK scale second).

UK and 19 per cent in Australia—and this is the key area of difference between the two countries.

The final income measure, shown to the right in Figure 4.1, equals original income, plus cash transfers, minus direct and indirect taxes and plus indirect benefits. The reason that it is slightly lower as a percentage of gross income in the UK than in Australia simply reflects the fact that, in the UK, marginally more taxes than benefits have been allocated (while the converse is true for Australia). These results suggest that, overall, the two welfare states rely upon relatively similar magnitudes of direct tax and direct benefits to achieve their redistributive goals.

Overall outcomes by quintile group

The remarkable impression of similarity gained from Figure 4.1 is reduced somewhat once the focus moves away from the average household within each country to look at the impact by income quintile. While the monetary outcomes are summarized by quintile group in Table 4.2, Figure 4.2 introduces a common metric, showing the average original and final incomes of each group as a percentage of the original and final incomes of the average household within each country. Figure 4.2 suggests a major difference in the distribution of original (or market) income within the two countries. Thus, while the original income of the poorest 20 per cent of households in the UK amounts to 14 per cent of the original income of the average UK household, the comparable figure for the bottom Australian quintile group is only 3 per cent. Yet, in contrast to this difference at the bottom end of the income spectrum, there is relatively little difference at the top end. In the UK, the original income of the most affluent 20 per cent of households equals 247 per cent of the original income of the average household in the UK while, in Australia, the original income of the top quintile group is 235 per cent of the original income of the average Australian household. The distribution of original income is thus more unequal in Australia than in the UK.

Despite this, after moving beyond original income by taking full account of the taxes and benefits examined within this study, the distribution of final income appears more equal in Australia than in the UK. Thus, the final income of the top quintile group of households in the UK amounts to 190 per cent of the final income of the average household in the UK—and is four times higher than the final income of the bottom quintile group in the UK. In Australia, the final income of the top quintile group is only 165 per cent of the final income of the average Australian household—and is only 3.8 times higher than the final income of the bottom quintile group in Australia. This suggests that the Australian tax and benefit programmes are more redistributive than the comparable UK programmes—an issue which we now examine in more detail.

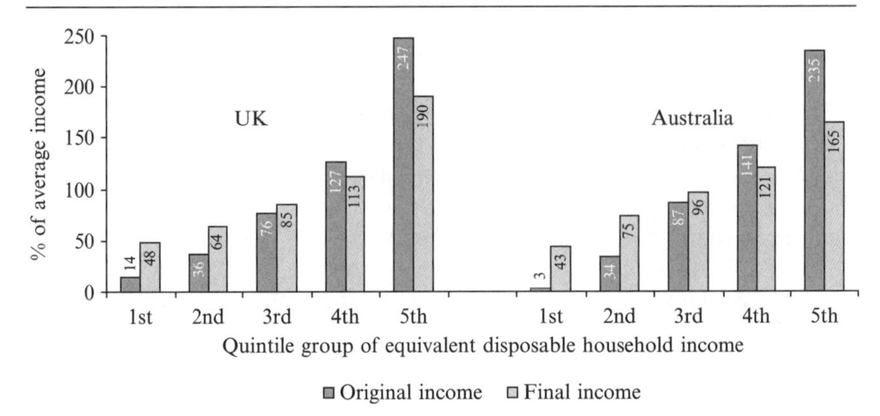

Figure 4.2 Original and final income as a percentage of average income, by quintile group, UK and Australia, 2001–02

Notwithstanding this suggestion of greater redistributive effect in the Australian programmes, it is notable that in both countries the bottom two quintile groups are significant net gainers, the middle quintile group is a marginal net gainer, and the top two quintile groups are net payers. This is well illustrated in Figure 4.2 where, after taking full account of direct and indirect taxes and benefits, the final incomes of the bottom three quintile groups in each country are higher than their original incomes.

Taxes and benefits by quintile group

Which tax and benefit programmes have the most significant impact in the two countries? The two darkest portions shown in Figure 4.3 are, respectively, direct benefits above the zero line and direct taxes below the zero line. Both of these two components are taken account of in the standard disposable income measures—and it is apparent from Figure 4.3 that they both play an important redistributive role. Presumably partly in response to the much lower original income for the bottom fifth, the distribution of direct benefits in Australia is much more pro-poor than in the UK. The bottom fifth in the UK receives 30 per cent of all direct benefits, compared with 35 per cent in Australia. And the Australian benefits are much more tightly targeted, with the top fifth in Australia receiving only 2 per cent of all direct benefits, compared with 6 per cent in the UK.

These patterns are emphasized in Figure 4.4, which shows direct benefits as a percentage of gross income in the two countries. The Australian direct benefits make up almost 90 per cent of the gross income of the bottom quintile group of households, falling sharply to less than 2 per cent for the top fifth. The slope of the UK line is less steep, reflecting the lower progressivity of direct benefits there, with such benefits amounting to just over 60 per cent of gross income

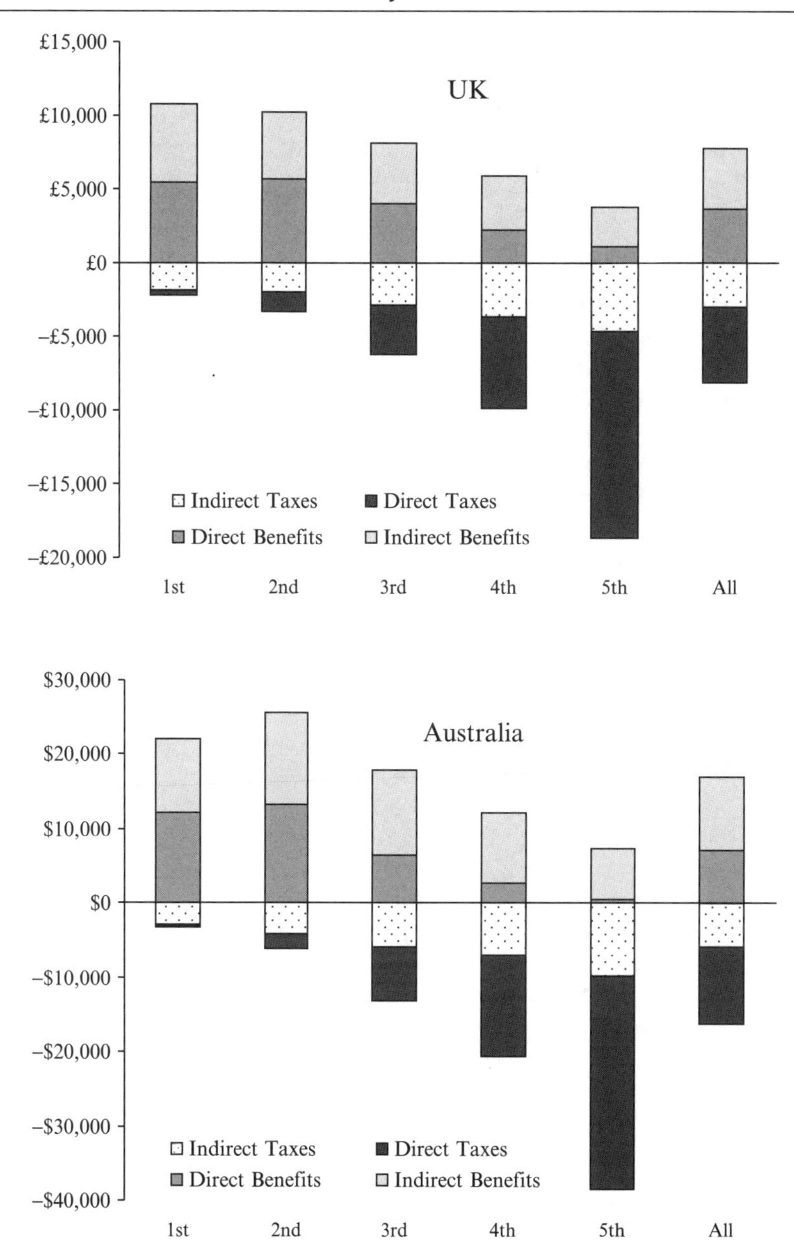

Figure 4.3 Summary of the effects of taxes and benefits on households, by quintile group, UK and Australia, 2001–02

for the bottom fifth and just over 4 per cent for the top fifth. These differences reflect the much greater emphasis on poverty alleviation in the Australian cash transfer system compared with the UK social insurance system (where benefits paid are often more directly dependent upon previous earnings). These results also echo those found by Whiteford, who concluded that the Australian system was more targeted than that of any other OECD country (2005: 13).

In respect of direct taxes, Figure 4.3 suggests that in both countries they play a more important redistributive role than even direct benefits. This is partly due to the higher quantum of funds transferred with, for example, direct taxes per household amounting to £5,089 a year in the UK, compared with only £3,715 of direct benefits (Table 4.2). While there are some minor differences, including that relatively more direct taxes are collected from the bottom quintile in the UK than in Australia, it is very clear from Figure 4.3 that in both countries the direct taxes collected from the top quintile group fund a large proportion of the income redistribution that occurs. As Figure 4.4 illustrates, the 'direct tax as a percentage of gross income' line is flatter in the UK than in Australia, presumably reflecting a less progressive direct tax schedule as well as differences in the underlying gross income distribution.[5]

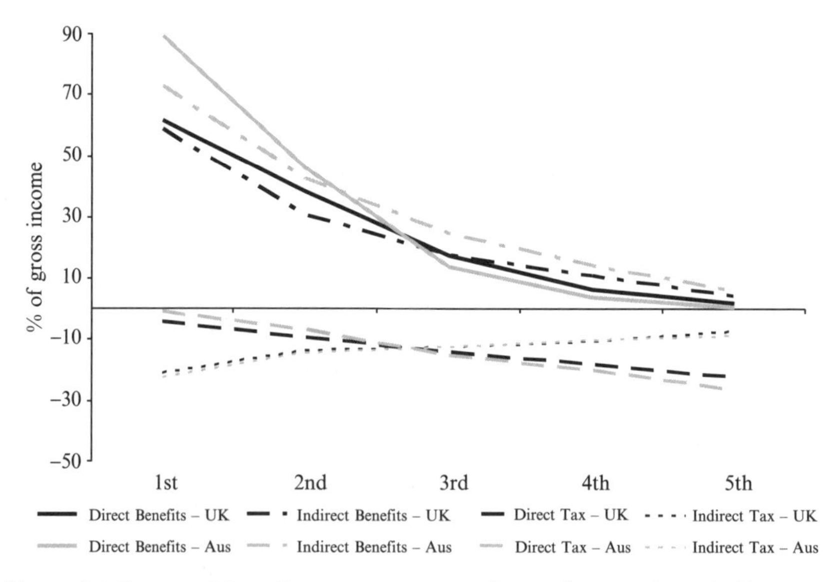

Figure 4.4 Taxes and benefits as a percentage of gross income, by quintile group, UK and Australia, 2001–02

[5] Although it must be noted here that since 2001–02 Australia has introduced a series of income tax cuts, which have particularly reduced the tax burden of high income taxpayers.

What about the two pieces of the jigsaw that are typically missing from income distribution analyses, namely indirect taxes and indirect benefits? In both countries, the 'missing' health, education and housing indirect benefits are extremely important, being worth more to the average household than direct benefits. This is particularly true in Australia, where the average household receives $10,010 in indirect benefits, compared with only $7,045 in direct benefits. In addition, while it is apparent from Figure 4.3 that indirect benefits are not as tightly targeted towards the poor as direct benefits, they are nonetheless still very significant for low income groups. For example, the bottom quintile in Australia receives 50 per cent more in indirect benefits than does the top Australian quintile group while, in the UK, the bottom quintile receives twice as much in indirect benefits as the top quintile group.

Figure 4.4 again emphasizes how progressive indirect benefits are, with the 'indirect benefits as a percentage of gross income' line being strongly downward sloping in both countries. However, in both countries the slope of the line is not as steep as for direct benefits, reinforcing the point that direct benefits are the most progressive element of the outlays system.

In both countries, indirect health benefits are more important to the average household than indirect education benefits. Further analysis suggested that the distribution of public health spending between the five quintile groups was remarkably similar (Table 4.2), but that a greater proportion of public education spending was directed towards the bottom quintile in the UK than in Australia. Thus, almost 30 per cent of total outlays on education in the UK were received by bottom quintile households, compared with only 14 per cent in Australia (Fig. 4.5).

However, the extent to which this is due to differences in policy between the two countries is not clear, as the picture is clouded by a very different distribution of children between quintiles in the two countries. For example, while acknowledging the slightly different definitions of 'children' used,[6] it appears that in Australia households in quintile group 2 and 3 contain on average about twice as many children as households in quintile group 1—whereas the UK has about the same number of children on average per household in each of these three groups (ONS 2003: 22). Thus, in summary, children appear more likely to be represented at the bottom of the income distribution in the UK than in Australia—a conclusion which is also borne out by OECD studies which find a higher rate of child poverty in the UK than in Australia (Whiteford 2006). This therefore seems to be one of the factors producing the variation in public education benefits received by each quintile group within each country. As a result, this provides an interesting illustration of how analyses of the comparative

[6] The UK definition of children extended up to 18-year-olds who were not married and were in full-time non-advanced further education, whereas the Australian definition extended up to 24-year-olds who were not married and were in full-time education.

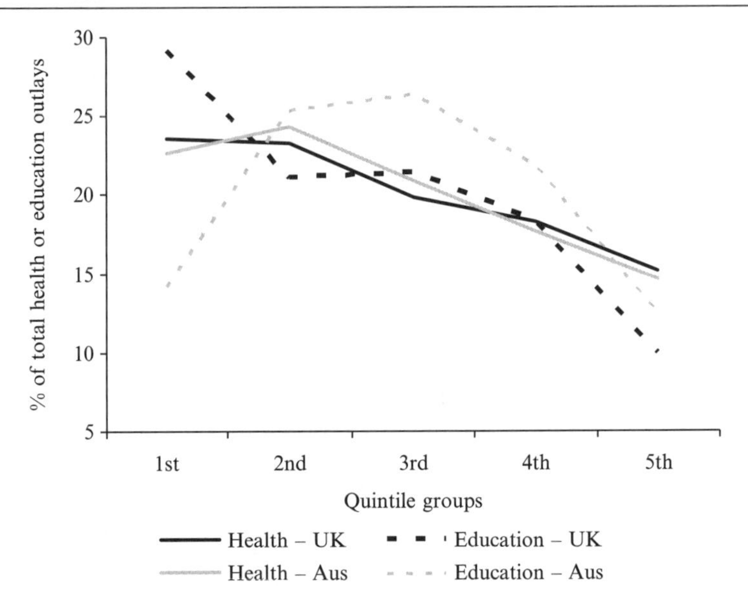

Figure 4.5 Proportion of total health and education outlays received by each quintile group, UK and Australia, 2001–02

redistributive impact of various tax and benefit programmes can be profoundly affected by differences in the underlying distribution of types of households across the income distribution within each country.

Returning now to the other typically neglected piece of the puzzle, indirect taxes, Figure 4.3 illustrates how indirect tax burdens are spread more equally across the distribution than direct tax burdens. While the direct tax burden paid by the bottom fifth is negligible in both countries, the indirect taxes paid have a significant impact on lower income households in both Australia and the UK. As Figure 4.4 demonstrates, the incidence of the indirect taxes included within the scope of this study is very similar in both countries, as the lines almost exactly overlap. The upward slope of the indirect taxes line in both countries shows us that indirect taxes are regressive—in contrast to the other three components of the redistributive picture included within this study.

4.3 Conclusions

Studies of income inequality and the redistributive impact of government typically use equivalent disposable income as their final measure of economic well-being. This measure incorporates original (that is, private) income, subsequently adding cash transfers received by government and subtracting income tax (and social security contributions paid, where applicable).

Measures of economic well-being that are based on equivalent disposable income ignore many of the mechanisms that the modern welfare state uses to ensure relatively equal access to essential goods and services and to attain redistributive goals. In particular, this measure excludes indirect benefits provided by welfare states, through the provision of free or subsidized health, education and other services. On the tax side, governments normally generate a significant proportion of their total tax revenue from taxes other than income tax. Overall, the exclusive concentration upon equivalent disposable income may give us a false picture of the extent and profile of redistribution achieved by modern welfare states.

This study represents a step in the direction of greater comprehensiveness, including health, education and housing indirect benefits and a range of indirect taxes within its scope and presenting broadly comparable results for the UK and Australia.

A number of interesting conclusions emerge. First, it is clear that in both countries excluding indirect benefits from the analysis of income redistribution is a serious omission. In the UK, the health, education and housing services consumed by the average household are worth eight per cent more than the cash benefits received—while the comparable figure for Australia is 42 per cent.

In both countries, indirect benefits are not as progressive in their incidence as direct benefits, but they are nonetheless still unambiguously pro-poor. As a result, they have an equalizing effect on the income distribution. In both countries they raise the share of all income received by the bottom quintile group of households substantially—by 2.7 percentage points to 9.9 per cent in the UK and by 2.6 points to 8.9 per cent in Australia (as the income measure is broadened from disposable income only to disposable income plus indirect benefits). Similarly, the income share of the top quintile group falls by 4.1 percentage points in the UK and 4.6 points in Australia as the income measure is broadened in this way.

Second, the study indicates that the usual exclusion of indirect taxes from income analyses results in an unduly optimistic view of the extent of income redistribution achieved by welfare states. In both countries, the subset of all indirect taxes considered are regressive and, on average, amount to around 60 per cent of the value of direct taxes collected. Thus, in both the Australian and the UK case, including indirect taxes results in an increase in measured income inequality. It can be argued that it is inappropriate to include within the measure of economic well-being both direct and indirect benefits, whose combined value then far exceeds the volume of income tax collected in a particular country—but then fail to take account of how those benefits were actually financed by excluding indirect (and other) taxes from the balance sheet.

Third, it is also evident that the assessment of levels of economic well-being may be biased by use of the equivalent disposable income measure, given the magnitude of the redistribution achieved through indirect benefits and indirect taxes in both Australia and the UK. This may occur within one country over time, if government expenditure or taxation patterns shift away from, or towards, direct benefits and direct taxes. Or it may occur when we are comparing different countries, whose degree of reliance upon direct benefits and/or direct taxes varies greatly. In this study, for example, adding indirect benefits and indirect taxes had a greater equalizing impact in the Australian case than in the UK.

Fourth, although only results by income quintile group were presented in this chapter, it is also clear from the original studies associated with the UK and Australian fiscal incidence research that the focus on equivalent disposable income may adversely affect our understanding of the economic well-being of different population sub-groups. The elderly and sole parents, for example, emerge as two key groups in both Australia and the UK whose final income is much higher than their disposable cash income (ONS 2003; Lloyd, Harding, and Warren 2005). This again echoes the findings of earlier studies, with Smeeding *et al.* noting that 'nonelderly single people and nonaged families without children find their relative income positions are worsened by the inclusion of noncash income' (1993: 253–4).

Finally, the results highlight the need for continuing research in this area. For example, the most appropriate method for imputing the value of health services to households still requires further exploration. Even if one accepts the 'insurance premia' rationale, this does not mean that the apparent value of such 'insurance' should vary only with age and gender (the traditional approach used by fiscal incidence analysts). If usage also varies greatly by other characteristics, such as income or race, then there is a case for using a more detailed imputation approach.

References

ABS (Australian Bureau of Statistics) (2001). *Government Benefits, Taxes and Household Income 1998–99*. Cat. No. 6537.0, Canberra: ABS.

ABS (Australian Bureau of Statistics) (2005). *Household Income and its Distribution, Australia 2003–05*. Cat. No. 6523.0, Canberra:ABS

Atkinson, A. B. and Micklewright, J. (1992). *Economic Transformation in Eastern Europe and the Distribution of Income*. Cambridge: Cambridge University Press.

——, Rainwater, L., and Smeeding, T. M. (1995). *Income Distribution in OECD Countries: Evidence from the Luxembourg Income Study*. OECD Social Policy Studies 18. Paris: Organisation for Economic Co-operation and Development.

Biewen, M. (2000). 'Income Inequality in Germany during the 1980s and 1990s'. *Review of Income and Wealth*, 46: 1–19.

Brewer, M., Goodman, A., Myck, M., Shaw, J., and Shephard, A. (2004). *Poverty and Inequality in Britain: 2004*. IFS Commentaries no. 96, London: The Institute for Fiscal Studies.

Canberra Group (Expert Group on Household Statistics) (2001). *Final Report and Recommendations*. http://www.lisproject.org/links/canbaccess.htm.

Devarajan, S. and Hossain, S. I. (1995). 'The Combined Incidence of Taxes and Public Expenditures in the Philippines'. Policy Research Working Paper no. 1543. Washington, DC: World Bank.

Dodge, D. R. (1975). 'Impact of Tax, Transfer and Expenditure Policies of Government on the Distribution of Personal Income in Canada'. *Review of Income and Wealth*, 21: 1–52.

Entin, S. (2004). *Tax Incidence, Tax Burden, and Tax Shifting: Who Really Pays the Tax?* Center for Data Analysis Report no. 04-12. Washington, DC: The Heritage Foundation.

Förster, M. and d'Ercole, M. (2005). *Income Distribution and Poverty in OECD Countries in the Second Half of the 1990s*. OECD Social, Employment and Migration Working Papers 22. Paris: Organisation for Economic Co-operation and Development.

Fullerton, D. and Metcalf, G. (eds) (2003). *The Distribution of Tax Burdens*. Cheltenham: Edward Elgar.

Gillespie, I. (1965) 'Effect of Public Expenditures on the Distribution of Income', in R. Musgrave (ed.), *Essays in Fiscal Federalism*. Washington: The Brookings Institute.

Harding, A., Lloyd, R., and Warren, N. (2006). 'The Distribution of Taxes and Government Benefits in Australia', in D. B. Papadimitriou (ed.), *The Distributional Effects of Government Spending and Taxation*. Basingstoke: Palgrave Macmillan, 176–201.

Immervoll, H., Levy, H., Lietz, C., Mantovani, D., O'Donoghue, C., Sutherland, H., and Verbist, G. (2005). 'Household Incomes and Redistribution in the European Union: Quantifying the Equalizing Properties of Taxes and Benefits'. Discussion Paper 1824. Bonn: IZA.

Lloyd, R., Harding, A., and Warren, N. (2005). *Redistribution, the Welfare State and Lifetime Transitions*. Refereed Proceedings from the Conference on 'Transitions and Risk: New Directions in Social Policy', Melbourne, 24 February 2005. http://www.public-policy. unimelb.edu.au/Conference2005/Har1.pdf.

Musgrave, R., Case, K., and Leonard, H. (1974). 'The Distribution of Fiscal Burdens and Benefits'. *Public Finance Quarterly*, 2: 259–312.

O'Higgins, M. and Ruggles, P. (1981). 'The Distribution of Public Expenditures and Taxes among Households in the United Kingdom'. *Review of Income and Wealth*, 27: 298–326.

ONS (Office for National Statistics) (2003). *The Effects of Taxes and Benefits on Household Income, 2001–02*. London: Office for National Statistics.

—— (2006). *The Effects of Takes and Benefits on Household Income, 2004–05*. London: Office for National Statistics.

Peacock, A.T. and Browning, P. R. (1954). 'The Social Services in Great Britain and the Redistribution of Income', in A. T. Peacock (ed.), *Income Redistribution and Social Policy*. London: Jonathan Cape,139–77.

Reynolds, M. and Smolensky, E. (1977). *Public Expenditures, Taxes and the Distribution of Income: The USA, 1950, 1961, 1970*. New York: Academic Press.

Ruggles, P. and O'Higgins, M. (1981). 'The Distribution of Public Expenditure among Households in the United States', in L. Osberg (ed.), *Economic Inequality and Poverty: International Perspectives*. Armonk, NY: M. E. Sharpe, 220–45.

Saunders, P. (2001). 'Household Income and its Distribution', in *Australian Economic Indicators*, Cat no. 1350.0. Canberra: Australian Bureau of Statistics.

Smeeding, T., Saunders, P., Coder, J., Jenkins, S., Fritzell, J., Hagenaars, A. J. M., Hauser, R., and Wolfson, M. (1993). 'Poverty, Inequality and Family Living Standards Impacts across Seven Nations: the Effect of Non-cash Subsidies for Health, Education and Housing'. *Review of Income and Wealth*, 39: 229–56.

Snively, S. (1987). *The 1981/82 Government Budget and Household Income Distribution*. Wellington: New Zealand Planning Council.

van der Berg, S. (2005). 'Fiscal Expenditure Incidence in South Africa, 1995 and 2000: a Report for the National Treasury'. Department of Economics, University of Stellenbosch.

Whiteford, P. (2005). 'The Welfare Expenditure Debate: "Economic Myths of the Left and the Right" Revisited'. Paper presented at the Australian Social Policy Conference, Sydney. http://www.sprc.unsw.edu.au/ASPC2005/papers/Paper7.pdf.

—— (2006). 'Family Assistance in OECD Countries: How does Australia Compare?' Presentation to the Department of Families, Community Services and Indigenous Affairs, 27 April, Canberra.

Wolff, E. and Zacharias, A. (2006). 'An Overall Assessment of the Distributional Consequences of Government Spending and Taxation in the United States, 1989 and 2000', in D. B. Papadimitriou (ed.), *The Distributional Effects of Government Spending and Taxation*. Basingstoke: Palgrave Macmillan, 15–68.

Wolfson, M. and Murphy, B. (1998). *New Views on Inequality Trends in Canada and the United States*. Ottawa: Statistics Canada.

5

Inequality within the household reconsidered

*Peter Burton, Shelley Phipps, and Frances Woolley**

> The choice between the different units [the individual or the household] depends in part on the empirical question of how far incomes are in practice shared, and on this there is very little evidence. Earlier it was suggested that within the nuclear family there is an important degree of income-sharing, but we know very little about just how *equally* income is divided among different members. (Atkinson 1975: 42, emphasis in original)

A key reason to study income distribution is a belief that people suffer as a result of inequalities in the distribution of income, consumption, and other resources. If our primary concern is with the well-being of individual children, women and men, then what matters is each person's access to resources. Studies of overall inequality frequently assume equal sharing within the household, neglecting inequality among household members (although in some cases, researchers recognize the problem but lack appropriate data to study it, for example, Corak 2005 and Osberg 2000). Inequality within households may even be invisible to those actually affected in so far as inequality can be both hidden within and perpetuated by customs and norms. Deeply ingrained traditions about who does what, or who eats what, may be seen simply as 'customs', with the role of traditions in maintaining and perpetuating inequality unrecognized. Yet, as researchers have begun to study the earnings, consumption and well-being of individuals within households, a large body of evidence is accumulating, from both developed and less developed countries, that individuals within families do not enjoy equal resources or outcomes.

This chapter begins with a conceptual discussion of what 'inequality within the household' might mean. We review approaches taken to studying this

* We gratefully acknowledge the financial support of the Social Sciences and Humanities Research Council of Canada and the excellent research assistance of Lynn Lethbridge.

topic in the past, summarize what has been learned, assess strengths and weaknesses of alternative streams of research and suggest possible directions forward. Like any survey, this one makes a contribution through identifying patterns and themes; marking commonalities and differences. A key difference between intra-household inequality and other forms of inequality is, as noted by Atkinson above, that just 'how equally income is divided among different members' is rarely directly observed by researchers. As a result, those interested in intra-household inequality have drawn from a wide variety of literatures—not only the mainstream income inequality literature but also sociological research, theoretical models of household decision-making, and development economics. One contribution of this chapter is to bring together this extremely wide and diverse literature, and highlight the strengths and weaknesses, both theoretical and empirical, of various approaches. Our primary aim in the first section is to provide a springboard for further research, to suggest valuable directions for future studies. While doing so, we highlight a number of often-neglected issues relevant more generally for the study of inequality in society.

The second major section of the chapter explores one potentially useful approach to learning more about inequality within families—to study what happens following exogenous changes in the relative incomes of family members. We exploit a unique feature of Canadian policy to illustrate how an exogenous increase in the income available to retired Canadian wives compared to their husbands (also retired) is associated with a change in household spending patterns. Increased income appears to be used not just to increase the private consumption of the retired women who receive it, but also for gifts and charitable donations. This emphasizes a point also raised in our review of existing research. That is, studying only the distribution of income or of expenditures on privately allocable items (for example, clothing, food) may not lead us to a full understanding of the distribution of well-being within households. Indeed, our findings call into question just what 'privately allocable' or 'public' means.

5.1 Conceptual overview of inequality within the household

> In our society most married women do share their husbands' income (perhaps not equally) and most children are supported by their parents, so that there is a very important degree of income-sharing. If the extent of these intra-family transfers was known with reasonable accuracy, then it would be possible to add them to the income of the wife and children, and we could then retain the individual unit. Such calculations of intra-family transfers are not likely to be possible. (Atkinson 1975: 41)

Any study of inequality begs two questions. First, inequality of what?—that is, inequality of income, consumption, happiness, life-expectancy or . . . ? Second, inequality among whom?—that is, inequality among individuals, or households, or wage earners, or ethnic/racial groups, or regions, or countries ...? Most studies of inequality study inequality in income, first, because the data are readily available and, second, because income represents potential spending power (Atkinson 1975: 31). Income data are typically collected at the level of the household. However, most researchers now want to study inequality among individuals, that is, researchers wish to use the individual as the unit of analysis.

The way most researchers infer individual incomes from household-level data is by dividing household income by a suitable equivalence scale (for example, 2.3 for a household of two adults and one child). The resulting figure is a 'needs adjusted' income, and this needs adjusted income is used in inequality measurement. Notice that this approach assigns each household member the same needs adjusted income, and therefore assumes equal sharing within the family. Although individuals are nominally the basic unit of analysis, possible inequality *within* households is not really addressed.

That this approach is not entirely satisfactory has long been recognized. This section surveys different approaches to learning about inequality within households: simulation exercises that fall very much within the mainstream income inequality research tradition; expansion of the mainstream approach by bringing in new information about household finances or time use; bargaining models of the household that give theoretical insights into what shapes intra-household income distribution; new estimation methods that provide more precise measures of intra-household income allocation; the rich development economics literature on the distribution of consumption within households; new research, some inspired by sociological or other disciplinary approaches, others inspired by the work of Amartya Sen and others, that looks beyond income and consumption to explore different notions of well-being. Much of this literature falls outside the standard inequality literature, hence a major contribution of this chapter is bringing all of these approaches together in one place.

Simulation approaches or 'How important might intra-household inequality be?'

Even if intra-household transfers are not known, it is still possible to estimate the sensitivity of inequality measurement to the assumed extent of intra-household transfers, in the spirit of the quotation from Atkinson above. For example, one could make two extreme assumptions: (a) all household members have the same needs adjusted income and (b) each household member only enjoys the income that he or she earns. It is then possible to contrast the income distributions under equal sharing and no sharing and find out the sensitivity of the income distribution to the assumed extent of sharing within the household.

Such an exercise is not entirely realistic. Some household members (for example, children, stay-at-home parents) have no income of their own, yet are much better-off than zero income would suggest. Clearly, income can be shared within the household, though it is not appropriate to assume that it is always equally shared. However simulation exercises are extremely valuable as indicators of the potential importance of intra-household inequality.

The number of such simulation studies is fairly limited. Jenkins (1991) simulates the effect of alternative sharing rules on the distribution of income within the household. Sutherland (1997) compares the distributional impact of tax/benefit changes on both individual and household inequality. Phipps and Burton (1995) estimate the sensitivity of Canadian poverty estimates to various assumptions about how income is shared within the family. The general conclusion of these studies is that 'the relative well-being of individuals within households is very sensitive to income-sharing assumptions employed' (Phipps and Burton 1995: 180).

What the simulation studies show is that sharing within households matters. If household members share their earnings, overall inequality is substantially reduced. If incomes are not fully shared among household members, then current estimates of overall inequality substantially understate the true extent of inequality.

Conventional methods, unconventional data

With this stylized fact well-established, recent research attempts to answer more directly the question posed by Atkinson over thirty years ago—'how *equally*' is it reasonable to assume income is shared?

One way of answering the 'how equally' question is to ask people directly about 'the extent of these intra-family transfers'. For example, inspired by the work of Pahl (1983), Woolley and Marshall (1994) use data on family financial management—who manages and controls the money within the household?—to infer the extent of intra-household income transfers. Woolley and Marshall use Canadian data, and in Canada it appears that family members typically perceive that most income is shared and most decisions are made jointly. Woolley and Marshall's (1994: 428) estimate of overall inequality taking into account the amount of inequality perceived by household members, based on responses to the question 'How do you feel about your individual income: Do you think of it as your own income or as a family income?', was almost identical to a household-based inequality measure. Adjusting for income transfers by looking at, for example, whether each family member looks after their own income or if it is pooled, produces a Gini coefficient 25 per cent higher than the Gini based on household equivalent income, but 9 per cent less than the Gini estimated from individual incomes. Even so, it is not obvious whether looking after money is a source of power or a tedious chore—or both. We need to be careful when using data about 'who manages the money' in that it does not necessarily reflect 'who enjoys the benefit of this income' (Woolley and Marshall 1994; Phipps and Woolley 2007).

Jenkins and O'Leary (1996) also use unconventional data within the context of a conventional approach to inequality measurement. This paper is one of the first to recognize explicitly, and to try to incorporate, the value of work done within the household or household production—into a measure of income inequality. To measure *overall* inequality within households, we need a measure of well-being that combines material resources and time, which are denominated in different units (dollars and hours). Jenkins and O'Leary resolve this dilemma by developing a measure of inequality that puts money values on time. Their 'extended' income measure adds the money value of time spent in home production (using both 'replacement' and 'opportunity' cost measures) to market income. They find, for the UK, that 'extended income' is distributed more equally than market income. While not their focus, it might be interesting to consider what this approach can tell us about inequality within households (for example, in terms of contributions to and/or receipt of benefit from extended income). Here, as elsewhere, the study of inequality within the household throws into stark relief problems that arise in inequality measurement more generally, but are sometimes ignored or dismissed.

Theoretical underpinnings

The papers discussed so far have, for the most part, been empirical papers. However the framework for empirical research is shaped by economic theory. For many years, economic researchers took the family as the fundamental unit of economic analysis, assuming away the possibility of inequality or conflict within families. Becker (1974) gave a theoretical justification for this 'unitary' model of the family. Ironically, by making clear the strong assumptions required for the family to act as a single unit, he paved the way for numerous papers that tested, and rejected, the unitary model.

In particular, the unitary model implies that households act as if all income within the household is pooled. This implication is known as the 'pooling hypothesis'. Pooling means, for example, that it does not matter for any observable household outcome whether government support for children is paid in the form of a tax deduction to the higher earner or a cash transfer to the lower earner, as long as the amount of the support is the same.

In the 1980s and 1990s, a number of papers appeared viewing intra-household resource allocation as a bargaining game. Taking what we will call a 'structural approach' to intra-household allocation, it is possible to model the division of income within the household as a non-cooperative game (Chen and Woolley 2001), or a cooperative game (McElroy and Horney 1981; Lundberg and Pollak 1993; and Agarwal 1997). The key feature shared by these models is that all make assumptions about the process underlying negotiation within the household, and identify variables—for example, divorce laws, government tax/transfer programmes, wages, prices, the presence of children, property laws—that would be predicted to influence the sharing of income within the household. The papers predict that income is not necessarily pooled. For example, paying child benefits directly to the lower earner might matter for the distribution of income within the household. To date, bargaining models have tended to concentrate on bargaining between husband/wife couples. Children as players are typically ignored though they may well play an important role (for example, arguing for a vacation at Disney World rather than in the south of France). One exception is Burton, Phipps, and Curtis (2002) who use a model in which children are players with high discount rates.

There is a growing body of empirical evidence suggesting that the variables identified by these structural models of household bargaining, such as the source of income (his versus hers) matters for a variety of observed household outcomes (most frequently, patterns of expenditure). In other words, the pooling hypothesis is rejected by the data. A large number of these papers use data from developing countries (for example, Haddad and Hoddinott 1994; Hoddinott and Haddad 1995; and Thomas 1990). A smaller set of papers test income pooling for developed countries (for example, Lundberg, Pollak, and Wales 1997; Bonke and Browning 2003; and Alessie, Crossley, and Hildebrand 2005).

From a theoretical point of view, one would expect the source of income to affect spending on household members' 'private' consumption (Chen and Woolley 2001). For example, money transferred directly to a teenager might be more likely to be spent on things for their own consumption (t-shirts) rather than something that is enjoyed by all household members (a public good such as housing). In line with these theoretical predictions, Phipps and Burton (1998) argue that it may not be appropriate to say that all income is either 'pooled' or 'not pooled'. They cannot reject pooling of income for housing, for example, but reject pooling for a variety of private consumption items (such as clothing) as well as for some public expenditures that may reflect gendered spheres of responsibility. For example, an extra dollar of the wife's income is more likely to be spent on childcare; an extra dollar of the husband's income is more likely to be spent on transportation. Yet beyond rejecting pooling, most existing studies using structural models do not work out the implications of their findings for the overall division of income within the household.

The structural models are methodologically superior to the old unitary models and are better at explaining observed household behaviour. From these models, we learn that government policy can influence the intra-household distribution of resources, which is vitally important for anyone interested in income inequality. Yet there are still major gaps. Data are needed to test between alternative structural models, children could be modelled as more than public goods or consumer durables, and there is much more to do in terms of integrating structural models with the economic inequality literature.

Assuming efficiency and a little bit more

The strength of the structural models of the household, that they explicitly model the process of household decision-making and identify variables which would be predicted to influence intra-household outcomes, is thought by others to be a weakness. Alternative approaches to analysing the household, pioneered by Apps and Rees (1997) and Chiappori (1988, 1992), take what can be thought of as a 'reduced form' approach to modelling the behaviour of husbands and wives. These approaches assume that the outcome of marriage is efficient—that is, the partners end up somewhere on the utility possibilities frontier. Given this starting point, researchers infer from observation of, say, expenditures on clothing or labour supply behaviour, how income is shared within the household. Proponents say they are making 'only a very weak and general assumption' (Chiappori 1988: 64); detractors say that several very strong assumptions are required to justify such analyses.

In Chiappori's (1988) paper, he argues that all intra-household resource allocation can be described by a single income 'sharing rule'; each person's income is assumed equal to their own earnings plus a share of the household's non-labour income (Chiappori, Fortin, and Lacroix 2002: 45). Household members act as if they first divide total income according to the sharing rule, which may depend on prices and incomes. Each agent then maximizes his (or her) utility, subject to the budget constraint thus defined (Bourguignon and Chiappori 1992: 359). Household members care about each other, but not about each other's consumption of specific goods and services: I value my partner's clothing expenditures only in so far as those expenditures make him or her happy. I do not care about my partner's clothing *per se*.

In order to find out about the sharing rule from available data, further assumptions are generally made. Most papers in the Chiappori tradition assume that all time not spent in paid work is leisure, a private good—there is no household production. From observation of how 'leisure' consumption changes in response to changes in prices and incomes, it is possible to infer how each agent's private consumption changes in response to prices and incomes. From there one can deduce the partial derivatives of the sharing rule and then by integration the sharing rule itself (up to a constant). An alternative approach is to find goods that can be assigned to individual household members, for example, women's and men's clothing, and (assuming that labour supply is fixed) infer the sharing rule from consumption of those goods—see Browning *et al.* (1994). More recent extensions of Chiappori's original research draw from theories of marriage markets to hypothesize that the male/female population ratio, divorce laws or the age gap between husband and wife are 'distribution factors' influencing the sharing rule (Chiappori, Fortin, and Lacroix 2002).

Perhaps the most compellingly attractive feature of the Chiappori approach is that it allows researchers to deduce a precise numerical estimate of how income is shared at the margin from, say, information about wives' and husbands' labour supply. For example, Chiappori *et al.* estimate that, at their sample mean, a $1 increase in household non-labour income increases the wife's consumption by 70 cents (2002: 66). Browning *et al.* (2003: 36) use expenditures on a variety of goods to estimate a female share that is 65 per cent in their benchmark case, and ranges from 60 to 77 per cent (based on 1992 data for Ontario, Canada).

Only one paper that we are aware of incorporates a sharing rule into a measure of intra-household inequality. Lise and Seitz (2004) find that a conventional measure of inequality (household equivalent income Gini) underestimates inequality at a single point in time by 30 per cent, as compared to a measure that explicitly models the household sharing rule, because it neglects the possibility of inequality within the household. However, it overstates the rise in inequality since the 1970s by two-thirds. Female labour force participation rose substantially in the 1970s and 1980s. Lise and Seitz find that increasing participation reduced intra-household inequality by increasing women's share of household income. Conventional measures overstate the rise in inequality because they ignore the reduction in inequality within the household.

Although work such as Lise and Seitz's is valuable, some of the female share estimates reported above (60% to 77%, say) are implausibly high. These empirical results suggest that precision may not be the same as accuracy. The Chiappori, Fortin, and Lacroix (2002) result may be driven by their assumption that all time not spent in paid work is assumed to be private leisure, and women spend significantly less time in paid work on average than men do. Indeed, as Apps and Rees (1997) point out, a critical limitation to the Chiappori approach is the neglect of household production (one exception is Aronsson, Sven-Olov, and Magnus 2001). Households exist, in large part, to care for the young and the old, to provide food and shelter to household members. Assuming away household production (and in a number of earlier papers in the literature, the presence of public goods within the household) eliminates that which constitutes the economic basis of the family unit.

Apps and Rees (1997) provide a critique of the Chiappori approach, and also summarize their own approach developed at the same time as, but independently of, Chiappori. The critical element of the Apps and Rees approach is that it allows for household production. The cost, however, of Apps and Rees' richer and more realistic description of the household is the model's greater informational requirements. Estimation of the sharing rule in the Apps and Rees framework requires data on consumption of both domestic and market goods.

Apps and Rees, critiquing early estimates of the sharing rule, argue that 'primary emphasis should now be placed on collecting data on individual consumptions of household members' (1997: 189). More recent research is moving in that direction, using information on consumption of both 'private' and 'public' goods within the household, as well as labour supply information. Yet there is still something odd about a framework where even quite recent empirical results suggest women's share of household consumption is almost twice that of men. More research about what actually happens within households will permit researchers to evaluate the realism of the assumptions made in the Chiappori approach. In particular, since empirical results are typically based on expenditures on a limited set of 'privately allocable' commodities, we need to know more about what it means for a good to be private or public within the household—something that will become more clear from the empirical evidence presented in the second part of this chapter.

Inequality of consumption within households

We now turn to evidence on inequality in consumption among family members. This brings us to a sharp distinction between intra-household inequality research and inter-household inequality research in general: the much greater focus on consumption as opposed to income inequality. A growing body of literature documents the existence of inequality within the household between men and women, adults and children, or boys and girls in the consumption of food, medical treatment or schooling in less developed countries (Haddad and Hoddinott 1994; Hoddinott and Haddad 1995; and Thomas 1990). The inequality is greater than can be explained by differences in needs, and is responsive to certain types of policy intervention.[1] Extrapolating these findings to other aspects of consumption suggests that overall levels of inequality are likely to be higher than household-level studies have suggested (Haddad and Kanbur 1990).

Any study of consumption inequality in developed countries must deal with a number of difficult issues. First, in developed countries, a large percentage of most households' budgets go towards housing, heating, a family car or other goods that are public in the sense that they provide at least some benefits for all members of the family. Family members do not necessarily benefit equally from a given public good—for example, a home near good schools may benefit children more, a home near the golf club may benefit adults more—but even so, thinking about 'who gets what' is conceptually difficult. Measuring 'who gets what' is even harder.

[1] For example, the Mexican programme PROGRESA has increased girls' school attendance and decreased their domestic work (Skoufias and Parker 2001).

Second, in rich countries, the link between individual consumption and individual well-being is less straightforward than it is in poor countries. Indeed, consuming more calories in a rich country may signal exhaustion and stress rather than privilege. Even if private consumption is identifiable, it is not always obvious that consumption attributed to a particular household member actually increases the well-being of that household member. For example, a baby may benefit by having warm clothing, but does not care whether it has designer labels; an eleven-year-old boy may abhor the suit and tie purchased by his mother (who loves it). Piano lessons could be another example of expenditures made on behalf on an individual but not necessarily appreciated by that individual. The empirical results later on in this chapter demonstrate that sometimes a household member's well-being is increased by other people's consumption.

A third and related point is that it is not clear when consumption differences within the household reflect individual preferences as opposed to systemic gender inequalities—difference does not imply injustice. For example, the daughter of one of the authors of this paper chooses to eat no meat, while the son eats ample portions. Researchers studying less developed countries typically interpret the lower meat consumption of girls as an indicator of gender bias.[2] In rich countries, is it right to interpret consumption of, say, meat solely as a matter of choice, or can anorexia be viewed as a form of gender inequality?

Fourth, measuring individual consumption is somewhat intrusive. In poor countries studies that involve, say, weighing the food given to all household members before it is consumed (see, for example, Del Ninno *et al.* 2001) are not uncommon; we are not aware of any attempts to measure intra-household inequality using direct measures of food consumption in developed countries. Generally, developed country statistical surveys will provide data on a household's budget for 'entertainment', but the amount spent on entertainment by any one household member is unidentified. Speculating on the reasons for this difference is beyond the scope of this paper; the point is that the needed data are generally unavailable.

Finally, within the context of the household, consumption of home-produced goods (home-cooked meals, clean houses, mowed lawns) are clearly also central to individual well-being. These are particularly hard to measure.

Despite these difficulties, there has been some progress towards measurement of intra-household consumption inequality. First, some helpful research has employed expenditure data. Classic early work by Lazear and Michael (1986, 1988) studies allocable expenditures on children compared to parents. If these results are extrapolated to other expenditures, including public goods,

[2] See, for example, Bouis (2003: 485–6), who finds that adult women in rural Bangladesh consume the same absolute amount of animal and fish products as pre-school boys.

Lazear and Michael estimate that children receive only 40 per cent of what their parents receive.

More recently, Cantillon and Nolan (2001) extend their research on multidimensional measures of deprivation, to study inequality within families. They use a 1997 Irish survey to present evidence of multidimensional differences in consumption between spouses, for example, having a vacation, having a waterproof coat.

Second, time use data have also been employed. While they do not measure the value of home production, time use data can at least help in understanding inequality in consumption of home-production. For example, some expenditures of time clearly benefit just one household member (for example, helping a particular child with homework). But, just as with expenditures of dollars, it is often the case that home production time is used to produce 'public goods' (for example, a clean house) which benefit all household members. And, there can be economies of scale for time just as for income (see Burton and Phipps 2004 for a discussion). As with income, we can attempt to measure inequality in the allocation of time within households. For example, Bittman and Wajcman (2004) demonstrate gender differences in the quality of leisure time available to men and women. In addition to the issue of inequality of benefits from time used for home production, there is also the issue of inequality in terms of who is doing the work. A further complication is that the (dis)utility associated with different time uses can differ across individuals and activities (some like to cook and some do not; some like their paid work and some do not) and this can vary from day to day for the same person.

Beyond measures of income and consumption

Tony Atkinson's early work on inequality emphasized quantitative measurement, providing solid foundations to a subject associated at the time with 'consulting one's prejudices' (Atkinson 1975: 257). One of the major developments during the time since Atkinson first began writing on these subjects has been an explosion of new data sources that go beyond income, consumption or wealth to measure well-being more directly. That is, we now have surveys which simply ask people how satisfied they are with their leisure, consumption or life overall. This approach avoids the difficulties discussed above about inferring who really benefits from the family car, or deciding whether not eating meat is a choice or a measure of hardship.

Large-scale quantitative surveys including measures of individual 'well-being' or 'satisfaction' provide a new way to study inequality within families. Studies using this approach have focused on self-reported happiness (Bonke and Browning 2003; Alessie, Crossley, and Hildebrand 2005), satisfaction with time for self (Phipps, Burton, and Osberg 2001), and self-assessed health status (Burton, Lethbridge, and Phipps 2006).

Qualitative techniques such as focus groups or unstructured interviews have also been used to study inequality within the household. Such studies offer much richness of detail and may be well-suited for probing processes but, on the other hand, are usually restricted to small samples and may lack generalizability. One study using qualitative methods is Middleton, Ashworth, and Braithwaite (1997) who found that mothers often report 'going without' in order to provide for their children. Thus, in some households apparently poor according to household income, children may not actually be deprived while their mothers are more deprived than 'equal sharing' would suggest.

The work of Amartya Sen has also called into question economists' focus on income and consumption. Instead, Sen argues, a better way of measuring welfare is through capabilities: what a person is capable of doing and being, for example, walking freely and without shame (although see, for example, Brandolini and D'Alessio 1998, for a discussion of implementation difficulties). Consumption is flawed as a measure of well-being because even if you derive some benefit from consumption of whatever is ultimately chosen, if it was not what you wanted, you might feel powerless. Having to ask for money to buy something you want may be utility-reducing, even if you usually get it. That is, it is not only personal consumption that matters for well-being within households, but also the power to make choices (see Sen 1990).

Moreover, agency can be used for different purposes. For example, altruism may mean that increases in bargaining power are used to increase expenditures on others rather than self. It is not necessarily the case that increases in bargaining power will be used to increase private consumption or leisure time. In the next section, we will examine the effect of increasing women's incomes through old age security. Our findings will highlight the distinction between well-being and personal consumption.

Describing levels of inequality within households is an extremely difficult yet important project and one that needs to be continued. Yet, as the preceding discussion indicates, an even harder task for research is to go beyond simply describing what exists. We should also try to find causal explanations for observed levels of within-household inequality. As Sen's arguments suggest, it is very important to understand how any outcome comes to be. Since it can be very difficult to find causal links between levels of two variables (for example, in a cross-section), one way to move forward in learning about inequality within households is to study how consumption patterns change in response to an exogenous shift of resources to one household member. We may not be able to determine, for example, whether a given expenditure pattern reflects the husband's or the wife's preferences. However, by examining the sensitivity of expenditures to changes in circumstances, we may gain some sense of the processes leading to inequality within the household. This may be very helpful for policy purposes. For example, Lundberg, Pollak, and Wales (1997) find that when mothers in the UK began to be paid family allowance, expenditures on children's clothing increased, a finding replicated by Kooreman (2000) using data from the Netherlands. The example in the second half of this chapter is also a contribution to this literature, finding another (rare) exogenous change in relative male and female incomes.

Such research is in the spirit of structural models of the household, as already discussed, determining how much a shift in the structural parameters matter. Notice, however, that understanding changes on the margin will not provide a complete understanding of underlying levels of inequality. But it is a start.

5.2 Old Age Security and the expenditures of retired Canadian couples

This section of the chapter takes advantage of a particular quirk of Canadian policy in an attempt to understand how an exogenous increase in wife's income relative to husband's income affects patterns of household expenditure. That is, we ask: if the wife's bargaining power increases, how will she use it? As noted by, for example, Lundberg, Pollak, and Wales (1997), differences in husbands' and wives' incomes are usually correlated with differences in their earnings, making it difficult to separate the effect of increased female share of household income and increased female labour force participation. Lundberg *et al.* get around this difficulty by studying a policy change resulting in a shift in transfer payment from fathers to mothers. Although we do not study a change in policy, we focus on retired couples who become eligible for a significant amount of transfer income purely on the basis of turning 65. A related paper is Lundberg, Startz, and Stillman (2003) who find female bargaining power to increase when husbands retire (and so have a smaller share of household market income).

In Canada, individuals aged under 65 in non-poor households receive no income guarantee. Individuals aged 65 and over receive a substantial amount of Old Age Security (OAS), a payment in excess of $5,000 (Canadian dollars) per year, regardless of personal income or past work history.[3] OAS was introduced for individuals aged 70 and over in 1952, replacing provincial means-tested pensions. The programme was changed in 1965 to provide benefits for individuals aged 65 and over; no major changes have occurred since.[4]

[3] There is a clawback on OAS for recipients whose personal (not household) 'net' income exceeds $62,144 in 2006 ('net' in this case refers to income net of some standard tax deductions). An individual with net income above $101,031 would have the full OAS taxed back. We do not have sufficient information in the SHS to calculate how many men and women actually exceed these thresholds (because we do not know net income). However, note that even the lower threshold amount is more than twice mean male personal income and more than four times mean female personal income for our sample (see Table 5.1).

[4] Although it would be ideal to be able to estimate a 'difference in difference' model exploiting significant changes in OAS, this is not possible since there have been no large changes to the programme since suitable microdata have been available.

We ask how household expenditures are affected by wives becoming eligible for OAS, given husbands are already in receipt of the benefit (Canadian husbands are, on average, about two years older than their wives). More specifically, our research strategy is to construct a sample of retired married couples. All husbands are retired and aged 65 or more. All wives are retired (or not engaged in paid work); some are aged 60 to 64 while others are aged 65 to 69. We then compare expenditure patterns for couples where the wife receives OAS with those of otherwise similar couples in which the wife has not yet started to receive OAS. This allows us to estimate the potential significance of intra-household inequality in Canada and developed countries in general.

Several caveats about this research design should, however, be made. First, a sample of retired married couples may not be fully representative of all married couples. Although there is no restriction in our data that they have been continuously married to each other (that is, some will have re-married following divorce or death of an earlier spouse), many couples with a wife aged 60 to 70 years will be in long-standing relationships. Thus, for example, they may be couples who are more than usually harmonious about financial matters. Second, although receipt of OAS is exogenous in so far as it does not depend on anything except turning 65, Canadians are certainly aware of the programme and may have adjusted behaviour prior to actual receipt of the wife's benefits. Finally, although we restrict attention to couples within a reasonably tight age band (wives are 60 to 70) to minimize the concern that changes in expenditure patterns will inevitably occur as couples age, it is obviously still true that the wives who are eligible for OAS are a few years older than the wives who are not, and this may explain part of what we observe in the data.

To carry out this research, we pool three years of microdata (2001, 2002 and 2003) from the public use versions of the Statistics Canada Survey of Household Spending (SHS). The SHS is a multi-stage, stratified sample drawn from the Labour Force Survey sampling frame. It is thus representative of Canadians living in the ten provinces and three territories (with the exception of those living on reserves, in institutions or who are members of the military; respondents from the north are contacted only every second year, beginning in 2001). Coverage is of about 98 per cent of the population in the ten provinces (slightly lower for the north). The survey is conducted from January to March each year, asking respondents about their spending habits, dwelling and household characteristics during the previous year. The survey is relatively difficult to complete (the response rate in 2003, for example, was 72 per cent) and is carried out during a personal interview using a paper questionnaire. Total sample size was 17,265 in 2003, 14,704 in 2002, and 16,901 in 2001.

In each year, we select married-couple households in which the husband is at least 65 years old and reports no paid work. Selected couples must further satisfy the requirements that the wife is aged between 60 and 69 and reports no paid work. We exclude older retired couples on the grounds that the expenditure patterns of more elderly households are likely to be rather different from those of the 'newly retired' (who may eat out, travel, garden, play golf, etc.). Thus, all husbands in the sample will be in receipt of OAS; about half the wives (those aged 65 and over) will receive OAS while the other half will not (those aged 60 to 64). Following these restrictions, we are left with 439 households in 2003, 386 in 2002 and 442 in 2001 that satisfy all of these requirements. Since these are relatively small samples, we pool the three years to obtain a total sample of 1267 retired couples; 481 in which the wife is aged 60 to 64 and so OAS-ineligible; 786 in which she is aged 65 through 69 and so OAS-eligible.

Table 5.1 reports sample means, overall as well as for the two sub-samples of couples with OAS-ineligible and OAS-eligible wives. We use sample weights for all analyses. As we would expect, household income before tax is higher when the wife as well as the husband is OAS-eligible ($39,195 versus $37,900—all dollar values are expressed in 2003 Canadian dollars). And, this is clearly a result of higher wife's income ($12,506 rather than $11,132), not higher husband's income ($26,689 when wives are aged 65 to 69 and $26,768 when wives are 60 to 64).

Table 5.1 next takes a preliminary look at expenditures on a variety of items which might plausibly be purchased by 'younger' retired couples: restaurant

Table 5.1 Variable means, by age

Variable	Wife aged 60–64	Wife aged 65–69	All
Income ($) of:			
Husband	26,768	26,689	26,719
Wife	11,132	12,506	11,987
Household	37,900	39,195	38,705
Expenditure ($) on:			
Restaurant food	1,073	961	1,003
Clothing for men and boys	525	572	554
Clothing for women and girls	865	893	883
Gifts of clothing and money	826	1,342	1,147
Donations	607	807	731
Entertainment	530	605	577
Gambling	339	395	374
Alcohol	533	495	510
Personal care	712	692	699
Gardening	258	268	265
% of sample:			
In a rural area	20.1	21.9	21.2
Atlantic Canada	8.0	8.8	8.5
Quebec	33.9	39.6	37.5
Ontario	30.9	25.6	27.6
West or North	27.1	25.9	26.4
2001	34.8	34.1	34.4
2002	32.8	30.1	31.1
2003	32.3	35.8	34.5
Sample size	481	786	1,267

Note: Expenditures and income are in 2003 Canadian dollars per year.

food, women's clothing, men's clothing, gifts to people (including all purchases of gifts plus money but not gifts in kind), charitable donations, entertainment (including expenditures on movie theatre, live sports events, live performing arts, admission to museums and other activities plus rental of cable and/or satellite services), gambling, alcohol, personal care and gardening. Restaurant food, male and female clothing and alcohol are also interesting to consider as these have been featured in earlier work on inequality within households (for example, Phipps and Burton 1998). Thus, we do not model all forms of expenditure; in particular, we have avoided any attempt to analyse purchase of durables (such as recreational vehicles or sports cars).

Not surprisingly, since household income is higher when wives as well as husbands receive OAS, average expenditures are higher for 7 of the 10 categories considered here (exceptions are restaurant food, alcohol, and personal care—see Table 5.1). In most cases, however, differences in means between the two groups are negligible. Expenditure categories that stand out as being noticeably higher when wives receive OAS are: gifts, increasing from $826 to $1,342 (or 62%); donations, increasing from $607 to $807 (or 33%); and to a lesser degree, gambling, increasing from $339 to $395 (or 17%); and entertainment, increasing from $530 to $605 (or 14%). Interestingly, expenditures on restaurant food *fall* by $113 (11%) despite the increase in household income.

Of course, it is important to go beyond simply comparing expenditure means for these two groups of 'younger' retired couples. Household spending patterns should certainly be influenced by characteristics such as the overall level of household income, urban versus rural residence, and so on. While the SHS provides only limited demographic information, we are able to control for region of residence (aggregating the four Atlantic provinces and the three Prairie provinces with the North), urban versus rural residence as well as for total household income and household income squared.[5] We also include dummy variables for survey year. We do not control for age of husband/wife, since we have already restricted our sample with respect to age. Recall that we have also restricted the sample to couples in which neither the husband nor the wife reports any paid work. We would like to control for education level but, unfortunately, this is not available in the data.

Given the controls for household income, urban/rural status and region, the variable of particular interest is the dummy variable for households in which the wife is aged 65 to 69 (and so eligible for OAS) relative to the base case in which the wife is aged 60 to 64 (and so not eligible). That is, our central question is whether or not there is a difference in household spending associated with an exogenous increase in wife's income compared to husband's.

[5] We experimented with alternative functional forms for income and obtained the same qualitative results.

To test this hypothesis, we estimate a Tobit model for each of the expenditure categories noted above. We use the Tobit specification since there are some couples with zero expenditures for each of the categories studied. Zero expenditure is least likely for personal care (less than 1% of the full sample); most likely for gifts (21% of the full sample). All Tobit models are estimated in share form to reduce potential problems of heteroskedasticity. That is, the dependent variable for each regression is expenditure on a particular category as a percentage of total expenditures.

For brevity, Table 5.2 presents just the estimated coefficient on the 'OAS-eligible' dummy for each of the expenditure categories. In 9 of the 10 cases, this coefficient is positive (alcohol is an exception with a negative coefficient). However, controlling for household income, urban/rural status and region of residence, the only statistically significant relationships apparent are for gifts, charitable donations and entertainment. For these three cases, more detailed reporting of regression results is provided in Table 5.3.

Since results reported in Table 5.3 are estimated Tobit coefficients, we cannot directly read off the estimated magnitude of the change in the share of

Table 5.2 Tobit regressions of the percentage shares of various categories of household expenditure: coefficient on dummy variable indicating the wife's age is 65–69

Expenditure	Coefficient (standard error)
Restaurant food	0.01
	(0.17)
Clothing for men and boys	0.07
	(0.09)
Clothing for women and girls	0.01
	(0.14)
Gifts of clothing and money	1.31***
	(0.37)
Donations	0.58***
	(0.20)
Entertainment	0.25***
	(0.08)
Gambling	0.18
	(0.18)
Alcohol	−0.16
	(0.14)
Personal care	0.00
	(0.08)
Gardening	0.05
	(0.06)

Notes: *** indicates significant at the 1% level. The dependent variable is the expenditure for a category expressed as a percentage of total household expenditures minus personal taxes. Other explanatory variables included in the model but not shown: household income, household income squared, a rural residence dummy, dummies for residence in Atlantic Canada, Quebec, and West or North, and year dummies for 2002 and 2003.

Table 5.3 Tobit regressions of the percentage shares of three categories of household expenditure

Variable	Gifts of clothing and money	Donations	Entertainment
Wife is 65–69	1.31***	0.58***	0.25***
	(0.37)	(0.20)	(0.08)
Household income ($ 000s)	0.14***	−0.02*	1.19E–3
	(0.02)	(0.01)	(0.01)
Household income ($ 000s) squared	−8.604E–4***	5.06E–4***	−3.71E–5
	(1.897E–4)	(9.088E–5)	(3.787E–5)
Rural residence	−0.95**	0.13	−0.18*
	(0.45)	(0.25)	(0.10)
Atlantic Canada	1.52	0.18	0.05
	(1.52)	(0.37)	(0.15)
Quebec	−0.67	−2.02***	−0.20**
	(0.46)	(0.25)	(0.10)
West or North	0.55	−0.50**	0.07
	(0.45)	(0.25)	(0.10)
2002	−0.86*	0.19	0.02
	(0.44)	(0.24)	(0.10)
2003	−0.33	−0.68***	2.23E–3
	(0.43)	(0.23)	(0.10)
Intercept	−1.83**	1.75***	1.68***
	(0.79)	(0.42)	(0.17)
Variance	6.19	3.40	1.43
	(0.14)	(0.08)	(0.03)

Notes: *, ** and *** indicate significant at the 10%, 5% and 1% levels respectively. The dependent variable is the expenditure for each category expressed as a percentage of total household expenditures minus personal taxes. All explanatory variables are dummies other than household income and its square.

expenditure devoted to the three categories in question. However, if we set all categorical variables equal to zero and household income at the sample mean, our estimated Tobit model predicts that couples will devote 3.2 per cent of total expenditure to gifts compared to 4.0 per cent if the wife is OAS eligible (an increase of 26%). Similarly, we calculate that the percentage share of total expenditures allocated to donations will increase from 2.3 to 2.7 per cent (an 18% increase). Finally, we calculate an increase from 1.8 to 2.0 per cent devoted to entertainment (a percentage increase of 13% in the share).

In terms of other estimated coefficients, we find expenditure shares increase with income at a decreasing rate for gifts until we reach a maximum share when household income is about $81,000 (about twice mean income for our sample). The relationship between income and expenditure share on donations might be described as 'U-shaped' with a minimum share when household income is about $20,000 (about half the mean for our sample). There is no apparent association between income and the share of expenditure devoted to entertainment. The only other result of note is that residence in a rural area decreases expenditure shares on both gifts and entertainment but notice that the magnitude of the association is only about 70 per cent of that estimated for 'being OAS eligible'.

Our findings, which suggest that retired women do not spend income under their control entirely on themselves, but on gifts for others (possibly grandchildren) is consistent with other literature. Cantillon and Nolan (2001), for example, find, using a 1997 Irish survey, that giving 'presents to friends or family at least once a year' is one area of consumption in which husbands are less likely than wives to have the item, perhaps indicating a greater 'taste' for gift-giving by women. Duflo (2000) finds that increases in pension income received by grandmothers in South Africa increased the health and nutrition of grandchildren (especially girls); the same was not true of pension income received by grandfathers. Andreoni, Brown, and Rischall (2003) find that men and women have different preferences for charitable giving, which seem to be resolved in favour of the husband's preferences. Our finding that OAS received by retired Canadian women is partially used to increase charitable giving is also consistent with the idea that when female bargaining power is higher, more income is used for charitable giving.

Notice that increased expenditures on both gifts and charitable donations means that increased power is at least partially used to increase expenditures on others rather than self. The point is not so much that grandmothers are selfless as it is that examining only apparently allocable private expenditures is too narrow a way of understanding how inequality of household bargaining power may affect household outcomes.

5.3 Conclusions

Simulations make it clear that there is a large potential for inequality within households, in both time and money. When researchers look for inequality within the household, they generally find some. Overall inequality is probably larger than studies using household-level data would suggest.

Presumably, the ultimate goal of this sort of research is to determine if inequality within families is a problem, then to understand what drives it, and finally to decide which policies might alleviate it. Yet major gaps remain in our understanding of all aspects of this agenda. There are, first of all, theoretical gaps. The unitary model, which suggests that households act as a single decision-making unit, cannot explain observed household behaviour. It must be rejected. Yet what is to be the alternative? There are a range of different structural models, and not much empirical evidence to prove one superior to the others. The reduced form models yield predictions of sharing rules but some of the best existing empirical research in this area produces implausible results. More work is needed to provide better models of processes within families, to account for externalities and public goods, to expand the scope of analysis beyond income and consumption to well-being and agency.

Hand in hand with more refined models, we need more refined testing of the assumptions and predictions of these models. For this, availability of data is clearly a central issue. We need to get beyond studying 'privately allocable' expenditures such as clothing, alcohol and tobacco. Studying only the distribution of expenditures on what are conventionally thought of as privately allocable items (for example, clothing, food) is unlikely to lead us to a full understanding of the distribution of well-being within households. Privately allocable goods like adult clothing have significant public characteristics: because of altruism, paternalism, or for purely selfish reasons (for example, you earn more if you go to work wearing an expensive suit) family members care about other family members' consumption of food and clothing.

Many studies find that when women have more money of their own, they tend to spend it on their children, either on children's clothing or, as we find in this chapter, on gifts. Thus, better data about expenditures on children—both in terms of money and time—would be helpful in understanding both the distribution of resources between men and women, and the distribution between adults and children. And, such data would not be particularly difficult to collect. We would also suggest collecting more data on individual savings and asset ownership, as well as on individual spending on charitable donations and gifts, as immediate priorities.

One thing that we all value, and that we all have in common, is time. More data on time use is needed. In particular, such data should integrate time and income/consumption. Again, this is certainly possible, and likely to produce interesting results, particularly if time use data were available for all family members. Measures of self-rated health status, happiness and over-all life satisfaction for all family members would again greatly facilitate work in this area. A perhaps more daunting task would be the collection of longitudinal data for the study of inequality within households since most empirical work in this area is currently cross-sectional.

In addition to improved theoretical models and better data for quantitative studies, we might consider new research techniques such as experiments or qualitative analysis (for example, focus groups, unstructured interviews) which might shed light on different aspects of the problem.

Yet all of this research will not have much impact on the existing literature on inequality without having some bridge to the more conventional income inequality literature, which calculates Gini coefficients, Atkinson indices and other distributional measures. One avenue is to keep on trying to make estimates of intra-household inequality more comparable with estimates of overall inequality—get better data, estimate models carefully, try to come up with both precise and accurate estimates of how income is shared within households. Another alternative is to make estimates of overall inequality using measures that work both within and between households—using, for example, happiness, life satisfaction, or other non-traditional, more ordinal measures of well-being.

We might then be in a position to understand how much of the inequality in, say, the distribution of happiness, is attributable to differences within households as compared to differences between households.

References

Agarwal, B. (1997). '"Bargaining" and Gender Relations: Within and Beyond the Household'. *Feminist Economics,* 3: 1–51.

Alessie, R., Crossley, T. F., and Hildebrand, V. (2005). 'Estimating a Collective Household Model with Survey Data on Financial Satisfaction'. Unpublished paper.

Andreoni, J., Brown, E., and Rischall, I. (2003). 'Charitable Giving by Married Couples: Who Decides and Why Does it Matter?' *The Journal of Human Resources,* 28: 111–33.

Apps, P. and Rees R. (1997). 'Collective Labor Supply and Household Production: Comment'. *Journal of Political Economy,* 105(1): 178–90.

Aronsson, T., Sven-Olov, D., and Magnus, W. (2001). 'Estimating Intrahousehold Allocation in a Collective Model with Household Production'. *Journal of Population Economics,* 14: 569–84.

Atkinson, A. B. (1975). *The Economics of Inequality.* Oxford: Clarendon Press.

Becker, G. S. (1974). 'A Theory of Marriage', in T. W. Schultz (ed.), *Economics of the Family.* Chicago: University of Chicago Press, 299–343.

Bittman, M. and Wajcman, J. (2004). 'The Rush Hour: The Quality of Leisure Time and Gender Equity', in N. Folbre and M. Bittman (eds), *Family Time: The Social Organization of Care.* New York: Routledge Press, 171–93.

Bonke, J. and Browning, M. (2003). 'The Distribution of Well-Being and Income Within The Household.' Unpublished paper.

Bouis, H. (2003). 'Commercial Vegetable and Polyculture Fish Production in Bangladesh: Impacts on Income, Food Consumption, and Nutrition', in A. R. Quisumbing (ed.), *Gender, Household Decisions, and Development: A Synthesis of Recent Research.* Washington, DC: International Food Policy Research Institute, 73–7.

Bourguignon, F. and Chiappori, P.-A. (1992). 'Collective Models of Household Behaviour: An Introduction'. *European Economic Review,* 36, 355–64.

Brandolini, A. and D'Alessio, G. (1998). 'Measuring Well-being in the Functioning Space'. Unpublished paper. Rome: Banca D'Italia. Presented at 26th General Conference of The International Association for Research in Income and Wealth, Cracow, Poland. http://www.iariw.org/papers/2000/brandolini.pdf.

Browning, M., Bourguignon, F., Chiappori, P. A., and Lechene, V. (1994). 'Income and Outcomes: A Structural Model of Intra-Household Allocation'. *Journal of Political Economy,* 102: 1067–96.

——, Chiappori, P.-A., and Lewbel, A. (2003). 'Estimating Consumption Economies of Scale, Adult Equivalence Scales, and Household Bargaining Power'. Working Paper 2003-12, Centre for Applied Microeconometrics, Institute of Economics, University of Copenhagen.

Burton, P. and Phipps, S. (2004). 'Families, Time and Money in Canada, Sweden, the UK and the US'. Paper presented at 28th General Conference of the IARIW, Cork, Ireland.

Burton, P., Lethbridge, L., and Phipps, S. (2006). 'Children with Disabilities and Chronic Conditions and Longer-Term Parental Well-being'. Unpublished paper.

——, Phipps, S., and Curtis, L. (2002). 'All in the Family: A Simultaneous Model of Parenting Style and Child Conduct'. *American Economic Review*, 92: 368–72.

Cantillon, S. and Nolan, B. (2001). 'Poverty Within Households: Measuring Gender Differences Using Non-monetary Indicators'. *Feminist Economics*, 7: 5–23.

Chen, Z. and Woolley, F. (2001). 'A Cournot-Nash Model of Family Decision Making'. *Economic Journal*, 111: 722–48.

Chiappori, P. A. (1988). 'Rational Household Labor Supply.' *Econometrica*, 56: 63–89.

—— (1992). 'Collective Labor Supply and Welfare'. *Journal of Political Economy*, 100: 437–67.

——, Fortin, B., and Lacroix, G. (2002). 'Marriage Market, Divorce Legislation, and Household Labor Supply'. *Journal of Political Economy*, 110: 37–72.

Corak, M. (2005). 'Principles and Practicalities for Measuring Child Poverty in the Rich Countries'. Working Paper No. 406. Luxembourg: Luxembourg Income Study.

Del Ninno, C., Dorosh, P. A., Smith, L. C., and Roy, D. K. (2001). *The 1998 Flood in Bangladesh: Disaster Impacts, Household Coping Strategies, and Response*. Research Report 122. Washington, DC: International Food Policy Research Institute.

Duflo, E. (2000). 'Child Health and Household Resources in South Africa: Evidence from the Old Age Pension Program'. *The American Economic Review*, 90: 393–8.

Haddad, L. and Hoddinott, J. (1994). 'Women's Income and Boy–Girl Anthropometric Status in the Cote D'Ivoire'. *World Development*, 22: 543–53.

—— and Kanbur, R. (1990). 'How Serious is the Neglect of Intra-Household Inequality?' *The Economic Journal*, 100: 866–81.

Hoddinott, J. and Haddad, L. (1995). 'Does Female Income Share Influence Household Expenditure Patterns? Evidence from the Cote D'Ivoire'. *Oxford Bulletin of Economics and Statistics*, 57: 77–96.

Jenkins, S. P. (1991). 'Poverty Measurement and the Within-Household Distribution: Agenda for Action'. *Journal of Social Policy*, 20: 457–83.

—— and O'Leary, N. C. (1996). 'Household Income Plus Household Production: The Distribution of Extended Income in the UK'. *Review of Income and Wealth*, 42: 401–19.

Kooreman, P. (2000). 'The Labeling Effect of a Child Benefit System'. *American Economic Review*, 90: 571–83.

Lazear, E. P. and Michael, R. T. (1986). 'Estimating the Personal Distribution of Income with Adjustment for Within-Family Variation'. *Journal of Labor Economics*, 4: S216–S239.

—— and Michael, R. T. (1988). *Allocation of Income Within the Household*. Chicago: University of Chicago Press.

Lise, J. and Seitz, S. (2004). 'Consumption Inequality and Intra-Household Allocations'. Department of Economics Working Paper 1019. Kingston, Ontario: Queen's University.

Lundberg, S. and Pollak, R. A. (1993). 'Separate Spheres Bargaining and the Marriage Market'. *Journal of Political Economy*, 101: 988–1010.

——, Pollak, R. A., and Wales, T. (1997). 'Do Husbands and Wives Pool their Resources? Evidence from the United Kingdom Child Benefit'. *Journal of Human Resources*, 32: 463–80.

——, Startz, R., and Stillman, S. (2003). 'The Retirement-Consumption Puzzle: A Marital Bargaining Approach'. *Journal of Public Economics*, 87: 1199–218.

McElroy, M. B. and Horney, M. J. (1981). 'Nash-Bargained Household Decisions'. *International Economic Review*, 22: 333–50.

Middleton, S., Ashworth, K., and Braithwaite, I. (1997). *Small Fortunes. Spending on Children, Childhood Poverty and Parental Sacrifice*. York: Joseph Rowntree Foundation.

Osberg, L. (2000). 'Poverty in Canada and the United States: Measurement, Trends and Implications'. *Canadian Journal of Economics*, 33: 847–77.

Pahl, J. (1983). 'The Allocation of Money and the Structuring of Inequality within Marriage'. *Sociological Review*, 31: 237–62.

Phipps, S. and Burton, P. (1995). 'Sharing within Families: Implications for the Measurement of Poverty among Individuals in Canada'. *Canadian Journal of Economics*, 28: 177–204.

—— and —— (1998). 'What's Mine is Yours? The Influence of Male and Female Incomes on Patterns of Household Expenditure'. *Economica*, 65: 599–613.

—— and Woolley, F. (2007). 'Control over Money and the Savings Decisions of Canadian Households. *Journal of Socio-Economics*, forthcoming.

——, Burton, P., and Osberg, L. (2001). 'Time as a Source of Inequality Within Marriage: Are Husbands More Satisfied with Time for Themselves than Wives?' *Feminist Economics*, 7: 1–22.

Safilios-Rothschild, C. (1976). 'A Macro and Micro-Examination of Family Power and Love'. *Journal of Marriage and the Family*, 37: 355–62.

Sen, A. K. (1990). 'Gender and Cooperative Conflicts', in I. Tinker (ed.), *Persistent Inequalities: Women and World Development*. New York: Oxford University Press, 123–49.

Skoufias, E. and Parker, S. W. (2001). 'Conditional Cash Transfers and Their Impact on Child Work and Schooling: Evidence from the PROGRESA program in Mexico'. *Economia*, 2: 45–96.

Sutherland, H. (1997). 'Women, Men and the Redistribution of Income'. *Fiscal Studies*, 18: 1–22.

Thomas, D. (1990). 'Intra-Household Resource Allocation: an Inferential Approach'. *Journal of Human Resources*, 25: 634–64.

Woolley, F. R. and Marshall, J. (1994). 'Measuring Inequality within the Household'. *Review of Income and Wealth*, 40: 414–32.

Part II

Multiple Dimensions

6

Inequality of learning in industrialized countries

*John Micklewright and Sylke V. Schnepf**

The importance of human capital in determining incomes leads quickly to interest in the extent of educational inequalities. Differences in education have a major impact on the distribution of earnings and on the number and characteristics of the poor. Inequalities in education also help produce disparities in well-being in dimensions other than income. These include both obvious dimensions—such as improved health and higher occupational status—and less obvious ones such as ability to perceive and take advantage of a range of opportunities: 'the educational level of the retired, for example, is relevant to their capacity to participate in society and to take part in the democratic process' (Atkinson *et al.* 2002: 128).

Our aim in this chapter is to compare within-country differences in educational outcomes across a large group of industrialized countries. Where are these differences greatest? We are immediately faced with the issue of how to measure levels of education. One option would be to focus on data on 'attainment', that is on levels of education that have been completed (or at least entered): primary, secondary, tertiary and so on. There are significant literatures within both economics and sociology that use this form of information to compare educational inequalities across countries. For example, Thomas, Wang, and Fan (2001) compare the distribution of the population across seven levels of attainment for 85 developing and industrial countries for the period 1960–90, attributing a given number of years of schooling to each level.

* This chapter stems from a research project undertaken with Giorgina Brown, of ISTAT, Rome, and Robert Waldmann, of University of Rome 'Tor Vergata', and we draw in part on unpublished work with them. The research was partly funded by UNESCO Institute for Statistics, Montreal (the views expressed are our own and should not be associated with UNESCO). We are grateful for comments to Stephen Jenkins and to seminar participants at the Institute for Fiscal Studies, London, and at Cornell and Princeton.

Other authors compare social class differences in attainment across countries, for example Müller (1996) and Shavit and Blossfeld (1993).

We take a different route, focusing on survey data that record what people actually know, as measured by performance in tests. These are a form of 'achievement' data. Recent years have seen several international surveys of learning achievement of children and 'functional' literacy of adults (the ability to function in modern society). Samples of individuals are administered standardized tests with the aim of comparing countries' levels of achievement or literacy and the factors that influence them. These surveys, with their purpose-built design for cross-national comparison, offer the hope of cutting through the problems of comparing national educational systems that are presented by attainment data.

But which achievement survey to use? There is the International Adult Literacy Survey (IALS), the Trends in International Mathematics and Science Study (TIMSS), the Programme for International Student Assessment (PISA), and the Progress in International Reading Literacy Study (PIRLS). Each survey aims to assess something different or to assess knowledge in a different way. They each refer to particular age groups or school grades. And they each have been the subject of criticism on one ground or another. Our main contribution is to compare results across the surveys. This contrasts with the typical analysis of the data, whether of inequalities or of any other aspect of achievement, that is restricted to a single source. We use TIMSS, PISA, and PIRLS.

These three surveys all refer to children of compulsory school age. We are therefore comparing differences in educational outcomes across countries that emerge *before* the decisions at the end of compulsory schooling and in the ensuing years that generate most of the variation in attainment in industrialized countries. These decisions, both by individuals and their families and by schools, colleges and universities, are strongly influenced by learning that has taken place during the compulsory school period. This learning also has direct effects on well-being in adult life.

We next describe the data and the tools we use to compare within-country differences in achievement scores. These tools are simple and allow for the fact we have multiple sources. We also take into account the nature of the achievement data, which are very different to income data. Our main results follow, in which we focus on a group of 21 countries present in all three surveys. We investigate where inequality is greatest, the association between inequality in learning and average levels of learning, the interpretation of measured levels of inequality, and differences in inequality at the top and bottom of the national distributions. In the concluding section we discuss future directions for the analysis of educational inequalities with achievement data.

6.1 Data and tools

The international achievement surveys

TIMSS, PISA, and PIRLS have similar sample designs. They all involve the selection of a sample of schools and then a single class (TIMSS and PIRLS) or a random sample (PISA) of pupils within each school. Typical sample size in any country is about 150 schools and about 30 pupils per school. TIMSS is perhaps the best well known. We use data on children in grade 8 (usually aged 13–14) from the 1995 and 1999 rounds of the survey (taking the data from the later year if a country participated in both rounds).[1] The PISA data relate to an age group—15 year olds—rather than a grade. We use data from the 2000 round. PIRLS focused on children in grade 4 (usually aged 9–10) and we use the data from the first round of the survey which was held in 2001.

The surveys differ in a number of ways other than the differences in the target population.[2] Notably, they vary widely in the type of achievement that they try to assess. PISA assesses ability in reading, science and maths, attempting to determine to what extent 'education systems in participating countries are preparing their students to become lifelong learners and to play constructive roles as citizens in society' (OECD 2001). (Note that 'education systems' should be interpreted as the combination of schools and families and not just schools.) The aim is to measure broad skills, and to see how students would be able to use what they have learned in real-life situations. While covering a similar age group to PISA and two of the same subjects—maths and science—TIMSS focuses more on measuring mastery of internationally agreed curricula. This may seem a narrow approach. But at least the concept of a curriculum agreed by educationalists is one that a lay person can begin to understand, even though the content of that curriculum is subject to debate. By contrast, at first sight the 'life-skills' approach of PISA may seem more nebulous. It may also be easier to carry out measurement of achievement against a standard in a culture-free way in TIMSS. PIRLS measures only achievement in reading. The survey organizers argue that their approach is similar to that in PISA, both being based on 'an expanded notion of literacy' (Campbell *et al.* 2001: 85).

These three sources provide information on achievement in a total of six tests. We restrict attention to the 21 countries present in all three surveys. This group comprises 14 OECD members, two other rich countries (Hong Kong and Israel), and five Central and Eastern European countries at lower levels of development (Russia, Latvia, Bulgaria, Macedonia, and Romania). Our findings therefore relate to a rather arbitrary group of countries, but one that is not

[1] About one third of the questions in 1999 were the same as in 1995. The others were intended to give results that were comparable. The precise selection of data is described in Brown *et al.* (2007).

[2] See Brown *et al.* (2007) for more discussion.

dissimilar to, for example, those present in the Luxembourg Income Study that is widely used to analyse inequality in incomes.

The answers that a respondent gives to the questions in the surveys are summarized by the organizers into a single score for the subject concerned—maths, science, reading—using an 'item response' model. (See Chapter 8 by Cappellari and Jenkins for an application of these models in a different context.) The purpose of the modelling is to estimate the unobserved distribution of proficiency in a subject from the observed answers to the test questions. While the raw scores to the test questions have a theoretical maximum, the unobserved proficiency distribution is unbounded and one of the purposes of the modelling is to allow for the implied censoring of high achievement in the raw scores. (See, for example, Beaton 2000.) The steps in the process used in each survey are similar but the precise model that is employed differs from survey to survey. Scores for each country are scaled by the survey organizers to have a mean among all persons in all participating countries (which is always a wider group than the 21 countries present in all three surveys that we consider here) of 500 points and a standard deviation of 100 points.[3]

Measuring inequality in learning

The achievement test data are recorded on a continuous scale. This suggests that in measuring inequality of learning we could select from the full range of tools that have been developed to measure inequality in incomes, and the differences in this inequality across countries. The tools of income inequality analysis have, after all, been applied in international comparisons of other non-income dimensions of well-being, including height as a proxy for health (for example, Pradhan, Sahn, and Younger 2003). And they have also started to enter the analysis of the international education surveys of the type used here. Denny (2002) uses methods developed for the measurement of poverty to analyse levels of low functional literacy in IALS, including, for example, Foster-Greer-Thorbecke indices.

We hesitate over use of more sophisticated measures, for three reasons. First, there is the practical problem of multiple sources of data. We draw on three surveys covering six different test distributions. This amount of information would considerably complicate any dominance analysis, for example, in which one tried to order (at least partially) the country distributions in a way that would be independent of the choice of a particular inequality index. One of our aims when using multiple sources is to condense the information they

[3] Survey organizers use the item response models to produce what in fact are five 'plausible values' of proficiency for each individual rather than a single figure. We follow the organizers' practice of calculating all summary statistics of the score distributions with each plausible value and then averaging the five resulting estimates.

contain and as a result we are drawn towards summary measures of learning inequality for each country that are easier to compare across tests and surveys.

Second, the nature of the achievement test data calls for caution in the use of the income inequality measurement toolbox. The test scores are *derived* data providing estimates of proficiency in different subjects. It is doubtful whether the measurement of the scores is on a ratio scale. Their nature is therefore quite different from that of data on income or height. The fact that scores are scaled by the survey organizers to have the same mean and standard deviation does not make them inherently comparable across tests. The choice of item response model influences the shape of the estimated proficiency distributions and can do so in ways that change the cross-country picture. Together with Giorgina Brown and Robert Waldmann, we have shown that rankings of countries by within-country differences in TIMSS changed quite sharply in some cases when the survey organizers applied retrospectively the model used in the 1999 survey round to the 1995 data, although the changes are much less when low income countries that we do not use in this chapter are excluded (Brown *et al.* 2007).[4] We are therefore reluctant to compare directly the *levels* of inequality indices of learning across the different tests since these are in part a function of the chosen item response model.[5]

Third, given the lack of much previous work focusing directly on learning inequality as measured by the achievement surveys, we want to explore the shape of the test score distributions in a little more depth than is made possible by the use of a single index. We therefore focus on quite crude measures: differences in quantiles of the test score distributions. We consider the 95th percentile minus the 5th percentile, P95–P5, the 95th minus the 50th, P95–P50, and the 50th minus the 5th, P50–P5. The use of the latter two measures can reveal whether differences in inequality across countries are more obvious in the top half or in the bottom half of the range of scores. (Any answers, of course, are conditional on the particular item response model used to produce the distributions in question.) We allow for sampling variation when comparing these measures across countries (taking into account the complex survey designs).[6] These measures of absolute differences in scores contrast with indices

[4] We use the re-modelled 1995 data for countries that did not take part in the 1999 round. These data are in principle consistent with those for 1999.

[5] We are certainly not the first to be cautious with data measuring achievement or ability. Atkinson (1975: 89) notes the comment of Mayer (1960) that 'there is at present really no such thing as *the* distribution of ability: the distribution depends on the measuring rod used and cannot be defined independently of it'. Atkinson warns 'the fact that most IQ tests lead to a distribution of scores which follows the normal distribution does not necessarily tell us anything about the distribution of abilities: it may simply reflect the way in which the tests have been constructed'.

[6] The derivation of standard errors of the quantile differences is described in Brown and Micklewright (2004) and uses the survey organizers' estimates of the standard errors of the quantiles. These estimates are not provided for the 10th and 90th percentiles, helping determine our choice of the 5th and 95th percentiles.

of inequality that are most commonly used in the analysis of incomes, which relate to relative differences, for example quantile ratios or the Gini coefficient. However, we have no particular reason to focus on relative, as opposed to absolute, differences, especially since we doubt whether our data measure achievement on a ratio scale. And by not presenting ratios of scores, we remove any temptation to try to compare levels of inequality in the achievement data with those shown by quantile ratios for earnings or income distributions, a comparison that we feel would not be valid.

6.2 Results

Where is inequality highest?

Table 6.1 shows the values of P95–P5 in each of the six tests. These values have been transformed into z-scores. That is, for each test we adjust a country's value of P95–P5, expressed in points of achievement score, by subtracting the mean value of P95–P5 for the 21 countries that we consider and by dividing by

Table 6.1 Z-scores for P95–P5 in PISA, TIMSS, and PIRLS

	Average rank (1)	Average z-score (2)	PISA reading (3)	PISA maths (4)	PISA science (5)	TIMSS maths (6)	TIMSS science (7)	PIRLS reading (8)
Hong Kong	3.0	−1.2	−1.8	−0.4	−1.3	−1.1	−1.7	−1.0
Netherlands	3.8	−1.1	−1.2	−1.1	0.0	−0.9	−0.9	−1.5
Sweden	5.6	−0.8	−0.7	−0.4	−0.5	−1.4	−0.9	−0.7
France	6.5	−0.8	−0.8	−0.9	0.6	−1.8	−1.4	−0.4
Canada	7.3	−0.7	−0.4	−1.3	−1.0	−1.0	−0.8	−0.2
Iceland	7.5	−0.6	−0.8	−1.3	−1.2	−1.0	−0.5	0.0
Czech Republic	7.3	−0.5	−0.1	−0.1	−0.3	−0.2	−0.6	−0.9
Latvia	8.1	−0.5	0.6	0.4	0.2	−0.5	−0.8	−1.2
Hungary	10.1	−0.2	−0.6	−0.1	0.6	0.5	−0.2	−0.8
Italy	10.1	−0.2	−1.0	−0.7	0.1	0.6	0.2	−0.3
Norway	9.9	−0.2	0.8	−0.6	−0.2	−0.8	−1.2	0.5
Russia	11.0	0.0	−0.7	0.5	0.4	0.5	0.9	−0.8
Greece	12.9	0.1	0.0	0.9	0.0	0.6	−0.2	−0.2
Germany	12.5	0.1	1.9	0.4	0.7	−0.5	0.6	−0.7
UK	13.5	0.5	0.4	−0.6	0.2	0.2	0.6	1.0
Bulgaria	14.9	0.6	0.6	1.0	−0.1	0.6	0.8	0.6
USA	16.8	0.7	1.2	0.0	0.4	0.7	1.2	0.6
Macedonia	16.0	0.9	−0.7	0.0	−1.7	1.4	1.2	2.1
New Zealand	17.1	0.9	1.4	0.0	0.3	0.9	0.7	1.5
Romania	16.7	1.0	0.5	1.5	−0.3	1.3	1.1	1.2
Israel	20.6	2.0	1.6	2.9	3.3	1.7	2.0	1.5

Note: Countries are ordered by average z-score. The z-score adjustment is described in the text. A negative z-score implies a lower difference between P95 and P5 than the average for the 21 countries, a positive z-score implies a larger difference than the average.

the standard deviation of the 21 values. The z-scores therefore show how far each country is above (positive values) or below (negative values) the mean value of P95–P5 for the test in question, expressed in standard deviations. This transformation represents our best effort to reduce problems of comparability across tests that are presented by the nature of the achievement score data. The z-scores for each test are shown in columns 3–8.

The first two columns show for each country its average z-score (column 2) and its average rank (column 1) in the orderings implied by the values in columns 3–8. The surveys, and not the tests, are weighted equally in calculating these averages. (This implies, for example, that the scores and ranks for each of the three PISA tests receive one-third of the weight given to the scores and ranks for the single PIRLS test.) These averages have some merit as quick summary statistics. If the different tests were to produce sharply differing orderings of the countries, the averaging would produce figures with little variation. A negative z-score or low rank in one 'league table' would likely be balanced by a positive z-score or high rank in another. The more the average z-scores and ranks vary the more the different tests must be in agreement. Having a low or high average rank can only result from ranking consistently well or consistently badly in individual tests. The countries are ordered in the table on the basis of the average z-scores (which corresponds closely to the ordering on average ranks). The shading in each of columns 3 to 8 indicates the third of the distribution of values for that test into which a country falls: dark shading for the seven countries with the largest values of P95–P5 for the test concerned, light shading for the seven countries with intermediate values, white for the seven countries with the smallest values.

The table shows that there is a reasonable degree of agreement between the six tests, taken as a whole: the average z-scores and average ranks *do* vary considerably. Leaving aside the maximum and minimum values, the average z-scores range from −1.1 to +1.0 and the average rank from 3.8 to 17.1. Hong Kong, the Netherlands, Sweden, France, Canada, and Iceland are the countries where the within-country differences tend to be smallest and Bulgaria, the USA, Macedonia, New Zealand, Romania, and Israel the countries where the biggest differences are found. Israel is a clear outlier, with the largest differences in most tests and often by a large margin. The group of the most unequal countries therefore includes both the poorest member of the 21-country pool, Macedonia, and one of the richest, the USA. It is notable that the group contains three Eastern European countries. The future path of educational inequalities in these countries is an obvious subject to track in further rounds of the international achievement surveys.[7]

The degree of agreement between the different tests, and in particular the different surveys, is encouraging. However, there is also some disagreement

[7] Inequalities in education in Central and Eastern Europe and the impact of economic and social change following the end of the communist period are discussed in Micklewright (1999) and UNICEF (2001).

between the figures and this means that caution is required when looking at results from just one source. Israel aside, no country is in the same third of the distribution of countries for all six tests, with the same shading throughout columns 3–8. Nine of the 21 countries have three different shadings. For example, inequality in learning in the UK is well below the average for maths in PISA but well above the average for reading in PIRLS, with values in the middle third of countries for the other four tests. Russia has below average values in both the PISA and PIRLS reading tests but the opposite in both the PISA and TIMSS maths and science assessments. This underlines the importance of looking at the whole set of tests before coming to any conclusions about a country's position.

When comparing results across the tests, one possibility is that differences may reflect the different age groups covered by the surveys. In particular, PIRLS surveys children of primary school age but PISA and TIMSS survey children of secondary school age. Factors affecting achievement may vary with age. Primary school systems are typically comprehensive, with schools all containing a mix of children of different abilities, but secondary schooling in some countries divides children into separate academic and technical schools. This may have the effect of increasing inequalities in achievement (see, for example, Wößmann 2003). For example, it is notable that Germany, a country that does separate children into quite different school types straight after primary schooling, has a below average value of P95–P5 for reading for the 9–10 year olds in PIRLS but the highest value of all the 21 countries for reading for the 15-year-olds in PISA.

However, in general the comparison of a country's position between any two tests needs to consider other factors as well. In principle, the difference between Germany's position in PISA and PIRLS might conceivably reflect something to do with the different nature of the two assessments, or the item response modelling, or the organization of the surveys in Germany. (And it should also be noted that Germany does not stand out in Table 6.1 in TIMSS or, especially, in the other two PISA subjects.) Why is it that, to take a very different example, Macedonia is the most unequal country in reading in PIRLS by some way, but has below average inequality in reading in PISA, and is the least unequal country of all in PISA science? The fact that there is much more agreement for Macedonia between PIRLS and TIMSS than between PIRLS and PISA suggests that the differences between the latter two surveys reflect more than age.

The broad agreement between the different tests, as reflected in the extent of variation in the average ranks and z-scores, implies that the observed patterns in the data are unlikely to reflect merely the noise from sampling variation. We can test this formally: taking all pairwise comparisons of P95–P5 between countries, about a half are significant at the 5 per cent level in the PISA and TIMSS tests and about three-quarters in PIRLS.[8] Naturally, differences between

[8] We do not apply the Bonferroni correction for multiple comparisons.

countries that are close in the ranking on any test are typically insignificant. But in PIRLS, for example, the values of P95–P5 for the eight countries with the smallest values are all significantly different from each of the values for the eight countries at the opposite end of the ordering.

Inequality in learning versus average learning

It is of obvious interest to investigate the relationship between inequality of learning and average levels of achievement. Are the countries where inequalities in education are smallest also those where average levels are greatest? Or does there appear to be a trade-off, so that a focus on reducing within-country differences has the effect of depressing the average? In their large cross-country study of attainment, measured by years of schooling, Thomas, Wang, and Fan (2001) find that the former pattern clearly holds: inequality falls as average years of education rises. This finding relates to inequality measured using the scale-invariant Gini coefficient. When the authors switch to using the standard deviation (which is not scale invariant), an inverted U-shape Kuznets curve for education is found, with inequality first rising with average years of schooling and then falling. The turning point comes at about 6 to 7 years of schooling, a level exceeded by industrialized countries. Hence for these countries, their results show inequality in attainment is inversely related to average attainment, irrespective of whether a scale-invariant measure of inequality is used or not.

In contrast to Thomas *et al.*, who had repeated observations on the same countries over time, we cannot investigate this issue adequately with our achievement data. All we can do is to use a single observation—based on the three surveys we use—for our cross-section of countries to show the association of inequality in learning with average levels. Figure 6.1 plots the average z-scores of P95–P5 given in column 2 of Table 6.1 against the average z-scores across the same six tests for P50, the median. (The z-score transformations for the medians are performed in an analogous fashion to those for P95-P5; the z-scores measure how far a country is above or below the mean value of P50 for the 21 countries, measured in units of standard deviations of P50.) There is a reasonably clear pattern: in broad terms, within-country differences are highest (positive z-scores) where average achievement is lowest (negative z-scores).

This accords with the pattern found for industrialized countries by Thomas *et al.* with their very different data.[9] (The use of scale-invariant measures of relative differences for the achievement data, such as the ratio of P95 to P5, would emphasize this pattern even more.) This said, our results for particular

[9] Note that our results are conditional on both school enrolment and attendance. Children that are not enrolled or who do not attend schools cannot be tested. This may be a non-trivial issue for the poorer Eastern European countries in our 21-country pool.

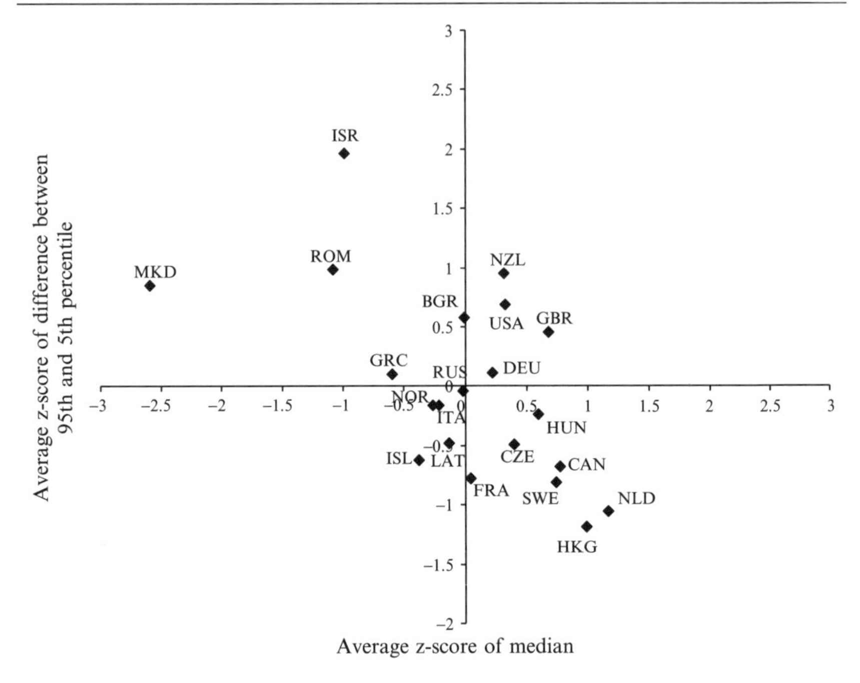

Figure 6.1 Average z-scores for P95–P5 and P50 in six tests in PISA, TIMSS, and PIRLS

Note: The z-score adjustment is described in the text. The values plotted are the average z-scores across the six tests (weighting surveys equally). The correlation between the two measures is –0.55.

countries do not always reflect the position found in the attainment data by Thomas *et al.* The USA appears as the most *equal* country in their study but one of the most unequal according to our achievement data. We also note that our work comparing results in TIMSS for different item response models (Brown *et al.* 2007) shows that the association of score dispersion and central tendency is not always robust to the choice of model, especially when low income countries (excluded here) are included in the analysis. With both types of data, attainment and achievement, the issue arises of whether the association between inequality and the average is simply a result of the nature of the data, or, to be more accurate, the nature of what is being measured. In principle, years of formal education have no upper bound, but in practice very few people will acquire successive doctorates. Hence we might expect inequality in years of schooling to fall as average years of education rises. In the case of the achievement data, the item response modelling in principle removes any problem of achievement scores being capped by a theoretical maximum score, but we have insufficient knowledge of the technique to judge whether there is any problem in practice.

How large are the within-country differences?

Up to this point we have not commented on the sizes of any of the within-country differences in achievement scores. How big are the inequalities in learning that we are measuring?

We need a metric for the achievement scores so that a given number of points can be interpreted in terms of something that is readily understood. The survey organizers provide what might be called partial metrics in the form of international benchmarks of achievement. These may be thought of as being similar to absolute international poverty lines, measured in, say, dollars per day.[10] For example, the PISA organizers define five levels of reading literacy. Children below level-2 are considered unable to 'locate straightforward information, make low-level inferences of various types, work out what a well-defined part of a text means and use some outside knowledge to understand it' (OECD 2001: 47). These thresholds are a useful guide but the metric they provide is partial. They tell one nothing directly about how to interpret any measure of the dispersion of scores, such as P95–P5 or the standard deviation. It is rather like having a tape measure to judge people's height that is blank except for a very few unevenly spaced marks, which are attached to labels describing something about height at that level in terms of what a person can or cannot do (e.g. 'see over others at a football game'). This measure can be used to find out the proportion of people with height at, or above, a given mark but it cannot be used to say something direct that compares the exact heights of two people.

Figure 6.2 suggests a way forward. The graphs show the distribution of science scores in the 1995 TIMSS round for a low inequality country, France, and for a country with above average inequality, Germany. The solid lines show the distributions for 8th grade pupils, which we use in Table 6.1. The dashed lines show the distributions for 7th grade pupils, who were also tested in TIMSS in 1995 and who faced the same test questions as the children in the 8th grade. The width of the distributions for the 8th grade children can be judged in terms of the change in average scores between 7th and 8th grades. In Germany, the value of P95–P5 is equal to 10.7 times the difference in these average scores. This is the highest for any country for which there are data on both grades, with the exception of the USA where the multiple is 13.3. But even in France, the country with the smallest value of P95–P5 in relation to the difference in average scores across grades, the figure is equal to 5.5.[11] The mean across all countries of the difference in average scores between the two grades

[10] The analogy may not extend to dollars expressed in purchasing power terms, however. A given level of achievement is likely to have different implications from country to country.

[11] The standard deviations for France and Germany, measured in the same way as multiples of the difference in average scores across grades, are 1.7 and 3.3 respectively. All the figures for TIMSS in this paragraph refer to the 1995 round.

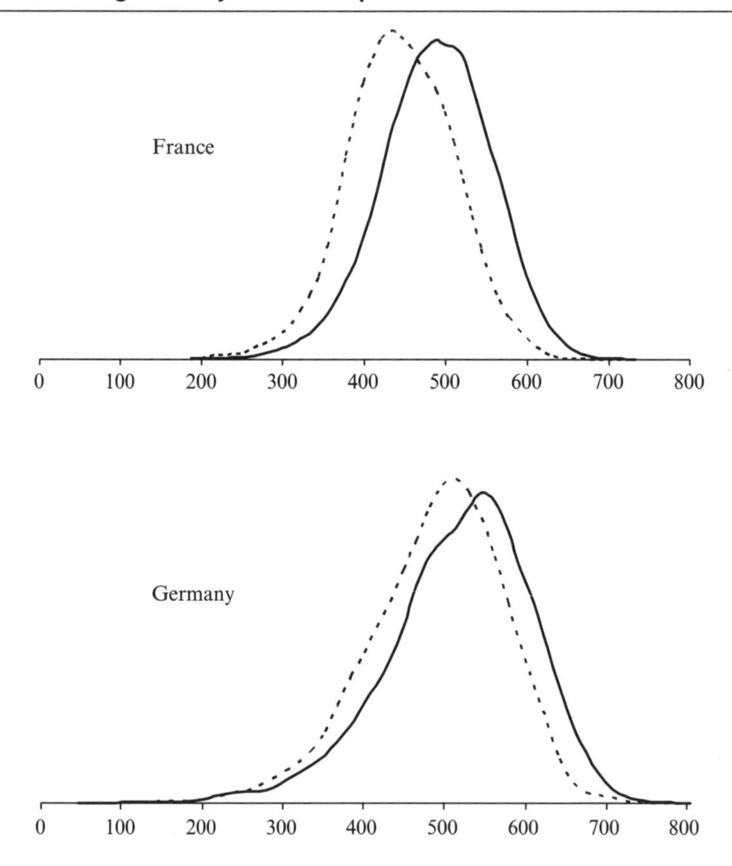

Figure 6.2 Distributions of TIMSS science scores, France and Germany

Note: The solid lines show the distributions for the 8th grade, the dashed lines show the distributions for the 7th grade.

is an alternative yardstick. On this basis, the P95–P5 science values range from a multiple of 6.1 in Hong Kong to 8.6 in Romania. The analogous multiples for maths in TIMSS 1995 range from 7.2 in France to 10.2 in Romania. Similar sorts of figures (although including lower values) are found for P95–P5 for reading in PISA, applying the difference in average scores between grades attended by the 15-year-olds in the survey.[12]

Viewed in this way, the differences within countries, including in low inequality countries, in a single school year or among children of the same age seem quite large everywhere. This should not come as a surprise, given

[12] In unpublished work with Giorgina Brown and Robert Waldmann, we have further investigated a possible metric by looking at differences between 7th and 8th grade TIMSS scores at various points of the distributions.

evidence from differences in achievement that are recorded in national surveys or national exam results.

Inequality at the top and the bottom

The last aspect of inequality of learning that we consider are differences in the top half of the distribution compared to those in the bottom half. One might be more concerned with the latter, arguing that it is the extent to which those of lower ability fall short of the average level of achievement that should be the principal focus for policy on differences in educational opportunity.

Figure 6.3 shows each country's average rank on P95–P50 and on P50–P5 across the six tests in PISA, TIMSS, and PIRLS. As in Table 6.1, the three surveys are weighted equally in these calculations. In general, larger inequalities in the top half of the distribution are certainly associated with larger inequalities in the bottom half. However, there is some variation about the 45-degree line. Countries above the line all do worse in rank terms on P95–P50 than on

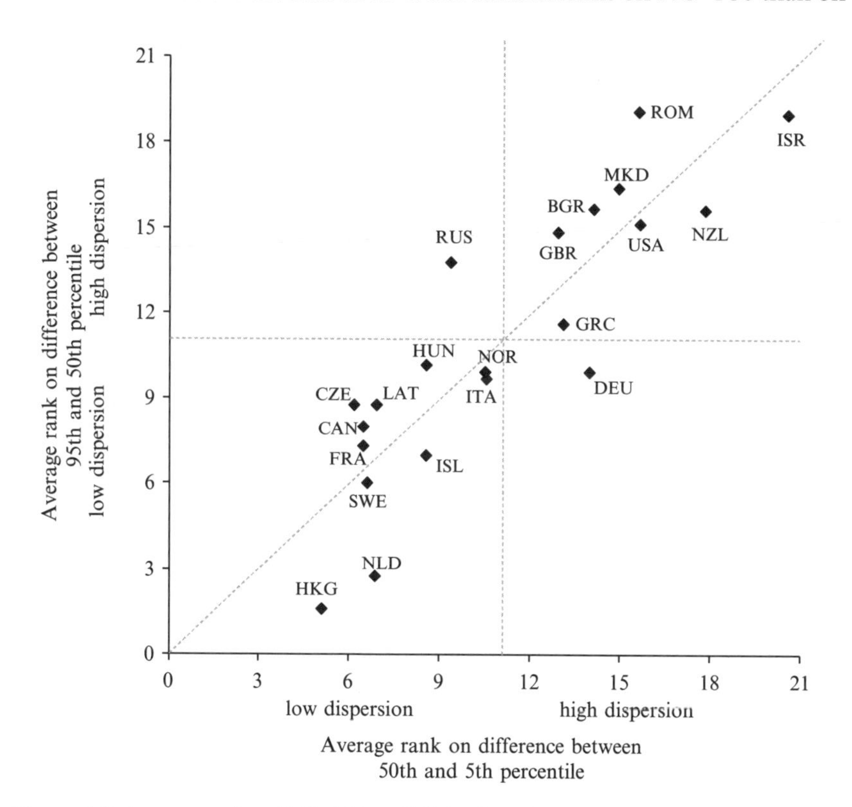

Figure 6.3 Average rank on P95–P50 and P50–P5 in 6 tests in PISA, TIMSS, and PIRLS
Note: Higher values of the average ranks indicate larger differences between the quantiles in question.

Table 6.2 Standard deviations of country values of selected score percentiles

	PISA reading	PISA maths	PISA science	TIMSS maths	TIMSS science	PIRLS reading
All 21 countries						
P5	42.5	59.8	39.2	40.9	38.4	44.0
P50	42.5	48.1	39.5	29.6	26.0	24.6
P95	38.4	36.4	34.8	24.3	25.7	20.1
14 OECD members						
P5	24.6	39.1	23.1	28.7	27.3	30.0
P50	20.1	31.5	21.9	20.6	23.0	16.0
P95	21.6	24.9	19.9	19.1	25.9	17.3

Note: The standard deviations relate to the scores in each survey unadjusted by any z-score transformation.

P50–P5: their levels of inequality in the top half of the distribution, compared to those of other countries, are larger (in rank terms) than their levels in the bottom half, again compared to other countries. It is noteworthy that all seven Central and Eastern European countries are in this category, although for several of these the average ranks on the top and bottom halves do not differ that much. Germany is perhaps the most obvious case below the line—Germany stands out more (in rank terms) for inequality in the bottom half of the distribution.

The actual values of P95–P50 and P50–P5 for each of the six tests reveal that the distributions almost invariably display mild negative skew, with P50–P5 somewhat larger than P95–P50. (The differences are modest but can just be seen easily for Germany in Fig. 6.2.) For reading in both PISA and PIRLS, and for maths in PISA, this is true for all the 21 countries that we consider and there are only a handful of exceptions for the other tests.

Table 6.2 uncovers a related aspect of the distributions, showing the variation in the 21 country values of P5, P50 and P95, measured in points scores. In every test, the standard deviation of P5 exceeds that of P95, and in most cases that of P50 as well. Countries vary more on levels of achievement for people near the bottom of each national distribution than they do for levels achieved by their high performers. (Like other results, this may or may not be robust to the choice of item response model, but the fact that the pattern is the same across surveys is worth noting.) The bottom half of the table shows this is also true for the subset of 14 OECD countries, although the differences in the standard deviations are in this case less marked.

6.3 Conclusions

Use of data from international surveys of learning achievement complements the analysis of differences in educational inequalities across countries that is based on attainment data. In order to avoid reliance on a single source, we have used data on six tests from three different surveys that relate to compulsory school age children, focusing on a pool of 21 countries covered in all the surveys. Our results show that (i) the surveys broadly agree on which countries in this pool have the greatest inequality in learning and which the least inequality, although care is often needed when drawing conclusions based on one source alone; (ii) lower inequality of learning and higher levels of average learning tend to be associated; (iii) differences in learning within all countries seem quite large in absolute terms; (iv) all surveys show more variation in low achievement across countries than in high achievement.

Future work in this area can head in several directions. First, there is the question of the extent to which differences in learning inequality across countries while at school help drive differences in inequality in earnings and other outcomes in later life. An important start to answering this question has been made by Bedard and Ferrall (2003), who compare inequality in achievement in international maths studies from 1964 and 1982 that were the forerunner of TIMSS, with earnings inequality recorded in survey data for the same population cohorts drawn from the Luxembourg Income Study. They find the two are positively associated. However, we feel they demand too much of the achievement data, since they make direct comparisons of the levels of inequality in achievement with the levels of earnings inequality. A complementary approach, adopted by Blau and Kahn (2005), is to use survey data that record both achievement scores and wages for the same individuals, although in this case the achievement scores do not relate to childhood, being collected at the same time as the wage data. Their study, based on the IALS data mentioned in the introduction, shows that greater inequality in cognitive skills in the USA than in other countries does help explain the higher US wage inequality, but only to a limited extent.

A second line of enquiry is to try to explain the observed differences in learning inequality in the international achievement surveys, resulting from family background, school institutions and combinations of the two (for example, Schütz, Ursprung, and Wößmann 2005; and Marks 2005). To date, such studies have been based on a single source and in line with our approach in this chapter we think that some comparisons of results across surveys is necessary. (A modest start is made in Micklewright and Schnepf 2004.) We think that it would be profitable to investigate the variation in results across different age groups. National studies based on panel data show inequalities in learning to be present at a very early age but to develop during childhood and the teenage years (for example, Feinstein 2003; Carneiro and Heckman 2003). In an ideal world one would compare such studies across countries, but, in the absence of suitable data, the cross-sections relating to different age groups in the international achievement surveys are a good place to start.

Third, there is a need for more methodological work that investigates the sensitivity of results on within-country differences in achievement to choice of item response model, and that provides more guidance on how to interpret the data produced by these models. We have noted that the modelling process certainly can influence results on learning inequalities (which qualifies our substantive results) and we have tried to be cautious in our use and interpretation of the data. These are not data that can be treated in the same way as those on income or stature.

References

Atkinson, A. B. (1975). *The Economics of Inequality.* Oxford: Clarendon Press.

——, Cantillon, B., Marlier, E., and Nolan, B. (2002). *Social Indicators. The EU and Social Exclusion.* Oxford: Oxford University Press.

Beaton, A. (2000). 'The Importance of Item Response Theory (IRT) for Large Scale Assessments' in S. Carey (ed.), *Measuring Adult Literacy. The International Adult Literacy Survey (IALS) in the European Context.* London: Office for National Statistics.

Bedard, K. and Ferrall, C. (2003). 'Wage and Test Score Dispersion: Some International Evidence'. *Economics of Education Review,* 22: 31–43.

Blau, F. and Kahn, L. (2005). 'Do Cognitive Test Scores Explain Higher US Wage Inequality?' *The Review of Economics and Statistics,* 87: 184–93.

Brown, G. and Micklewright, J. (2004). 'Using International Surveys of Achievement and Literacy: a View from the Outside'. Working Paper 2. Montreal: UNESCO Institute for Statistics.

——, Micklewright, J., Schnepf, S. V., and Waldmann, R. (2007). 'International Surveys of Educational Achievement: How Robust are the Findings?' *Journal of the Royal Statistical Society, Series A,*170: 623–46.

Campbell, J., Kelly, D., Mullis, I., Martin, M., and Sainsbury, M. (2001). *Framework and Specifications for PIRLS Assessment 2001—2nd Edition.* Chestnut Hill, MA: Boston College.

Carneiro, P. and Heckman, J. (2003). 'Human Capital Policy', in J. Heckman and A. Krueger (eds), *Inequality in America: What Role for Human Capital Policies?* Cambridge MA: MIT Press, 77–240.

Denny, K. (2002). 'New Methods for Comparing Literacy across Populations: Insights from the Measurement of Poverty'. *Journal of the Royal Statistical Society, Series A,* 165: 481–93.

Feinstein, L. (2003). 'Inequality in the Early Cognitive Development of British Children in the 1970 Cohort'. *Economica,* 70: 73–98.

Marks, G. (2005). 'Cross-National Differences and Accounting for Social Class Inequalities in Education'. *International Sociology,* 20: 483–505.

Mayer, T. (1960). 'The Distribution of Ability and Earnings'. *The Review of Economics and Statistics,* 42: 189–95.

Micklewright, J. (1999). 'Education, Inequality and Transition'. *Economics of Transition,* 7: 342–76.

—— and Schnepf, S. V. (2004). 'Educational Achievement in English-Speaking Countries: Do Different Surveys Tell the Same Story?' Discussion Paper 1186. Bonn: IZA.

Müller, W. (1996). 'Class Inequalities in Educational Outcomes: Sweden in Comparative Perspective', in R. Erikson and J. O. Jonsson (eds), *Can Education be Equalised? The Swedish Case in Comparative Perspective*. Boulder, CO: Westview Press, 145–82.

OECD (Organisation for Economic Cooperation and Development) (2001). *Knowledge and Skills for Life—First Results from PISA 2000*. Paris: OECD.

Pradhan, M., Sahn, D., and Younger, S. (2003). 'Decomposing World Health Inequality'. *Journal of Health Economics*, 22: 271–93.

Schütz, G., Ursprung, H. W., and Wößmann, L. (2005). 'Education Policy and Equality of Opportunity'. Discussion Paper 1906. Bonn: IZA.

Shavit, Y. and Blossfeld, H.-P. (eds) (1993). *Persistent Inequalities: A Comparative Study of Educational Attainment in Thirteen Countries*. Boulder, CO: Westview Press.

Thomas, V., Wang, Y., and Fan, X. (2001). 'Measuring Educational Inequality: Gini Coefficients of Education'. Policy Research Working Paper 2525. Washington: The World Bank.

UNICEF (United Nations Children's Fund) (2001). *A Decade of Transition*. Regional Monitoring Report 6. Florence: UNICEF Innocenti Research Centre.

Wößmann, L. (2003). 'Schooling Resources, Educational Institutions and Student Performance: the International Evidence'. *Oxford Bulletin of Economics and Statistics*, 65: 117–70.

7

On the multidimensionality of poverty and social exclusion

*Brian Nolan and Christopher T. Whelan**

While poverty is still most often measured in terms of income, it has long been said that poverty is 'not just about money'. The widespread adoption of the terminology of social exclusion/inclusion in Europe reflects *inter alia* the concern that focusing simply on income misses an important part of the picture. There is an increasing emphasis on the multidimensionality of poverty and social exclusion, and on the need to incorporate indicators relating to dimensions other than income. Thus the set of indicators adopted by the European Union (EU) to monitor social inclusion at the Laeken Council in 2001 include not only measures of income poverty and income inequality, but also educational disadvantage, health inequalities, unemployment and worklessness;[1] such a multidimensional approach has been adopted in many of the EU member states and other developed countries. A central role has also been assigned to multidimensionality in measuring progress in alleviating poverty in developing countries, as illustrated by the Millennium Development Goals now dominating the development agenda.

Typically the implementation of a multidimensional approach to poverty and social exclusion is pursued on a fairly *ad hoc* basis, even when the level of sophistication in the actual analysis is high; furthermore, the underlying rationale for adopting such an approach is often not spelt out and its implications followed through. Here we start by trying to clarify exactly why and when a multidimensional approach might be necessary or helpful (concentrating on the industrialized world). The point that needs to be stressed at the outset is that a clear distinction needs to be maintained between *conceptualizing, measuring, understanding* and *responding* to poverty. One can make a case for

* The authors are grateful for helpful comments from the editors, and to our colleague Bertrand Maître for comments and assistance.

[1] See Atkinson *et al.* (2002).

a multidimensional approach to each of these, but they are not the same case, they have different implications, and one does not simply follow from the other. The fact that poverty may be best thought of as a multidimensional concept does not in itself mean that the poor can be identified only by using a multidimensional approach; nor does identifying the poor unidimensionally (via income, for example) imply that poverty can be understood only in that fashion, or that policies should be directed towards that single dimension.

Starting at the level of conceptualization, a strong case can be made for the notion that poverty and social exclusion are inherently multidimensional concepts. Most research now takes as the point of departure that people are in poverty when 'their resources are so seriously below those commanded by the average individual or family that they are, in effect, excluded from ordinary living patterns, customs and activities' (Townsend 1979). Such a definition has also been adopted by the European Union and nationally by many countries.[2] It is echoed in the definition of poverty put forward by the influential National Research Council panel in the USA as insufficient resources for basic living needs, defined appropriately for the United States today (Citro and Michael 1995).

The linkage between concept and measurement then has to be thought about carefully, however, distinguishing two different aspects of measurement: identifying and counting the poor versus capturing what it means to be poor. In some circumstances, a single indicator might be perfectly adequate to identify empirically those experiencing poverty or social exclusion in a particular society. To take the example most relevant to actual measurement practice, it could be that household income, accurately measured, is sufficient to identify those who would be generally thought of as poor or socially excluded. They might well be experiencing all sorts of other types of deprivation and exclusion—poverty is in that sense multifaceted—and documenting what being poor entailed would require the use of appropriate indicators across various dimensions. However, the poor could still be accurately identified via their income alone, if income were indeed very strongly associated with those other dimensions of deprivation and exclusion. The need for a multidimensional measurement approach in identifying the poor or the excluded is an *empirical* matter, rather than something one can simply read off from the multidimensional nature of the concepts themselves.

In a similar vein, identifying the poor is only the first step in understanding the causes of poverty, and the measure employed does not determine the best approach to exploring those causes. The mechanisms whereby individuals and

[2] The EC Council adopted the following definition in the mid-1980s: 'The poor shall be taken to mean persons, families and groups of persons whose resources (material, cultural and social) are so limited as to exclude them from the minimum acceptable way of life in the Member State in which they live.'

groups are excluded could in fact be straightforward—in a pure caste society, for example, where birth determines outcomes. In that case, a single dimension may well serve to both identify the poor and capture the key mechanism underlying their poverty. However, in the societies we are concerned with here, even if income were the key determinant of poverty and exclusion and sufficed to identify the poor, the factors affecting income at household level and its distribution at societal level are extremely complex, encompassing most obviously the way the labour market, education and tax and transfer systems are structured. Poverty in the highly complex societies of the industrialized world—irrespective of how it is measured—can only be understood by taking a variety of causal factors and channels into account.

Focusing finally on policy, the way poverty is measured should not in itself imply a particular set of policy prescriptions to combat it, or a narrow versus broad approach to doing so. Measuring poverty via income does not in itself imply that the only way to tackle poverty is to directly target the incomes of the poor and try to raise them via social transfers. It could well be that such a policy would be ineffective and that a successful anti-poverty strategy aimed at raising incomes has to directly tackle low education, poor housing, regional development and so on. A multi-sectoral anti-poverty strategy involving 'joined up government' can be justified on the basis of the complex and interlocking nature of the underlying causal mechanisms and structures, irrespective of the measurement approach employed.

So we now move on to some key issues to be faced in employing a multidimensional approach in this context. We first contrast the adding-up of aggregate-level indicators with the use of micro-data to investigate the relationships between different dimensions at individual/household level and the extent of multiple deprivation. We discuss how non-monetary indicators obtained at micro-level have two complementary advantages in analysing poverty and social exclusion: they help to do a better job than income on its own in identifying the poor, and also directly capture the multifaceted nature of poverty and exclusion. We then explore and illustrate a particular approach to incorporating a multidimensional perspective into the analysis of poverty and social exclusion, via the application of latent class analysis to data for Ireland and for the 'old' EU member states.

7.1 Multidimensional measures of poverty and social exclusion: the aggregation issue

The most common way to use multidimensional indicators of poverty and social inclusion is to identify at the country level some statistics relating to different dimensions or aspects and track how they evolve over time and/or vary across countries. Taking the indicators of social inclusion which the EU has adopted as an example, these are each produced and presented as an aggregate for the country in question—the percentage below relative income thresholds, the long-term unemployment rate, the proportion of early school leavers, and so on, in each country at a particular time. The phenomena they aim to capture could be entirely distinct or intimately related to each other, but the indicators are stand-alone and have nothing to say about these inter-relationships. One can look at whether there are obvious patterns across the indicators—whether high unemployment normally goes with a high proportion below relative income thresholds, for example—but that is supplementary to the main emphasis, which is simply to see the direction of change each is displaying or whether one country does better or worse than another on each.

An issue that pervades the use of such multidimensional indicators is how to assess whether things are getting better or worse overall in a given country, or whether one country is doing better than another in some summary sense. Different indicators may well move in different directions for a particular country over time, and in cross-sectional comparisons countries may well not be ranked the same way by different indicators. Do we simply assume that the different dimensions are non-comparable and indicators relating to them should be presented separately, or do we try to aggregate or arrive at an overall assessment across dimensions—and if so how is this best done?

In the extensive literature on quality of life, there has been a longstanding practice of summarizing across dimensions to produce a single index.[3] In a development context the UNDP's Human Development Index (HDI), constructed from indicators of life expectancy, education and standard of living, has received a great deal of attention (and a HDI variant for developed countries is also now produced). On the other hand, the Laeken indicators are very deliberately presented individually with no attempt to produce an overall 'score' across the dimensions—indeed, Atkinson *et al.* (2002) argue that this should be avoided precisely because the whole thrust of the European social agenda is to emphasize the multidimensionality of social disadvantage. Proponents of summary measures aggregating across dimensions argue that they serve the twin functions of summarizing the overall picture and facilitating communication to a wide audience. However, the arguments against are also well illustrated by the on-going controversy around the use of the HDI. The general problem is how to reach agreement not only on the best indicators to use but also on the weight to give to different ones. If a society has a relatively low level of average income but above-average life expectancy, to use perhaps the most obvious but striking example, how would we place a value on one versus the other in constructing a summary measure? Such indices, in consequence, are always arbitrary in fundamental and unavoidable ways.[4]

[3] See Hagerty *et al.* (2001) for a review.

[4] Arguments for and against an aggregate index are reviewed in Micklewright (2001).

However, combining what are already aggregate indicators to produce a summary measure is to be distinguished from aggregation at the level of the individual. At the individual level, linking information across dimensions allows us to see for example where unemployment, poverty and ill-health are found together, which not only allows the extent of 'multiple deprivation' to be captured, but is also invaluable in investigating the causal factors involved. It is on this individual-level application of a multidimensional approach that we concentrate in the rest of this chapter. At this level, aggregation issues still have to be faced: having distinguished different dimensions and measured whether the individual is 'deprived' on each, how is such information to be summarized across dimensions?

Tsui (2002) and Bourguignon and Chakravarty (2003) have explored this issue from a welfare-theoretic perspective. Tsui provides an axiomatic justification for aggregating across different deprivation dimensions into a single cardinal index, and distinguishing the poor as those above some threshold score on that index. Bourguignon and Chakravarty, on the other hand, seek to take into account that one may want to define a poverty threshold *for each dimension* or attribute, providing a framework for counting the number of poor in different dimensions and combining that information into a statistic summarizing the overall extent of poverty. For example, this could count as 'poor' all those who are poor on *any* dimension, while more sophisticated measures take into account different weightings of dimensions and the degree of substitutability one builds in between them, and this can be linked to assumed properties of the social welfare function. The simplest summary measure of the individual's well-being is the number of dimensions in which they are deprived, which Atkinson (2003) refers to as the 'counting approach'. He brings out how this can be seen within the same welfare theoretic framework, and also highlights the role of assumptions made regarding the degree of concavity of the social welfare function and the weighting of different attributes or dimensions. Since there are likely to be differing views about the best form for the deprivation measure, the dominance approach—familiar from comparisons of income inequality—seeks to identify circumstances under which one can nonetheless say that 'multidimensional deprivation in country A is lower than in country B'.

Before considering how best to combine individual-level information across dimensions, however, the logically prior issues relate to why dimensions of poverty or deprivation need to be distinguished in the first place, and what is the best way of doing so. As we tried to clarify in the previous section, the rationale for a multidimensional approach and its implications depend on whether one is focused on conceptualizing, measuring, understanding or responding to poverty and social exclusion. In the next section we hone in on the measurement of poverty at individual/household level, and on why—despite economists' predilection for relying on income—a multidimensional approach might be preferable.

7.2 Measuring poverty: what is wrong with a unidimensional approach?

As we have seen, poverty in advanced societies is generally understood to have two core elements: it is about inability to participate, due to inadequate resources. Most quantitative research then employs a unidimensional approach to distinguishing the poor: it uses income. Many ways of establishing an income cut-off are employed, including by reference to budget standards, expenditure patterns, or social security support rates. The most common practice in Western Europe in recent years has been to rely on relative income lines, with thresholds such as 50 per cent or 60 per cent of median or mean income being used.[5] The broad rationale is that those falling more than a certain 'distance' below average income are unlikely to be able to participate fully in the life of the community.

However, it has been recognized for some time (Ringen 1988) that low income may be an unreliable indicator of poverty in this sense, failing in practice to identify those who are unable to participate in their societies due to lack of resources. This has been demonstrated in a variety of studies of different industrialized countries employing non-monetary indicators of deprivation.[6] Such indicators are based on survey questions asking people whether they have items such as a car, a television or a washing machine, or whether they can do certain things such as have a substantial meal regularly, heat their home adequately, go on holiday, or have friends in for a social occasion. Generally, a significant proportion of those below income poverty thresholds do not display (relatively) high deprivation scores in terms of such non-monetary indicators, whereas some households above the income lines do. This finding is confirmed by our own analyses of data from the European Community Household Panel survey (ECHP) for 11 of the EU-15 countries. We examined the relationship between falling below an income threshold set at 70 per cent of the country's median income and being located above a deprivation threshold set to capture an identical fraction of the population (see Whelan *et al.* 2001). The deprivation measure employed, which we refer to as Current Life-Style Deprivation (CLSD), is a 13-item index that has been shown to exhibit high levels of reliability across these countries. For ten countries the degree of overlap ranged from one-third to less than a half; for Denmark the overlap was only one-sixth. In the more affluent Northern European countries current income seems to provide a particularly poor indicator of permanent income or command over resources.

[5] See for example Förster and Pearson (2002) and Eurostat (2000).

[6] These include Townsend (1979), Mack and Lansley (1985), Gordon *et al.* (2000), Bradshaw and Finch (2003), Mayer (1993), Nolan and Whelan (1996), Muffels (1993), Halleröd (1995), Kangas and Ritakallio (1998), Tsakloglou and Papadopoulous (1998).

It is worth teasing out why one might expect current income to have serious limitations in capturing poverty.[7] A household's standard of living will depend crucially on its command over resources and its needs compared with others in the same society. While disposable cash income is a key element in the resources available to a household, it is by no means the only one. Savings accumulated in the past add to the capacity to consume now, and servicing accumulated debt reduces it. Similarly, the level of past investment in consumer durables influences the extent to which resources must be devoted to such expenditure now. The most substantial investment made by many households is in owner-occupied housing, and the flow of services from this investment—the imputed rent—should in principle be counted among available resources but very often is not. Non-cash income—in the form of goods and services provided directly by the State, notably health care, education and housing—may also comprise a major resource for households. Cash income itself may fluctuate from year to year, so that current income is an imperfect indicator of long-term or 'permanent' income. Since consumption cannot always be fully smoothed over time and households take time to adjust to income 'shocks', shorter-term income is still important but needs to be set in the context of the way income has evolved over time.

Turning to needs, these also differ across households, in a manner that is difficult to capture adequately at the conceptual, much less empirical, level. Most obviously, differences in household size and composition affect the living standards a particular level of income will support. It is customary to seek to take this into account by dividing household income by the number of 'equivalent adults' in the household, but the equivalence scales employed may or may not satisfactorily achieve this objective. Households may also vary in a variety of other ways that affect the demands on their income, such as the ages of the adults and children and their health status. Capturing the implications of chronic disability is particularly difficult. Work-related expenses such as transport and child care may also affect the net income actually available to support living standards and avoidance of deprivation. Finally, geographical variation in prices may mean that the purchasing power of a given income varies across households depending on their location.

Also one cannot be confident that income itself has been measured comprehensively and accurately. Household surveys face (intentional or unintentional) mis-reporting of income. They also find it particularly difficult to adequately capture income from self-employment, from home production, from capital, and from the imputed rent attributable to homeowners. One would be particularly concerned about the reliability of very low incomes observed in surveys—particularly in countries with what are thought to be effective social safety-nets—but other incomes may also be mis-measured to an unknown extent.

[7] See the discussions in for example Atkinson *et al.* (2002) and Mayer (1993).

These conceptual and measurement issues all arise within a standard economic framework, unlike arguments that this framework itself misses important features of the phenomenon of poverty. We argued earlier that a single indicator such as income could in certain circumstances suffice to identify the poor, if not to capture the complexity of the phenomenon. But that the evidence for a range of countries strongly suggests that those circumstances do not in fact prevail there; it is hazardous to draw strong conclusions about whether a household is poor from current income alone.

There is then a range of responses to recognition of these difficulties. One is clearly to work to improve the depth and accuracy of measures of resources and needs and our understanding of how they relate to one another—notably by using expenditure as an indicator of longer-term resources, using panel data to capture income over a longer period, measuring stocks of assets and liabilities as well as income flows, incorporating non-cash benefits into 'income', and exploring ways of capturing needs associated with, for example, disability. All these are important areas to pursue, and progress is being made on various fronts in different countries. However, obtaining a full picture of command over resources and how it relates to needs remain problematic. This is illustrated by the results of analysis of the relationship between deprivation and income using data from the ECHP that follows people from one year to the next. This shows that deprivation levels do indeed rise with the persistence of low income (Whelan, Layte, and Maître 2002, 2003). However, when we define persistent poverty as experiencing a consecutive three-year spell in poverty in the course of a five-year window of observation and construct a comparable deprivation indicator, the extent of mismatch remains substantial. Results for nine EU-15 countries showed that while the extent of overlap is higher than in the cross-sectional case, it exceeds 50 per cent only in the case of Ireland (Whelan, Layte, and Maître 2004).[8]

A complementary rather than alternative route is to use non-monetary indicators to measure levels of deprivation directly, and see whether these can assist in improving the measurement of poverty. Reflecting on the conceptual and measurement problems we have described in relation to reliance on income certainly suggests that non-monetary indicators could have significant potential in identifying the poor. For example, where income is currently unusually, genuinely low, for the household, thus impacting on savings, or where income has been misreported as low, non-monetary indicators might correctly show a higher standard of living than income. Where the household benefits from non-cash support from the state, this should enable them to attain a higher standard of living and this should again be reflected in lower levels of deprivation, *ceteris*

[8] See also Berthoud, Bryan, and Bardasi (2004). Correcting for measurement error in relation to both income poverty and deprivation dynamics does not alter these conclusions (Whelan and Maître 2006).

paribus. Where a household faces particular needs that act as a drain on income, due to disability for example, then once again deprivation levels as reflected in non-monetary indicators should be higher than others on the same income. Where prices are considerably higher in one part of the country than another, lower levels of deprivation for those in the low-cost regions should again in principle be reflected in appropriate non-monetary indicators.

The problem though is how to be sure one is capturing genuine differences in levels of deprivation rather than variation in choices and tastes. Deprivation itself conceptually relates to being denied the opportunity to have or do something; the difficulty is in empirically inferring a constrained opportunity set from what people do not have or do. It is this concern about the role choice may play in the outcomes observed that underpins the reluctance of many economists to rely on non-monetary deprivation indicators in measuring poverty. The survey questions on which the indicators are based often go beyond simple absence of an item or activity to try to hone in on deprivation that is 'enforced' by lack of money—for example, by a follow-up question on whether those without an item did not want or could not afford it—although an element of subjectivity inevitably remains. Furthermore, deprivation (like income) will be measured in surveys only with error.

Despite these concerns, the evidence suggests that such non-monetary indicators contain valuable information, and when combined with information on financial constraints, do help in identifying those who are experiencing exclusion due to lack of resources. This evidence takes a number of forms. One is that those on low income and displaying particular types of deprivation generally have much higher levels of self-assessed economic strain than those on low income alone. Another is that 'low income plus deprivation' is generally more strongly related to factors that are widely believed to increase the risk of poverty in many countries—such as unemployment, disability, lone parenthood, divorce—than low income alone. Finally, those identified as 'low income plus deprived' using a specific set of indicators generally also display higher levels of other types of deprivation than those on low income alone (Nolan and Whelan 1996; Halleröd 1995). As well as helping in identifying the poor, non-monetary indicators obtained in household surveys can be very valuable in the second element of the measurement process, namely capturing the multifaceted nature of poverty and social exclusion.

Curiously, many of the studies employing non-monetary indicators have not explored the dimensionality of the deprivation measures themselves, although simply summing across a range of items to construct summary deprivation indices may involve 'adding apples and oranges'. The inter-relationships among deprivation items have been explored using national data by, for example, Muffels (1993), Nolan and Whelan (1996), and using data from the ECHP by Whelan *et al.* (2001) and Eurostat (2003). Using factor analysis, Whelan *et al.* (2001) identified five distinct dimensions with ECHP data:

(i) *Economic strain*—comprising items such as food and clothing, a holiday at least once a year, and being able to replace worn-out furniture.
(ii) *Consumption deprivation*—comprising items such as a car, phone, colour television, video, microwave and dishwasher.
(iii) *Housing facilities*—housing services such as the availability of a bath or shower, an indoor flushing toilet and running water.
(iv) *Housing deterioration*—the existence of problems such as a leaking roof, dampness and rot in window frames and floors.
(v) *Neighbourhood environment problems* relating to noise, pollution, vandalism and crime, and inadequate space and light.[9]

A striking finding was that this structuring was common across each of the participating EU countries, greatly facilitating comparative analysis.

Distinguishing dimensions of deprivation in this way is an important step in selecting a sub-set of indicators which, when combined with low income, helps identify the poor.[10] However, it also provides a fruitful approach to capturing different dimensions of poverty and exclusion, and how levels of deprivation on these vary over time and across countries. Thus Eurostat (2003, 2005), for example, has used ECHP data to compare levels of deprivation in EU countries across different dimensions, and the European Quality of Life Survey (EQLS) has allowed for such comparisons across all 25 member states and the three Candidate countries. Distinguishing dimensions in this way also allows the relationships between dimensions and the extent of multiple deprivation to be investigated. Both national and cross-country studies suggest that the numbers experiencing high levels of deprivation across a number of dimensions are often quite modest.

In Figure 7.1, using the first wave of the ECHP, we provide a very simple illustration of the extent to which the notion of substantial levels of multiple deprivation constitute a myth—although one that has been particularly difficult to dispel. The definition of multiple deprivation employed is deliberately minimalist, simply counting the number of individuals lacking at least one item on each of the five dimensions. Obviously, adopting an alternative criterion, such as being located in the bottom quartile on a dimension, would produce substantially lower estimates of multiple deprivation. Nevertheless, even with this minimalist definition, only in Portugal and Greece is the number reporting deprivation on all five dimensions appreciably above zero. Furthermore, outside Greece, Portugal and Spain the percentage reporting

[9] The labels of some of these dimensions have been changed from the original names to bring them in line with recent EUROSTAT usage.

[10] We have argued that the economic strain set, or economic strain plus secondary set, of indicators are most suitable for this purpose in the ECHP (Whelan *et al.* 2001). However, developing a methodology to combine deprivation indicators with low income to capture poverty in a way that is meaningful across countries over time is a considerable challenge (see Atkinson *et al.* 2005 for a discussion).

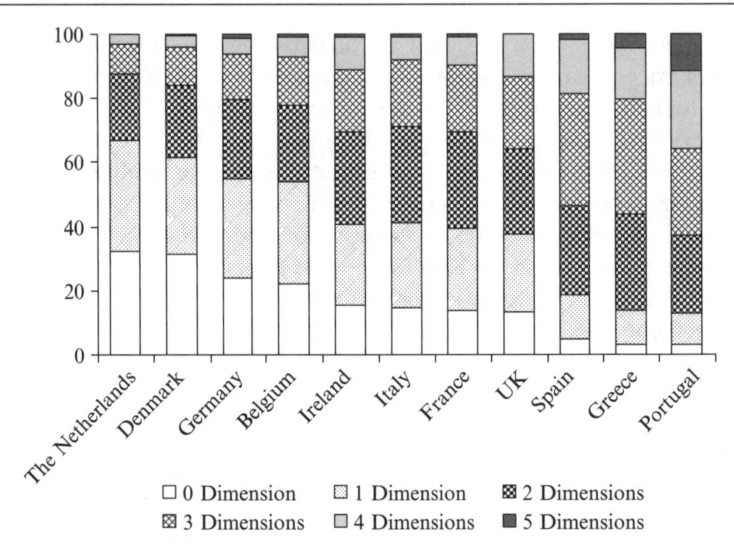

Figure 7.1 Number of dimensions on which persons experience an enforced lack on at least one item, ECHP 1994 (% of persons)

deprivation on four or more dimensions does not exceed 13 per cent and in most cases is substantially lower. Similarly the number reporting that they lack on three or more dimensions is mostly less than one-third. Thus, even in this minimal form, multiple deprivation is a minority phenomenon.

The other avenue for research opened up by this approach is exploration of the factors underlying different dimensions of deprivation, and their implications for policy. It is worth noting, in particular, the weak relationship between low income, either current or persistent, and housing facilities, housing deterioration, and even more so neighbourhood environmental problems—where no substantial relationship even to persistent low income was found across countries in the ECHP (Whelan, Layte, and Maître 2003). Such factors as age, household composition, urban/rural location and tenure status play an important role in predicting housing and neighbourhood-related dimensions; this serves to bring out the force of the argument that a multidimensional approach is needed to understand the causes of poverty and frame policy responses.

7.3 A latent class approach to incorporating multidimensionality

Implicit in the notion of multidimensional measurement of exclusion is the assumption that there is no one 'true' indicator of the underlying concept. Instead what is measured is a sample of indicators that tap different aspects of a complex phenomenon. There is considerable appeal in trying to move beyond rather *ad hoc* approaches to develop a measurement model that enables us to understand the manner in which the indicators are related to the latent concept. One way of doing so is by employing the methodology of latent class analysis. Building on Moisio (2005), we illustrate its application to the multidimensional analysis of poverty and social exclusion, focusing first on Ireland, then on 13 'old' members of the EU for which appropriate ECHP data is available.

The basic idea of latent class analysis is long established (Lazarsfeld and Henry 1968). The associations between a set of categorical variables, regarded as indicators of an unobserved typology, are accounted for by membership of a small number of latent classes. Latent class analysis assumes that each individual is a member of one and only one of *N* latent classes, and that the observed correlations between a set of indicators is due to their common association with some underlying factor; thus, conditional on latent class membership, the indicators are assumed to be mutually independent of each other. This is a variant of the familiar idea that the correlation between two variables may be a result of their common dependence on a third variable; in estimating latent class models that explanatory variable is unobserved and must be identified statistically. Latent class analysis can be thought of as a categorical analogue of factor analysis, with the crucial difference in this context that one is seeking to identify groups of individuals rather than clusters of variables.

Given three dichotomous variables the latent class model for variables *A*, *B*, *C* is

$$\pi_{ijkt}^{ABCX} = \pi_t^X \pi_{it}^{\bar{A}X} \pi_{jt}^{\bar{B}X} \pi_{kt}^{\bar{C}X}$$

where π_t^X denotes the probability of being in latent class $t = 1, \ldots, T$ of latent variable X; $\pi_{it}^{\bar{A}X}$ denotes the conditional probability of obtaining the ith response to item A, from members of class $t = 1, \ldots, T$, and $\pi_{jt}^{\bar{B}X}, \pi_{kt}^{\bar{C}X}$ denote the corresponding probabilities for items B and C respectively.

Conditional independence can also be represented as a log-linear model

$$F_{ijkt}^{ABCX} = \eta \tau_i^A \tau_j^B \tau_k^C \tau_t^X \tau_{it}^{AX} \tau_{jt}^{BX} \tau_{kt}^{CX}$$

In this case, the cell frequencies in the complete fitted table are represented as the product of a set of parameters corresponding to the fitted marginals of the conditional independence model. We use the ℓEM Programme to estimate the relevant model (Vermunt 1997).[11]

[11] The parameters of the model are estimated by an iterative procedure using the EM algorithm (Dempster, Laird, and Rubin 1977).

Because our objective is to identify an overall economically vulnerable class that can be contrasted with the remainder of the population, we develop models with two latent classes.[12] Goodness of fit measures include the likelihood ratio chi-square test (G^2), the reduction in the corresponding statistic for the benchmark independence model and the percentage of cases misclassified.

In this context two underlying classes can be specified, those who are vulnerable to economic exclusion, whom we label as 'economically vulnerable', and those who are insulated from such exclusion. For each of the applications we describe, people are allocated in one or other of these classes based on estimation of a latent class model with three indicators: where the person is situated in relation to a four-category income poverty variable, a dichotomous deprivation score variable, and whether their household reported having great difficulty or difficulty in 'making ends meet'. Thus, in each case our analysis is based on an observed $4 \times 2 \times 2$ table.

Our application of this approach is to Irish data from the first full wave of the EU-SILC survey conducted in Ireland in 2004. The income poverty indicator we employ in the latent class model is a four-category variable indicating whether the household was below 50 per cent of median equivalized income, between 50 per cent and 60 per cent, between 60 per cent and 70 per cent, or over 70 per cent of median income. The basic deprivation indicator is a dichotomous variable that distinguishes those scoring two or more on an 11-item index of economic strain (Whelan, Maître, and Nolan 2006); the third indicator is whether the household reported great difficulty making ends meet. The estimated model using these three indicators to distinguish those inside versus those outside the vulnerable class, misclassifies less than 0.5 per cent of cases and returns a G^2 value of 11.3 with 4 degrees of freedom which involve a reduction in the value of the benchmark independence model of 99.7 per cent: see Whelan and Maître (2007).

The model identifies one in five of the population as being 'economically vulnerable'. As shown in Figure 7.2, at all three income poverty lines the economically vulnerable are, approximately, four times more likely to be below the relevant threshold. At the 50 per cent line the respective percentages are 30 per cent and 6 per cent and these rise to 70 per cent and 18 per cent at 70 per cent of median income. The contrast between economic vulnerability and income poverty is clearly illustrated by these results. At the 60 per cent line, where the number income poor is almost identical to that economically vulnerable, 54 per cent of those below the income threshold are vulnerable. Furthermore, there is no tendency for the association between income poverty and vulnerability to strengthen as the income threshold is made more stringent. In fact, the opposite is the case with the odds of being vulnerable rather than non-vulnerable for the income poor versus non-poor declining from 10:1

[12] An alternative approach would be to use a wider range of indicators and compare the results for models with varying numbers of latent classes.

at the 70 per cent line to 8:1 at the 60 per cent line and finally to 6:1 at the 50 per cent line.

The economically vulnerable are also sharply differentiated from the non-vulnerable in terms of their exposure to subjective economic stress (that is, difficulty making ends meet) with the respective figures being 78 per cent and 12 per cent. However, while these disparities are substantial, the primary factor differentiating the latent classes is their risk of experiencing an enforced lack of two or more of the items making up the economic strain index (that is, experiencing basic deprivation). While 65 per cent of the vulnerable group fall into this category this is true of only 1 per cent of the non-vulnerable.

The profile of multiple deprivation captured by this notion of economic vulnerability is a good deal more restricted than that normally referred to in the social exclusion literature. However, the capacity of the vulnerable/non-vulnerable distinction to differentiate is not restricted to the indicators that enter into the latent class analysis. This is illustrated by risk levels for the vulnerable versus non-vulnerable groups for the other three deprivation dimensions distinguished earlier. We find that 88 per cent of the vulnerable class lack at least one consumption item compared to 30 per cent of the non-vulnerable. For the housing facilities dimension, the respective figures are approximately 23 per cent and 6 per cent. Finally, half the economically vulnerable class experience deprivation in terms of their local neighbourhood environment compared to three out of ten of the non-vulnerable. Thus there is a strong association with economic vulnerability for each of the dimensions, but one that varies in strength and is in all cases weaker than for the indicators

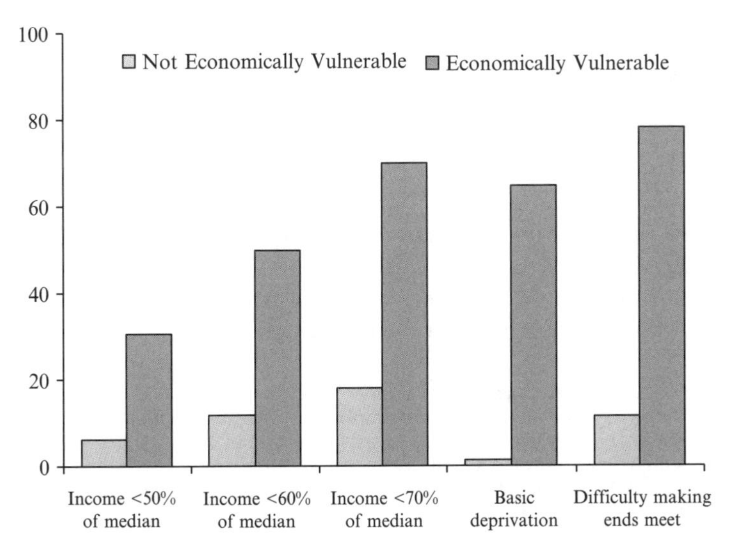

Figure 7.2 Risk of income poverty for different poverty lines and risk of basic deprivation and great difficulty making ends meet, Ireland EU-SILC, 2004 (%)

entered into the latent class analysis. The correlation is strongest for consumption deprivation and weakest for neighbourhood environment. Thus in identifying an economically vulnerable group we have distinguished a group that is also distinctive across a range of other dimensions. However, multiple deprivation, in the rather minimal sense of enforced lack of at least one item on each of these three dimensions, is a relatively rare phenomenon: even among the vulnerable class it does not exceed 15 per cent, and outside this class it falls to 3 per cent.

Different dimensions of deprivation certainly tend to be positively correlated, and this is reflected in the fact that each is positively associated with economic vulnerability. However, both the scale of deprivation and the strength of the association with economic vulnerability vary across dimensions. This means that the level of multiple deprivation is modest, even among the economically vulnerable.[13] Overall it is still hard to avoid the conclusion that the emphasis on such deprivation in the poverty and social exclusion literature has been misplaced. While there is clearly a common element influencing the different dimensions of deprivation, each type is clearly influenced by a range of rather different factors.

7.4 Multidimensionality and welfare regimes

As Leisering and Liebfried (1999) argue, the focus on multiple deprivation has been encouraged by perspectives that focus on outcomes rather than processes and neglect the dynamic nature of poverty and social exclusion. However, in rejecting such static perspectives it is equally important to be clear that a dynamic probabilistic perspective is entirely consistent with the notion that poverty and social exclusion are highly structured by socio-economic factors. To illustrate this, we apply the same analytical approach as in Section 7.3 to data for 13 'old' EU countries participating in the ECHP.[14] Once again, position vis-à-vis relative income poverty thresholds, deprivation score, and self-assessed difficulty making ends meet provide the ingredients for the estimation of the latent class model. The deprivation measure in this instance is a 13-item CLSD deprivation index referred to earlier with each item weighted by the proportion of households in the country possessing the item.[15] In most

[13] Social isolation, often thought of as another dimension of exclusion, is weakly correlated with other forms of deprivation—see for example Gallie, Paugam, and Jacobs (2003).

[14] Luxembourg has not been included in our analysis. Data from the first wave is used to maximize sample size; this was generally 1994, though Austria only joined the survey in 1995 and Finland in 1996. For an extension of such analysis to the EU-25 and the three candidate countries, see Whelan and Maître (2005*b*).

[15] This score is used to distinguish those above and below a deprivation threshold set in each country so that the percentage above it is the same as the number below the 70% relative income threshold.

countries, less than 1 per cent of cases are misclassified, and the model fit once again supports the notion that the relationships between the three indicators arise because of the division of the samples into two latent classes.[16]

We then distinguish four clusters of countries in terms of 'welfare regime', and evaluate the extent to which economic vulnerability and its socio-economic patterning are consistent with the theoretical assumptions underlying the welfare regime typology (Esping-Andersen 1990; Goodin *et al.* 1999). Denmark and Finland are in the social democratic regime, with its emphasis on a substantial redistributive role, seeking to guarantee adequate economic resources independently of market or familial reliance. The Netherlands, Germany, Austria, Belgium, and France are in the corporatist regime, with its emphasis on welfare as primarily a mediator of group-based mutual aid and risk pooling, with rights to benefits depending on being already inserted in the labour market. The UK and Ireland are in the liberal regime, which acknowledges the primacy of the market and confines the state to a residual welfare role, social benefits typically being subject to a means test and targeted on those failing in the market. Italy, Spain, Greece, and Portugal we will take as constituting a distinctive welfare regime, with family support systems playing a distinctive role and the benefit system being uneven and minimalist in nature (Ferrera 1996).

We find that the level of economic vulnerability increases from 18 per cent in the social democratic countries to 20 per cent in the corporatist cluster welfare, climbing sharply to 30 per cent in the liberal welfare regimes and peaking at 31 per cent in the residualist Southern countries.[17] Just as we would expect, the level of vulnerability increases sharply as the buffering effect of the welfare state diminishes.

The manner in which vulnerability is structured by socio-economic factors would also be expected to vary across regimes. To assess this we look at the relationship between vulnerability and being in the manual versus non-manual social class and being unemployed versus at work, using the odds ratio of the vulnerable versus non-vulnerable as the measure of association. For manual versus non-manual social class, the odds ratio rises from 1.9 in the social democratic regime to 4.4 for the corporatist group, and to 5.7 for the liberal cluster before peaking at 7.9 for the residualist welfare regime. So the extent and character of welfare activity has a striking effect on the social class patterning of economic vulnerability. This is also clear in the case of unemployment but as would be expected unemployment has its sharpest effect in the liberal welfare regime. The odds ratio rises from 6.4 in the social democratic

[16] The percentage of cases misclassified varies between 0.41% and 1.25%. For a detailed discussion of goodness of fit statistics, see Whelan and Maître (2005*a*).

[17] In calculating welfare regime figures, we average across countries rather than weighting by population because our interest is theoretical rather than descriptive.

countries to 10.9 in the corporatist cluster before almost doubling to 20.2 for the liberal welfare regime; by contrast, it is only 7.8 for the residualist Southern cluster, reflecting the relatively high levels of vulnerability among those at work there, particularly small employers and farmers.

Overall, the social democratic regime is associated with low levels of economic vulnerability and weak differentiation by social class and employment status. For the corporatist group, consistent with the greater emphasis on insider–outsider distinctions, both the level of vulnerability and their socio-economic structuring are stronger. The liberal welfare regime exhibits both a high level of vulnerability and particularly sharp inequalities in risk of exposure to such vulnerability, especially with regard to unemployment. The residualist regime is associated with the highest vulnerability rates and the sharpest class differentials, but such inequalities are less directly connected to experience in the labour market. The multidimensional approach based on latent class analysis thus produces findings relating to the scale and socio-economic patterning of economic vulnerability that are entirely consistent with expectations deriving from welfare regime theory. This contrasts with the fashionable emphasis by Beck (1992), Leisering and Leibfried (1999) and others on individual life-course events as determinants of poverty and social exclusion, rather than more traditional structural factors such as social class and labour force trajectories (see also Layte and Whelan 2002).

7.5 Conclusions

Multidimensionality has become pervasive in debates about poverty and social exclusion, but with considerable confusion about what assigning it a central place would mean in practice—for research or policy-makers—and indeed about why that would be such a good idea in the first place. This chapter has tried to clarify exactly why a multidimensional approach might be necessary or helpful in this context, distinguishing conceptualizing, measuring, understanding and responding to poverty. It then explored in particular how a multidimensional approach might be taken to analysis of poverty and social exclusion using micro-data at the level of the individual and household. It argued that non-monetary indicators obtained at micro-level have two complementary advantages in analysing poverty and social exclusion. The first is that they help to do a better job than income on its own in identifying the poor. The second is that they can also be used to distinguish different dimensions of deprivation and exclusion, to directly capture the multifaceted nature of poverty and exclusion—which involves distinguishing those dimensions in the first place, which we also discussed. We then explored the application of a particular way of incorporating multidimensionality directly into the analysis of poverty by the application of latent class analysis. This was illustrated using data for Ireland and for the 'old' EU member states.

Going beyond income alone but still using only a small number of indicators of social exclusion, these empirical analyses identified an economically vulnerable class. Both the size and profile of this group varied systematically across socio-economic groups and welfare regimes, and the vulnerable group were exposed to enhanced risk across a range of dimensions. However, variability in both levels of deprivation across dimensions and in the strength of differentiation by economic vulnerability meant that the extent of multiple deprivation is quite limited, even for 'the vulnerable' among whom it is almost entirely concentrated. Ability to identify high-risk multidimensional profiles relating to economic vulnerability does not imply that the range of complex phenomena that come under the heading of social exclusion can be treated simply as by-products of levels and patterns of economic vulnerability. These findings reinforce the notion that a multidimensional approach—using non-monetary indicators as well as income, and distinguishing among different dimensions of deprivation rather than using a single summary deprivation index—is productive in deepening our understanding of poverty and social inclusion.

References

Atkinson, A. B. (2003). 'Multidimensional Deprivation: Contrasting Social Welfare and Counting Approaches'. *Journal of Economic Inequality*, 1: 51–65.

——, Cantillon, B., Marlier, E., and Nolan, B. (2002). Social *Indicators: The EU and Social Inclusion*. Oxford: Oxford University Press.

——, ——, —— and —— (2005). *Taking Forward the EU Social Inclusion Process*. Report for High-Level Conference organized by the Luxembourg Presidency of the EU, Luxembourg. http://www.ceps.lu/eu2005_lu/inclusion.

Beck, U. (1992). *Risk Society. Towards a New Modernity*. London: Sage.

Berthoud, R., Bryan, M., and Bardasi, E. (2004). *The Relationship between Income and Material Deprivation Over Time*. Department for Work and Pensions Report 219. Leeds: Corporate Document Services.

Bourguignon, F. and Chakravarty, S. (2003). 'The Measurement of Multidimensional Poverty'. *Journal of Economic Inequality*, 1: 25–49.

Bradshaw, J. and Finch, N. (2003). 'Overlaps in Dimensions of Poverty'. *Journal of Social Policy*, 32: 513–25.

Citro, C. F. and Michael, R. T. (1995). *Measuring Poverty: A New Approach*. Washington, DC: National Academy Press.

Dempster, A., Laird, N., and Rubin, D. B. (1977). 'Maximum Likelihood from Incomplete Data via the EM Algorithm'. *Journal of the Royal Statistical Society, Series B*, 39: 1–38.

EU Commission (1992). *Towards a Europe of Solidarity: Intensifying the Fight against Social Exclusion, Fostering Integration*. Communication from the Commission, Brussels.

Esping-Andersen, G. (1990). *The Three Worlds of Welfare Capitalism*. Cambridge: Cambridge University Press.

Eurostat (2000). *Income, Poverty and Social Exclusion in Member States of the European Union*. Luxembourg: Office for Official Publications of the European Communities.

—— (2003). *European Social Statistics: Income Poverty and Social Exclusion (2nd Report)*. Luxembourg: Office for Official Publications of the European Communities.

—— (2005). 'Material Deprivation in the EU'. *Statistics in Focus*, 05/2005.

Ferrera, M. (1996). 'The Southern Welfare State in Social Europe', *Journal of European Social Policy*, 6: 17–37.

Förster, M. and Pearson, M. (2002). 'Income Distribution and Poverty in the OECD Area: Trends and Driving Forces'. *OECD Economic Studies*, 34: 7–39.

Gallie, D., Paugam, S., and Jacobs, S. (2003). 'Unemployment, Poverty and Social Isolation: Is There a Vicious Circle of Social Exclusion?' *European Societies*, 5: 1–31.

Goodin, R. E., Headey, B., Muffels, R., and Dirven, H. J. (1999). *The Real Worlds of Welfare Capitalism*. Cambridge: Cambridge University Press.

Gordon, D., Adelman, L., Ashworth, K., Bradshaw, J., Levitas, R., Middleton, S., Pantazis, C., Patsios, D., Payne, S., Townsend, P., and Williams, J. (2000). *Poverty and Social Exclusion in Britain*. York: Joseph Rowntree Foundation.

Hagerty, M., Cummins R., Ferriss A., Land, K., Michalos, A., Peterson, M., Sharpe, A., Sirgy, J., and Vogel, J. (2001). 'Quality of Life Indexes for National Policy: Review and Agenda for Research'. *Social Indicators Research*, 55: 1–96.

Halleröd, B. (1995). 'The Truly Poor: Direct and Indirect Measurement of Consensual Poverty in Sweden'. *European Journal of Social Policy*, 5: 111–29.

Kangas, O. and Ritakallio, V. (1998). 'Different Methods – Different Results? Approaches to Multidimensional Poverty', in Andress, H. J. (ed.), *Empirical Poverty Research in a Comparative Perspective*. Aldershot: Ashgate, 167–203.

Layte, R. and Whelan, C. T. (2002). 'Cumulative Disadvantage or Individualization: A Comparative Analysis of Poverty Risk and Incidence'. *European Societies*, 4: 209–33.

Lazarsfeld, P. F. and Henry, N. W. (1968). *Latent Structure Analysis*. Boston: Houghton Mifflin.

Leisering, L. and Leibfried, S. (1999). *Time and Poverty in Western Welfare States: United Germany in Perspective*. Cambridge: Cambridge University Press.

Mack, J. and Lansley, S. (1985). *Poor Britain*. London: Allen and Unwin.

Mayer, S. (1993). 'Living Conditions Among the Poor in Four Rich Countries'. *Journal of Population Economics*, 6: 261–86.

Micklewright, J. (2001). 'Should the UK Government Measure Poverty and Social Exclusion with a Composite Index?', in *Indicators of Progress: A Discussion of Approaches to Monitor the Government's Strategy to Tackle Poverty and Social Exclusion*. CASE Report 13. London: London School of Economics, 45–50.

Moisio, P. (2005). 'A Latent Class Application to the Multidimensional Measurement of Poverty'. *Quantity and Quality—International Journal of Methodology*, 38: 703–17.

Muffels, R. (1993). 'Deprivation Standards and Style of Living Indices', in J. Berghman and B. Cantillon (eds), *The European Face of Social Security*. Aldershot: Avebury, 43–60.

Nolan, B. and Whelan, C. T. (1996). *Resources, Deprivation and Poverty*. Oxford: Clarendon Press.

Ringen, S. (1988). 'Direct and Indirect Measures of Poverty'. *Journal of Social Policy*, 17: 351–66.

Townsend, P. (1979). *Poverty in the United Kingdom*. Harmondsworth: Penguin.

Tsakloglou, P. and Papadopoulous, F. (2002). 'Aggregate Level and Determining Factors of Social Exclusion in Twelve European Countries'. *Journal of European Social Policy*, 12: 211–25.

Tsui, K. (2002). 'Multidimensional Poverty Indices'. *Social Choice and Welfare*, 19: 69–93.

Vermunt, J. K. (1997). 'ℓEM: A General Programme for the Analysis of Categorical Data'. Tilburg University.

Whelan, C. T. and Maître, B. (2005*a*). 'Vulnerability and Multiple Deprivation Perspectives on Economic Exclusion in Europe: A Latent Class Analysis'. *European Societies*, 7: 423–50.

—— and —— (2005*b*). 'Economic Vulnerability, Multidimensional Deprivation and Social Cohesion in the Enlarged European Community'. *International Journal of Comparative Sociology*, 46: 216–39.

—— and —— (2006). 'Comparing Poverty and Deprivation Dynamics: Issues of Reliability and Validity'. *Journal of Economic Inequality*, 4: 303–23.

—— and —— (2007). 'Levels and Patterns of Material Deprivation in Ireland: After the Celtic Tiger'. *European Sociological Review*, 23: 139–54.

——, Layte. R., and Maître, B. (2002). 'Multiple Deprivation and Persistent Poverty in the European Union'. *Journal of European Social Policy*, 12: 91–105.

——,——, and —— (2003). 'Persistent Income Poverty and Deprivation in the European Union'. *Journal of Social Policy*, 32: 1–18.

——, ——, and —— (2004). 'Understanding the Mismatch between Income Poverty and Deprivation: A Dynamic Comparative Analysis'. *European Sociological Review*, 20: 287–302.

——, Maître, B., and Nolan B. (2006). 'Measuring Consistent Poverty in Ireland with EU-SILC Data'. Working Paper 165. Dublin: Economic and Social Research Institute.

——, Layte, R., Maître, B. and Nolan, B. (2001). 'Income, Deprivation and Economic Strain: An Analysis of the European Community Household Panel'. *European Sociological Review*, 17: 357–72.

8

Summarizing multiple deprivation indicators

*Lorenzo Cappellari and Stephen P. Jenkins**

It is widely agreed nowadays that being poor does not simply mean not having enough money. It means, more generally, a lack of access to resources enabling a minimum style of living and participation in the society within which one belongs—as in the definition of poverty adopted by the European Union, for example.[1] In short, poverty is not only about low income, but also about deprivation. The emphasis on deprivation reflects, in part, theoretical concerns that low income provides an 'indirect' measure rather than a 'direct' measure of poverty, as emphasized by Ringen (1988). In addition, there are more purely empirical concerns about an exclusive focus on low income. The snapshot picture provided by income measures from cross-section surveys may be misleading because, with income smoothing, current living standards may not reflect current income, and, in any case, there may be substantial measurement errors particularly at the bottom end of the income distribution. A large body of research has pointed out that the people who have a low income are not the same as the population who are most materially deprived: see *inter alia* Berthoud, Bryan, and Bardasi (2004), Bradshaw and Finch (2003), Callan, Nolan, and Whelan (1993), Perry (2002), and Chapter 7 of this book.

These are not simply academic concerns. Assessments of deprivation are fundamental parts of national anti-poverty strategies in several countries.

* The research was supported by ISER's funding from the ESRC and the University of Essex. Earlier versions of the chapter were presented at the IARIW 2004 and ECINEQ 2005 conferences and to seminars at the Work and Pensions Economists Group and DIW Berlin. We are grateful for comments and suggestions from Richard Berthoud, Bruce Bradbury, Mark Bryan, Steve McKay, John Micklewright, Brian Nolan, Lucinda Platt, Sophia Rabe-Hesketh, and Brendan Whelan, but responsibility for the views expressed lies entirely with the authors.

[1] 'Persons whose resources (material, cultural and social) are so limited as to exclude them from the minimum acceptable way of life in the Member State to which they belong' (EEC 1985).

Summary indices of deprivation are used in combination with measures of low income to produce pictures of 'consistent poverty' in the National Action Plan Against Poverty and Social Exclusion in Ireland (http://www.socialinclusion.ie/poverty.html). In the UK, progress towards the eradication of child poverty is to be monitored not only using income poverty measures but also with measures of 'material deprivation' (Department for Work and Pensions 2003). Deprivation indicators are included in the main EU surveys for social monitoring, the European Community Household Panel and the EU-SILC surveys. They are part of a wider portfolio of social indicators being developed at a European level: see Atkinson *et al.* (2002) and Eurostat (2005).

This chapter examines some methodological issues concerning the construction of a deprivation scale from multiple deprivation indicators, issues that have received little attention in the deprivation literature. We draw on the literature on item response modelling from psychometrics and educational testing as it has a long history of addressing similar measurement issues.[2] Deprivation indicators are like test scores (i.e. whether an answer to a particular test question is right or wrong), and summarizing deprivation indicators with a deprivation scale is like summarizing test scores with a scale of academic ability. Our particular interest is in assessing the ubiquitous practice of constructing a deprivation scale as a raw (or weighted) sum of a relatively small set of dichotomous indicators.

We argue that the theoretical foundations of these 'sum-score' scales are weak and that the item response modelling approach provides a more promising way to summarize multiple deprivation indicators (section 8.1). An application based on British Household Panel Survey data is used to illustrate these points (section 8.2). As it happens, both approaches provide very similar pictures of the patterns of deprivation and their determinants, and so our results might be construed as providing an empirical rationale for the sum-score approach. We address this issue in the final sections of the chapter, where we combine further discussion of the relative merits of sum-score and item response modelling approaches with suggestions of ways in which the latter approach could be developed further (sections 8.3 and 8.4).

We are concerned with what Atkinson (2003) referred to as the 'counting' approach to deprivation. His cogent analysis discusses it from the perspective of social welfare measurement, considering the configurations of deprivation indicators that would allow one to say that deprivation is higher in one case than another for complete classes of summary indices—a dominance approach. By contrast, we consider the derivation of particular summary scales

[2] Similar methods were used by Kuklys (2004) to analyse housing and health 'functionings'. Moisio (2004) also related multiple indicators to a latent variable, as we do. The key difference is that our deprivation variable is a continuous one whereas his is discrete: he considers two latent classes—'poor' and 'non-poor'. The latent class approach is also used by Nolan and Whelan in Ch. 7.

of deprivation and use statistical measurement models to provide the framework for assessing them.[3] Both Atkinson's (2003) and our approach serve to highlight the assumptions underpinning deprivation scale construction.

We focus on only one set of measurement issues concerning deprivation indicators. Issues such as which deprivation indicators should be included in a sample survey (McKay and Collard 2004), survey methods topics such as question wording, or whether different sets of indicators should be used for different population subgroups (McKay 2004; Berthoud, Blekesaune, and Hancock 2006) are not considered here. Nor do we consider whether there is a critical level of deprivation above which households are judged to be in hardship, an issue analogous to the derivation of a poverty line when assessing income poverty.

8.1 Multiple deprivation indicators and a unidimensional deprivation scale

From deprivation indicators to a deprivation scale

There are many ways to define and measure 'deprivation', whether overall deprivation or specific dimensions of deprivation, but there are features common to them all:

- *multiple indicators*—the picture of household circumstances is based on multiple indicators of lack or possession of necessities (by contrast, income poverty is summarized using only one indicator);
- *combined into a single scale*—lack or possession of each item or activity (usually recorded as a zero or one in the indicator variables) is aggregated into a numerical scale (a simple or weighted sum).

Most derivations of scales of overall deprivation are inspired by, and derive from, Townsend's (1979) approach to poverty measurement. This was later refined in the Breadline Britain studies (Mack and Lansley 1985; Gordon and Pantazis 1997) and by Gordon *et al.* (2000).[4] In these studies, the multiple binary indicators refer to whether households lack various items and activities that are perceived as necessities and their lack is because they cannot afford them rather than because they do not want them, that is, an 'enforced lack'. Examples of the indicators include 'having heating to warm living areas of the home', to 'able to visit friends and family', and 'having meat, fish or vegetarian equivalent every other day'. The Policy Studies Institute index of overall

[3] All our statistical models are parametric ones. For a non-parametric approach to related issues, see Spady (2006).

[4] Deprivation scales of the type considered in this chapter are primarily a European phenomenon. We know of no similar US studies, for instance. There are US studies of material hardship and income: see e.g. Mayer and Jencks (1989).

'hardship' is similar in structure, except that it uses a prevalence-weighted sum of indicators rather than a simple unweighted sum (Vegeris and McKay 2002; Vegeris and Perry 2003).

Other studies have developed separate measures to summarize each of a number of separate dimensions of deprivation. For example, the ESRI Dublin research team have developed scales of basic lifestyle deprivation, secondary lifestyle deprivation, housing deprivation, and so on: see, for example, Nolan and Whelan (1986*a*, 1986*b*), Layte, Nolan, and Whelan (2000), and Whelan *et al.* (2001). (They have studied deprivation in Ireland and compared deprivation across EU countries.) A UK application using their methods is Calandrino (2003). The indices of material well-being and of accommodation and housing conditions developed by the Policy Studies Institute have a close familial resemblance (Vegeris and McKay 2002; Vegeris and Perry 2003). Although the measures cited each focus on different dimensions of deprivation, they are constructed in the same way as the measures of overall deprivation: multiple indicators are combined into a single numerical scale.

To simplify the arguments, we shall begin by assuming that one is interested in a single dimension of deprivation, call it 'basic lifestyle' deprivation. We do not observe basic lifestyle deprivation—it is a latent variable—but wish to make inferences about its distribution from a set of K dichotomous deprivation indicators observed for each of N households.[5] In practice, K is relatively small (often less than 10) and N is relatively large (several thousand).

The most commonly used deprivation scale is the sum of the dichotomous indicators. This 'sum-score' index D_i is

$$D_i = \sum\nolimits_k I_{ik} \qquad [1]$$

for each household $i = 1, \ldots, N$, and for each deprivation indicator I_{ik}, $k = 1, \ldots, K$. Alternatively, the sum-score index may be created as a weighted sum, $\sum_k w_k I_{ik}$. With prevalence weighting, for example, a higher weight (w_k) is given to an indicator for which the prevalence in the population is lower. (If few people in the population do not have an item, then arguably its lack should contribute less to overall deprivation.) We focus on [1].

The rationale for using the sum-score D_i as a deprivation scale is rarely considered. The view that is implicit in most studies is, we suspect, that the sum-score index is consistent with the classical measurement model:[6]

[5] We refer to households as the unit of analysis as the deprivation indicators are typically collected in surveys using questions directed at one person who responds on behalf of the household as a whole. We assume that the choice of the indicators has already been resolved. The number of indicators for each household may in fact vary because of survey item response. We return to this issue in section 8.4.

[6] For an authoritative discussion of measurement models in the psychometric literature, see Nunnally and Bernstein (1994).

$$I_{ik} = D_i^* + \varepsilon_{ik}, \qquad [2]$$

where D_i^* is the underlying 'true' but latent measure of deprivation and ε_{ik} is a measurement error term with zero mean, assumed to be independent of D_i^*, and mutually independent. The model implies that the average of the observed indicators for each household is equal to $D_i^* + (1/K)\sum_k(\varepsilon_{ik})$. With sufficiently large K, the sample mean of the equation errors would tend to zero, so that the arithmetic average of the observed indicators for each household would equal the household-specific latent deprivation level. The sum-score which is what is typically used in practice—the total score rather than the average—preserves the ranking of households by D^*.

The problem with rationalizing the sum-score in this way is that the classical measurement model cannot hold in the current context because the observed deprivation indicators are dichotomous variables, not continuous ones. One needs an approach that incorporates this fundamental characteristic of the data. Item response models (IRMs) provide such a framework. How large K is will be an issue that we return to.

One parameter item response models

The simplest IRM is the one parameter model, characterized by the following equations:

$$I_{ik}^* = \gamma_k + D_i^* + \varepsilon_{ik},$$
$$I_{ik} = 1 \text{ if } I_{ik}^* > 0 \text{ and } I_{ik} = 0 \text{ otherwise.} \qquad [3]$$

The error terms, ε_{ik}, are independently distributed with mean zero, and have a fixed and common variance. The data structure corresponds to what economists would recognize as a balanced panel except that the repeated observations per household come from the different indicators rather than from different points in time. Model specification is completed by assumptions about the functional form for the distribution of the error terms (for example whether logistic or normal) and whether the household-specific measures of latent deprivation should be treated as a set of fixed parameters or as random effects.

The larger that γ_k is, the more likely that the value of the corresponding indicator I_{ik} is one given any level of deprivation D_i^*. Therefore each γ_k can be straightforwardly interpreted as representing the intrinsic cheapness of the indicator, expressed in latent deprivation terms.[7] Households are less likely to report the lack of items that have smaller γ_k, other things being equal. The model also implies that the larger that a household's deprivation is, the greater

[7] In the item response modelling literature, $-\gamma_k$ summarizes the 'item difficulty' of a binary test score item in which a correct answer scores one and an incorrect answer scores zero.

the probability that each of the observed binary indicators equals one and, moreover, the effect of increasing D_i^* is the same for every item.

The Rasch model is the one-parameter IRM arising when the error term has a logistic distribution and the D_i^* are treated as fixed effects. In this model, the observed sum-score D_i is a sufficient statistic. That is, given D_i, the pattern of responses on the K indicators provides no further information about D_i^*. All units with the same D_i have the same D_i^*.

But can one actually estimate D_i^* given information on K observed indicators? It is well known that conditional maximum likelihood methods are able to provide estimates of each γ_k as $N \rightarrow \infty$, given K fixed, but the D_i^* parameters cannot be estimated. In addition, standard maximum likelihood estimates of the D_i^* parameters are inconsistent as $N \rightarrow \infty$, given K fixed. Consistency requires $N \rightarrow \infty$, $K \rightarrow \infty$, and $N/K \rightarrow \infty$ (Mollenaar 1995), and yet the number of indicators is typically small. Intuitively, the problem is that, as far as the estimation of each D_i^* is concerned, the relevant sample size is the number of indicators, K. This number is usually small.

The standard way forward is to assume, instead, that the D_i^* are random individual effects. In this case, standard maximum likelihood methods may be used to estimate each of the intrinsic cheapness parameters γ_k. The main advance is that, in addition, one can derive predicted values for each D_i^* using 'empirical Bayes' (EB) methods.[8] The intuition is that one gets a good fix on each household's D_i^* by updating the information about the assumed shape of the latent variable distribution (the 'prior') using the information about household's observed responses and the item response parameters. The predicted deprivation score for each household is the expected value of this updated ('posterior') distribution. Put another way, to predict the latent variable for the given household, one combines the observed responses for a given household with the assumptions of the model relating observed indicators to the latent variable for every household. The 'empirical' tag arises because one does the predictions using sample estimates of the parameters (γ_k), rather than their true values, which are not observed. The EB predictor also has a nice interpretation of minimizing the mean square error of prediction over the sampling distribution of the responses taking the model parameters as known.

With EB prediction of latent deprivation, one has a more secure methodological foundation, with deprivation scales consistently founded on a measurement model. This is a substantial advantage. There are several points to note, however. First, the small-sample properties of EB predictors from IRMs are not well-known (Hoijtink and Boomsma 1995). The relevant sample size is the number of deprivation indicators. Intuitively speaking, the larger that K is, the more information one has, and hence the better the prediction. Second,

[8] See Skrondal and Rabe-Hesketh (2004, Ch. 7) or Hoijtink and Boosma (1995) for discussions of EB methods.

the orderings of households in terms of EB predictions and sum-scores are likely to be closely related, since the probability that a household is counted as deprived according to each and every observed indicator is an increasing function of D_i^*. However, the association is not perfect (and also likely to vary with K). For any given sum-score value, there will be a distribution of EB predictions of D_i^* because the same sum-score may be achieved from different combinations of indicator scores. We illustrate this later.

The third point is that the one parameter IRM incorporates strong assumptions that are likely to be unrealistic. For example, in the one parameter random effects probit IRM, the correlation between any pair of item deprivations is the same, regardless of which pair is considered: $\text{corr}(I_{ik}^*, I_{im}^*) = \rho$, for all $k \neq m$, where $\rho = var(D_i^*)/[1 + var(D_i^*)]$. This strong assumption may be tested using a multivariate probit model in which no restrictions are placed on the cross-equation correlations: $\text{corr}(I_{ik}^*, I_{im}^*) = \rho_{km}$. See section 8.2. A more common way of avoiding the equi-correlation assumption is to incorporate additional parameters into the IRM. We consider this and other generalizations to the IRM specification next.

Two parameter item response models and other specification issues

The two parameter IRM weakens the assumption that a given change in D_i^* has the same impact on each deprivation indicator probability. This is done by introducing indicator-specific 'discrimination' parameters, otherwise known as 'factor loadings' into the one parameter random effects IRM:[9]

$$I_{ik}^* = \gamma_k + \lambda_k D_i^* + \varepsilon_{ik},$$
$$I_{ik} = 1 \text{ if } I_{ik}^* > 0 \text{ and } I_{ik} = 0 \text{ otherwise.} \qquad [4]$$

For model identification, it is usually assumed that $\lambda_1 = 1$. The equi-correlation assumption no longer holds, since $\text{corr}(I_{ik}^*, I_{im}^*)$ is a function of λ_k and λ_m. The parameter estimates can be estimated by maximum likelihood, and one can derive estimates of D_i^* by EB methods, subject to the caveats mentioned earlier.

One of the emerging themes of the chapter is the importance of having a relatively large number of deprivation indicators. One catch to this is that the more indicators that you use, the less likely it is that they refer to a single latent deprivation trait. This issue may be illustrated with reference to the research of, *inter alia*, Whelan *et al.* (2001). Using 24 deprivation indicators, they applied confirmatory factor analysis to identify three dimensions of deprivation: basic lifestyle deprivation, secondary lifestyle deprivation, and housing

[9] In the item response modelling literature, λ_k summarizes the extent to which the item (question) differentiates between individuals with different levels of academic ability (D_i^*).

deprivation. Then they used a separate sum-score index to summarize deprivation within each dimension. IRMs such as [4] can be straightforwardly extended from being one factor models, as in [3] and [4], to having two or more factors (Goldstein 1980; Skrondal and Rabe-Hesketh 2004). The advantage of following the IRM approach is that both the specification of the number of factors, and the relationship between deprivation indicators and factors, are encompassed within a single model-based framework, and not split into two separate and potentially inconsistent steps.

IRMs also provide a consistent way in which to incorporate heterogeneity in household characteristics into the analysis, both in terms of modelling observed responses, and for exploring the determinants of latent deprivation itself. We consider these two aspects in turn.

First, we observe that binary deprivation indicators are typically derived from a two-part question. The first part asks whether the household has an item or participates in some activity and, if the response is negative, the second part asks whether the lack was because it could not be afforded. If the answer to this second part is yes, then the deprivation indicator scores one, and is zero otherwise. (Specific examples are provided in section 8.2.) It is conceivable that there are systematic differences in observed responses because, even among households people with the same latent deprivation D_i^*, there are heterogeneous views about what they 'want', about what they understand by affordability, or about the interpretation of specific questions (for example relating to what 'adequate' means). For example, some people may give greater priority to a warm home than to having friends around, and this may be reflected in their responses to whether they cannot afford something that they do not have.

In principle, it is straightforward to introduce covariates into the IRM to address this issue. For example, one may rewrite [4] as follows:

$$I_{ik}^* = \gamma_k + \lambda_k D_i^* + \beta_k X_{ik} + \varepsilon_{ik},$$
$$I_{ik} = 1 \text{ if } I_{ik}^* > 0 \text{ and } I_{ik} = 0 \text{ otherwise.} \qquad [5]$$

Non-zero values of β_k indicate differential reporting propensities, or what is known as 'item bias' or 'differential item functioning' in the IRM literature. From this perspective, one may interpret the deprivation indicator regressions of Desai and Shah (1988) as being estimates of a one parameter IRM allowing for item bias but also assuming all cross-equation error correlations were equal to zero.

The IRMs discussed earlier can also be extended to model the determinants of the latent deprivation trait jointly with the estimation of the IRM parameters. The measurement component of the model is supplemented with a 'structural' equation of the form:

$$D_i^* = \alpha' Z_i + \xi_i, \qquad [6]$$

where ξ_i is a normally distributed i.i.d. error term with mean zero and fixed variance. This is an example of a multiple-indicator multiple-cause (MIMIC) model. One of the issues that we consider in the empirical illustration to follow is whether the conclusions that one would draw about the impact of covariates on deprivation differs depending on whether they are derived from an IRM model supplemented with equation [6], or the conventional approach of regressing sum-scores on covariates.

Some people commenting on our research have objected to the incorporation of item bias parameters as in equation [5], stating that this conflates two distinct activities: the measurement of deprivation, on the one hand, and analysis of the determinants of deprivation, on the other hand. Their argument is that the level of deprivation should be assessed entirely in terms of deprivation indicator response patterns, and so characteristics should not play a role in the measurement model.

Our view is that there is an important distinction between analysis of the determinants of observed deprivation indicators (D_i), analysis of the determinants of the latent deprivation variable (D_i^*), and estimation of D_i^*.[10] Item bias refers to the first of these issues, how different people with the same latent deprivation may report different indicator prevalence, and the structural equation [6] is the framework for addressing the second issue. In principle, estimation of D_i^*—the third issue—may be achieved using EB methods applied to models incorporating item bias and an equation for the determinants of latent deprivation. The problem is that, in practice, it is difficult to estimate models that incorporate both item bias and a structural equation. Often the same characteristic appears in both parts (X_{ik} and Z_i have common elements), and it is difficult to identify its separate contributions from a statistical point of view. We ignore item bias from now on for this reason.[11]

To sum up so far, we have argued that an IRM approach provides a coherent approach to the derivation of a deprivation scale, and that its methodological foundations are more secure than those of the commonly used sum-score approach. In the next section, we contrast the two approaches in an empirical illustration.

[10] Analysis of how the observed responses on the indicator variables vary with characteristics is of interest in its own right, of course, quite separately from interest in underlying deprivation (the focus here).

[11] An alternative way to address the heterogeneity in response issue would be to estimate different models for different population subgroups, for example elderly people versus younger people, or separately for different minority ethnic groups. This would also provide scope for using different sets of indicators for the different groups. The indicators of material deprivation recently introduced in the UK Family Resources Survey differ for adults and for children (Department for Work and Pensions 2003).

8.2 Empirical illustration: basic life-style deprivation in Britain

Data

We used data from Wave 6 (survey year 1996) of the British Household Panel Survey (BHPS). The advantages of the BHPS data are that they are based on a large national population sample and (from Wave 6 onwards) have contained a battery of questions about deprivation in addition to more conventional indicators of household living standards such as income. We used Wave 6 data rather than some later year to minimize any potential impact of panel attrition on sample selection.

We focus on 'basic life style' deprivation, summarized using seven binary indicator variables. The first six variables summarize responses to questions put to the household reference person, asking whether he or she would like to be able to do the following, but have to do without because they cannot afford it (an 'enforced lack'):

- keep your home adequately warm (1.9%);
- eat meat, chicken, fish every second day (3.1%);
- buy new, rather than second-hand, clothes (5.3%);
- have friends or family for a drink or meal at least once a month (6.5%);
- replace worn out furniture (13.4%);
- pay for a week's annual holiday away from home (20.1%).

Each variable was scored one if there was an enforced lack of the relevant item or activity and zero otherwise; the percentage in parentheses is the fraction of the sample with an enforced lack. The seventh binary indicator variable summarized difficulties in meeting housing costs: that is, whether the responding household[12]

- had any difficulties paying for their accommodation in the last twelve months (6.9%).

Those reporting payment problems scored one on this variable; otherwise it was zero.

These seven indicators are representative of those used in the literature. They are a subset of those used by Townsend (1979) and the later Breadline Britain studies. They were introduced to the BHPS when that survey was used to contribute data to the UK component of the European Community Household Panel (ECHP)—the same variables were available on a harmonized basis for all countries in the survey. The list corresponds closely to those used to summarize basic life-style deprivation in the many ECHP-based studies of

[12] Only individuals renting their accommodation (other than those receiving a 100% rent rebate) or buying with a mortgage were at risk of an enforced lack.

deprivation by the research team from ESRI Dublin: see *inter alia* Layte *et al.* (2001) and Whelan *et al.* (2001). See also Eurostat (2005). The indicators overlap with the ten indicators proposed for measurement of adult material deprivation by the UK Department for Work and Pensions (2003).

Summary statistics

There were 4,859 households with non-missing information on all seven indicators from an overall sample of 5,064 households. Sixty-nine per cent experienced no enforced lack according to any of the seven indicators; put another way, 31 per cent of the sample experienced an enforced lack of at least one item. Fifteen per cent were deprived of two items, and 8 per cent of three items, 4.4 per cent of four items, and 2.8 per cent were deprived of 4–7 items. Only one household was deprived of all seven items. The number of unique response patterns was 88, which is 66 per cent of the total number possible ($128 = 2^7$).

The 'reliability' of a sum-score deprivation scale is often assessed with reference to estimates of the Cronbach alpha statistic (α), even though the theory underlying it refers to a classical measurement model with continuous indicators. (See Nunnally and Bernstein 1994 for further discussion.) The α summarizes the extent to which the indicators in a summative scale correlate well with each other. If each indicator were statistically independent of each of the other indicators, then $\alpha = 0$. At the other extreme, if all are perfectly correlated with each other, then $\alpha = 1$. Our estimate of α for the sample as a whole is 0.653, which lies within the bounds of what is usually considered to be acceptable, though is lower than the 0.81 reported by Whelan *et al.* (2001). At the same time, we should not put too much emphasis on the estimated α because we have discrete rather than continuous indicators.

Item response model estimates

Estimates of item response models are shown in Table 1.[13] Model 1 is the basic one-parameter model. Reassuringly, the ordering of the indicators by the estimates of the 'intrinsic cheapness' parameters (γ_k) corresponds to the ordering by prevalence of enforced lack reported in the previous subsection. For any given level of D_i^*, the probability of reporting an enforced lack is lowest for keeping the home adequately warm, and highest for having a week's holiday away. For example, if $D_i^* = 0$, the probability of lacking an adequately warm

[13] All IRM parameter estimates and EB predictions were derived using the program modules gllamm and gllapred in Stata (http://www.gllamm.org). The exception was the multivariate probit version of the one parameter model: see Cappellari and Jenkins (2003).

Table 8.1 Estimates of probit random effects item response models

Indicator	One parameter IRM (1)		One parameter IRM (multivariate probit) (2)		Two parameter IRM (3)			
	γ_k	(SE)	γ_k	(SE)	γ_k	(SE)	λ_k	(SE)
Home adequately warm	−3.12	(0.07)	−2.09	(0.04)	−1.83	(0.06)	1	
Meat etc. every second day	−2.80	(0.06)	−1.86	(0.04)	−1.59	(0.06)	1.34	(0.18)
New rather than second hand clothes	−2.44	(0.05)	−1.62	(0.03)	−1.26	(0.06)	1.54	(0.20)
Friends or family visit at least once a month	−2.29	(0.05)	−1.52	(0.03)	−1.08	(0.05)	1.44	(0.18)
Difficulties paying for accommodation	−2.22	(0.05)	−1.48	(0.03)	−1.07	(0.04)	0.80	(0.10)
Replace worn out furniture	−1.69	(0.04)	−1.11	(0.02)	−0.43	(0.05)	1.62	(0.20)
Week's annual holiday away	−1.28	(0.04)	−0.85	(0.02)	0		1.57	(0.19)
ρ	0.57	(0.01)	[a]		[b]			
	−7517.8		−7669.7		−7473.7			

Notes: [a] Unrestricted cross-equation error correlations. Likelihood ratio test of model 1 versus model 2: $\chi^2(303.8, \text{d.f.} = 20)$, $p < 0.001$. [b] estimates of cross-equation error correlations not shown. Estimate of var(D_i^*) from model 3 is 0.702 (SE = 0.15).

home is 0.001, and of lacking a week's holiday away is 0.017. If $D_i^* = 1$, the probabilities are 0.100 and 0.390.[14]

The equi-correlation assumption for the errors incorporated by Model 1 is relaxed in Model 2, and a likelihood ratio test rejects the former in favour of the latter (χ^2(303.8, d.f. $= 20$), $p < 0.001$). The ordering of the intrinsic cheapness parameters in terms of relative magnitude is the same, however. The same is true when we move to Model 3, the two-parameter model that relaxes the assumption that a given change in D_i^* has the same impact on each deprivation indicator probability. Note also the substantial improvement in log-likelihood relative to the other models. There is substantial variation in the estimated factor loadings (λ_k), with relatively low values for difficulties in paying for accommodation keeping the home adequately warm, and the highest value for replacement of worn out furniture.

From these estimates, we can derive EB predictions of each household's latent deprivation score D_i^*, and see how these compare with their rankings by the sum-score. A comparison based on the two-parameter IRM estimates (Model 3) is shown in Figure 8.1. It is clear that the two scales order

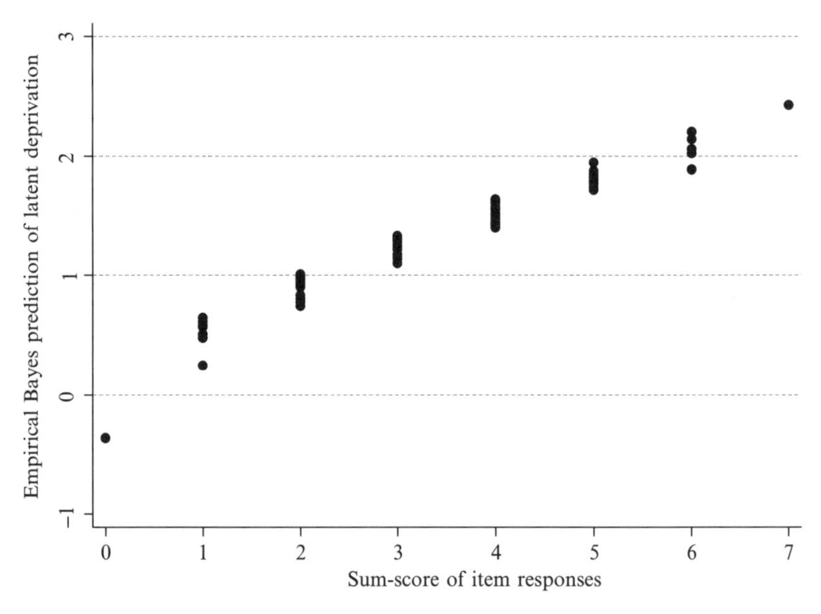

Figure 8.1 Empirical Bayes and sum-score deprivation scales are highly correlated

Notes: EB estimates derived from two-parameter IRM (model 3 in Table 8.1). The correlation between the two series is 0.97.

[14] The precise values of the predicted probabilities depend on the type of binary model (logit, probit, cloglog) that one uses. This issue is discussed by Goldstein (1980).

households in a very similar way. The scatterplot is close to a straight line, and the correlation between the two scales is 0.97. (The corresponding scatterplot using EB predictions from the one-parameter IRM is even more like a straight line.) There is only limited variation in predicted D_i^* scores at each sum-score value. And it is only at sum-scores of 5 and 6 that there are overlaps in predicted D_i^* scores.

The close association between the two scales is underlined further when we examine the household type breakdown of the worst-off 30 per cent of the sample. Table 8.2, columns (a) and (b), show that the composition of this group is the same according to the two scales. The largest group, comprising almost one-fourth of this worst-off group, is non-elderly working couples with children.

The determinants of deprivation are examined next. The impact of a set of covariates on latent deprivation D_i^* is considered using the two parameter IRM supplemented with the specification shown in equation [6]. This is compared with estimates from a regression of the sum-score on the same set of covariates, using ordered probit methods. (There are eight sum-score categories.) The regressors used are similar to those used in earlier deprivation studies: the numbers of adults and children in the household, the sex of the household head, the age of the household head and age-squared, whether the household contained at least one full-time worker, and the log of household annual income. See Table 8.3.

Table 8.2 Composition of the worst-off 30 per cent, by deprivation measure

		Column percentages	
Household type	Sum-score	Two parameter IRM	
		(a)	(b)
Elderly (household head of pension age)			
Single man	2.3	2.3	2.2
Single woman	9.9	9.9	9.8
Couple	6.3	6.3	6.2
Non-elderly			
Single, kids, full-time worker	5.5	5.5	5.3
Single, kids, no full-time worker	11.5	11.5	12.6
Single, no kids, full-time worker	5.8	5.8	5.6
Single, no kids, no full-time worker	9.1	9.1	9.9
Couple, kids, at least one full-time worker	24.4	24.4	23.9
Couple, kids, no full-time worker	7.1	7.1	7.3
Couple, no kids, at least one full-time worker	10.1	10.1	9.5
Couple, no kids, no full-time worker	3.8	3.8	3.9
Other	4.2	4.2	4.1
Total	100.0	100.0	100.0
N (households)	1430	1430	1425

Notes: (a): two parameter random effects IRM without covariates (Model 3 in Table 8.1).
(b): as (a), except model also includes determinants of deprivation (see Table 8.3).

The two modelling approaches yield similar results in the sense that corresponding coefficient estimates have the same sign and are precisely estimated. Deprivation is higher the more adults or the more children there are in the household, or if the household head is a woman. Deprivation is lower for households with at least one full-time worker, and the higher the household income. The magnitudes of the corresponding coefficients are not entirely comparable because the scale of the dependent variables differs: for example, the sum-score ranges from 0 to 7, whereas the range of D_i^* is much smaller (see Fig. 8.1). This explains why the magnitude of each coefficient in the sum-score regression is greater than that for its counterpart in the latent deprivation regression. But one can say that there are close similarities nonetheless. Ratios of coefficient estimates from one model are very similar to corresponding ratios from the other model. For example, the ratio of the estimated coefficient on the number of adults to the estimated coefficient on the number of children is 1.11 in the latent deprivation regression and 1.14 in the sum-score regression. Deprivation has an inverse U-shaped relationship with age in both regressions, with a maximum at age 35 according to the latent deprivation regression, compared to age 32 according to the sum-score regression.

8.3 Discussion

We have argued the case for an IRM approach to the derivation of deprivation scales from multiple deprivation indicators. Our empirical illustration has shown, however, that in practice, the IRM and conventional sum-score approaches yield very similar pictures of the distribution of deprivation in terms

Table 8.3 The determinants of deprivation: two approaches compared

	Dependent variable			
	Latent deprivation (a)		Sum-score (b)	
Regressors	Coeff.	(SE)	Coeff.	(SE)
Number of adults	0.136	(0.03)	0.165	(0.02)
Number of children	0.122	(0.02)	0.145	(0.02)
Female household head	0.170	(0.08)	0.199	(0.04)
Age of household head (years)	0.028	(0.01)	0.032	(0.01)
Age squared	−0.0004	(0.0001)	−0.0005	(0.0001)
One or more full-time workers	−0.219	(0.05)	−0.260	(0.05)
Log(income)	−0.491	(0.06)	−0.579	(0.03)
Constant	3.321	(0.42)		
log*L*	−7029.0		−4292.1	
N (households)	4671		4680	

Notes: (a) Specification based on equation [6] embedded in two parameter random effects IRM (other parameter estimates not shown). (b) Ordered probit regression of sum-score on covariates.

of the association between the distributions of scores, who is found to be worst-off, and also the determinants of deprivation. At one level, then, we have provided an entirely practical argument for the continued use of the sum-score approach. It is very simple to implement and to understand, and appears to provide the same conclusions.

This case for the sum-score approach is not decisive. There are some strong arguments in favour of exploring the IRM approach further in the deprivation context. The approach can handle missing indicator information in a straightforward manner, using what economists would call unbalanced panel methods. (For simplicity, we did not use them in this chapter.)

In addition, there are intrinsic advantages of using a consistent model-based framework for thinking about measurement. The framework can incorporate models of the relationship between the latent deprivation and explanatory variable, and can also be extended to have more than one latent deprivation variable. This approach contrasts with the two-step one which first uses confirmatory factor analytic methods to identify deprivation variables (even though, strictly speaking, these methods were developed for continuous variables), and then constructs sum-scores for each dimension identified at the first step. More generally, the specification of the IRMs has highlighted the nature of the assumptions underlying the construction of a deprivation scale. In the conventional sum-score approach, these assumptions are left implicit and typically ignored.

We have highlighted the important role played by the number of indicators available for the properties of the measures and estimation. Underlying this point is the common sense idea that there is little information that a small number of dichotomous indicators can communicate about a particular household's circumstances and or help us discriminate between different households. The maximum number of distinct response combinations is only 2^K.

This suggests that the more indicators there are, the better (subject to their being relevant to deprivation, of course). More information about the different circumstances of households might also be gained by using different types of indicators. For example, one could use polytomous variables with ordered categories, or indeed continuous variables. IRMs can be generalized to use combinations of dichotomous, ordered polytomous and continuous indicators, albeit at the cost of additional complexity. See Skrondal and Rabe-Hesketh (2004) for discussion of the principles and Ribar (2005) for an application.

Another way to get additional repeated observations on households is to use panel survey data in which there are responses on the same deprivation items at multiple points in time. The most extensive study to date of deprivation indicators using panel data is that by Berthoud, Bryan, and Bardasi (2004), who considered the longitudinal evolution of a sum-score scale calculated at each annual interview. By contrast, we have in mind an extension to the IRM approach that takes explicit account of the repeated observations per household or individuals. In the same way that researchers have argued in favour of using repeated observations on income at each interview to calculate a measure of (unobserved) 'permanent' income, one could use the repeated observations on deprivation indicators over time to get a better measure of latent deprivation.

Precisely what the specification of a 'panel' IRM would look like is unclear, and an interesting topic for future research. (Ribar 2005 is the only related study that we are aware of.) For example, an empirical regularity identified by Berthoud, Bryan, and Bardasi (2004) is that there is a decline in average deprivation sum-scores over time as living standards improve—in the same way that income poverty rates decline if the poverty line is fixed in real terms. This led them to standardize their sum-scores: the year-specific average score was deducted from each household's score and the result divided by the year-specific standard deviation (Berthoud, Bryan, and Bardasi 2004: Ch. 4). From an IRM perspective, one might ask what precisely it is that the passage of time is affecting—is it the intrinsic cheapness parameters or latent deprivation itself that changes over time, or both? If it is the former, then one might think of an IRM estimated from panel data in which there are interview-specific intrinsic cheapness parameters (γ_k varying with calendar time). If it is the latter, then one would incorporate interview-specific factor loading parameters (λ_k varying with calendar time).

8.4 Conclusions

There has been remarkably little discussion of fundamental measurement issues in the deprivation literature of the type that we have considered here, and especially little that takes account of the dichotomous nature of the indicators that are commonly used. In part, this may be because deprivation analysts have considered other measurement issues to have a greater priority for attention, for example the choice of the set of indicators itself, and the precise wording of questions about them in surveys.

We acknowledge that these are important issues. Nonetheless, we would argue that the issues we have raised also deserve some further consideration, especially as deprivation scores are being used increasingly to monitor social progress in national and cross-national contexts. Although we found in our illustrative application that IRM and sum-score approaches provided very similar descriptions of patterns of deprivation and their determinants, this need not be the case outside this setting. And it may partly reflect the small number of indicators in the first place.

There is an interesting contrast with this growing deprivation literature and the extensive literature on international comparisons of educational test scores based on harmonized surveys such as Programme for International Student Assessment (PISA), Trends in International Mathematics and Science

Study (TIMSS), and Progress in International Reading Literacy Study (PIRLS). (See Chapter 6.) In addition to survey issues, pure measurement issues have been given substantial attention, and IRM approaches are much used. One key difference is that these surveys provide a large number of indicators.

References

Atkinson, A. B. (2003). 'Multidimensional Deprivation: Contrasting Social Welfare and Counting Approaches'. *Journal of Economic Inequality*, 1: 51–65.

——, Cantillon, B., Marlier, E., and Nolan, B. (2002). *Social Indicators. The EU and Social Exclusion*. Oxford: Oxford University Press.

Berthoud, R., Bryan, M., and Bardasi, E. (2004). *The Relationship between Income and Material Deprivation over Time*. Department for Work and Pensions Research Report 219. Leeds: Corporate Document Services.

——, Blekesaune, M., and Hancock, R. (2006). *Are 'Poor' Pensioners Deprived?* Department for Work and Pensions Research Report 364. Leeds: Corporate Document Services.

Bradshaw, J. and Finch, N. (2003). 'Overlaps in Dimensions of Poverty'. *Journal of Social Policy*, 32: 513–25.

Calandrino, M. (2003). 'Low-Income and Deprivation in British Families'. Working Paper Number 10. London: Department for Work and Pensions.

Callan, T., Nolan, B., and Whelan, C. T. (1993). 'Resources, Deprivation, and the Measurement of Poverty'. *Journal of Social Policy*, 22: 141–72.

Cappellari, L. and Jenkins, S. P. (2003). 'Multivariate Probit Regression using Simulated Maximum Likelihood'. *The Stata Journal*, 3: 278–94.

Department for Work and Pensions (2003). *Measuring Child Poverty*. London: Department for Work and Pensions.

Desai, M. and Shah, A. (1988). 'An Econometric Approach to the Measurement of Poverty'. *Oxford Economic Papers* 40: 505–22.

EEC (1985). 'On Specific Community Action to Combat Poverty (Council Decision of 19 December 1984) 85/8/EEC'. *Official Journal of the EEC*, 2: 24.

Eurostat (2005). 'Material Deprivation in the EU'. *Statistics in Focus—Population and Social Conditions, 21/2005*. Eurostat: Luxembourg.

Goldstein, H. (1980). 'Dimensionality, Bias, Independence and Measurement Scale Problems in Latent Trait Test Score Models'. *British Journal of Mathematical and Statistical Psychology*, 33: 234–46.

Gordon, D. and Pantazis, C. (1997). *Breadline Britain in the 1990s*. Aldershot: Ashgate.

——, Adelman, L., Ashworth, K., Bradshaw, J., Levitas, R., Middleton, S., Pantazis, C., Patsios, D., Payne, S., Townsend, P., and Williams, J. (2000). *Poverty and Social Exclusion in Britain*. York: Joseph Rowntree Foundation.

Halleröd, B. (1994). 'A New Approach to the Direct Consensual Measure of Poverty'. Social Policy Research Centre Discussion Paper No 50. Sydney: University of New South Wales.

Hoijtink, H. and Boomsma, A. (1995). 'On Person Parameter Estimation in the Dichotomous Rasch Model', in G. H. Fischer and I. W. Mollenaar (eds), *Rasch Models: Foundations, Recent Developments, and Applications*. New York: Springer-Verlag, 53–67.

Kuklys, W. (2004), 'Measuring Standards of Living in the UK—an Application of Sen's Functioning Approach Using Structural Equation Models'. Working Paper on Strategic Interaction 11-2004. Jena: Max Planck Institute.

Layte, R., Nolan, B., and Whelan, C. (2000). 'Targeting Poverty: Lessons from Monitoring Ireland's National Anti-Poverty Strategy'. *Journal of Social Policy*, 29: 553–75.

——, Maître, B., Nolan, B., and Whelan, C. T. (2001). 'Explaining Levels of Deprivation in the European Union'. *Acta Sociologica*, 44: 105–22.

Lord, F. M. and Novick, M. R. (1968). *Statistical Theories of Mental Test Scores*. Reading, MA: Addison-Wesley.

Mack, J. and Lansley, S. (1985). *Poor Britain*. London: George Allen & Unwin.

Mayer, S. E. and Jencks, C. (1989). 'Poverty and the Distribution of Material Hardship'. *Journal of Human Resources*, 33: 88–114.

McKay, S. (2004). 'Poverty or Preference? What do "Consensual Deprivation Indicators" Really Measure?' *Fiscal Studies*, 25: 201–23.

—— and Collard, S. (2004). 'Developing Deprivation Questions for the Family Resources Survey'. IAD Research Division Working Paper No. 13. London: Department for Work and Pensions.

Moisio, P. (2004). 'A Latent Class Application to the Multidimensional Measurement of Poverty'. *Quality and Quantity*, 38: 703–17.

Mollenaar, I. (1995), 'Estimation of Item Parameters', in G. H. Fischer and I. W. Mollenaar (eds), *Rasch Models: Foundations, Recent Developments, and Applications*. New York: Springer-Verlag, 39–51.

Nolan, B. and Whelan, C. (1996*a*). 'Measuring Poverty Using Income and Deprivation Indicators: Alternative Approaches', *Journal of European Social Policy*, 6: 225–40.

—— and Whelan, C. (1996*b*). *Resources, Deprivation and Poverty*. Oxford: Clarendon Press.

Nunnally, J. C. and Bernstein, I. H. (1994). *Psychometric Theory*, 3rd edn. New York: McGraw-Hill.

Perry, B. (2002). 'The Mismatch Between Income Measures and Direct Outcome Measures of Poverty'. *Social Policy Journal of New Zealand*, 19: 101–27.

Ribar, D. (2005). 'The Persistence of Financial Strains Among Low-Income Families: an Analysis of Multiple Indicators'. Unpublished Paper. Washington, DC: Department of Economics, The George Washington University.

Ringen, S. (1988). 'Direct and Indirect Measures of Poverty'. *Journal of Social Policy*, 17: 351–65.

Skrondal, A. and Rabe-Hesketh, S. (2004). *Generalized Latent Variable Modeling: Multilevel, Longitudinal, and Structural Equation Models*. Boca Raton, FL: CRC Press.

Spady, R. H. (2006). 'Identification and Estimation of Latent Attitudes and their Behavioral Implications'. Working Paper CWP12/06. London: Centre for Microdata Methods and Practice, Institute for Fiscal Studies.

Townsend, P. (1979). *Poverty in the United Kingdom*. Harmondsworth: Penguin.

Vegeris, S. and McKay, S. (2002). *Low/Moderate-income Families in Britain: Changes in Living Standards*. DWP Research Report No. 164. Leeds: Corporate Document Services.

—— and Perry, J. (2003). *Families and Children Study 2001: Report on Living Standards and the Children*. DWP Research Report No. 190. Leeds: Corporate Document Services.

Whelan, C., Layte, R., Maître, B., and Nolan, B. (2001). 'Income, Deprivation and Economic Strain: an Analysis of the European Community Household Panel'. *European Sociological Review*, 17: 357–472.

9

Robust multidimensional poverty comparisons with discrete indicators of well-being

Jean-Yves Duclos, David Sahn, and Stephen D. Younger

Most poverty analysts agree that poverty is multidimensional in theory. In practice, empirical poverty studies are overwhelmingly univariate, with most economists limiting their attention to poverty defined in terms of having low income or low consumption expenditure. This chapter is part of a larger research agenda that aims to bring the empirical literature closer to the widely accepted theory.[1] In particular, we show that it is both interesting and practicable to make poverty comparisons when poverty is measured using more than one dimension of well-being. These comparisons, which can be across groups, policies, or time in a single population, or across different populations, are robust in several ways. By using the stochastic dominance methods introduced by Atkinson (1987) and others, we are able to make comparisons that are robust to the choice of the poverty line and that are also valid for many poverty measures. This relieves us of the need to choose one specific poverty line and one specific poverty measure for our analysis. As in the univariate literature, our comparisons make use of cumulative density functions (CDF) or what are sometimes called poverty incidence curves. In our multidimensional setting, these CDFs are multivariate functions rather than univariate ones, defined over multiple dimensions of well-being rather than only income.

Multivariate poverty comparisons bring an additional complication compared to univariate comparisons: poverty measures must aggregate the various dimensions of well-being. There is a large literature that discusses different options for such aggregations.[2] But, as with the choice of the poverty line or

[1] See, for example, Duclos, Sahn, and Younger (2006*a*, 2006*c*).

[2] The best-known of these is the Human Development Index (United Nations Development Programme 1990), which also involves arbitrary aggregations across individuals. A recent WIDER

poverty measure, we prefer to avoid the choice of a specific indexation or aggregation procedure. Such aggregation involves value judgements about the relative importance of each dimension of well-being which are necessarily arbitrary. Instead, the comparisons that we develop are valid for broad classes of aggregation rules. In this sense, the approach in this chapter is genuinely multidimensional.[3]

Atkinson and Bourguignon (1982) pointed to another novel feature of multivariate approaches to poverty measurement: the distinction between 'union' and 'intersection' definitions of multivariate poverty. According to the union definition, a person is considered to be poor if he falls below the poverty line in either dimension. According to the intersection definition, the person is considered poor only if he falls below the poverty line in both dimensions. The comparisons that we develop are applicable to measures incorporating both types of definition.

Finally, statistical tests of poverty comparisons remain rare in the literature. Because we derive the sampling properties of the poverty estimators that we propose, our conclusions can be checked for their robustness to sampling variability.

The particular innovation that distinguishes this chapter from our previous work on multidimensional poverty comparisons is that we consider comparisons for which one or more of the indicators of well-being is a discrete variable. This is of considerable practical importance since dimensions of well-being such as literacy and political enfranchisement are usually considered to be discrete. In addition, variables that are intrinsically continuous are sometimes recorded in the form of a discrete variable: for example, income may be grouped into ranges rather than exact amounts being reported; respondents may be asked to rank their health status on a scale from 1 to 5, and so on. The methods that we use also provide a way to avoid the arbitrary choice of household equivalence scales in standard univariate poverty comparisons, a method first developed by Atkinson (1992) and Atkinson and Bourguignon (1987).

Our intellectual debt to Tony Atkinson is obvious throughout the chapter. Atkinson (1987) pioneered the use of stochastic dominance techniques in poverty analysis. Atkinson and Bourguignon (1982) is a seminal contribution to the literature on comparisons of well-being in multiple dimensions. And Atkinson (1992) and Atkinson and Bourguignon (1987) developed a specific example of the general problem that we consider in which welfare is measured in two dimensions, income, a continuous variable, and household size, a discrete one.

Section 9.1 provides our main theoretical results for robust poverty comparisons when well-being is measured in one continuous dimension and one discrete dimension. We consider two cases, corresponding to whether or

conference on Inequality, Poverty, and Human Well-Being examined many more such indices. See http://www.wider.unu.edu/conference/conference-2003-2/conference2003-2.htm.

[3] See http://www.undp-povertycentre.org/md-poverty for examples of alternative non-index approaches to capturing and comparing multidimensional poverty.

not the class of poverty measures of interest is continuous at the poverty line. The most well-known example of a unidimensional poverty measure that is discontinuous at the poverty line is the headcount index. This causes no particular difficulty for univariate poverty dominance, but the situation is different for multidimensional poverty dominance, as we show. Section 9.2 provides an estimator as well as the sampling distribution for the tests proposed in section 9.1. Section 9.3 extends the results of section 9.1 to the case of one continuous and two (or more) discrete dimensions of well-being.

Section 9.4 provides four examples of the practical application of these methods using data for countries at different levels of development. The first compares the poverty impact of two different transfer payments in Romania, child allowances and social security pensions. Following Atkinson (1992), Jenkins and Lambert (1993), and Chambaz and Maurin (1998), we consider poverty in two dimensions, income and household size. This allows us to avoid the arbitrary choice of an equivalence scale. The second example considers poverty measured in the dimensions of household consumption per capita and adult literacy, using data from Peru in 1985 and 1994. The hyperinflation of 1990 caused consumption to fall significantly over this period, for the literate and illiterate alike. However, because literacy rose, our multidimensional poverty comparisons do not allow us to conclude that poverty worsened over the period. The third example compares poverty in Ecuador between 1998 and 1999, also a period of substantial macroeconomic turmoil. We measure poverty in the dimensions of household consumption per capita and area of residence, where we suppose that urban residence is preferable to rural. In this case, we find that even though univariate comparisons of consumption poverty are inconclusive, multivariate intersection poverty measures do improve. The final example uses British Household Panel Survey data to illustrate poverty comparisons for the case where there are one continuous and two discrete dimensions. In particular, we examine poverty in the dimensions of income per adult equivalent, education status as measured by highest degree obtained, and a dichotomous indicator of whether the respondent has health problems that limit her/his activities. We find that multivariate poverty defined in this way declined between 1994 and 2002 for a very broad range of poverty lines. We also explore the likelihood that these rather demanding dominance tests reject the null using trivariate comparisons across all the waves of the BHPS. Proofs of all theorems may be found in the Appendix.

9.1 Multivariate poverty comparisons for discrete and continuous measures of well-being

Suppose that a population can be split into K exhaustive and exclusive population subgroups, whose population share is denoted by $\phi(k), k = 1, \ldots, K$. Hence $\sum_{k=1}^{K} \phi(k) = 1$. We can define these subgroups using a discrete welfare measure such as literacy, political enfranchisement, access to a public service, or physical capabilities. Alternatively, we can differentiate households by their relative needs, using information about household size and composition, type of activities, or area of residence. In either case, the important point is that these discrete differences in the characteristics of households or individuals suggest that, for a given value of the continuous measure of well-being, some specific groups have lower overall well-being than other groups. This can be because the discrete variable is itself a measure of well-being (e.g. being illiterate is worse than being literate, being able to vote is better than not being able to, etc.), or because it indicates differences in needs, prices, or poverty lines (e.g. a large household has greater needs than a small one, an urban area has a higher poverty line than a rural one, etc.). In addition, we can suppose that there is some uncertainty as to the precise value of these differences.

We assume that the K subgroups can be ordered in increasing value of a discrete measure of well-being in such a way that, at common values of the other, continuous, measure of well-being, individuals in subgroup 1 are more deprived than individuals in subgroup 2, who are more deprived than individuals in subgroup 3, and so on. For now, we assume that there is only one discrete variable (and thus a one-dimensional ordinal ranking of the K subgroups at some common value of the continuous measure), but we will later generalize the analysis to the case of several such discrete variables.

As is standard in the literature, for simplicity we limit our attention to poverty measures that are additive, that is, measures that are (weighted) sums of each individual's poverty status. This allows us to define poverty in each of the population subgroups as:

$$P(k; z(k)) = \int_0^{z(k)} \pi_k(x) f(x; k) dx \quad [1]$$

where x is a continuous measure of well-being. $f(x; k)$ is the probability density function for living standards, x, for subgroup k, that is, broadly speaking, the number of people in group k with income equal to x, normalized such that $\int f(x; k)dx = \phi(k)$. This ensures that group k's contribution to overall poverty is weighted by its share in the population. $z(k)$ is subgroup k's poverty line in the dimension of x. $\pi_k(x)$ is the contribution to subgroup k's poverty of an individual in that subgroup with living standard equal to x. Since the non-poor do not, by definition, contribute to total poverty, we have that $\pi_k(x) = 0$ if $x > z(k)$. For those below the poverty line, $\pi_k(x)$ equals one for the headcount poverty measure, $z(k)-x$ for the poverty gap measure, etc. Total poverty in the population is given by the sum of each subgroup's poverty:

$$
\begin{aligned}
P(z(1), \ldots, z(K)) &= \sum_{k=1}^{K} \int_{0}^{z(k)} \pi_k(x) f(x; k) dx \\
&= \sum_{k=1}^{K} P(k; z(k)).
\end{aligned} \qquad [2]
$$

For expositional simplicity, we will sometimes denote $P(z(1), \ldots, z(K))$ simply by P.

An example of such a poverty index is the sum across groups of the *FGT* poverty indices (Foster, Greer, and Thorbecke 1984) for each group, where each group has its own poverty line. Denote the $FGT(\alpha)$ index for subgroup k and parameter α, multiplied by the population share of group k, by

$$
P^{\alpha}(k; z(k)) = \int_{0}^{z(k)} (z(k) - x)^{\alpha} f(x; k) dx. \qquad [3]
$$

Total poverty as measured by the *FGT* index is then:

$$
P^{\alpha}(z(1), \ldots, z(k)) = \sum_{k=1}^{K} P^{\alpha}(k; z(k)). \qquad [4]
$$

Note that $P^0(z(1), \ldots, z(K))$ is the population headcount, with each subgroup k being assigned its specific poverty line $z(k)$. Similarly, $P^1(z(1), \ldots, z(K))$ is the average poverty gap in the population, again with each subgroup k being assigned its specific poverty line $z(k)$.[4] Other multidimensional additive poverty indices can be defined along similar lines, extending, for instance, the unidimensional Watts (1968) or Chakravarty (1983) poverty indices.

Rather than focus on any one poverty index, however, we wish to establish conditions under which poverty will be lower in one group than in another for any poverty index belonging to a broad class of indices, in the tradition of the stochastic dominance approach to poverty comparisons (Atkinson, 1987; Foster and Shorrocks 1988*a*, *b*, *c*). The conditions for such poverty dominance differ for poverty indices that are continuous rather than discontinuous at the poverty line. We treat the continuous case first because it is somewhat simpler.

Poverty indices that are continuous at the poverty line

Define $\Pi^1(z(1), \ldots, z(K))$ to be a class of multidimensional first-order poverty indices.[5] $\Pi^1(z(1), \ldots, z(K))$ includes all of the additive P indices defined in equation [2] that satisfy three conditions:

[4] We will also make use of poverty indices for which poverty is measured at the same poverty line for each group, denoted $P^{\alpha}(z(1), \ldots, z(k)) = \sum P^{\alpha}(k, z)$, where the poverty line z is independent of the group k.

[5] These indices are called 'first order' because the proof of Theorem 1 makes use of the first integral of the income distribution, i.e. the cumulative density function. A similar (but smaller)

$$z(1) \geq z(2) \geq \ldots \geq z(K) \quad [5]$$

$$\pi_1^{(1)}(x) \leq \pi_2^{(1)}(x) \leq \ldots \leq \pi_K^{(1)}(x) \leq 0, \forall x \quad [6]$$

$$\pi_k(z(k)) = 0, \forall k = 1, \ldots, K \quad [7]$$

where $\pi_1^{(1)}(x)$ is the first-order derivative of $\pi_1(x)$ with respect to x. The first condition says that the poverty lines in the continuous dimension for the subgroups can be ordered from the poorest (neediest) group to the richest (least needy) group. This is a sensible ordering since we assume that for the same value of x, group k has lower well-being than group $k+1$, and so on.

The second condition orders the first derivatives of $\pi_k(x)$ with respect to x. This assumption says that the impact of an increase in x is no smaller the poorer the person is along discrete dimension k. Roughly speaking, this assumption says that x and k are substitutes in the production of well-being. In most circumstances, this is a reasonable assumption—improving one dimension of well-being for those who are poorer in another dimension should generate greater poverty reduction than the same improvement for those who are richer in that dimension. However, it is possible that complementarity in the production of two dimensions of well-being might force a reversal. For example, consider poverty measured in two dimensions, ownership of paintings (a continuous variable) and ability to see (a discrete state). Even though it is reasonable to consider being blind as worse than being able to see, other things being equal, transferring paintings from those who can see to those who cannot will not increase their well-being or reduce poverty measured in these two dimensions, but the opposite transfer would.[6] We do not consider such cases in this chapter, in part because we feel that they are less empirically relevant.

The third condition assumes continuity of the poverty measure at the poverty line for each subgroup k.

Define $\Delta P(z(1)\ldots, z(K)) = P_A(z(1)\ldots, z(K)) - P_B(z(1)\ldots, z(K))$, and $\Delta P^\alpha(z(1)\ldots, z(K))$ and $\Delta P^\alpha(k; z(k))$ analogously. The above assumptions lead to the following result for all poverty measures in the class $\Pi^1(z(1), \ldots, z(K))$:

Theorem 1. (First-order poverty dominance for heterogeneous populations)

$$\begin{aligned}
&\Delta P(\zeta(1), \ldots, \zeta(K)) > 0, \\
&\forall P(\zeta(1), \ldots, \zeta(K)) \in \Pi^1(\zeta(1), \ldots, \zeta(K)) \\
&\text{and } \forall \zeta(k) \in [0, z(k)], k = 1, \ldots, K \\
&\text{iff} \sum_{k=1}^{i} \Delta P^0(k; \zeta) > 0, \forall \zeta \in [0, z(i)] \text{ and } \forall i = 1, \ldots, K.
\end{aligned} \quad [8]$$

class of second order indices uses a second integration of the density, and so on for higher orders of poverty measures.

[6] Bourguignon and Chakravarty (2003) and Duclos, Sahn, and Younger (2006*a*, 2006*c*) have more detailed discussions of this assumption for the continuous case.

Proof: See the Appendix for a method of proof that follows Jenkins and Lambert (1993) and Chambaz and Maurin (1998).

Recall that $P^0(k;\ \zeta)$ is the $FGT(0)$ measure, or headcount, for subgroup k and poverty line ζ, times the population share of subgroup k. Hence $\sum_{k=1}^{i} P^0(k;\zeta)$ shows, as a proportion of the total population, the number of individuals below ζ in the i most deprived, or neediest, subgroups. $\sum_{k=1}^{i} P^0(k;\zeta)$ can then be termed the cumulative headcount index at the poverty line ζ for the i most deprived subgroups. The first-order dominance condition [8] requires that this cumulative headcount be greater in bivariate distribution A than in bivariate distribution B, whatever the number i of groups that we wish to include, and at all common poverty lines $0 \leq \zeta \leq z(i)$. Note, however, that it does not require that every subgroup k have independently more poverty in A than in B, nor does it require that the population headcount (with each subgroup being assigned its own particular poverty line rather than a common line ζ) be greater in distribution A than in distribution B.

To see this more clearly, consider the case of poverty comparisons involving only two groups of individuals, $K = 2$, with $z(1)$ being the poverty line of the more deprived group and $z(2)$ the poverty line of the less deprived group. Multidimensional dominance is checked first by comparing the headcount of those in group 1 whose value of x falls below poverty lines ζ between 0 and $z(1)$, and then by comparing the combined poverty headcounts of the two groups at all common poverty lines between 0 and $z(2)$. This is illustrated in Figure 9.1, where $\zeta(1)$ and $\zeta(2)$ denote the poverty lines at which poverty in each of the two subgroups is assessed. For $\Pi^1(z(1), z(2))$ dominance, we need to compare the global poverty headcount at all of the combinations of poverty lines on the $\zeta(1)$ axis up to $z(1)$, that is, up to point G, and on the 45-degree line (up to point E). Comparing poverty for the combination of poverty lines on the $\zeta(1)$ axis amounts to checking the sign of $\Delta P^0(1;\zeta)$ for $\zeta \in [0, z(1)]$. Comparing poverty for the combination of poverty lines on the 45-degree line (until point E) amounts to checking the sign of $\sum_{k=1}^{2} \Delta P^0(k;\ \zeta)$ for $\zeta \in [0,\ z(2)]$.

If the dominance conditions in [8] are met, then we obtain a robust ordering of multidimensional poverty. Indeed, we can then assert with confidence that all of the multidimensional poverty indices contained in $\Pi^1(\zeta(1),\ \ldots,\ \zeta(K))$ will show more poverty in A than in B, and this, regardless of the selection of any particular combination of poverty lines, so long as they belong to the set defined by $\zeta(k) \in [0, z(k)], k = 1,\ \ldots, K$.

Poverty indices that are discontinuous at the poverty line

Even though Theorem 1 makes use of the headcount poverty measures $P^0(k;\ \zeta)$ to check for poverty dominance, the theorem does not establish poverty dominance for the headcount, because the theorem is applicable only to

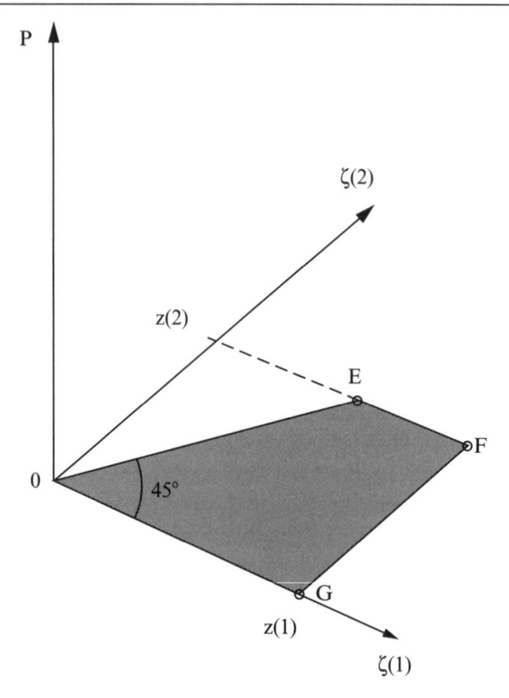

Figure 9.1 Domain for dominance testing

poverty measures that are continuous at the poverty line.[7] The dominance condition needed to include the headcount and other indices that are discontinuous at the poverty line in the manner of, for example, Bourguignon and Fields (1997), is more stringent. Replace assumption [7] by the following:

$$\pi_1(x) \geq \pi_2(x) \geq \ldots \geq \pi_K(x) \geq 0, \forall x. \qquad [9]$$

This condition requires that the poverty measure for group k evaluated at a given x be at least as great as the poverty measure in the next neediest group $k+1$ evaluated at the same value of x. This must hold for all k and for all x. A larger class $\tilde{\Pi}^1(z(1), \ldots, z(K))$ of additive poverty indices then includes all the P indices defined in equation [2] that satisfy assumptions [5], [6], and [9]. The traditional headcount index, by which total poverty is measured by assigning each subgroup its own poverty line, belongs to $\tilde{\Pi}^1$ but not to Π^1. We thus expect the dominance conditions for $\tilde{\Pi}^1$ to be correspondingly more demanding. The definition of $\tilde{\Pi}^1(z(1), \ldots, z(K))$ leads to the following equivalence:

[7] The difference is that Theorem 1 refers to sums of group-specific poverty measures at a common poverty line ζ, while the actual headcount must apply to each group's specific poverty line $z(k)$.

Theorem 2. (First-order poverty dominance without continuity)

$$\Delta P(z(1), \ldots, z(K)) > 0,$$

$$\forall P(z(1), \ldots, z(K)) \in \tilde{\Pi}^1(z(1), \ldots, z(K))$$

$$\text{iff} \begin{cases} \sum_{k=1}^{i} \Delta P^0(k; \zeta) > 0, \forall \zeta \in [0, z(i)] \text{ and } \forall i = 1, \ldots K \\ \text{and} \\ \sum_{k=1}^{i} \Delta P^0(k; z(k)) > 0, \forall i = 1, \ldots K. \end{cases} \qquad [10]$$

Proof: see the Appendix.

The first condition in [10] is identical to the one already discussed in [8]. In addition, we must check that the cumulative headcount differences are positive when each group k has its specific poverty line set to $z(k)$. That is the second condition in [10]. In the two-group case of Figure 9.1, this adds to the previously-discussed test locations one more test at point F on the figure. More importantly, however, note also that the combinations of poverty lines over which the $\tilde{\Pi}^1(z(1), \ldots, z(K))$ ranking is robust are far more restricted than for the previous result. In fact, dominance by [10] ensures robustness only at the exact combination of lines $\{z(1), \ldots, z(K)\}$. To extend the results to all of the poverty lines $\zeta(k)$ contained in $[0, z(k)]$ as we did in the continuous case, we must also check the sign of the cumulative headcount when each subgroup is assigned its specific poverty line, instead of a common value ζ. This new condition would need to be checked for all combinations of poverty lines (other than $\{z(1), \ldots, z(K)\}$) for which we would wish the poverty ordering $\tilde{\Pi}^1$ to be robust. For the two-group case, this requires checking for dominance at all of the combinations of poverty lines defined by the shaded area of Figure 9.1. This is clearly a more stringent condition than that stated in Theorem 1, and it explains why we might wish to limit the generality of poverty orderings to a continuous class such as $\Pi^1(\zeta(1), \ldots, \zeta(K))$.[8]

Higher-order dominance comparisons

It is possible to extend the above reasoning to any arbitrary order of dominance. For a given order of dominance s, we would assume continuity at the poverty line up to the $(s-1)$th order. We would also require conditions on the sth order derivative $\pi_k^{(s)}(y; z(k))$, and on the ranking of these derivatives across population subgroups. Ordering conditions would use the sums of the $P^{s-1}(k; \zeta)$ curves.

[8] See Atkinson (2003) for a discussion of this.

For second-order dominance, this would require that $\pi_1^2(x) \geq \ldots \geq \pi_K^2(x) \geq 0, \forall y$. Indices in Π^2 would then be convex in y and thus decreasing in mean-preserving equalizing transfers of living standards; that is, they would obey the Pigou-Dalton principle of transfers within each group. The convexity of $\pi_k(x)$, and thus the importance of the Pigou-Dalton principle of transfers, would also be assumed to be decreasing in k and hence increasing in the needs of the subgroups. At a given x, the greater the needs of a subgroup of individuals, the greater the poverty-relieving effect of a mean-preserving equalizing transfer within that subgroup. The dominance conditions would then use $P^1(k;\zeta)$, the average poverty gap in subgroup k for a poverty line ζ multiplied by the population share of subgroup k, and would cumulate it across the i most deprived subgroups to give $\sum_{k=1}^{i} P^1(k;\zeta)$. When this cumulative average poverty gap is greater in A than in B, whatever the number i of neediest subgroups included, and at all common poverty lines $0 \leq \zeta \leq z(i)$, poverty in A is unambiguously greater than in B for all of the indices in $\Pi^2(\zeta(1), \ldots, \zeta(K))$ and at all of the poverty lines $\zeta \in [0, z(i)]$. For the 2-group case, the graphical combinations of poverty lines over which this condition must be tested are the same as in the discussion of Figure 9.1 for condition [8].[9]

9.2 Estimation

Suppose that we have two random samples of N independently and identically distributed observations[10] drawn from the joint distribution of membership into group k and of the indicator of well-being x, one sample from each of two distributions A and B. These samples from A and B could be paired in the sense that they could form a panel with which to make poverty comparisons at two points in time, or to represent two different states for a single cross-section, for example poverty comparisons with and without a particular tax or transfer payment. But there are also cases in which distributions A and B are independent, such as when we wish to compare poverty for one population at two points in time with two independent cross-section samples of that population. We can write these observations, drawn from a population $L = A, B$, as (k_i^L, x_i^L), $i = 1, \ldots, N$. A natural estimator of the sum of the dominance curves $\sum_{k=1}^{j} P_L^{\alpha}(k; z(k))$ is then given by:

$$\sum_{k=1}^{j} \hat{P}_L^{\alpha}(k; z(k)) = \frac{1}{N} \sum_{i=1}^{N} \left(z(k_i^L) - x_i^L\right)_+^{\alpha} I(k_i^L \leq j) \qquad [11]$$

[9] More discussion of this can be found in Duclos and Makdissi (2005).

[10] Most survey data are not i.i.d. because the survey is both stratified and clustered. See for instance the discussion of survey design effects by Stata Corporation (2005). While this does not affect our poverty estimates, it will affect our estimates of the standard errors. In particular, it is likely that the standard errors that we report in the examples below will be too small because of the clustering of the survey data.

where $I(\cdot)$ equals 1 if the argument is true and 0 otherwise. Expression [11] has the convenient property of being a simple sum of IID variables. We can then state:

Theorem 3. For $L = A, B$ and $M = A, B$, let the joint population moments of order 2 of $(z(k^L) - x^L)_+^\alpha I(k^L \leq j)$ and $(z(k^M) - x^M)_+^\alpha I(k^M \leq j)$ be finite, for all $j = 1, \ldots, K$.

Then $N^{1/2}\left(\sum_{k=1}^{j} \hat{P}_L^\alpha(k; z(k)) - \sum_{k=1}^{j} P_L^\alpha(k; z(k))\right)$ and

$N^{1/2}\left(\sum_{k=1}^{j} \hat{P}_M^\alpha(k; z(k)) - \sum_{k=1}^{j} P_M^\alpha(k; z(k))\right)$ are asymptotically normal with mean zero and with asymptotic covariance structure given by:

$$\lim_{N\to\infty} N \operatorname{cov}\left(\sum_{k=1}^{j} \hat{P}_L^\alpha(k; z(k)), \sum_{k=1}^{j} \hat{P}_M^\alpha(k; z(k))\right) = E\big((z(k^L) - x^L)_+^\alpha I(k^L \leq j)(z(k^M) - x^M)_+^\alpha I(k^M \leq j)\big) - \sum_{k=1}^{j} P_L^\alpha(k; z(k)) \sum_{k=1}^{j} P_M^\alpha(k; z(k)). \quad [12]$$

Proof: see the Appendix.

When A and B are independent, we need only replace N by either N_A or N_B and note that the covariance between the independent estimators of A and B will then be zero.

9.3 Multiple discrete variables

In principle, it is straightforward to extend Theorems 1 or 2 to the case of one continuous and multiple discrete measures of well-being: we only need to combine the discrete variables into one grouping. So, for example, if we have a literacy indicator and an enfranchisement indicator, each with only two possible values, then we create a combination of these variables with four values: illiterate/disenfranchised, literate/disenfranchised, illiterate/enfranchised, and literate/enfranchised. The only problem with this strategy is that the ordering of the four outcomes from poorest to richest (or most to least needy) is not always clear. While illiterate/disenfranchised is obviously the worst outcome, and literate/enfranchised is the best, we cannot say which of the other two is better or worse. To overcome this, we must check the dominance conditions of Theorem 1 or 2 using both of the possible orderings. Formally, the result is obtained for Theorem 1 by supposing two discrete indicators, say k and k^*, with K and K^* different possible values, and by assuming that the poverty indices $P(z(1, 1), z(1, 2), \ldots, z(1, K^*,), z(2, 1), \ldots, z(K, K^*))$ defined over these two discrete and one continuous indicators satisfy the following conditions:

$$z(k, k^*) \geq z(l, k^*) \text{ if } k < l \qquad [13a]$$

$$z(k, k^*) \geq z(k, l^*) \text{ if } k^* < l^* \qquad [13b]$$

$$\pi^{(1)}_{k,k^*}(x) \leq \pi^{(1)}_{k+1,k^*} \leq 0, \forall x, k, k^* \qquad [14]$$

$$\pi^{(1)}_{k,k^*}(x) \leq \pi^{(1)}_{k,k^*+1} \leq 0, \forall x, k, k^* \qquad [15]$$

$$\pi_k(z(k, k^*)) = 0, \forall k = 1, \ldots, K \text{ and } \forall k^* = 1, \ldots, K^*. \qquad [16]$$

Define the class of such poverty indices as $\dot{\Pi}^1((z(1,1), \ldots, z(K, K^*)))$ and, as above, let

$$P^\alpha(k, k^*; z) = \int_0^z (z - x)^\alpha f(x; k, k^*)dx \qquad [17]$$

where $f(x; k, k^*)$ is the probability density at x in groups k and k^* normalized such that its integral over x gives the population share of those in groups k and k^*. We then have:

Theorem 4. (First-order poverty dominance for two discrete indicators and one continuous one.)

$$\begin{aligned} &\Delta P(\zeta(1,1), \ldots, \zeta(K, K^*)) > 0, \\ &\forall P(\zeta(1,1), \ldots, \zeta(K, K^*)) \in \dot{\Pi}^1(\zeta(1,1), \ldots, \zeta(K, K^*)) \text{ and} \\ &\forall \zeta(k, k^*) \in [0, z(k, k^*)], k = 1, \ldots, K, k^* = 1, \ldots, K^* \\ &\text{iff } \sum_{k=1}^{i} \sum_{k^*=1}^{j} \Delta P^0(k, k^*; \zeta) > 0, \forall \zeta \in [0, z(i, j)] \text{ and} \\ &\forall i = 1, \ldots, K, j = 1, \ldots, K^*. \end{aligned} \qquad [18]$$

The proof is analogous to that of Theorem 1. Again, this is equivalent to checking the dominance conditions of Theorem 1 using all of the possible orderings of the discrete indicators.

9.4 Applications

Our first example in this section obviates the equivalence scale problem by using the method first suggested by Atkinson (1992). We ask which type of transfer payment reduces poverty more in Romania, child allowances or social security pensions? Because the answer may depend on the choice of equivalence scale, we will avoid that choice altogether. Instead, we use bivariate dominance tests where the second dimension of well-being is household size, an indicator of greater needs. The neediest group is households with six or more people,[11] the next neediest contains households with five people, and so on. The data come from the Romania Integrated Household Survey (Government of Romania 1994). The other well-being variable is household income, plus the relevant transfer payment (child allowances or social security pensions). We have standardized these payments so that they have the same mean, thus ensuring that the tests do not merely reflect the fact that one programme is very large relative to the other.

Table 9.1 gives the *t*-statistics for the differences in the dominance curves of the neediest group, the two most needy groups, and so on, through to the difference for all groups, as required by Theorem 1. The difference is the ordinate of the dominance curve for income plus child allowances minus that for income plus social security pensions, so a positive *t*-statistic indicates that social security pensions are more poverty-reducing than child allowances, and vice-versa for a negative statistic. For large households, child allowances reduce poverty by more than social security payments, regardless of the poverty line chosen. But this result is reversed once we include households with only two people, where the dominance curves now cross or are not statistically different from each other, and where social security payments appear to be more beneficial to poorer households. The same pattern holds for higher order dominance comparisons, that is, for $s=2$ and $s=3$, involving the poverty gap and poverty severity curves, respectively. This suggests that we cannot make any robust statement about the comparative poverty-reducing impact of these two transfer payments without excluding households of size 2 and 1. Thus,

Table 9.1 *t*-statistics for differences between household income and size with child allowances vs. with social security (Romania)

	Household size					
Household income	6 or more	5 or more	4 or more	3 or more	2 or more	1 or more
43,527	−34.2	−29.6	−23.4	−11.9	20.1	31.8
63,000	−41.8	−36.4	−30.2	−16.6	17.4	26.3
78,602	−48.1	−42.5	−35.3	−20.6	13.3	18.2
94,671	−52.8	−46.2	−39.0	−23.8	8.0	10.5
112,460	−55.7	−50.2	−42.0	−27.1	2.9	4.4
129,630	−57.7	−50.8	−42.6	−27.0	−0.2	1.1
147,520	−58.8	−51.5	−44.2	−28.9	−5.6	−4.1
...	...	...	...	...	...	...
756,240	−8.3	−8.4	−7.5	−5.9	−2.2	−1.4

Notes: Values in column 1 are the vingtiles of the distribution of expenditures. A positive *t*-statistic in columns 2 through 7 indicates greater poverty for income plus child allowances than for income plus social security pensions. The '. . .' indicate 11 further test points for which all the *t*-statistics are negative and significant.

Source: Authors' calculation from the Romania Integrated Household Survey, 1994.

[11] There are very few households with more than six people in the sample.

any dominance result derived with a particular equivalence scale will not be robust to the choice of that scale in this case, a result that is not too surprising given the very different demographic profiles of households receiving these two transfers.

Our second example considers a case in which poverty is measured in two dimensions, household expenditure per capita and adult literacy (a binary discrete variable). We consider the change in poverty in Peru between 1985 and 1994, using data from the *Encuesta Nacional de Hogares sobre Medición de Niveles de Vida* for those two years. This period spanned a significant economic crisis, including the hyperinflation of 1990–91. Real income fell significantly during this period, but literacy increased, from 82 to 87 per cent. Table 9.2, summarizing the dominance comparison, has a similar format to Table 9.1, but the groups are now defined by literacy.[12] We assume that, for a given level of expenditure, adults who cannot read and write have lower well-being than those who can. Thus, the first group is the illiterate population. The *t*-statistics are for the 1985 dominance curve minus the 1994 curve. For the entire sample (both illiterate and literate people), column 3 shows a clear worsening of poverty due to the economic crisis. However, for poverty lines at or above the 40th percentile of the expenditure distribution (2634 nuevo soles, the Peruvian currency), column 2 shows that the conditions of Theorem 1 are not met, once we take into account the need for the difference in the dominance curves to be statistically different from zero. Even though poverty among illiterate Peruvians increased unambiguously during this period, the theorem requires that poverty normalized by the population share of the cumulative groups increase. But the illiteracy rate fell from 18 to 13 per cent between 1985 and 1994, which means that $P^0(k;\zeta)$ (which includes the normalization) for the illiterate group was greater in 1985 than 1994 at poverty lines above 2634 nuevo soles, so the dominance is inconclusive. In effect, the larger population share for illiterate people in 1985 overwhelms the greater prevalence of poverty among the smaller group of illiterate people in 1994.

In the previous example, using a bivariate poverty comparison impedes our ability to get a clear dominance between distributions, even though the univariate expenditure distribution shows a statistically significant difference in poverty. Although the stricter conditions for multivariate dominance might make us think that this is likely to be the norm, it is also possible that, when there is no univariate dominance in the continuous dimension, bivariate comparisons may produce clear cut dominance results, as we demonstrate in our next example.

Atkinson and Bourguignon (1982) distinguish 'union' from 'intersection' definitions of multivariate poverty. In the former, you are considered poor if you fall below the poverty line in either dimension. In the latter, you are considered poor only if you fall below both poverty lines. Duclos, Sahn,

[12] The comparison is for those fifteen years old or older.

Table 9.2 *t*-statistics for differences between per capita expenditures for literate and illiterate Peruvians, 1985 minus 1994

Expenditure per capita	Illiterate	All
915	−15.2	−17.4
1,166	−15.9	−24.6
1,436	−16.4	−29.7
1,663	−14.6	−33.9
1,883	−10.9	−36.7
2,122	−7.9	−39.5
2,350	−5.3	−41.8
2,634	−0.8	−43.2
2,926	5.8	−45.1
...	...	...
12,842	287.6	−27.8

Notes: Values in column 1 are the vingtiles of the distribution of deflated expenditures per capita, measured in nuevo soles per capita per month. A positive *t*-statistic in columns 2 and 3 indicates greater poverty in 1985 than in 1994. The '...' indicate 9 further test points for which all the *t*-statistics in column 2 are positive and significant, and those in column 3 are negative and significant.

Source: *Encuesta Nacional de Hogares sobre Medición de Niveles de Vida*, 1985 and 1994.

and Younger (2006*a*) show that union poverty comparisons require univariate dominance in both dimensions, but intersection poverty comparisons do not. They give examples of cases in which there is no univariate dominance in one or both dimensions, but there is bivariate dominance for a set of intersection poverty measures. A similar result is possible in the present case of one discrete and one continuous measure of well-being. Table 9.3 compares poverty in Ecuador between 1998 and 1999, also a period of significant macroeconomic turmoil. The comparison is in two dimensions: real household expenditures per capita and area of residence, where we suppose that well-being is lower in rural than in urban areas, other things being equal.[13] The third column shows that there is neither univariate dominance in the dimension of household expenditures nor bivariate dominance as defined in Theorem 1. However, column 2 shows that income poverty did decline unambiguously in rural areas for any choice of poverty line. Suppose that any reasonable poverty line in the dimension of area of residence is chosen such that rural residents are poor and urban residents are not.[14] Then intersection poverty measures will consider only those in rural areas (and with incomes below the poverty line in that dimension) as poor. Column 2 shows that there is a dominance result for these intersection poverty measures, even though there is no univariate income

[13] This might be because urban areas have better public services, or because only urban areas have sufficient population density to bring forth certain markets—for entertainment or public transport, e.g. such goods simply are not available in rural areas, lowering welfare there.

[14] We are not saying that only income poor people live in rural areas and *vice versa*. We refer to poverty in the dimension of area of residence.

Table 9.3 *t*-statistics for differences between household expenditures per capita for rural and urban residents in Ecuador, 1998 minus 1999

Expenditure per capita	Rural	All
35,401	2.5	1.0
48,323	4.0	2.5
56,506	3.9	2.9
66,447	5.0	1.6
75,234	6.9	1.2
84,304	6.5	0.0
92,862	6.2	0.2
101,830	5.5	−1.2
111,330	7.4	−1.2
123,420	7.9	−1.4
135,690	7.6	−1.5
149,940	7.7	−1.3
167,140	7.1	−2.1
186,530	6.8	−1.7
208,850	8.6	−0.7
242,520	10.3	−1.0
288,660	11.8	−1.3
365,330	14.6	−0.8
541,410	19.6	−1.1

Notes: Values in column 1 are the vingtiles of the distribution of real expenditures per capita, measured in sucres per capita per month. A positive *t*-statistic in columns 2 and 3 indicates greater poverty in 1998 than in 1999.

Source: *Encuesta sobre Condiciones de Vida*, 1998 and 1999.

poverty dominance in this case. (Note also the importance here of taking into account statistical significance in checking for univariate poverty dominance.)

Our final example illustrates the case of poverty comparisons involving one continuous variable and two discrete ones. The data come from the fourth and twelfth waves of the British Household Panel Survey, carried out in 1994 and 2002, respectively. We measure well-being in the dimensions of real income per adult equivalent, education status, and health status. The latter two variables are discrete ones. Education status refers to the highest qualification attained, and health status to whether or not the respondent reported that his or her daily activities were limited by ill-health.[15] As Theorem 4 shows, poverty dominance requires comparisons across all the possible cumulative combinations of education and health status, regardless of the order of accumulation. Despite these rather demanding criteria, we find that multidimensional poverty declined over this period in Britain for income poverty lines up to the 55th percentile of income distribution.[16] The poverty rate in this period

[15] We use only the observations with data available in all waves of the survey. While not strictly necessary—each of the waves is representative of the British population—using this subsample provides a way to ensure that the measure of self-reported health status is consistent across the various waves of interviews.

[16] The table for these results is large (20 × 20) and thus not reported here. It is available from Duclos, Sahn, and Younger (2006*b*).

was about 19 per cent, so it is safe to conclude that multivariate poverty declined during this period for all reasonable poverty lines.

As a more general check of this correspondence, we made trivariate poverty comparisons for each wave of the first 12 waves of the BHPS (except the ninth) for these combinations of variables: income/education/health; income/education/happiness; and income/health/happiness.[17] We set the maximum poverty line at the median of the joint income distribution for all waves. For the income/education/health comparisons similar to the one reported above, the multivariate comparison rejects the null in favour of dominance in 15 of the 43 cases in which the univariate comparison for income per adult equivalent rejects the null.[18] For the income/happiness/education comparisons, we reject the null in the multivariate tests in 26 of 43 cases. But in the income/health/happiness comparisons, we reach the same conclusion in only 7 of 43 cases.[19] Thus, whereas use of the multivariate comparisons makes it more difficult to find a statistically significant change in poverty over time, it does not make such a conclusion impossible.

9.5 Conclusions

This chapter has drawn on two literatures to which Tony Atkinson was an early and influential contributor: one uses stochastic dominance methods to make general poverty comparisons (Atkinson 1987), and another studies poverty comparisons involving multiple dimensions (Atkinson 1992; Atkinson and Bourguignon 1982). Drawing on both those literatures, we have shown that it is possible to make robust multidimensional poverty comparisons when one or more of the dimensions of well-being is summarized using a discrete variable. This is useful because many of the measures of well-being that are available are either inherently discrete or are recorded as such. We have also seen that to make such comparisons, it is important to distinguish between discontinuous headcount-like multidimensional poverty indices and continuous ones. The importance of this distinction is well understood in the univariate poverty literature, being linked *inter alia* to whether poverty indices obey the Pigou-Dalton principle. Finally, we have derived the sampling

[17] The happiness question is 'Have you recently been feeling reasonably happy, all things considered?' The possible responses are: more so than usual, about the same as usual, less so than usual, much less than usual. Wave 9 did not include this question, so we did not use that wave in our comparisons.

[18] These are the only interesting comparisons. If the univariate comparison fails to reject the null, the multivariate comparisons must also fail to do so, so the correspondence is perfect in that case.

[19] In the latter two cases, the correspondence is considerably higher if we lower the maximum reasonable poverty line to the 40th percentile.

distributions for our multivariate poverty comparisons, so that they can be stated in a statistically meaningful way.

The examples presented highlight several key points about multivariate poverty comparisons that distinguish them from the standard univariate case. First, because multivariate comparisons appear to be more demanding than univariate ones, there is a concern that these tests will not be able to reject the null of non-dominance in practice. While this is true for most of the comparisons that we consider, we found many cases in which the null is rejected using surveys with sample sizes of a few thousand households. Second, there are cases when a multivariate poverty comparison rejects the null for an intersection definition of poverty even when the univariate income comparison does not. This can occur when income poverty declines for a subset of the poorest groups of households but does not for all households. Third, for a lower range of poverty lines, it is also possible for multivariate poverty to increase even if the share of households in the poorest subset of discrete groups declines. This happens if income poverty among the poorest groups rises so much that the number of poor people in those groups increases even though the total number of poor people in the population declines. Each of these examples shows how a multivariate analysis can be richer and more subtle than poverty comparisons based on income alone.

These conclusions point to some of the ways in which robust multidimensional poverty analysis can and should move forward in the future. For example, it is an empirical issue whether methods such as those proposed in this chapter have empirical power to detect differences in multidimensional poverty across time and space. When dominance testing succeeds, robust poverty conclusions can be drawn—as illustrated by the analysis in this chapter—but much remains to be done in order to check how frequently such robust rankings arise.

If dominance testing fails, two different views can be expressed. First, it can be concluded that alternative poverty measurement procedures may produce different poverty rankings of the two distributions being compared, and that trying to rank them in terms of their poverty is therefore imprudent. This may be viewed as a negative result, but it also alerts us to the potential sensitivity of poverty comparisons to the measurement procedure used. Secondly, it can be argued that poverty dominance methods are insufficiently informative in such cases and that there is a need to focus on a more limited subset of measurement procedures. The definition and the interpretation of such subsets remains an important area for future research. How this more limited focus can help generate poverty rankings more often is also an issue that further work could usefully address.

It is also clear that statistical inference issues need to be taken more seriously in the applied welfare literature. In much current applied work on poverty, poverty estimates are treated as if they were true population values. The statistical inference procedures derived in this chapter also need to be extended since the standard errors we reported do not take into account, for example, survey design features such as clustering and stratification. See Duclos and Araar (2006: Chs 16 and 17) for a discussion of this issue. Finally, dominance testing involves tests of multiple null hypotheses, and how to take into account the joint distribution of the test statistics is an important topic for future research.

Appendix

Proof of Theorem 1.
The proof follows the line of Atkinson (1992) and Jenkins and Lambert (1993). We first use [2] to integrate by parts the difference ΔP. We find:

$$\begin{aligned} \Delta P = & \sum_{k=1}^{K} \pi_k(z(k))\Delta P^0(k; z(k)) \\ & - \sum_{k=1}^{K} \int_0^{z(k)} \pi_k^{(1)}(x)\Delta P^0(k; x)dx. \end{aligned} \quad [19]$$

Recall the continuity assumption that $\pi_k(z(k)) = 0, \ \forall k$. For $\Delta P > 0$, we thus need to show that

$$\sum_{k=1}^{K} \int_0^{z(k)} \pi_k^{(1)}(x)\Delta P^0(k; x)dx < 0. \quad [20]$$

Recall that $\pi_k^{(1)}(x) = 0$ if $x > z(k)$; combined with [5], we can then rewrite [20] as:

$$\int_0^{z(1)} \sum_{k=1}^{K} \pi_k^{(1)}(x)\Delta P^0(k; x)dx < 0. \quad [21]$$

The inner sum in [21] can be rewritten as:

$$\sum_{k=1}^{K} \pi_k^{(1)}(x)\Delta P^0(k; x) = \quad [22]$$

$$\pi_K^{(1)}(x) \sum_{l=1}^{K} \Delta P^0(l; x) + \left(\pi_{K-1}^{(1)}(x) - \pi_K^{(1)}(x)\right) \sum_{l=1}^{K-1} \Delta P^0(l; x) \quad [23]$$

$$+\ldots+\left(\pi_1^{(1)}(x)-\pi_2^{(1)}(x)\right)\Delta P^0(1;x) \tag{24}$$

Denoting $\pi_{K+1}^{(1)}(x)\equiv 0$, we can thus rewrite the right-hand-side of [21] as

$$\int_0^{z(1)}\sum_{i=1}^{K}\left[\left(\pi_i^{(1)}(x)-\pi_{i+1}^{(1)}(x)\right)\sum_{k=1}^{i}\Delta P^0(k;x)\right]dx. \tag{25}$$

Note that by the definition of the class of indices $\Pi^1(\zeta(1),\ldots,\zeta(K))$, $\pi_i^{(1)}(x)-\pi_{i+1}^{(1)}(x)\leq 0,\ \forall i=1,\ldots,K$, with strict inequality for some values of i over some range of $x\in[0,\zeta(i)]$ (for the indices to be non-degenerate). Hence, if $\sum_{k=1}^{i}\Delta P^0(k;\zeta)>0, \forall\,\zeta\in[0,z(i)]$ and $\forall i=1,\ldots,K$, then it must be that [21] holds for all $P(z(1),\ldots,z(K))\in\Pi^1(z(1),\ldots,z(K))$. But this also implies that $\Delta P(\zeta(1),\ldots,\zeta(K))>0$, $\forall P(\zeta(1),\ldots,\zeta(K))\in\Pi^1(\zeta(1),\ldots,\zeta(K))$, and $\forall\zeta(k)\in[0,z(k)],\ k=1,\ldots,K$. This proves the sufficiency of condition [8].

For the necessity part, it suffices to consider any particular case in which $\sum_{k=1}^{i}\Delta P^0(k;\zeta)\leq 0$, for some $\zeta\in[z^-(i),z^+(i)]$ and for some value of i. Consider then a poverty index that belongs to $\Pi^1(z(1),\ldots,z(K))$ such that $\pi_k^{(1)}(x)-\pi_{k+1}^{(1)}(x)=0$ everywhere, except for $k=i$ and over that range $\zeta\in[z^-(i),z^+(i)]$ over which $\sum_{k=1}^{i}\Delta P^0(k;\zeta)\leq 0$. Then, by [25], $\Delta P\leq 0$ for that index, which therefore shows the necessity of condition [8].

Proof of Theorem 2.

Consider again equation [19]:

$$\begin{aligned}\Delta P=&\sum_{k=1}^{K}\pi_k(z(k))\Delta P^0(k;z(k))\\&-\sum_{k=1}^{K}\int_0^{z(k)}\pi_k^{(1)}(x)\Delta P^0(k;x)dx.\end{aligned} \tag{26}$$

The second line of condition [10] guarantees the non-negativity of the second line of [26], as shown before in the proof of Theorem 1. Denoting again $\pi_{K+1}^{(1)}(y)\equiv 0$, rewrite the first term on the right-hand side of [26] as:

$$\sum_{i=1}^{K}\left[(\pi_i(z(i))-\pi_{i+1}(z(i+1)))\sum_{k=1}^{i}\Delta P^0(k;z(i))\right]. \tag{27}$$

Note that by the definition of the class of indices $\tilde{\Pi}^1(z(1),\ldots,z(K))$, $\pi_i(z(i))-\pi_{i+1}(z(i+1))\leq 0,\ \forall i=1,\ldots,K$. Hence, if $\sum_{k=1}^{i}\Delta P^0(k;z(k))>0,\ \forall i=1,\ldots,K$, then the first part on the right-hand-side of [26] is also non-negative. The combination of the first and of the second parts of condition [10] guarantees that $\Delta P>0$.

The necessity of condition [10] proceeds as for the proof of Theorem 1.

Proof of Theorem 3.
For each distribution, the existence of the appropriate population moments of order 1 lets us apply the law of large numbers to [11], thus showing that $\sum_{k=1}^{j} \hat{P}_L^{\alpha}(k; z(k))$ is a consistent estimator of $\sum_{k=1}^{j} P_L^{\alpha}(k; z(k))$. Given also the existence of the population moments of order 2, the central limit theorem shows that the estimator in [11] is root-N consistent and asymptotically normal with asymptotic covariance matrix given by [12].

References

Atkinson, A. B. (1987). 'On the Measurement of Poverty'. *Econometrica*, 55: 749–64.

—— (1992). 'Measuring Poverty and Differences in Family Composition'. *Economica*, 59: 1–16.

—— (2003). 'Multidimensional Deprivation: Contrasting Social Welfare and Counting Approaches'. *The Journal of Economic Inequality*, 1: 51–65.

—— and Bourguignon, F. (1982). 'The Comparison of Multi-Dimensional Distributions of Economic Status'. *Review of Economic Studies*, 49: 183–201.

—— and —— (1987). 'Income Distribution and Differences in Needs', in G. R. Feiwel (ed.), *Arrow and the Foundations of the Theory of Economic Policy*. New York: New York Press, 350–70.

Bourguignon, F. (1989). 'Family Size and Social Utility: Income Distribution Dominance Criteria'. *Journal of Econometrics*, 42: 67–80.

—— and Chakravarty, S. R. (2003). 'The Measurement of Multidimensional Poverty'. *Journal of Economic Inequality*, 1: 25–49.

—— and Fields, G. (1997). 'Discontinuous Losses from Poverty, Generalized P[alpha] Measures, and Optimal Transfers to the Poor'. *Journal of Public Economics*, 63: 155–75.

Chakravarty, S. R. (1983). 'A New Index of Poverty'. *Mathematical Social Sciences*, 6: 307–13.

Chambaz, C. and E. Maurin (1998). 'Atkinson and Bourguignon's Dominance Criteria: Extended and Applied to the Measurement of Poverty in France'. *Review of Income and Wealth*, 44: 497–513.

Davidson, R. and Duclos, J.-Y. (2000). 'Statistical Inference for Stochastic Dominance and for the Measurement of Poverty and Inequality'. *Econometrica*, 68: 1435–65.

Duclos, J. -Y. and Araar, A. (2006). *Poverty and Equity: Measurement, Policy and Estimation with DAD*. New York: Springer.

—— and Makdissi, P. (2005). 'Sequential stochastic dominance and the robustness of poverty orderings'. *Review of Income and Wealth*, 51: 63–88.

——, Sahn, D., and Younger, S. D. (2006*a*). 'Robust Multidimensional Spatial Poverty Comparisons in Ghana, Madagascar, and Uganda'. *The World Bank Economic Review*, 20: 91–113.

——, ——, —— (2006*b*). 'Robust Multidimensional Poverty Comparisons with Discrete Indicators of Well-being'. CIRPEE Working Paper 06-28. Montreal: University of Laval. http://132.203.59.36/CIRPEE/cahierscirpee/2006/files/CIRPEE06-28.pdf.

——, ——, —— (2006*c*). 'Robust Multidimensional Poverty Comparisons'. *The Economic Journal*, 116: 943–68.

Foster, J. E., Greer, J., and Thorbecke, E. (1984). 'A Class of Decomposable Poverty Measures'. *Econometrica*, 52: 761–76.
—— and Shorrocks, A. F. (1988*a*). 'Poverty Orderings'. *Econometrica*, 56: 173–7.
—— and —— (1988*b*). 'Poverty Orderings and Welfare Dominance'. *Social Choice Welfare*, 5: 179–98.
—— and —— (1988*c*). 'Inequality and Poverty Orderings'. *European Economic Review*, 32: 654–62.
Government of Romania (1994). *Romania Integrated Household Survey*.
Jenkins, S. P. and Lambert, P. J. (1993). 'Ranking Income Distributions when Needs Differ'. *Review of Income and Wealth*, 39: 337–56.
McClements, L. D. (1977). 'Equivalence Scale for Children'. *Journal of Public Economics*, 8: 191–210.
Stata Corporation (2005). *Stata Reference Manual, Release 9*. College Station. Texas: Stata Press.
United Nations Development Program (1990). *Human Development Report*. New York: Oxford University Press.
Watts, H. W. (1968). 'An Economic Definition of Poverty', in D. P. Moynihan (ed.), *On Understanding Poverty*. New York: Basic Books.

Part III

Public Policy

10

A guaranteed income for Europe's children?

*Horacio Levy, Christine Lietz, and Holly Sutherland**

In the Introduction to his 'Public Economics in Action', Atkinson (1995) expressed his conviction that 'the proposal of a *basic income/flat tax*, or variations on its central elements... should be on the agenda for any serious discussion of tax and social security reform for the twenty-first century' (Atkinson 1995: 1). Some ten years after the publication of this work, the basic income/flat tax proposal (BI/FT), or variations of it, are gaining ground in the public debate

* This paper is based on work carried out as part of the MICRESA (Micro Level Analysis of the European Social Agenda) project, financed by the *Improving Human Potential* programme of the European Commission (SERD-2001-00099). We are indebted to all past and current members of the EUROMOD consortium and especially to Herwig Immervoll and Stephen Jenkins for helpful comments. However the views expressed, as well as any errors, are the responsibilities of the authors. In particular, this applies to the interpretation of model results and any errors in its use. EUROMOD is continually being improved and updated and the results presented here represent the best available at the time of writing.

EUROMOD relies on micro-data from twelve different sources for 15 countries. These are the European Community Household Panel (ECHP) User Data Base made available by Eurostat; the Austrian version of the ECHP made available by the Interdisciplinary Centre for Comparative Research in the Social Sciences; the Panel Survey on Belgian Households (PSBH) made available by the University of Liège and the University of Antwerp; the Income Distribution Survey made available by Statistics Finland; the Enquête sur les Budgets Familiaux (EBF) made available by INSEE; the public use version of the German Socio Economic Panel Study (GSOEP) made available by the German Institute for Economic Research (DIW), Berlin; the Living in Ireland Survey made available by the Economic and Social Research Institute; the Survey of Household Income and Wealth (SHIW95) made available by the Bank of Italy; the Socio-Economic Panel for Luxembourg (PSELL-2) made available by CEPS/INSTEAD; the Socio-Economic Panel Survey (SEP) made available by Statistics Netherlands through the mediation of the Netherlands Organization for Scientific Research—Scientific Statistical Agency; the Income Distribution Survey made available by Statistics Sweden; and the Family Expenditure Survey (FES), made available by the UK Office for National Statistics (ONS) through the Data Archive. Material from the FES is Crown Copyright and is used by permission. Neither the ONS nor the Data Archive bears any responsibility for the analysis or interpretation of the data reported here. An equivalent disclaimer applies for all other data sources and their respective providers cited in this acknowledgement.

on tax and social policy reform in some countries. A good example of that is the Green Paper on Basic Income published by the Irish Government in 2002 (Department of the Taoiseach 2002).

This chapter analyses a variation of the BI/FT which has been suggested as an instrument to tackle child poverty in the European Union: a 'Child Basic Income' (CBI). Taking up ideas set out by Atkinson (2005), we consider a CBI that consists of an income that would be unconditionally guaranteed to every child by each member state. Analysing the impact of such a proposal not only allows us to form judgements about the advantages and disadvantages of the approach, it also helps us to learn more about the existing social protection systems, as well as to consider some issues about the implementation of social policies at the European level. For example, we can assess the extent to which existing levels of financial support for children through national benefits and tax concessions fall short of illustrative minimum levels of income, and then calculate the cost of bringing the amount of support up to these levels for all children. Alternatively, measures of child poverty based on household income can be used to estimate the cost in each country of providing guaranteed incomes for children such that potential EU-wide child poverty reduction targets are met. The cost of implementing a CBI could be met at national or, instead, at EU level. Here, once more, we approximate the original BI/FT idea by investigating the effect of financing the child basic income with the implementation of a new 'European flat tax'.

Atkinson (1995) mentions the use of tax-benefit microsimulation models as one of the research fields in public economics that is relevant to the examination of the BI/FT proposal. Tax-benefit models have evolved in the last decade and here we employ one example of these recent developments: the European tax-benefit microsimulation model EUROMOD. We investigate the impact of different CBI levels in all 15 countries that constituted the European Union prior to the enlargement of May 2004 (EU-15).[1]

The chapter is organized as follows. Section 10.1 discusses why child basic income is a policy option for tackling child poverty in the EU. Section 10.2 addresses the issues involved in putting a CBI into practice and assessing its impact. Section 10.3 presents some methodological issues related to the use of EUROMOD; it explains how simulations are used to assess the current level of spending on children and determine the CBI levels, as well as some of the key definitions and assumptions that are used in the analysis. Section 10.4 measures the impact of different levels of CBI on aggregate spending on children and on child poverty rates. Section 10.5 explores the impact of financing a CBI through a flat tax. Section 10.6 considers the implications for transfers first across the EU-15 member states and secondly between generation groups.

[1] See Immervoll *et al.* (1999) for a general description. Sutherland (2001) provides a discussion of technical issues. The version of EUROMOD used in this chapter is 31A.

Finally, Section 10.7 concludes, focusing particularly on what microsimulation analysis can tell us about designing policy to achieve common objectives in the European Union, and suggesting an agenda for further work.

10.1 Child Basic Income as a policy to tackle child poverty in the EU

Child poverty has recently emerged as one of the key issues in EU social policy. As pointed out by Atkinson *et al.* (2005), whereas just a few countries expressed concern about child poverty in their first National Action Plans on Social Inclusion in 2001, this problem has been recognized by more countries in later years. Recently, the European Commission acknowledged that '[m]aterial deprivation among children must be a matter of serious concern, as it is generally recognised to affect their development and future opportunities' and urged member states towards 'developing a focus on eliminating poverty and social exclusion among children' as one of the six key priorities 'over the course of the next 2 years' (European Commission 2004*a*: 2, 7).

Economic indicators of living standards, in particular household income, reveal just one of the dimensions that affect the well-being of children. Therefore, combating child poverty requires a combination of different types of policies that in conjunction are able to protect children from all dimensions of poverty. Of course, the child's family income is a key dimension and is widely known to be correlated with other aspects of well-being (Gregg and Machin 2001). Hence, cash transfers to families with children are policies that are highly relevant to the development of a system that provides effective protection for children. It is income adequacy that the BI naturally addresses and on which this chapter focuses.

Different types of policies or policy packages can be used to transfer income to families with children. Financial support to families with children may be provided through means-tested benefits targeted on lower income families. Tax concessions can be used to increase the disposable income of families that are subject to income tax. Transfers may also be targeted on special groups using non pecuniary restrictions such as benefits that depend on the labour market status of parents (or other characteristics), or by introducing child complements to benefits not strictly related to children such as housing benefit. Finally, cash support can be guaranteed to all children by unconditional refundable tax credits and (universal) child benefits.

A 'basic income guarantee for families with children' has been advocated by Esping-Anderson as part of 'combined strategies' for 'promoting a broad European goal of—simply—abolishing child poverty altogether' (Esping-Andersen 2002: 66). This view is also shared by the High-Level Group on the future of social policy in an enlarged European Union which includes among its policy recommendations: 'To reduce child poverty, including through a basic income for children delivered by Member States' (European Commission 2004*b*: 56).

In its original and purest form a *basic income* is an unconditional income transfer granted to every individual, irrespective of any personal circumstances such as employment or marital status. It guarantees an adequate level of income for each person, replacing all tax concessions and social benefits and, therefore, becoming the sole cash transfer. For more on the Basic Income proposal, see Parker (1989), Van Parijs (1992), Atkinson (1995), and Callan *et al.* (2000). A pure child basic income would consist of a generous unconditional child payment that would replace all existing child contingent tax concessions and cash transfers. A variation of this form of CBI could involve the setting of a universal level of child minimum income that would be unconditionally guaranteed to every child. Under the principle of subsidiarity, each member state could choose its own preferred method to deliver this basic income. This seems to be the interpretation of the High-Level Group on the future of social policy in an enlarged European Union when it proposes a 'basic income for children, under which all Member States guarantee that the child benefit and other payments for children will reach a specified percentage of the median household income in that country' (European Commission 2004*b*: 44). Atkinson (2005) suggested setting the level of the CBI to be that necessary to reach a specific child poverty target (for example, to halve the child poverty rate or reduce it to a certain level).

This mixed form of child basic income is explored in the following sections of this chapter. Different levels of CBI are analysed by adding an amount to the existing level of child-contingent support such that the total matches the specified CBI level of income for each child in each country, without reducing payments that exceed the CBI level. We make no judgement about how the CBIs should be delivered in practice. The aim is simply that the same level of guarantee should apply to each child.

These CBI schemes have budgetary costs. In order to maintain budget neutrality with respect to the current system, governments would have a number of options: reduce expenditure on other areas of the budget; raise any or some of the current revenues, or create new taxes. The pure Basic Income is usually twinned with a Flat Tax (FT). The pure FT would tax all income sources from the first euro with the same tax rate (without allowances or deductions) and would replace the existing income tax and social security contributions. The key feature of the Flat Tax proposal is its simplicity. By using a single rate, some of the most complex aspects of taxation such as the definition of a tax unit, the period of assessment and the aggregation and definition of different types of income become irrelevant. This would significantly reduce administration costs for government, employers, and taxpayers, as well as reduce evasion.

Here, we retain the existing tax and social insurance contribution systems and meet the additional cost of the CBI with an additional flat tax levied on all non-benefit income including pensions (before deducting existing taxes and contributions). In the next section we explain in further detail the steps, options and assumptions taken to implement the CBI and FT package in EUROMOD.

10.2 Implementing a Child Basic Income

We are interested in exploring how a level of guaranteed income for each European child can contribute to the goal of reducing child poverty. In order to do so, we take the following steps.

The level of the CBI is set as a proportion of median household income. One option is to set the level in relation to the *national* median. This means that the cash value varies according to the level of national income and a CBI of 20 per cent of income ranges from €107 per child per month in Portugal to €394 in Luxembourg. (Table 10.1 shows the levels of median income. All money values cited are in 2001 prices.) Alternatively, we may wish to use the CBI to redistribute to children in the lower-income countries of EU-15, and may set the CBI in relation to the EU-15 median income. In this case the level for the 20 per cent CBI is €242 per month for each child. This will have less effect on children in the richer countries that also have generous child support systems, and very dramatic effects on lower income countries with little in the way of existing support. In each case we experiment with CBIs set in relation to different proportions of median income in order to establish the trade-offs between the size of the guarantee, its net cost and the reduction in child poverty.

Because we have chosen to finance the CBI with a flat tax (FT), it is relatively straightforward to introduce in a uniform way in all countries. Raising existing national taxes would introduce variation in effects depending on the structure of existing tax systems. Since the focus of this study is on support for children rather than financing mechanisms, the FT is a useful device. On the other hand, a flat tax levied at the national level, sufficient to pay for the national cost of the CBI, would be very expensive for countries with low existing levels of child-contingent support, which also tend to be those with lower incomes. Conversely, a flat tax set as a EU-15 tax with a common rate applied everywhere, would have the effect of redistributing from higher to lower income countries and from countries with smaller shares of children in the population to those with relatively many. It is this second option which we explore. Table 10.1 shows, for example, that a flat tax of 2.3 per cent would finance a CBI set at 20 per cent of median income (in either national or EU-15 terms).

Table 10.1 Average payments per child by levels of child basic income (CBI) and rates of flat tax

	AT	BE	DK	FI	FR	GE	GR	IR	IT	LU	NL	PT	SP	SW	UK	EU-15	Flat tax rate %
Median income	1327	1287	1581	1304	1339	1371	603	1209	987	1969	1375	534	809	1289	1480	1210	
Without CBI	184	176	163	140	159	158	22	151	54	342	87	35	26	117	185	126	0.00
CBI 10	186	179	201	161	178	170	62	162	102	343	143	57	81	142	207	153	0.52
CBI 20	268	258	331	266	273	277	121	253	197	420	276	107	162	258	308	250	2.35
CBI 30	399	384	478	393	402	412	180	368	295	596	412	160	243	386	446	369	4.61
CBI 40	531	513	633	522	536	548	240	486	394	789	550	214	324	514	592	492	6.92
EU-CBI 10	185	178	176	155	173	164	121	162	121	342	128	121	121	136	194	157	0.60
EU-CBI 20	245	244	268	248	250	247	241	253	241	349	244	242	242	243	265	249	2.33
EU-CBI 30	364	361	373	365	364	364	362	368	362	398	363	363	363	362	368	364	4.51
EU-CBI 40	484	481	487	484	484	484	483	486	483	496	484	484	484	483	485	484	6.77

Notes: All monetary amounts are € per month. Median income is household equivalized disposable income in 2001 prices. CBI payments are themselves independent of household size and are the same for all children.
CBI xx: child basic income set at xx per cent of the national median income.
EU-CBI xx: child basic income set at xx per cent of the EU-15 median income.

Source: EUROMOD.

We can assess the effect on the child poverty rate using a poverty line set at the national or at the EU-15 level. The latter results in a high proportion of children being classified as poor in relatively low-income countries and relatively few being so classified in higher income countries. For example 61 per cent of children in Greece and 8 per cent in the UK are classified as poor using a poverty line set as 60 per cent of the EU-15 median compared with 18 per cent and 21 per cent, respectively, using the national median. For simplicity we confine our analysis to using national poverty lines, although we return to this issue in the concluding section.

There is again a choice between defining targets for poverty reduction at the national level or at the EU-15 level. For example, halving the child poverty rate might be achieved at the EU-15 level without it being achieved in each individual country. In this chapter, we consider two illustrative nationally-determined targets: halving the rate of child poverty and reducing the rate to 5 per cent. EUROMOD estimates of the 2001 child poverty rate range from 6.1 per cent in Denmark to 28.3 per cent in Portugal. Halving the rate is a more demanding target in Denmark than reducing to 5 per cent. The reverse is the case in Portugal.

Throughout, we use the euro as the unit with which to measure income.[2] One of the attributes of a CBI with a common monetary value across countries is transparency. All euro-zone citizens would be aware of the minimum level of cash support that their children, and other EU children, should be receiving.

10.3 Data and methods

Our analysis makes use of EUROMOD to identify the net public spending on cash benefits (including tax concessions) that households receive by virtue of the presence of each child. It is this concept that we consider as the foundation of the CBI. If this 'child contingent' income is less than the specified CBI level for any particular child, then the amount is topped up to that level.[3] Child contingent income is obtained by using EUROMOD to re-calculate household incomes while disregarding children in the calculation of benefits and taxes received by the household. This calculation is not generally the same as simply counting up the value of 'child' and 'family' benefits. In many systems alternative benefits would to some extent substitute for these income sources if they did not exist, or if the children were not present. For example, alternative housing benefit schemes may exist for parents and non-parents; social

[2] For the three countries not in the euro-zone, conversion from national currencies to euro uses market exchange rates as at 30 June 2001: 7.4488 for Denmark, 9.2942 for Sweden and 0.61405 for the United Kingdom. No adjustment is made for differences in purchasing power.

[3] Strictly speaking, the calculation applies to all children in each household, rather than each child individually. Thus in systems where existing payments depend on age or parity (or some other child-level characteristic) there is some averaging in our calculations that would not take place in a truly individual child-based system.

assistance benefits may fill the gap left by family benefits. Indeed some child-related components may be taxable and in this case their absence would result in a reduction in tax liability. Generally, the removal of tax concessions for children will result in taxes rising. EUROMOD re-calculates liabilities and entitlements and thus measures the net effect of child-contingent tax-benefit components (see Corak, Lietz, and Sutherland 2005).

The datasets that are used in the current version of EUROMOD are listed in the Appendix. The choice of dataset is based on the judgement of national experts about the most suitable dataset available for scientific research. Throughout, we consider policies as they existed on 30 June 2001. In most cases the input datasets refer to a period a few years prior to this and the original incomes derived from them are updated to this point in time. This process relies on indexing each income component that is not simulated by appropriate growth factors, based on actual changes over the relevant period.[4] In general no adjustment is made for changes in population composition.

Our analysis is based upon the following definitions and assumptions. Children are defined as individuals younger than 18 years. We assume that income is shared within the household such that household disposable income can be used to indicate the economic well-being of each individual within the household. When comparing across households, incomes are equivalized using the modified OECD scale, as has become standard for EU comparisons since the recommendation by Eurostat. Generally, the individual is taken as the unit of analysis. So our focus is on each child, rather than on parents or families containing children. Household disposable income is defined as original income added up over each household member plus between-household receipts (maintenance and alimony), minus taxes (income tax, social contributions and other direct personal taxes) plus cash benefits. Non-cash benefits are not included.

Individuals are defined to be poor if they live in a household with equivalized household disposable income below 60 per cent of the median (where the median is calculated across individuals). The child poverty rate is defined as the number of children living in poor households expressed as a proportion of the number of all children. Implementing the CBI and the FT will affect median incomes. However, we make use of a poverty threshold that is fixed according to the baseline median. In practice we would expect median income, and hence the relative poverty threshold to be influenced not only by the direct effects of the CBI and FT, but also by behavioural adjustments to the new policy regime. These are not considered in this analysis.

We do not model non-take up of benefits or tax avoidance or evasion. Thus it is assumed that the legal rules apply and that the costs of compliance are zero.

[4] This process is documented in EUROMOD Country Reports. See http://www.iser.essex. ac.uk/msu/emod/countries/.

This can result in the over-estimation of taxes and benefits so in this case might under-estimate the cost and impact of the CBI. Although the method of delivering the CBI is not determined and is assumed to be the choice of national administrations, it is likely that take-up rates would be high simply because the common level of total payment for all children is likely to minimize any stigma or information problems that underlie non-take up behaviour.

The level of the CBI is calculated in relation to common proportions of equivalized household disposable income, both within each country and across the EU-15. The proportions used are 10, 20, 30 and 40 per cent. Average spending per child for each of these eight levels of CBI is shown in Table 10.1, along with the actual average child contingent payment under the 2001 tax-benefit systems. The average payment when a CBI is implemented is typically larger than the CBI level itself (which can be calculated from median income, also shown in Table 10.1). This is because, especially at lower levels of CBI, some children receive a greater level of support under the existing system than provided by the CBI. Nevertheless, for all levels of CBI considered, the average payment under the CBI is larger than the average under the existing system: some children always benefit even at low levels of the guarantee. For the 20 per cent CBI, the average payment for children in the whole EU-15 is €250 per month, in contrast to €126 without the CBI. At this CBI level, the average payment is highest in Luxembourg (€420) and Denmark (€331), and lowest in Portugal (€107) and Greece (€121). The average payment depends not only on the median income level in the country concerned, but also on the distribution of payments under the actual system. The more that existing payments are targeted on particular groups of children (leaving others with low or no payments), the higher the increase in average payment (and the aggregate cost) once the CBI is introduced.

The EU-set CBI results in less variation in average payment across countries than does the CBI set in relation to national income levels. At the 20 per cent level, the range is from €349 in Luxembourg (only a little higher than €342, the average before any CBI) to €241 in Italy and Greece. At higher levels of EU-CBI the average payment in each country starts to converge to the EU-15 average (€484), although some variation remains as in a few countries, under the actual 2001 system, a few children receive child contingent payments in excess of the value of 40 per cent of median income.

10.4 The effect of the level of per-child spending on child poverty rates

Aside from questions about the design and effects of the CBI, the relationship between child poverty rates and the level of per-child payments is of interest.

As might be expected, the higher the average payment, the lower the child poverty rate. For the EU-15 as a whole, an increase of €100 per month per child results in a reduction in child poverty of about five percentage points. However, as shown by Figure 10.1, which plots the relationship for each country in comparison with the EU-15 average, there is considerable cross-country variation in this relationship.

The existing position—actual 2001 child poverty rates and average child contingent spending under 2001 tax-benefit systems—is also plotted as a single point (an open square for the individual countries and a diamond for the EU-15). This is identifiable separately from the line in the case of the EU-15 and some individual countries (for example Greece and Spain). In countries where a 10 per cent CBI makes little difference to the incomes of the poor, this point representing the actual situation is shown close to, or on, the line (for example, Austria and Belgium). In interpreting this figure it is important to remember that, apart from the points showing the 'actuals', the structure of the spending takes on a more and more 'universal' character as the amount of spending rises and a greater proportion of children are covered by the CBI. The relationships between child poverty rates and spending would be different if the extra spending were targeted on particular groups of children. In particular, if it were targeted on children in low income households, the slope of the curves would be steeper. If it were targeted on higher income households with children (perhaps through tax allowances), the curves would be flatter.

The steepness of the curves depends on several factors. One influence is the distribution of household incomes below the poverty line. A high concentration just below the line will result in a relatively large reduction in child poverty for a relatively small additional payment. On the other hand, if poor children are very poor, large payments are needed to reduce the child poverty rate. Second, the gradient depends on the composition of the households in which poor children live. If one child shares its household with many adults, it will take a large child payment to lift the whole household out of poverty. Conversely, if it is lone parents with several children who are poor, a relatively small increase in per-child payment is sufficient to lift the household above the poverty line. Third, the shape depends on the nature of the existing system, to which the CBI provides a top-up. If support levels of current policies are low for poor children, then relatively modest levels of CBI will involve some increase in poor children's incomes and a reduction in the child poverty rate. On the other hand, if support is already targeted on the poor, modest levels of CBI may result in income increases for households with middle and high incomes. Poverty reduction would then require CBI levels above the current level of support for low income households, which may be substantially above the average level of support.

Figure 10.1 shows that several countries have curves that are relatively flat at lower levels of spending. This is particularly the case in the UK where, under

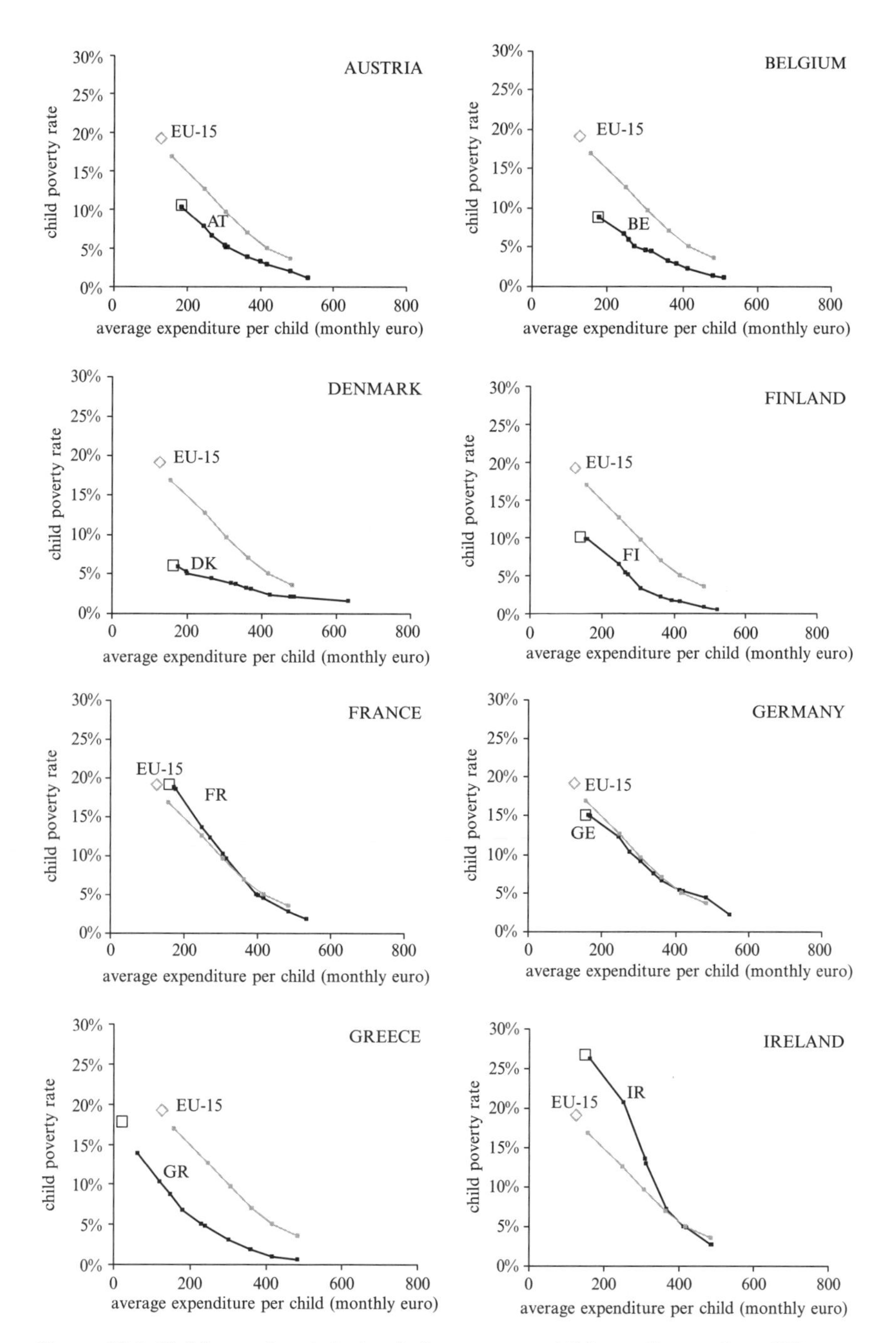

Figure 10.1 Child poverty rate by level of average per-child spending under a CBI

Notes: The single point shown by an open square (diamond) shape indicates the actual 2001 position for each country (EU-15). The other points shown on the continuous lines plot the relationship between per child spending and child poverty at each level of the CBI and EU-CBI (EU-CBI) calculated in this chapter: 10, 20, 30 and 40 per cent, and the levels required to halve child poverty and to reduce it to 5 per cent.

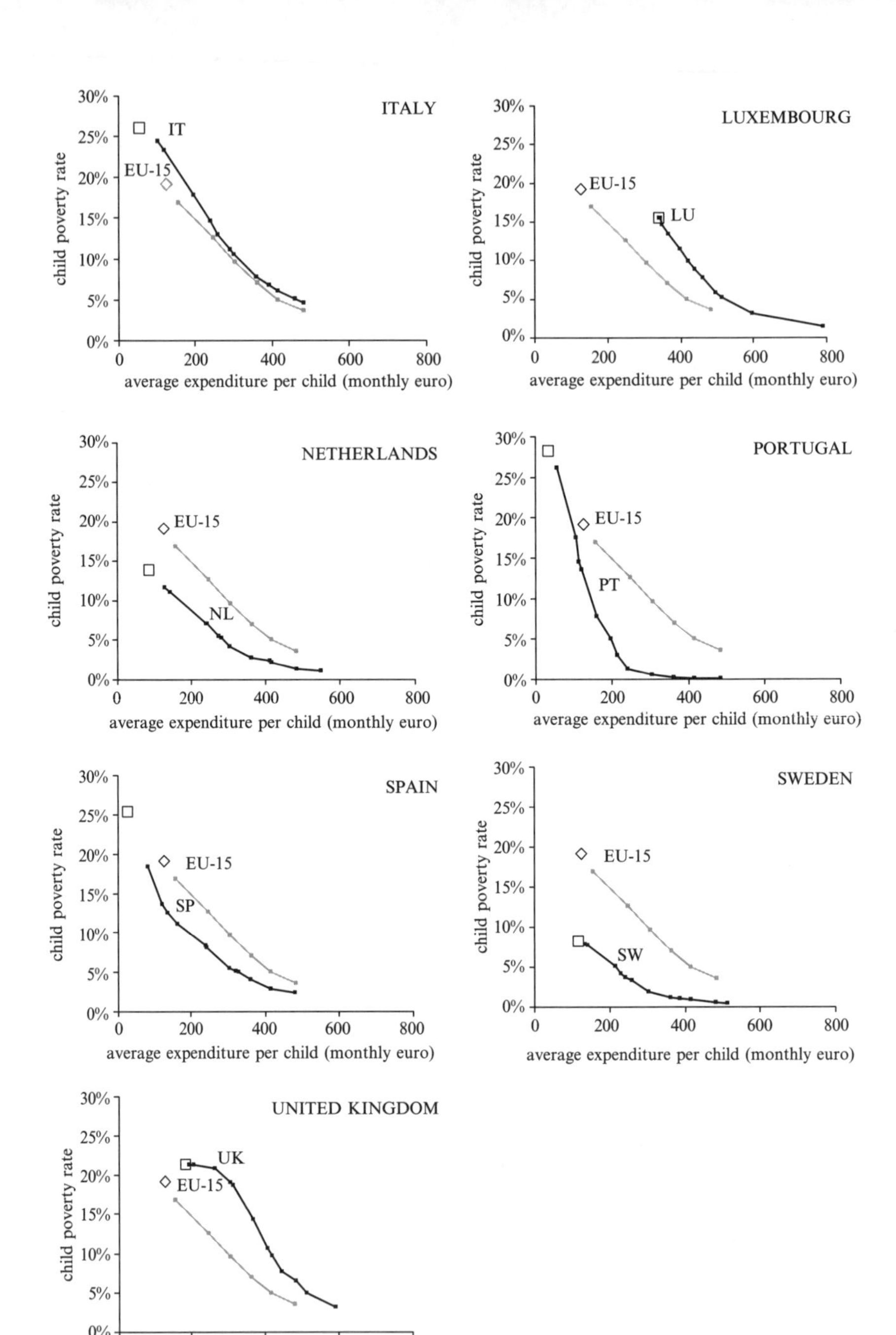

Figure 10.1 (*Continued*)

Source: EUROMOD.

the existing system, the largest payments are made to children in households with the lowest incomes. The gradient is particularly steep in Portugal and also in Ireland, showing the potential for relatively modest increases in child payments to reduce child poverty in these countries. At the other extreme, in Denmark and Belgium, where poverty rates are already low, large increases in payments are needed for modest reductions in child poverty.

These curves can be used as the basis for establishing the level of CBI that would be required to meet particular targets for child poverty reduction. Table 10.2 shows more precisely the level of CBI necessary to achieve the two illustrative targets we have just discussed. The level of guaranteed income per child that achieves a halving of the national child poverty rate ranges from €113 in Portugal and €136 in Spain, to €403 in the UK and €443 in Luxembourg. Expressed as a percentage of national equivalized household disposable income the cost varies from 17 per cent in Spain to 27 per cent in Italy and the UK.

Reducing child poverty to a common low rate in all countries requires a different pattern of extra resources. In the three Nordic countries and Belgium, where the child poverty rate is already lower than 10 per cent, less is required. In the Southern countries, and in Ireland and the UK, achieving 5 per cent is much more demanding than halving the high existing rate. The necessary level of child guaranteed payment corresponds to between 10 per cent of national equivalized household disposable income in Denmark and 47 per cent in Italy. When considered in relation to EU median, rather than the national median, the range in this case becomes narrower and varies from 13 per cent in Denmark to 42 per cent in the UK.

However, when considering the size of the CBI needed for the targets to be reached, it is also necessary to take account of the need to pay for the cost of the CBI. Some of the burden will fall on households near the poverty line if budget neutrality is to be achieved through a flat tax. This is considered in the next section.

10.5 Paying for the CBI with a flat tax

The flat tax is implemented as a fixed percentage on all gross income including pensions but excluding other benefits.[5] This departs from the definitions of the national income tax bases to varying extents, and is distinct from all national income tax structures because it does not involve a tax-free allowance. The rates of flat tax, common to all countries, necessary to finance each of the levels of CBI range from 0.52 per cent for the nationally-set 10 per cent CBI to 6.92 per cent for the nationally-set 40 per cent CBI (see Table 10.1). The

[5] See Levy, Lietz, and Sutherland (2006) for definitions of these income sources.

Table 10.2 Meeting targets for child poverty: levels of CBI necessary to achieve (a) halving the child poverty rate and (b) a child poverty rate of 5 per cent

	AT	BE	DK	FI	FR	GE	GR	IR	IT	LU	NL	PT	SP	SW	UK
2001 actual child poverty rate %	10.5	8.8	6.1	10.1	19.1	15	17.7	26.8	26	15.5	13.8	28.3	25.3	8.2	21.4
(a) halving the child poverty rate															
CBI in monthly €	301	319	347	268	315	340	149	302	263	443	242	113	136	229	403
% of national equivalized median	23	25	22	21	23	25	25	25	27	23	18	21	17	18	27
% of EU-15 equivalized median	25	26	29	22	26	28	12	25	22	37	20	9	11	19	33
(b) a child poverty rate of 5%															
CBI in monthly €	309	274	156	268	397	421	231	410	463	501	283	198	329	215	513
% of national equivalized median	23	21	10	21	30	31	38	34	47	25	21	37	41	17	35
% of EU-15 equivalized median	26	23	13	22	33	35	19	34	38	41	23	16	27	18	42

Notes: The child poverty rate is the proportion of all children living in households below 60 per cent of the national median equivalized household disposable income. The same poverty line is used for measuring child poverty after the introduction of the CBI, even though median income is likely to change.

Source: EUROMOD.

combined impact of the eight variants of CBI and Flat Tax on child poverty is shown in Table 10.3.

As already shown in Figure 10.1, CBIs at the level of 10 per cent of national median disposable income have little effect on child poverty in most countries. The exceptions are the four Southern countries, especially Spain and Greece, and to some extent Denmark and the Netherlands. Child poverty rates in all countries are significantly reduced by CBIs of 20 per cent of national income and are reduced below 4 per cent by a 40 per cent CBI in all countries except the four Southern countries.

The common EU-set CBI implies lower levels of CBI for higher-income countries and higher levels for low income countries. In this case, even a 10 per cent EU-CBI has a dramatic effect in Greece, Portugal and Spain (reducing child poverty rates by 7, 15 and 11 percentage points respectively), and at 40 per cent it all but eradicates child poverty in these countries. On the other hand, as might be expected, the effect is smaller in higher income countries. Those still facing child poverty rates of more than 4 per cent under a 40 per cent EU-CBI include Luxembourg, UK, Italy and Germany.

A 20 per cent EU-CBI actually results in an increase in child poverty in Luxembourg and the UK, as does a 10 per cent EU-CBI in Austria. The explanation is that the EU flat tax, which is applied at the same rate in each country, pushes some households with children below the poverty line and this is not entirely offset by the numbers pushed above the line by the modest level of CBI. In Luxembourg and Austria, as shown in Table 10.1, the average payment is not much higher under the CBI set at 20 per cent of the median than under the actual system. Households in these countries are paying the flat tax but not receiving much CBI in return. In the UK, the current system is income-targeted to the extent that low income households do not benefit greatly (see Fig. 10.1). The national versions of the CBI have a bigger effect in these three relatively high-income countries because the national CBIs, set relative to national median incomes are larger than the EU CBI, set relative to the EU median (see Table 10.1).

10.6 Transfers between countries and across generations

The Flat Tax and CBI combination involves re-distribution between countries. Thus there are gainers and losers: countries that are net recipients or contributors. We identify them in terms of the proportional change in national household disposable income that occurs as a result of the CBI/FT. The net national effect of each CBI/FT combination is shown in Figure 10.2 for the national CBIs, and in Figure 10.3 for the EU-set versions. Countries are ranked by the budgetary effect under the 40 per cent version, shown by the darkest bars. A positive value indicates that the country is a net recipient; a negative

Table 10.3 Child poverty rates (%) under the 2001 tax-benefit system and with CBI, financed by a EU-15 flat tax

	AT	BE	DK	FI	FR	GE	GR	IR	IT	LU	NL	PT	SP	SW	UK	EU-15
2001 actual child poverty rate	10.5	8.8	6.1	10.1	19.1	15.0	17.7	26.8	26.0	15.5	13.8	28.3	25.3	8.2	21.4	19.2
CBI 10	10.3	8.7	5.0	9.7	18.5	15.0	13.8	26.2	24.4	15.5	11.1	26.2	18.3	7.7	21.4	17.8
CBI 20	7.1	6.2	3.7	6.1	13.4	11.1	10.5	20.8	18.8	11.0	5.7	18.2	11.6	3.6	19.7	13.5
CBI 30	3.6	3.0	2.2	2.0	5.5	5.5	7.4	7.3	12.4	3.9	2.4	9.1	8.9	1.2	8.2	6.9
CBI 40	1.3	1.2	1.6	0.6	2.5	2.5	5.4	3.0	7.8	1.8	1.2	4.6	5.9	0.6	3.6	3.7
EU-CBI 10	10.7	8.8	6.1	10.0	18.9	15.0	10.3	26.4	23.5	15.5	11.9	13.7	13.9	7.9	21.7	17.1
EU-CBI 20	8.8	6.9	4.4	7.2	14.9	13.0	4.9	20.8	15.4	15.6	7.6	1.5	8.7	3.9	21.6	13.3
EU-CBI 30	4.4	3.4	3.8	2.3	8.4	7.1	2.0	7.3	8.4	13.4	3.0	0.3	4.5	1.4	14.8	7.6
EU-CBI 40	2.3	1.7	2.2	1.1	3.4	4.5	0.7	3.0	5.3	7.8	1.7	0.1	2.8	0.6	7.0	4.0

Notes: The child poverty rate is the proportion of all children living in households below 60 per cent of the national median equivalized household disposable income. The same poverty line is used for measuring child poverty after the introduction of the CBI-FT system (even though median income is likely to change).

Source: EUROMOD.

value shows that the country is a net contributor. By design, the effect at the EU-15 level is budget neutral, and is not shown.[6]

The rankings are not identical in the two Figures. Lower-income countries are more likely to be at the higher-gaining end under the EU-set scheme than under the national schemes. It should also be noted that the figures are not drawn to the same scale. The net gain in Ireland is of the same magnitude under both schemes (around 5 per cent of household income), but other countries gain much more under the EU-set scheme. Generally the EU scheme involves more redistribution across countries, as would be expected.

Some countries are net contributors under both versions of the scheme and at all levels of CBI that have been investigated. These tend to be countries with a lower share of children in their populations, with higher income (receiving less CBI under the EU-CBI scheme) and with already generous and/or

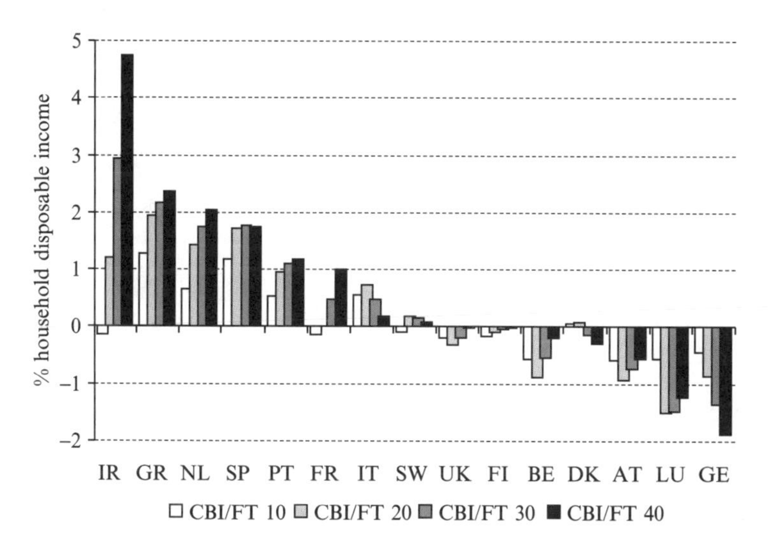

Figure 10.2 Gainers and losers with a national CBI/FT: the net budgetary effect of the CBI/FT as a proportion of national household disposable income

Notes: Countries are ranked by the amount they gain from the CBI/FT 40 scheme (shown by the black bars), as a proportion of national household disposable income. A downward pointing bar indicates a loss. The paler bars indicate the gain/loss at lower levels of CBI.

Source: Authors' calculations using EUROMOD.

[6] The net effect is made up of the additional spending on the CBI less the revenue from the Flat Tax. The separate effects of these are given in Levy, Lietz, and Sutherland (2006).

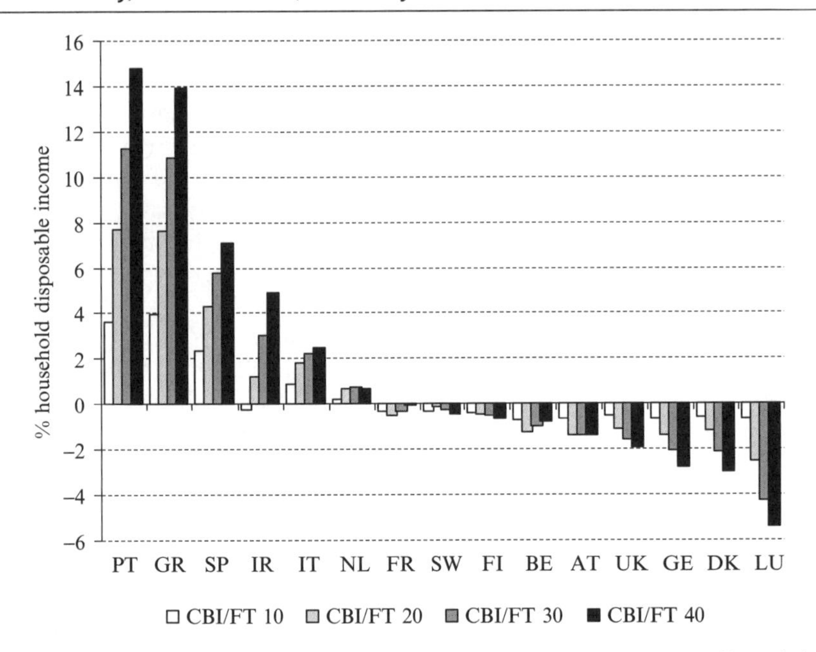

Figure 10.3 Gainers and losers with an EU-set CBI/FT: the net budgetary effect of the CBI/FT as a proportion of national household disposable income

Notes: As for Fig. 10.2. Fig. 10.3 is not drawn to the same scale as Fig. 10.2: the Irish gain is about the same size under both the national and EU-set CBI.
Source: Authors' calculations using EUROMOD.

comprehensive child-contingent cash support systems (benefiting less from the CBI but paying their share of the FT). Such countries include Austria, Belgium, Germany and Luxembourg. A second set of countries are always net gainers. These are countries that have lower incomes, or a higher share of children, or less-developed child cash support systems. They include Greece, Italy, Portugal, Spain, and also the Netherlands. The inclusion of the Netherlands in this group may be surprising but, whereas it does not have low income relative to the rest of the EU, it does have a high share of children (the fourth highest, according to the information in the Appendix). It also has the fifth lowest level of existing spending on children through the cash benefit and tax systems, higher than the four Southern countries only (see Table 10.1), a finding confirmed using stylized family analysis by Bradshaw and Finch (2002: Table 11.3).

The remaining countries gain in some circumstances and lose in others. Interestingly it is not always the case that the net gain or loss increases monotonically with the CBI level. For example, in the UK moving from the national CBI of 10 per cent to that of 20 per cent increases the net cost. However, the net cost falls as the CBI level increases to 30 per cent and vanishes as it reaches 40 per cent. This is because the UK gains little from small amounts of CBI as it already has a relatively generous cash support system for children. But, because of its relatively high share of children in the population—the UK has the sixth highest in the EU-15 (see the Appendix)—as the level of CBI rises beyond a certain level the CBI spending as a percentage of overall disposable income in the UK catches up with the EU-15 average. Italy provides a contrasting example. Given its less-developed child support system, it benefits substantially more than the EU-15 average at low CBI levels. However, as the level increases the relatively low proportion of children in Italy results in a lower rate of increase in spending on the CBI than for the EU-15 as a whole.

Within each country, whether or not the country as a whole is a net loser or gainer, we can anticipate that there will be significant shifts in resources towards children and away from households without children. Indeed for all levels of CBI, changes in income for households with children are more positive than for households as a whole.[7] But there are losers as well as gainers among households with children and the group as a whole is not always better off. With the 10 per cent EU-CBI, children are on average net losers in Austria, Belgium, Denmark, Germany, Luxembourg and the UK. In Luxembourg, even the 40 per cent EU-CBI results in children as a group being worse off, and the national 10 per cent CBI also results in children being losers in Austria, Belgium and Luxembourg.

For the EU-15 as a whole, 40 per cent CBIs financed by the FT result in a shift of resources to children equivalent to 14 per cent of disposable income for households containing children. The corresponding increases for the 10 per cent CBI and 20 per cent CBI are 1 per cent and just under 5 per cent of disposable income respectively. This applies whether the CBI is set nationally or at the EU-15 level. The choice between national or EU-level CBI does affect the extent of re-distribution toward children within countries. It is greater under the EU-CBI in the Southern countries and greater under the nationally-set CBIs in Denmark, Germany, Luxembourg and the UK.

Our calculations demonstrate rather starkly that, in improving the level of guaranteed cash support for children, there is a choice over the nature of the re-distribution that takes place to free up the necessary resources. One option is to rely on re-distribution within a country, from the 'older' and the childless (which has not been considered directly here). Another is redistribution across countries from those with small population shares of children to those with large shares. A third is redistribution from relatively rich to relatively poor countries. A fourth—which is closely related to the third—is redistribution from countries with well-developed child support systems, to those without. Depending on the balance between these options, different countries are

[7] The results for households with children are provided in Levy, Lietz, and Sutherland (2006).

net gainers and children—within countries and across the EU-15—benefit to varying extents.

10.7 Conclusions

This is a first attempt to quantify the scale of guaranteed child payments needed to meet specific child poverty targets in the countries of EU-15. We have considered child basic incomes which are made up of existing child payments, including tax concessions, topped up to meet a series of common standardized levels of per-child income. Our main focus has concerned the implications of the way these common income levels are specified, on the redistribution between countries and from the childless to households with children, and how differences between countries have an impact on the effects of the schemes. Apart from the impact on child poverty rates we have not explored the distributional effects of these universal schemes within countries. This is for brevity and is clearly an interesting subject for further work.

Halving child poverty rates in all member states could be achieved with CBIs set at between 18 per cent and 27 per cent of national median income. A CBI corresponding to a common proportion of 25 per cent of national median income would at least halve child poverty in all countries except Italy and the UK. Reducing the child poverty rate to 5 per cent is a less demanding task in a few countries and a much more demanding task in others. Using an EU-CBI of 40 per cent of EU-15 median income would meet this target in all cases except Luxembourg and the UK. These proportions correspond to average levels of payment that are much higher than under any existing system. At the same time, rather lower levels of CBI are quite effective at reducing child poverty in countries with less well-developed child-contingent systems, particularly in Greece, Spain, and Portugal and also to some extent in Italy. This indicates that a rather different form of CBI might be an effective policy choice in these countries. A guaranteed universal child payment at a low level relative to the CBIs considered here has been examined for the Southern European countries by Matsaganis *et al.* (2006).

A variant that has not been considered in this chapter is the effect of the EU-set CBI on child poverty measured against a line set in relation to the EU-15 median income. This would highlight attention on the Southern European countries where high proportions of households with low income relative to the EU median are located. The CBI, and particularly the EU-set CBI, has a strong impact in these countries because of the low level of existing child-contingent payments. The effect on child poverty rates when using the higher poverty line is a matter for empirical investigation. But the main focus would then be on the equalizing of the average level of incomes across countries, rather than the distribution within countries and across generations.

We have chosen to meet the cost of the CBIs with a flat tax, using a common EU-15-wide tax rate on all non-benefit gross income. The combined schemes are budget-neutral across EU-15 but involve substantial cross-country subsidization. While clearly not on any current policy agenda in the form presented here, we consider the implications for between-country transfers to be informative, both in illuminating existing inequalities and in highlighting some of the issues to be addressed in setting targets and standards within the European Union. The CBI/FT schemes also involve a shift in resources from the (currently) childless to those with children, since the flat tax is levied on all incomes. As implemented here, childless households with any non-benefit income, including some on very low pension incomes, contribute to the cost of the CBIs. They are not protected by adult BIs as in the classical version of the BI/FT scheme. This indicates that financing a child BI with a general flat tax is not a practical proposition on its own. Other financing mechanisms, perhaps using existing tax bases and schedules, would be more appropriate.

One of the factors that determine whether a country is a net contributor or beneficiary is the nature and level of the existing system of child-contingent support. Countries with relatively high standards of child support tend to be net contributors. One reaction to this would be to ask why countries that already prioritize their own children should also be required to support children in other countries. In a dynamic perspective, this could be expected to lead to a 'race to the bottom' in terms of non-CBI spending on children, as countries try to maximize transfers from other member states. On the other hand, the extent of within-country re-distribution has its limits, particularly in the lower-income countries, and if child poverty reduction targets are to be both ambitious and achievable across the whole EU, some cross-country transfer might be needed to meet them.

However, if the CBI takes the form of a top-up to existing measures, the 'race to the bottom' effect is accentuated: the less adequate the nationally-financed system, the larger the burden on the EU-financed top-up. This suggests that either the top-up CBI should be nationally financed, with any cross-country subsidization using an independent mechanism, or that the CBI should not depend (inversely) on the generosity of the existing system. A second factor that affects the relative size of the national financing burden is the share of children in the population. Countries with low fertility tend to be those that contribute. Given the importance of children as the labour force and taxpayers of the future (among other things), it can be argued that it is reasonable that there should be some community-level support for this resource. Member states with difficulties in increasing fertility might contribute to, or 'invest in', the support of children of other member states, who will be part of the European labour force of the future. However, this is only sustainable if there is also some sharing of responsibility for the support of incomes in old age. A companion to the CBI might be the common provision of an adequate retirement income, guaranteed at the EU level (Atkinson *et al.* 2002).

Appendix EUROMOD Datasets

Country	Base Dataset for EUROMOD	Date of collection	Reference time period for incomes	Sample size		Number of children as % of total population[a]
				Households	Children	
Austria	Austrian version of European Community Household Panel	1999	annual 1998	2,672	1,687	21.3
Belgium	Panel Survey on Belgian Households	1999	annual 1998	3,653	2,245	24.0
Denmark	European Community Household Panel	1995	annual 1994	3,215	1,666	23.3
Finland	Income distribution survey	2001	annual 2001	10,736	7,493	22.0
France	Budget de Famille (HBS)	1994/5	annual 1993/4	11,291	7,448	24.0
Germany	German Socio-Economic Panel	2001	annual 2000	7,020	3,743	18.7
Greece	European Community Household Panel	1995	annual 1994	5,168	3,089	21.3
Ireland	Living in Ireland Survey	1994	month in 1994	4,048	4,534	30.8
Italy	Survey of Households Income and Wealth	1996	annual 1995	8,135	4,353	18.6
Luxembourg	PSELL-2	2001	annual 2000	2,431	1,426	22.2
Netherlands	Sociaal-economisch panelonderzoek	2000	annual 1999	4,329	2,694	23.9
Portugal	European Community Household Panel	2001	annual 2000	4,588	2,392	21.2
Spain	European Community Household Panel	2000	annual 1999	5,048	2,642	18.9
Sweden	Income distribution survey	2001	annual 2001	14,610	7,182	22.0
UK	Family Expenditure Survey (HBS)	2000/1	month in 2000/1	6,634	4,071	22.9

Note: [a] calculated using weights.

References

Atkinson, A. B. (1995). *Public Economics in Action: The Basic Income/Flat Tax Proposal*. Oxford: Clarendon Press.

—— (2005). 'EUROMOD and the Development of EU Social Policy', EUROMOD Working Paper EM1/05. Colchester: ISER, University of Essex.

——, Bourguignon, F., O'Donoghue, C., Sutherland, H., and Utili, F. (2002). 'Microsimulation of Social Policy in the European Union: Case Study of a European Minimum Pension'. *Economica*, 69, 229–43.

——, Cantillon, B., Marlier, E., and Nolan, B. (2005). *Taking Forward the EU Social Inclusion Process*. Independent report commissioned by the Luxembourg Presidency of the Council of the European Union. http://www.ceps.lu/eu2005_lu/report/final_report.pdf.

Bradshaw, J. R. and Finch, N. (2002). *A Comparison of Child Benefit Packages in 22 Countries*. Department for Work and Pensions Research Report No. 174. Leeds: Corporate Document Services.

Callan, T., Nolan, B., Walsh, J., McBride, J., and Nestor R. (2000). *Basic Income in Ireland: A Study for the Working Group on Basic Income*. Dublin: Economic and Social Research Institute.

Corak, M., Lietz, C., and Sutherland, H. (2005). 'The Impact of Tax and Transfer Systems on Children in the European Union'. Innocenti Working Paper No. 2005-04. Florence: UNICEF Innocenti Research Centre.

Department of the Taoiseach (2002). *Basic Income: A Green Paper*. Dublin: Department of the Taoiseach.

Esping-Andersen, G. (2002). 'A Child-Centred Social Investment Strategy', in G. Esping-Andersen, D. Gallie, A. Hemerijck, and J. Myles (eds), *Why We Need a New Welfare State*. Oxford. Oxford University Press, 26–67.

European Commission (2004*a*). *Joint Report on Social Inclusion 2004, Statistical Annex*. Luxembourg: Office for Official Publications of the European Communities.

—— (2004*b*). *Report of the High-Level Group on the Future of Social Policy in an Enlarged European Union*. Luxembourg: Office for Official Publications of the European Communities.

Gregg, P. and Machin, S. (2001). 'The Relationship Between Childhood Experiences, Subsequent Educational Attainment and Adult Labour Market Performance', in K. Vleminckx and T. Smeeding (eds), *Child Well-Being, Child Poverty and Child Policy in Modern Nations: What Do We Know?* Bristol: The Policy Press, 129–50.

Levy, H., Lietz, C., and Sutherland, H. (2006). 'A Basic Income for Europe's Children?' EUROMOD Working Paper EM4/06, Colchester: ISER, University of Essex.

Immervoll, H., O'Donoghue, C., and Sutherland, H. (1999). 'An Introduction to EUROMOD'. EUROMOD Working Paper EM0/99. Colchester: ISER, University of Essex.

Matsaganis, M., O'Donoghue, C., Levy, H., Coromaldi, M., Mercader-Prats, M., Rodrigues, C. F., Toso, S., Tsakloglou, P. (2006). 'Reforming Family Transfers in Southern Europe: is There a Role for Universal Child Benefits?' *Social Policy and Society*, 5: 189–97.

Parker, H. (1989). *Instead of the Dole*. London: Routledge.

Sutherland, H. (2001). 'EUROMOD: An Integrated European Benefit-Tax Model, Final Report', EUROMOD Working Paper EM9/01. Colchester: ISER, University of Essex.

van Parijs, P. (1992). *Arguing for Basic Income: Ethical Foundations for a Radical Reform*. London: Verso.

11

The impact of minimum wages on the distribution of earnings and employment in the USA

Stephen Bazen

Effective minimum wages necessarily have an impact on the earnings distribution. Whether employment is reduced or not, the introduction of, or an increase in, the minimum wage will decrease earnings inequality (unless the pay of workers earning more than the minimum increases more than proportionately). The nature of this distributional impact will depend on the direct and induced effects of the minimum wage on both earnings and employment. Being the lowest wage rate in the economy, the direct effect is to raise the wage of some employees compared to what they otherwise would have earned. Apart from this mechanical distributional effect, there are also a number of indirect distributional effects. (See, for example, Freeman 1996 for a detailed account.) A minimum wage could reduce poverty and discrimination, and may improve incentives to work. These indirect effects occur to the extent that low paid workers are in low income households, that women figure disproportionately among workers on low wages, and higher wages for certain low paying occupations induce certain individuals to leave unemployment. The extent of these effects will depend, first, on how high the minimum wage is set relative to the existing earnings distribution and, second, on whether there are adverse effects on the employment of the workers concerned. This chapter begins by examining the impact of minimum wages on the distribution of earnings and then proceeds to assess the effects on employment using evidence from the USA.

On the employment effects associated with minimum wages, the study by David Card and Alan Krueger (1994) of the effect of a rise in the minimum wage in New Jersey fast-food restaurants, had a marked impact on the economics profession. They found that the rise in the minimum wage increased employment. Furthermore, in their subsequent book (Card and Krueger 1995) they re-examined earlier studies and presented evidence supporting the claim that, during the 1980s and early 1990s in the USA, minimum wage hikes had no significant negative employment effects. The so-called new economics of the minimum wage is thus based on a wider body of evidence than the New Jersey study. Their work has given rise to a renewed interest in the employment consequences and the economic relevance of minimum wages more generally.

However, recent studies for the United States have suggested that the employment effects may be less empirically relevant than the impact on the distribution of earnings. Ironically, it is the decline in the real and relative value of the federal minimum wage rather than an increase in it that lies behind this conclusion. (The federal minimum wage was frozen at $3.35 between 1981 and 1989.) During the 1980s, earnings inequality increased and various explanations were advanced such as the impact of foreign trade from low wage countries (see, for example, Wood 1994) and changes in the relative demand for skills brought about by technological progress (see Katz and Autor 1999). As will be seen later, studies have found that between a quarter and three quarters of the increase in earnings inequality could be the result of the freezing of the federal minimum wage, which resulted in its erosion in real and relative terms and led to the collapse of the floor supporting the earnings distribution.

Such a phenomenon is rarely found in countries other than the USA. In almost all countries with minimum wages, the minimum is uprated on a regular basis. It thus remains a binding constraint on wages and ensures the continual presence of a floor to the earnings distribution. In the USA, the federal minimum wage is uprated at the will of Congress and each proposed increase is accompanied by an intense debate on the relative merits of the measure and its effect on employment. The federal minimum can remain unchanged for several years; the last five increases were in 1981, 1990, 1991, 1996 and 1997. At the time of writing (2006), a proposal for an uprating has just been voted down. However, individual states can also set minimum wage rates and a minority do so. One of the key issues in research into the impact of minimum wages is the difference between the effects of state- and federally-set minimum wages. One of the main findings to emerge from this chapter is that the conclusions of the new economics of the minimum wage are based mainly on evidence about the effect of changes in state-level minimum wages. The freezing of the federal minimum wage during the 1980s had a substantial effect on the earnings distribution, and it was its subsequent uprating in 1990–91 that led to a reduction in teenage employment.

11.1 The impact of the minimum wage on the distribution of earnings

The economic impact of a minimum wage depends on how it affects the distribution of earnings that would have prevailed in its absence. We will refer to the latter as the underlying distribution of earnings and this is represented by the dotted curve in Figure 11.1. The direct effect on the earnings distribution is to sweep up the proportion (*P*) of affected workers in the lower tail and raise their wages up to the minimum (*m*). *P* is equal to the shaded area at the lower extreme of the earnings distribution. Unless all of the workers concerned are laid-off, this sweeping-up effect creates a spike in the wage distribution at the minimum. In Figure 11.1, this entails an increase in wages up to *m* for all workers earning less than the minimum. If this is the only effect on earnings and if there is no impact on employment, the vertical distance between points *a* and *b* will be equal to *P*. If the employment of the affected population is reduced, the vertical distance will be less than *P*.

However, this is unlikely to be the sole effect of the minimum wage, since all wage differentials among the lowest paid are eliminated. There may be substantial increases in pay for the very lowest paid and negligible increases for those earning just less than the minimum wage prior to its imposition. In addition, differentials between those earning above the minimum and those below it are narrowed, and in some cases cut substantially. This could have consequences for the shape of the earnings distribution beyond the lower tail (the part below the minimum wage).

First, to the extent that differences in wages represent payments for better quality workers, rewards for taking responsibility, or incentives to certain types

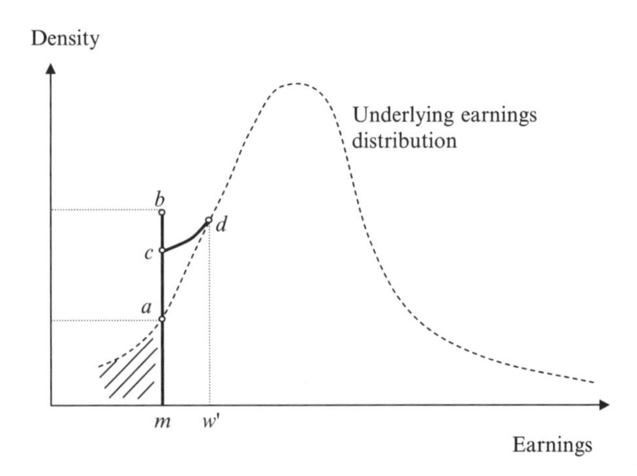

Figure 11.1 The distributional impact of introducing a minimum wage

of employee, the elimination or severe narrowing of wage differentials could cause difficulties in employee relations with the employer or among employees themselves. There could be adverse effects on productivity and discipline, and increased turnover. Within the directly affected population (those initially earning less than *m*), some workers' pay may rise beyond the minimum wage. This means that the distance *ab* will be less than *P* and that the earnings distribution to the right of *m* will be altered by the addition of a branch like *cd* in Figure 11.1. If this kind of mechanism operates, then it will also give rise to further induced wage increases in the part of the earnings distribution initially above the minimum wage. Thus for a non-negligible rise in the minimum, employers will, in all probability, need to raise the wages of those earning more than the minimum wage, and to re-establish some kind of hierarchy among those whose wages are all pushed up to the minimum. These effects will not occur all the way up the earnings distribution since firms will resist the pressures on costs.

A second indirect effect was highlighted by Teulings (2003). If substitution is possible between workers affected by the minimum wage and those initially earning more, demand for the latter type of worker may increase and lead to higher wages. This additional mechanism would also have the effect of creating a branch like *cd* in Figure 11.1. A third possible effect may result if collective bargaining is widespread. One of the major reasons for having collective bargaining is to establish (by agreement) wage scales that are regarded as fair. If seniority and experience are given prominence, collectively agreed wage scales would be re-based on the minimum wage or possibly above it. (This kind of effect was feared in the United Kingdom in the 1980s when trade unions claimed that they would aim to re-establish wage differentials were a national minimum wage to be introduced.) These indirect or spill-over effects will mean that the initial reduction in earnings inequality that a minimum wage brings about will be tempered, as some of the wage differential among different types of employee is restored. It is important to stress, however, that these effects occur at the lower end of the earnings distribution and therefore have a limited impact on the overall distribution.

Minimum wages and changes in earnings inequality in the United States

As has already been pointed out, research into the impact of minimum wages experienced a major revival in the 1990s following work by David Card and Alan Krueger. While their findings on employment have been the main focus of commentary, criticism and reassessment, they also addressed the issue of the extent to which minimum wages 'bite'. In each of their case studies, and in their state level analysis of the employment effects of both state and federal minimum wages, they first examined the impact of the minimum wage on earnings. This was assessed by regressing the average (log) wage on the proportion of workers potentially affected by the minimum wage or by examining the difference in differences of log wages for affected and non affected states. In all studies, there was a statistically significant effect of minimum wages on earnings levels for the affected group. To a large extent, this is not unexpected if the minimum wage is binding. If the distribution is truncated, so that the affected population is eliminated from the distribution, mean earnings necessarily increase (unless those earning above the minimum see their wages reduced). If there is a direct, sweeping-up effect, mean earnings will also mechanically increase, an effect that will be even greater if there are indirect spill-over effects.

Card and Krueger were concerned with the impact of increases in minimum wages. It is now becoming clear that a substantial part of the increase in earnings inequality experienced in the United States in the 1980s could have been due to the decline in the real value of the federal minimum wage after 1981, rather than changes in skill composition, international trade or technology. One of the first studies to formally analyse the issue was by Dinardo, Fortin, and Lemieux (1996), who concluded that the decline in the minimum wage was responsible for a quarter of the increase in earnings inequality. This calculation was based on estimating the form that the earnings distribution would have in the absence of a minimum wage and then inferring the change in the distribution when a minimum wage is imposed. In terms of the framework presented above, they estimated the direct effect of the minimum wage under the assumptions that there are no effects on earnings above the minimum, and also that there are no adverse effects on employment.

Their analysis was deepened by Lee (1999) who examined the impact of both state and federal minimum wages on earnings differentials in the lower half of the distribution. Rather than examine the entire distribution, Lee estimated the impact of minimum wages on the ratio of lowest decile to median earnings and found that nearly all of the increase in earnings inequality in the 1980s was due to the decrease in the value of the minimum wage relative to median earnings. For example, the distribution of earnings in 1982 showed a clear spike at the minimum wage (see Fig. 11.2). After the 1981 federal hike, the federal minimum was frozen for eight years and the lowest quantiles of the earnings distribution followed the downward movement of the real and relative value of the minimum wage, to such an extent that the distribution for 1989 just prior to the federal hike implemented in 1990 was similar to the kind of distribution that would prevail in the absence of a minimum wage.

Teulings took the analysis of the distributional impact a step further. Dinardo, Fortin, and Lemieux examined only the direct effect on the earnings distribution just mentioned—the sweeping-up of workers paid below it up to the minimum wage. Lee looked at the impact on quantile-median ratios, which blurs the direct and indirect effects on the shape of the earnings distribution. Teulings attempted to estimate the direct effect and the effect on the

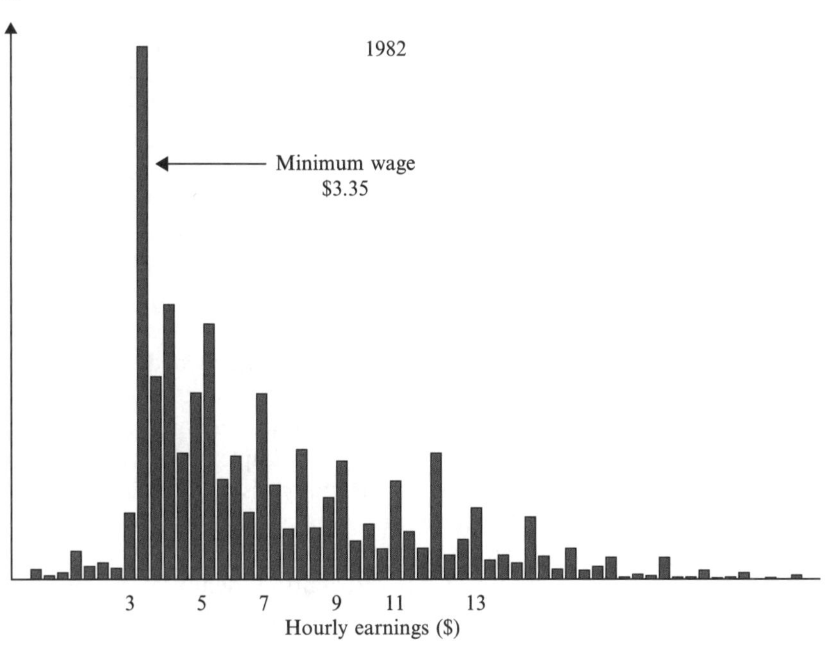

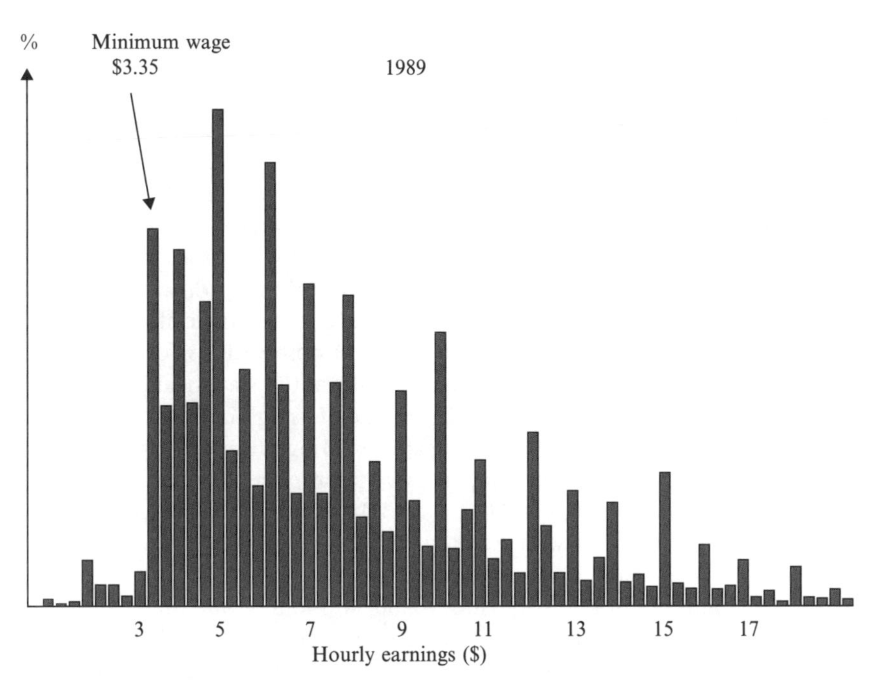

Figure 11.2 The distribution of hourly earnings in the USA in 1982 and 1989
Source: Author's calculations from the Current Population Survey.

return to human capital of changing the minimum wage. He formally tested and strongly rejected the hypothesis that there were no spillover effects on earnings higher than the minimum wage. He concluded that 'minimum wages can explain the whole of the increase in wage inequality in the lower half of the wage distribution during the 1980s' (2003: 831). In fact he found the effect on earnings just above the minimum to be more pronounced than the direct effect on those in the lower tail. Furthermore, the indirect effect diminishes as one moved up the earnings distribution.

A recent study by Neumark, Schweitzer, and Wascher (2004) attempted to take into account employment effects in the analysis of the distributional impact of the minimum wage. Rather than compare two distributions—those with and without a minimum wage (or increase in the minimum wage)—they examined what happens to individuals' earnings, hours and employment following minimum wage increases implemented at the state and federal level during this period. Their study also differs in that they examined lagged effects of the minimum wage, so that any initial impact may be subsequently tempered or exacerbated. Each effect was assessed at different points in the hourly earnings distribution, delimited in terms of proximity to the forthcoming minimum wage. In line with other studies of the impact on the hourly earnings distribution, their results showed a strong direct (sweeping up) effect in the year of the minimum wage increase, an effect which is tempered but not cancelled out a year later. There were initially indirect (ripple) effects on earnings up to possibly 1.5 times the minimum wage but they found that these were all cancelled out subsequently, except for individuals earning within ten per cent of the minimum wage.

In order to take into account any employment adjustments which may undermine the positive distributional effect, Neumark, Schweitzer, and Wascher (2004) presented estimates of the probability that an individual is employed, and of the number of weekly hours worked conditional on being employed. The employment impact is, in general, not statistically significant. Their estimates were based on nearly 850,000 observations for the period 1979–92 and, arguably, one could require substantial statistical significance if there really is any effect. For example, instead of using a critical value of 1.96 for the absolute t-statistic when testing statistical significance, a critical value based on the Schwarz criterion may be more appropriate. In the current case, this would be equal to $\ln(\sqrt{850{,}000}) = 6.83$. In any case, for the employment effects, the reported t-statistics are only -1.85 for individuals earning within 10 cents, and -2.1 for those earning within 10 per cent, of the minimum wage. The highest absolute t-statistic (-2.86) was found much further up the distribution for those initially earning 20 to 30 per cent more than the minimum wage. These results are not consistent with the notion that the positive, direct distributional impact found around the minimum wage is undermined by loss of employment among the affected population. The only context in which Neumark, Schweitzer, and Wascher (2004) appear to have found an employment adjustment was in terms of hours of work (and then only with a one year lag after the increase in the minimum wage) which decreased for those earning within 10 cents and 10 per cent of the minimum. On the basis of their calculations, taking into account the statistically questionable employment effect and this apparently more robust hours effect, they suggested that weekly labour income may decline for those earning within 10 cents of the minimum wage by a small amount.

It appears, then, that in the USA, the federal minimum wage plays a key role in supporting the bottom of the earnings distribution. When it is not uprated regularly, earnings inequality tends to increase as there are no forces preventing wages from stagnating and declining relative to other earnings. The freezing of the federal minimum wage in the United States for most of the 1980s provides clear evidence of this tendency, and may be the main reason why earnings inequality rose over the period. However, as mentioned at the outset, whether there were adverse effects on employment or not, an effective minimum wage would be expected to have an inequality-reducing effect on the dispersion of earnings.

11.2 Minimum wages and employment

Four of these five studies of the impact of minimum wages on the earnings distribution mentioned above share a common assumption, namely that any detrimental employment effects are negligible or non-existent. However, any reduction in the employment of the affected groups raises doubts over the beneficial nature of the impact on the earnings distribution. This is, first, because the distributional effects only benefit workers who remain in employment. A second and less obvious issue is whether there are beneficial distributional effects for certain workers at the expense of others. In the early 1980s, the assumption of negligible employment effects would have been rejected as unrealistic since a consensus view had emerged that minimum wages had a statistically significant, negative impact on teenage employment (but not the employment of other groups). The survey by Brown, Gilroy, and Kohen (1982), for example, concluded that a 10 per cent increase in the federal minimum wage reduced teenage employment by between 1 and 3 per cent.

This consensus was questioned by David Card and Alan Krueger who found that the 1992 increase in the minimum wage in New Jersey increased employment in fast food restaurants. And this study was not the only piece of research in which no negative employment effects were found. Earlier papers by Card (1992*a*, 1992*b*), Card, Katz, and Krueger (1994), Holzer, Katz, and Krueger (1991), and Katz and Krueger (1990, 1992), found no significant effects associated with rises in the federal minimum, the state-specific minimum wages set in California and Texas, or increases in both types of minimum in a panel of US states. Card and Krueger (1995) brought together this material in a book, adding a critical re-examination of earlier research.

Many economists regarded the findings of Card and Krueger (1995) as the advent of a new approach to analysing the operation of the labour market and an abandoning of the competitive model. Others were dismissive of their findings and continued to adhere to a competitive framework especially in the market for low-skill labour. Among researchers working in the area of the impact of minimum wages, there have been a number of attempts to examine the robustness of their results. (Card and Krueger encouraged this work by providing free and complete access to the data sets, questionnaires and computer programs they used.)

There are essentially two issues at stake: why their results differ from those obtained in previous research, and the extent to which the idea that minimum wage increases have no effect on employment is applicable in the USA. The first issue concerns research methodology, whereas the second one is a more substantive economic question. Research has centred on three aspects: the validity of the New Jersey study, the apparent absence of effects of federal minimum wage hikes using time-series data, and the analysis of state and federal minimum wage increases on state employment levels.

The impact of 1992 New Jersey minimum wage increase

The federal minimum wage had been frozen at $3.35 throughout the 1980s following concerns about negative effects on teenage employment and due to an administration hostile to intervention in the labour market. It was subsequently raised to $4.25 in two stages, to $3.85 in April 1990 and $4.25 in April 1991. Due to lack of activity on the federal front during the 1980s, a number of states implemented their own minimum wage increases. (Not all states have minimum wage legislation and those that do have it do not always set minimum rates independently of the federal system.)

This continued to a lesser extent after the federal increases of the early 1990s. The state of New Jersey, having left its minimum wage unchanged throughout the 1980s, increased it from $4.25 to $5.05 in April 1992, a sizeable hike of 18 per cent. In order to test the hypothesis that increases in the minimum wage reduce employment, Card and Krueger (1994) undertook a telephone questionnaire survey of the effects on employment, wages and other variables in a sample of fast-food restaurants between the first and third quarters of 1992 in New Jersey, and also in the neighbouring state of Pennsylvania (where the minimum wage remained unchanged in 1992 at $4.25). Such establishments typically employ a significant part of their workforce on wages equal to, or close to, the legal minimum wage. Since employment levels in fast-food restaurants in contiguous states are likely to be influenced by the same general economic environment, any difference that shows up in employment variations over the period can be attributed to the minimum wage increase in New Jersey. This is a quasi-experimental approach, in which the New Jersey fast-food restaurants constitute the treatment group and those in Pennsylvania the control group.

Card and Krueger's main findings concerning the effect of the minimum wage are presented in Table 11.1. More than half of the New Jersey restaurants increased their employment levels over the period covered and average employment per restaurant increased by +0.59 full-time equivalent workers (FTEs). On the basis of these two observations it is not possible to deduce that these effects are due to the minimum wage. There could have been other demand-side factors that gave rise to increased employment during the eight month period studied. This is why the Pennsylvania sample is critical in the evaluation of the impact of the minimum wage. However average employment fell in Pennsylvania −2.26 FTEs, suggesting that in the absence of the minimum wage, increased employment would have fallen in New Jersey. The difference in differences estimate of +2.75 gives the impact of minimum wages in New Jersey so that, while employment rose on average by one part-time worker in New Jersey, in the absence of the minimum wage increase it would have fallen by more than two full-time workers (i.e. the change in employment in the control group). Overall, the impact of the minimum wage rise was to raise average employment by more than two and a half full-time workers relative to what it would have been in the absence of the increase. These findings stand up to a large number of robustness checks that were undertaken by Card and Krueger (using the same sample) such as using different weights, adding controls, taking into account ownership and geographical situation.

The Card and Krueger study has been criticized on at least two fronts. First, it is claimed that it is defective because it comes up with a result that is at odds with the conventional theoretical conclusions and the large amount of evidence that seems to converge on a narrow range of negative elasticities.

Table 11.1 Summary of Card and Krueger's study of fast-food restaurants

	New Jersey	Pennsylvania
Percentage of restaurants where employment:		
Decreases	44.0	53.3
Increases	51.5	41.3
Average number of full-time equivalent employees per restaurant:		
February	20.44	23.33
November	21.03	21.17
Change	+0.59	−2.16
Difference-in-differences	+2.75	

Source: Card and Krueger (1995) Tables 2.2 and 2.5.

Second, it is claimed the way the study was undertaken undermines the conclusion and that, had it been done properly, the opposite conclusion would have been obtained (that minimum wage rises reduced the employment of some of those who would have earned less). Neumark and Wascher (2000) obtained data drawn from payroll records from a sample of restaurants in the states of New Jersey and Pennsylvania. They found that the impact of the minimum wage hike on employment in this sample was the opposite of that found by Card and Krueger. Using Zip codes, they were able to find restaurants in the same chains and in the same local areas as the Card and Krueger sample (although a perfect match was not possible because the codes did not correspond to exact addresses), and contacted these restaurants requesting data from their payroll records for the period covered in the Card and Krueger study. They found that, in New Jersey, employment declined relative to employment in Pennsylvania, and that regression estimates suggested that the minimum wage elasticity was around –0.2.

In their reply, Card and Krueger (2000) re-analysed these data and in addition introduced a further data source (made available by the US Bureau of Labor Statistics), derived from employer declarations of payroll records made for unemployment insurance purposes, and which covered fast-food restaurants in New Jersey and Pennsylvania. The data suggest that it was the Neumark-Wascher sample and, in particular, the sample of Pennsylvania restaurants, that might not be representative. Using the Bureau of Labor Statistics data, Card and Krueger found the same result as in their original study. The minimum wage increase had no negative impact on fast-food employment (although the coefficients are positive but not significant as in the original study).

Time-series evidence

That a substantial increase in a minimum wage can have no adverse effect on employment is a major finding. However it is not clear that this result generalizes to other situations, whether the effect on employment is in other sectors (where there is international competition for example), or in other states. In particular, one of the main concerns expressed by critics was that the Card and Krueger results were at odds with the consensus view based essentially on time-series evidence. In their survey article, Brown, Gilroy, and Kohen (1982) concluded that increases in minimum wages had a negative effect on teenage employment with elasticity estimates in the range –0.1 to –0.3 for the period from 1954 to 1979.

The standard specification for the time-series regression equation used in the studies surveyed had the following form:

$$E = g(MWK, X, U, \text{Time Trend, Time Trend Squared, Seasonal dummies}) \quad [1]$$

where E is the employment-population ratio for 16–19 year-olds, X is a vector of supply-side control variables, U is the unemployment rate among men aged 25–54 (a proxy for cyclical factors). MWK is the so-called Kaitz index which is defined as $(C \times M)/W$, where M is the value of the federal minimum wage, W is the average manufacturing wage, and C is the coverage rate. (At first the federal minimum did not apply to all workers and coverage was extended progressively until the early 1970s.)

In their book, Card and Krueger (1995) re-assessed the time-series evidence based on the specification shown in [1], and claimed that there had been 'publication bias' in favour of studies that had found negative employment effects. The basis of their claim was that studies using more data did not find smaller standard errors (or larger absolute t-ratios) for the minimum wage coefficient, as would be the case if the effect was well-defined in a statistical sense. Furthermore, they re-estimated the standard model using data up to 1993 and found that, while the coefficient was still negative, it was both smaller in absolute value and no longer statistically significant.

The US time-series data provide a useful basis for testing the impact of minimum wages on employment. After the increase to $3.35 in 1981, the federal minimum wage was frozen until 1990 when the federal minimum was increased by 28 per cent to $4.25 (in two steps over two years). This context provides an excellent opportunity for evaluating the validity of the consensus view since, if the earlier research findings were correct, an increase in teenage employment relative to trend should be observed (because the real and relative values of the minimum had declined). Bazen and Marimoutou (2002) re-estimated this equation for the period 1954–79, and found that it substantially over-predicted teenage employment over the period during which the minimum wage was frozen, 1982–89. The econometric basis for the consensus view appears to be unsound.

The econometric analysis of time-series data has undergone a revolution since 1980 when this consensus emerged. The earlier practice of correcting for serial correlation and introducing deterministic trends in order to isolate the effects of economic variables has been found to be inappropriate, except in very special circumstances. A more flexible specification of cyclical, trend and seasonal influences using a stochastic rather than deterministic specification, produces a model that provided very accurate forecasts of employment over the period when the minimum wage was unchanged. Furthermore, the estimated model revealed that, for the period 1954–79, minimum wages had a small but statistically significant negative impact on teenage employment, with a short-run elasticity of -0.1 and a long-run elasticity of between -0.2 and -0.3. The range of elasticities is similar to that reported by Brown, Gilroy, and Kohen (1982). The estimated model successfully predicted a downturn in teenage employment over 1990–92 when the minimum wage was increased and the model remained on track until the end of the period studied (1999).

Williams and Mills (2001) arrived at similar conclusions using a VAR approach.

The time-series evidence therefore tells a very different story from the New Jersey studies. It is important to bear in mind however that the former concerns a large number of federal rises whereas the New Jersey fast-food studies relate to a single rise implemented at state level. In this light, that two different conclusions are found does not necessarily mean the results are conflicting. Minimum wages can have different effects on employment in different contexts.

Panel data evidence on the impact of state and federal minimum wage increases

Combining cross-section and time-series information by using panel data on states over time would appear to be particularly appropriate in the light of the different results obtained in the Card and Krueger case study compared to the time-series approaches. Furthermore, the effects of both state and federal minimum wages can be assessed in a single empirical framework. Neumark and Wascher (1992), for example, used data from the annual Current Population Survey for the period 1973–89 and estimated an equation similar to [1], replacing time trends with time dummies, and introducing state fixed effects:

$$E_{st} = \phi_s + \phi_1 U_{st} + \phi_2 P_{st} + \phi_3 S_{st} + \theta MWK_{st} + \lambda_t + \upsilon_{st} \qquad [2]$$

where υ_{st} is the error term for state s in year t, P_{st} is the proportion of the state population that is aged 16–19, S_{st} is the proportion of 16–19 year-olds enrolled in school, and MWK_{st} is the state level Kaitz index. The equation was estimated with state fixed effects ϕ_s and time fixed effects λ_t. Neumark and Wascher found a negative and statistically significant effect of minimum wages on teenage employment, so long as the school enrolment rate was included among the control variables. If excluded, the effect of the minimum wage was positive though statistically insignificant. Card, Katz, and Krueger (1994), and Card and Krueger (1995), questioned the exogeneity of the enrolment rate and its almost mechanical link to the dependent variable (the employment–population ratio).

Burkhauser, Couch, and Wittenberg (2000) used monthly rather than annual data from the Current Population Survey for 1979 to 1992 to estimate the impact of both state and federal minimum wage increases on teenage employment. Burkhauser, Couch, and Wittenberg use the same specification as preferred by Card and Krueger (1995), that is, without the school enrolment rate, and with the minimum and average wages entered separately:

$$E_{st} = \phi_s + \phi_1 U_{st} + \phi_2 P_{st} + \theta_1 w_{st} + \theta_2 m_{st} + \lambda_t + \upsilon_{st} \qquad [3]$$

where w_{st} is the logarithm of average usual earnings of adult workers in state s in month t, and m_{st} is the logarithm of the prevailing minimum wage—the higher of the state or the federal minimum wage.

The estimates of Burkhauser, Couch, and Wittenberg (2000) threw up an interesting finding that goes some way to explain why Card and Krueger (1995) found no evidence of negative effects in their analysis of these data. When the equation was estimated with time dummies as Card and Krueger did, the minimum wage elasticity estimate was −0.07 but not statistically significant (t-ratio = −1), whereas when they were excluded, the elasticity was larger in absolute value (−0.4) and highly significant (t-ratio = −10). Burkhauser, Couch, and Wittenberg showed that this difference was due to the almost perfect correlation between the time dummies for years when the federal minimum wage was raised and the minimum wage variable.

Although Burkhauser, Couch, and Wittenberg do not mention it, these results suggest that the state level minimum wage increases implemented during this period had no significant effects on teenage employment. In order to explore the hypothesis that only federal minimum wage increases have a negative effect on teenage employment, Bazen and Gallo (2005) used annual panel data from the Current Population Survey. Between 1982 and 1989, the only increases in minimum wages in the USA were those implemented by a small minority of mainland states, and these occurred from 1985 onwards. When Bazen and Gallo (2005) re-estimated [3] over the period 1985–89 without the time dummies, the minimum wage coefficient was positive but not statistically significant (see Table 11.2). However, the same model estimated over 1990–91 when the federal minimum was raised from $3.35 to $4.25 produces a negative and statistically significant coefficient on the minimum wage variable.

These two findings stand up to a number of specification checks (for example estimating the model recursively and using dummies to represent the minimum wage increases). In the period 1992–95, there were only six state minimum wage increases (including the New Jersey increase) and, when estimated over this sub-period, the model produced a small positive, though statistically insignificant, coefficient (see Table 11.2). For the 1996–97 increases in the federal minimum (from $4.25 to $5.05), Bazen and Gallo (2005) again found a negative coefficient, though it was not statistically significant. These results, which are also implicit in the findings of Burkhauser, Couch, and Wittenberg, suggest that since 1982 only federal minimum wage increases have had a negative impact in teenage employment. State minimum wage increases by and large had no effect on employment.

Card and Krueger's (1995) study provides serious evidence that minimum wages can be increased without deleterious effects on employment. This conclusion stands up to outside observation and re-analysis. Their New Jersey results do not, however, generalize to minimum wage increases at the federal

Table 11.2 Panel data estimates of the effects of state and federal minimum wage increases

	1984–89	1990–91	1984–91	1991–95	1996–97	1991–97
State minimum wage (log)	0.168		0.173*	0.009		0.009
	[0.141]		[0.074]	[0.267]		[0.179]
Federal minimum wage (log)		−0.173**	−0.223**		−0.109	−0.111
		[0.069]	[0.074]		[0.069]	[0.091]
Unemployment rate	−0.0053	−0.0095	−0.0067	−0.0019	−0.0012	−0.0019
	[0.0032]	[0.0062]	[0.0062]	[0.0065]	[0.017]	[0.0025]
Teenage population ratio	−0.634	0.183	−0.412**	0.345	0.174	0.276
	[0.648]	[1.024]	[0.074]	[1.221]	[0.783]	[0.579]
Average adult earnings	0.085	−0.094	0.050	0.122	0.128	0.121
	[0.089]	[0.186]	[0.074]	[0.145]	[0.188]	[0.070]
Uncentred R^2	0.115	0.339	0.212	0.077	0.071	0.075
Number of observations	240	96	336	192	96	288

Notes: Bootstrap standard errors in brackets. * statistically significant at 5% level. ** statistically significant at 1% level.

Source: Bazen and Le Gallo (2005), Tables 2, 5, 6 and 7.

level. Time-series analyses examine the effects of federal minimum wage increases and, when the econometric model is appropriately specified, a significant negative effect is found. In a panel data analysis, however, state minimum wage increases are found to have no negative effect on employment whereas federal increases do, at least in the period 1984–97. This empirical conclusion provides an answer to the puzzling question of why Card and Krueger found no evidence of significant negative employment effects in a variety of contexts where individual states had increased their minimum wages, whereas the time-series data (when properly modelled) suggested that increases in federal minimum wages have a negative impact on teenage employment.

11.3. Conclusions

Recent research into the impact of minimum wages in the United States suggests that during the 1980s and 1990s, the effect on the distribution of earnings is more empirically relevant (in terms of size and statistical significance) than any employment effects. The distributional effect is found for both state and federal minimum wages, whereas any employment effects that are found for this period pertain only to sporadic and sizeable hikes in the federal minimum wage. Furthermore, these effects while statistically significant are of limited size and relate to teenage employment.

More research is required on the nature of the federal–state dichotomy concerning the employment effects of minimum wages. It is not obvious in theoretical terms why a minimum wage hike implemented at the state level should have a different effect on employment to one implemented at the federal level. One possibility is that the states that increased their minima during the 1980s tended to do so several times. Only 12 states used their own legislation between 1984 and 1989, and seven of these increased their minimum more than once (four of these did so three times or more). The majority of the increases were therefore relatively small and concentrated in a small number of states (in the New England division). Given the regularity of the increases, the minimum wage remained a binding constraint in these states, and so firms could not use the slack federal constraint to adopt a strategy based on employing more low-wage labour.

By 1990, states that had implemented increases had minimum wages of between $3.55 and $4.25, and the increase in the federal minimum in 1990 from $3.35 to $3.85 had relatively little impact on employers in these states. In contrast, low-wage employers in states without local legislation, during the period in which the federal minimum was frozen, may have taken advantage of the slack federal constraint. When this regime came to an end and an effective wage floor was reinstated, employers found their employment levels unprofitable. Sporadic hikes in the federal minimum create abrupt regime changes in states without a binding local minimum wage and, as a consequence, have adverse effects on employment. A gradualist approach in which minimum wages are raised regularly by small amounts thereby maintaining a floor to wages may not give rise to a significant employment impact as firms operate within a stable regime. Furthermore, this approach would maintain a floor under the earnings distribution and prevent earnings inequality from increasing in the lower half of the earnings distribution.

This conclusion is broadly supported by evidence from other countries. In particular, the introduction of a national minimum wage in the United Kingdom in 1998 appears to have had a significant inequality-reducing effect on the earnings distribution. Since its introduction, the minimum has been regularly uprated thereby maintaining a firm floor under the earnings distribution with no discernible effect on employment (see, for example, Metcalf 2002). In France, successive annual increases in the last 15 years have led to a doubling of the proportion of workers affected by the minimum wage, from 8 per cent in 1993 to 16 per cent in 2005. This degree of compression of the lower tail of the earnings distribution may have worrying consequences. In France, there is concern that firms find it difficult to provide appropriate incentives for supervisory workers, that wage rates that have been collectively agreed by firms and unions are overtaken by the minimum wage set by government and that some groups of workers remain on the minimum wage for substantial parts of their working lives. The evidence presented here suggests that research could be usefully directed into assessing the nature and consequences of the modification of the lower tail of the earnings distribution that results from minimum wage increases. Of particular interest are the issues of how firms' internal pay structures are modified and what happens to workers in the affected population over time.

References

Bazen, S. and Le Gallo, J. (2005). 'The Answer to the US Minimum Wage Puzzle? Only Federal Minimum Wage Hikes have a Negative Effect on Teenage Employment'. Paper presented at the LoWER Annual Conference, ZEW Mannheim, Germany, April.

—— and Marimoutou, V. (2002). 'Looking for a Needle in a Haystack? A Re-Examination of the Time Series Relationship Between Teenage Employment and Minimum Wages in the United States'. *Oxford Bulletin of Economics and Statistics*, 64: 699–725.

Bound, J. and Johnson, G. (1992). 'Changes in the Structure of Wages in the 1980s: an Evaluation of Alternative Explanations'. *American Economic Review*, 82: 371–92.

Brown, C., Gilroy, C., and Kohen, A. (1982). 'The Effect of the Minimum Wage on Employment and Unemployment'. *Journal of Economic Literature*, 20: 487–528.

——, ——, and —— (1983). 'Time Series Evidence on the Effect of the Minimum Wage on Teenage Employment and Unemployment'. *Journal of Human Resources*, 18: 3–31.

Burkhauser, R., Couch, K. A., and Wittenberg, D. C. (2000). 'A Reassessment of the New Economics of the Minimum Wage Literature using Monthly Data from the CPS'. *Journal of Labor Economics*, 18: 653–702.

Card, D. (1992a). 'Using Regional Variation in Wages to Measure the Effects of the Federal Minimum Wage'. *Industrial and Labor Relations Review*, 46: 22–37.

——, (1992b) 'Do Minimum Wages Reduce Employment? A Case Study of California 1987–1989'. *Industrial and Labor Relations Review*, 46: 38–54.

—— and Krueger, A. (1994). 'Minimum Wages and Employment: a Case Study of the Fast-Food Industry in New Jersey and Pennsylvania'. *American Economic Review*, 84: 772–93.

—— and —— (1995). *Myth and Measurement: The New Economics of the Minimum Wage*. New Jersey: Princeton University Press.

—— and —— (2000). 'Minimum Wages and Employment: a Case Study of the Fast-Food Industry in New Jersey and Pennsylvania: Reply'. *American Economic Review*, 90: 1397–420.

——, Katz, L., and Krueger, A. (1994). 'Comment on David Neumark and William Wascher, "Employment Effects of Minimum and Sub-minimum Wages: Panel Data on State Minimum Wage Laws" '. *Industrial and Labor Relations Review*, 48: 487–96.

Deere, D., Murphy, S., and Welch, F. (1995). 'Employment and the 1990–1991 Minimum Wage Hike'. *American Economic Review, Papers and Proceedings*, 85: 232–7.

Dinardo, J., Fortin, N., and Lemieux, T. (1996). 'Labor Market Institutions and the Distribution of Wages 1973–92'. *Econometrica*, 64: 610–43.

Freeman, R. (1996). 'The Minimum Wage as Redistributive Tool'. *Economic Journal*, 106: 639–49.

Holzer, H., Katz, L., and Krueger, A. (1991). 'Job Queues and Wages'. *Quarterly Journal of Economics*, 106: 739–68.

Katz, L. and Autor, D. (1999). 'Wage Inequality', in O. Ashenefelter and D. Card (eds), *Handbook of Labor Economics, Volume 3*. Amsterdam: North Holland.

—— and Krueger, A. (1990). 'The Effect of the New Minimum Wage Law in a Low-Wage Labor Market'. *Industrial Relations Research Association Proceedings*, 43: 254–65.

—— and —— (1992). 'The Effect of the Minimum Wage on the Fast Food Industry'. *Industrial and Labor Relations Review*, 46: 6–21.

Kennan, J. (1996). 'The Elusive Effects of Minimum Wages'. *Journal of Economic Literature*, 33: 1949–65.

Lee, D. (1999). 'Wage Inequality During the 1980s: Rising Dispersion or Falling Minimum Wage?' *Quarterly Journal of Economics*, 114: 35–78.

Manning, A. (2003). *Monopsony in Motion*. Cambridge, MA: MIT Press.

Metcalf, D. (2002). 'The National Minimum Wage: Coverage, Impact and Future'. *Oxford Bulletin of Economics and Statistics*, 64: 567–82.

Neumark, D. and Wascher, W. (1992). 'Employment Effects of Minimum Wages and Subminimum Wages: Panel Data on State Minimum Wage Laws'. *Industrial and Labor Relations Review*, 46: 55–81.

—— and —— (2000). 'Minimum Wages and Employment: a Case Study of the Fast-Food Industry in New Jersey and Pennsylvania: Comment'. *American Economic Review*, 90: 1362–96.

——, Schwarzer, M., and Wascher, W. (2004). 'Minimum Wage Effects Throughout the Wage Distribution'. *Journal of Human Resources*, 39: 425–53.

Teulings, C. (2003). 'The Contribution of Minimum Wages to Increasing Wage Inequality'. *Economic Journal*, 113: 801–33.

Williams, N. and Mills, J. (2001). 'The Minimum Wage and Teenage Employment: Evidence from Time Series'. *Applied Economics*, 33: 285–300.

Wood, A. (1994) *North–South Trade, Employment and Inequality: Changing Fortunes in a Skill-Driven World*. Oxford: Oxford University Press.

12

Training, minimum wages and the distribution of earnings

*Alison L. Booth and Mark L. Bryan**

> The Government believes that work is the best route out of poverty and is committed to making work pay by improving incentives to participate and progress in the labour market. Through the Working Tax Credit and the National Minimum Wage, the Government has boosted in-work incomes, improving financial incentives to work and tackling poverty among working people. (HM Treasury 2006: 92)

Work is widely seen as representing the 'best route out of poverty', as the quotation above makes clear. In the UK in 2004–05, working-age adults had a 48 per cent chance of being poor if they belonged to a workless household, compared to only a 23 per cent chance if they lived in a working household (DWP 2006: 71).[1] Nevertheless, having a job may not be sufficient to lift low skilled workers and their families out of poverty. In fact most of the working-age poor (57%) are in households that contain one or more working adults (DWP 2006: 68). This suggests that, as well as getting people into work, an effective anti-poverty strategy will need to increase the earnings of low-skilled individuals when they do work. This in turn will further increase the incentives to participate.

In recent years in the UK, policy to increase low earnings has been based on the introduction of a national minimum wage and the expansion of in-work tax credits (see Brewer and Shephard 2004, and Sutherland 2001). These measures provide a direct boost to earnings and thereby help reduce poverty and inequality. But the longer term prospects of low-paid workers are also likely to depend on improving their skills.[2]

* Part of this research was supported by an ARC Discovery Award.

[1] Poverty is defined here as a net equivalized disposable household income before housing costs of less than 60% of the median. A working household is a household containing at least one adult in work.

[2] There have been various initiatives to encourage basic training amongst low-paid workers. One of the latest measures is a Train to Gain programme, which, from 2006, will offer subsidized training to low-skilled workers in small firms.

Our aim in this chapter is to look at work-related training in relation to the overall wage distribution and in particular to focus on the interaction between the national minimum wage and the training of low-paid workers. The proposition that a minimum wage would restrict training opportunities open to workers was initially suggested by Rosen (1972) and followed from developments in human capital theory. With competitive labour markets, human capital theory predicts that the introduction of a minimum wage will reduce investment in training by covered workers who can no longer contribute to training costs through lower wages. If, instead, the labour market for the low paid is imperfectly competitive and workers are credit constrained, then a minimum wage can increase investment in the general component of training (Stevens 1994; Chang and Wang 1996; Acemoglu and Pischke 1999; Booth and Zoega 2004).[3] This arises because the monopsonistic character of the labour market introduces a wedge between the wage and the marginal product. If this wedge increases with general training, so that wages are compressed, then the firm can keep some of the surplus generated by general training. Since the introduction of a minimum wage acts to compress wages, it can induce employers to train their unskilled workers (Acemoglu and Pischke 2003).

Our chapter is set out as follows. In section 12.1, we demonstrate that work-related training is disproportionately received by workers who are towards the middle and top of the distribution of wages. In section 12.2, we address the issue of whether or not training affects the longer-term job prospects of British workers. We find, using panel data, that training has statistically significant positive effects that do not seem to decline over our seven-year estimating period. In section 12.3, we summarize the results of our earlier work (Arulampalam *et al.* 2004*a*; Bryan 2005) that uses difference-in-difference methods to estimate whether or not the introduction of the national minimum wage in 1999 in Britain had an adverse effect on the training of low-paid workers. Overall, there is no evidence that the minimum wage introduction reduced the training of affected workers, and some evidence that it increased it by around 8 to 11 percentage points. The findings do not support models of training investment based on competitive labour markets, but are consistent with more recent theories involving imperfect labour market competition. In the final section, we argue that the minimum wage therefore has the potential to reduce wage inequality in the longer term, since available empirical evidence for Britain shows that minimum wages are associated with a small increase in work-related training for the low paid, and have not adversely affected the employment of British workers.[4]

[3] General training refers to skills that are useful to other firms as well as to the firm providing the training.

[4] For evidence on the employment effects of the introduction of the national minimum wage in Britain, see *inter alia* Stewart (2002, 2004) and Machin, Manning, and Rahman (2003).

12.1 How training incidence varies across the hourly wages distribution

It is well known that more highly educated workers have a higher probability of receiving work-related training (see *inter alia* Arulampalam, Booth, and Bryan 2004*b*, Bassanini *et al.* 2007, and references therein). It is also well-documented that work-related training has a positive effect on wages and year-on-year wages growth (see the survey by Blundell *et al.* 1999). Although, to our knowledge, no research has documented variation in the incidence of work-related training across the hourly wage distribution, we did report in Arulampalam, Booth, and Bryan (2003*b*: Appendix Table A.2) summary statistics using data from ten countries derived from the European Community Household Panel (ECHP).[5] The figures suggested that, in most of the European countries analysed, low-paid workers received substantially less training than their higher-paid counterparts. For Britain, the ECHP data revealed that training participation for men in the bottom fifth of the wage distribution was 43 per cent of training participation of men in the top fifth of the wage distribution whereas, for women, the corresponding figure was 47 per cent. This compares with the mean across all countries of 30 per cent for men and 19 per cent for women. The country with the most equal distribution of training incidence was the Netherlands, being 131 per cent for men and 117 per cent for women, while the most unequal for men was Ireland at 15 per cent and Italy for women at 15 per cent. The highest training incidence countries in our ECHP sample were Britain, Denmark, and Finland.

To explore in more detail the variation in training incidence across the British wages distribution, we next report information on training and wages from Waves 8–10 of the British Household Panel Survey (BHPS), conducted over survey years 1998 to 2000. This window was chosen to be comparable with the analysis reported in section 12.3.[6] The BHPS is a nationally representative panel survey of private households in Britain. We pool observations from three waves, where our sample includes all employed (private sector and public sector) men and women aged between 18 and 60 years. We then position these men and women within the hourly wage distribution. The hourly wage data for each year are obtained from the annual survey points.[7]

[5] See Arulampalam, Booth, and Bryan (2003*b*) for full details of how these figures were calculated.

[6] We are constrained to start our analysis of the minimum wage and training at Wave 8 of the BHPS since that was when the training questions in the BHPS were altered to elicit more detailed information about specific training events. As discussed by Booth and Bryan (2007), the responses are not directly comparable to those from previous waves. Secondly, Waves 8 and 10 bracket the introduction of the minimum wage in 1999. Stopping our analysis at Wave 10 allows us to examine the impact of the introduction of the National Minimum Wage rather than estimating the impact of subsequent increases in the minimum wage, as we explain in greater detail in section 12.3.

[7] Gross hourly wages were calculated as hourly wages = (usual gross pay per month × 12/52) / [(usual standard weekly hours) + 1.5 × (usual weekly paid overtime hours)].

Figure 12.1 Training incidence for men and women across the hourly wages distribution

Source: Authors' calculations from unweighted BHPS data, waves 8–10 pooled.

We construct, from responses to the training questions, a training incidence variable. This is an indicator variable measuring whether a worker attended any training schemes or courses (employer-provided or not) that were intended to increase or improve skills in the current job, received since 1 September in the previous year.[8] The measure excludes spells of full-time education and leisure courses.

Training incidence is 17 per cent in the bottom tenth of the hourly wage distribution. It then increases to around 20 per cent in the second and third tenths, and continues to increase to a peak of just over 40 per cent in the ninth decile group before declining to 36 per cent for the top tenth. Average training incidence for the entire sample is 28.5 per cent and there are 12,531 person-year observations.

Figure 12.1 shows training incidence separately for men and women over the decile groups of the combined wage distribution. The profile for women is

[8] The survey asks for details of up to three training events received since 1 September of the previous year. The precise question is: 'Was this course or training: (i) To help you get started in your current job? (ii) To increase your skills in your current job? (iii) To improve your skills in the current job? (iv) To prepare you for a job or jobs you might do in the future? (v) To develop your skills generally?' The categories are not mutually exclusive. We combined categories (ii) and (iii) to create variables that measured training intended to increase or improve skills in the current job. Some 85% of reported training events are covered by this definition. See Booth and Bryan (2007), for a detailed analysis of the training data.

even more skewed than for the figures for all workers just discussed. Only 16 per cent of women in the bottom tenth receive training, compared to 45 per cent in the ninth decile group. For men the gradient is less steep, with 20 per cent receiving training in the bottom decile group compared to 37 per cent for the ninth group. The low incidence of training at the bottom of distribution affects women disproportionately because they are concentrated in this part of the distribution. More than two-thirds of workers in the bottom two decile groups are women and, in fact, they account for over a quarter of all women. Although, overall, women have slightly higher training incidence than men (29.4% compared to 27.5%), this reflects the fact that the minority of women in the higher part of the distribution get substantially more training than their male counterparts.

How is this information relevant to minimum wages? Workers covered by the national minimum wage are in the lowest decile group. Figure 12.1 indicates that, overall, they receive less work-related training than any other decile group. In particular, those above the 8th decile are more than twice as likely to receive work-related training as workers in the bottom decile group. And for women (who make up two-thirds of UK minimum wage workers, LPC 2005) the gradient is steeper. This lack of human capital acquisition may impede the wage growth of these low paid workers. Whether or not the national minimum wage affects the training incidence of low paid workers is therefore of considerable interest, since it could further advantage or disadvantage them through affecting their wage position.

In section 12.3 we investigate whether or not the introduction of the national minimum wage did affect the training receipt of low-paid workers. If the minimum wage affects training incidence, then in the longer term workers might be indirectly affected by the minimum wage through its training effects, as well as through the more direct employment effects much discussed in the literature. If the introduction of the minimum wage reduces the amount of training of workers at the bottom of the wage distribution, it is likely to worsen the longer-term wage prospects of the low paid. On the other hand, if its introduction increases training incidence of low paid workers, then it has the potential to improve their longer-term wage prospects.

As background to our analysis of the minimum wage effects, the next section provides an illustration, using BHPS data, of how training can affect long-term wage growth.

12.2 A longer-term perspective

In this section, we demonstrate the potential longer-term effects of work-related training by estimating its impact on individuals' long-term wage prospects. To do this, we clearly need more waves of data than the three utilized in the analysis in section 12.1. We therefore use wages data from Waves 7–14 of the BHPS, spanning the period 1997 to 2004. The training data are from Waves 8 to 14.[9] Because we wish to estimate the impact of *accumulated* training events on wages growth over the period 1997 to 2004, our main estimating sub-sample is a balanced panel comprising men and women who were aged 18 to 53 years in 1997 and who were employed at all waves.

Of course, by estimating on this balanced panel, we are of necessity dropping individuals with discontinuous labour market histories over that period. These may be lower-paid individuals, and may potentially include some workers who lost their jobs following the introduction of the minimum wage (though, as we note later, there is little evidence that the minimum wage has caused job losses). We are therefore estimating on a rather selected sample. To check the sensitivity of our results to this criticism, we also re-estimated our wages growth specifications on a larger sample of individuals including those who moved in and out of work over the period 1997 to 2004. We report on those estimates towards the end of this sub-section.

The preceding analysis in section 12.1 showed that higher-paid workers get more training, and therefore it would not be surprising to find that workers who do well in the long-term also receive more training over the years. The aim of our analysis is to measure the causal effect of training on wages, while netting out the correlation between the two that would exist even if training had no effect. To do this, it is necessary to control for factors which raise wages but are also associated with higher training. Some of these factors, such as education, are observed in the BHPS data but others, like career orientation, are not. Our estimation method is therefore based on changes in wages between 1997 and 2003. This technique eliminates unobserved individual-specific effects that are time-invariant, since these are differenced out. The set of characteristics used in the estimation includes age, education, and marital status, occupation, industry, part-time and temporary contract status, trade union coverage and firm-size. In our basic wage equation, the growth of wages is modelled as a function of changes in these characteristics. We also estimate an extended specification which also allows wage growth to depend on the levels of observed characteristics in 1997. The detailed list of controls is given in the notes accompanying Table 12.2.

Accumulated training is measured as the total number of times training was experienced over Waves 8–14. We constructed two measures which are reported in Table 12.1: first, the number of waves in which training was received (accumulated incidence) and, second, the total number of events reported (up to 3 per wave). There are several reasons for using these aggregate measures rather than year-by-year indicators. First, Booth and Bryan (2005) showed, using the BHPS,

[9] Since the training data are derived by retrospective recall over the 12 months since the previous interview, it is appropriate to use wages data from Wave 7 onwards and training data from Wave 8 onward.

Table 12.1 Receipt of training over BHPS Waves 8–14

Sample	Accumulated training measure [1]	Mean training (unconditional) [2]	Percentage receiving training [3]	Mean training (conditional) [4]	Minimum training (conditional) [5]	Maximum training (conditional) [6]
Employed all Waves 7–14	Incidence	2.00	70.6	2.83	1	7
	Counts	3.56	70.6	5.04	1	20
Employed at least in Waves 7 and 14	Incidence	1.95	70.8	2.76	1	7
	Counts	3.45	70.8	4.87	1	20

Notes: Unconditional mean in column [2] calculated over all observations. Conditional mean in column [4] calculated over trainees (individuals receiving one or more training event).

that most of the wage increase following training is realized when workers subsequently change jobs. We argued that this finding is consistent with imperfections in labour or credit markets allowing training firms to receive some of the return to general training. Alternatively, if it is costly to evaluate general human capital, workers may only receive the full returns to training when they are interviewed for new jobs (Hart and Ritchie 2002). Training may also raise wages indirectly through future promotions (Melero 2004), and some training may not be used immediately or may serve as a basis for future skills acquisition. The way that wages respond to training is likely to differ across course types and jobs, and so the cumulated training measure will reflect the average of these effects over the seven-year observation window.

A second consideration is that workers who receive training in one year are much more likely to get training again the next year. In our estimating sample, 52 per cent of workers trained in one year also received training the following year, while only 18 per cent of workers who were not trained in the first year got training the next year. Thus training is highly serially correlated and in practice it can be difficult to separate the effects arising from different years (the multicollinearity problem). Finally, if there is measurement error in the training variables (for example, if respondents do not recall some training events), then a cumulative measure may be preferred because it will 'average out' measurement error.

Column [1] of Table 12.2, panel (a), reports the basic estimates of the effects of accumulated training incidence on wage growth for the sample employed at all waves, controlling for changes in their labour market characteristics between Waves 7 and 14. Training incidence takes a value of one if an individual has experienced at least one training course between two consecutive waves. Summing across waves, the maximum value for accumulated training incidence that an individual can accumulate is 7, while the minimum—for someone who has received no training over the entire period—is zero. The estimated coefficient on accumulated training incidence is 0.015 and this is statistically significant at the 5 per cent level. Thus an individual who has, for example, experienced at least one training event each year across all waves will experience wages growth that is over 10 per cent higher than an otherwise identical individual who has experienced no training [i.e. $0.015 \times 7 = 0.105$]. Table 12.1 shows that 71 per cent of the sample received training at some point over the period and that mean accumulated training incidence for those receiving any training was 2.8. Thus the average trainee (receiving training in nearly 3 waves) is expected to experience wage growth of over 4 per cent compared to workers who get no training.

Column [2] of Table 12.2, panel (a), shows the result when also controlling for the levels of workers' characteristics in Wave 7, thus allowing wage growth profiles to differ across, for example, education groups and industries. This specification also allows for the possibility that women experience different wage growth to men (although this coefficient was not significant). The estimated training coefficient in this extended specification is a little smaller, at 0.013, but still significant at the 5 per cent level.

Table 12.2 The effect of training on wage growth between BHPS Wave 7 and Wave 14

	Base year characteristics			
	Excluded [1]	Included [2]	Excluded [3]	Included [4]
Panel (a): Sample employed at all Waves 7–14				
Accumulated training incidence	0.0146***	0.0125**		
	(2.95)	(2.24)		
Accumulated training counts			0.0064***	0.0053**
			(2.82)	(2.11)
R-squared	0.128	0.157	0.127	0.157
Panel (b): Sample employed at least in Waves 7 and 14				
Accumulated training incidence	0.0132***	0.0127**		
	(2.88)	(2.46)		
Accumulated training counts			0.0061***	0.0058**
			(2.87)	(2.43)
R-squared	0.121	0.140	0.122	0.141

Notes: The dependent variable is the change in the log hourly wage between Waves 7 and 14. Additional control variables included in all specifications are: changes in age, age squared, highest qualification (6 levels), marital status (with gender interaction), whether covered by a trade union, firm size (3 categories), one-digit occupation and industry, public sector affiliation, temporary or fixed-term contract and part-time status. The regressions reported in panel (b) include as well the number of Waves 8–13 in which the respondent was missing from the survey, in self-employment, in full-time study, on a government scheme or not in employment (unemployed or not participating). Absolute robust *t*-statistics are shown in parentheses. * statistically significant at 10% level. ** statistically significant at 5% level. *** statistically significant at 1% level. Sample sizes are 1,518 for Panel (a) and 2,275 for Panel (b).

Of course, the value of a training course may drop over time if the embodied skills become obsolete. For this reason we experimented with including accumulated incidence in quadratic form (not reported in the tables). The quadratic term is negative, suggesting diminishing returns, but is not statistically significant.

The specifications reported in columns [1] and [2] of Table 12.2, panel (a), do not use all the training information available from the questionnaire. This is because the incidence measure effectively treats someone with one training event between waves the same way as someone with at least three training events (the maximum reported from one wave to the next). In the specifications reported in columns [3] and [4] we therefore use a richer training measure—accumulated counts. This ranges between 0 and 21. The upper bound of 21 is for individuals who have experienced 3 or more training events across each of the waves, while the lower bound is for individuals who have received no training over the entire sample period. As shown in Table 12.1, individuals experienced 3.45 events on average, with a maximum in the sample of 20 events. The estimated coefficient on accumulated counts, reported in column [3] of Table 12.2, panel (a), is 0.006. This is statistically significant at the 5 per cent level. For example, someone who has experienced at least three training events each year across all waves will experience wages growth that is over 12 per cent higher than an otherwise identical individual with no training. The expected wage growth of the average trainee (experiencing 5 training events) is somewhat lower, at 3 per cent, than for a worker with no training. Column [4] shows that the results are very similar using the extended specification which includes the levels of the explanatory variables in Wave 7 (the base year).[10]

As for the equations using accumulated training incidence, we also experimented with including accumulated training counts in quadratic form. Again, the quadratic terms were negative, suggesting diminishing returns, but they were not statistically significant.

Finally, we checked the sensitivity of the results to the inclusion of workers with lower labour market attachment. We re-estimated all specifications using a larger sample which included those additional people who were in employment in both Waves 7 and 14, but who did not respond to the survey or who were not in employment in some of the intervening years. To control for these intermittent histories, we added to the estimating equations the number of waves for which individuals did not respond, were self-employed, in full-time study, on a government scheme, or out of employment (non-participating or unemployed). Only being out of employment had a negative effect on wage growth (of 5.5% in absolute terms for each wave of missing employment), and the training effects are almost identical to the previous results, as shown in Table 12.2, panel (b).

[10] In all specifications we also tested whether the returns to training were different for women, by interacting the training variable with a dummy variable for women. The interaction coefficients were statistically insignificant, suggesting no differential returns.

In summary, we find, using Waves 7 to 14 of the BHPS, that work-related training has a long term effect on wages. Thus training can potentially affect the longer term upward wage mobility of British workers.

12.3 Training and the national minimum wage

Background

The national minimum wage was introduced in the UK on 1 April 1999. Its introduction followed a period of 6 years, from the abolition of the Wages Councils, without any statutory wage-floor except for agriculture. It constituted a major policy intervention aimed at increasing the earnings of low-skilled employees and helping low-income households out of poverty. It has also provided an excellent opportunity for evaluation of the effects of a minimum wage.

Research, most recently Bryan and Taylor (2004), has confirmed that the minimum wage is well targeted at the bottom of the income distribution of working households.[11] In this section, we focus on whether the minimum wage also has a more indirect effect on workers' longer-term prospects by affecting their training and therefore potentially their wages. We begin with the theoretical background and then present evidence from the BHPS.

As noted at the start of this chapter, there are good theoretical reasons why minimum wages are expected to affect training. In a perfectly competitive labour market, a binding minimum wage will prevent wages from being lowered to pay for the costs of training. The introduction of a minimum wage is therefore likely to restrict training, in particular general training financed by low-paid workers themselves. However, if the labour market is *imperfectly* competitive, a minimum wage can have the opposite effect by compressing wages at the bottom of the wage distribution. Imperfect competition means that the gains in productivity due to training accrue to employers and not to minimum wage workers, and so firms can find it profitable to pay for training. Depending on other factors, such as whether or not workers are credit constrained, the existence of training contracts and the mix of general and specific training, the overall effect of a minimum wage can be to increase training (Acemoglu and Pischke 2003). These differing predictions about training parallel the familiar predictions about employment. In a perfectly competitive labour market a minimum wage is likely to destroy jobs, while in an imperfectly competitive labour market employment may increase.

How do the arguments about training relate to the UK labour market? The possibility that workers share in the cost of major training events—and that a minimum wage might be a disincentive to some forms of training—was

[11] It is less well targeted at the bottom of the income distribution of all households, because the poorest households typically do not contain wage earners.

recognized in the design of the national minimum wage. The national minimum wage does not apply to young apprentices in their first year, and a lower 'development' rate applies to workers receiving some other forms of accredited training (lasting at least 26 days) in new jobs. The Low Pay Commission (LPC) monitors the workings of the national minimum wage and concluded that, without the apprenticeship exemption, initial training in some sectors would drop (LPC 2005: 150). But the LPC has also found little evidence that employers use the trainees' development rate and has recommended that it be abolished (LPC 2005: Ch. 5). At the same time, the Commission recognizes that the national minimum wage might actually spur employers to increase training in order to raise their workers' productivity (see for example, LPC 2001: 60).

So far, there has been very little formal empirical work using representative data to evaluate the overall impact of the national minimum wage on training receipt. Indeed to our knowledge the only empirical work in this area prior to our own was undertaken for the USA (see Schiller 1994; Neumark and Wascher 2001; Grossberg and Sicilian 1999; Acemoglu and Pischke 2003; and for a summary see Arulamapalam, Booth, and Bryan 2003*a*).

In the remainder of this section, we discuss the results of our earlier work using representative British survey data to examine the effects of the introduction of the national minimum wage on training.

The effect of the UK national minimum wage on training receipt

Our data description in section 12.1 revealed that low paid workers do not receive much training. It is therefore interesting to see what the introduction of the national minimum wage did to them, especially in view of the various theories predicting diverse effects. The studies by Arulampalam, Booth, and Bryan (2004*a*) and Bryan (2005) provided the first investigation of the training effects of the UK national minimum wage. The research utilized important new data from the BHPS—both on training and whether or not individuals' wages were increased to comply with the national minimum wage—facilitating a comparison of training evolution across affected and unaffected groups.

The data used were from Waves 8 to 10 (1998–2000) of the BHPS, which spanned the introduction of the national minimum wage and thereby allowed a comparison of training before and after its implementation.[12] As in the above analysis, training was defined to cover courses intended to increase or improve skills in the current job. The outcome variables were the change in training incidence and the change in training intensity. Training intensity

[12] We used the data from 1998 onwards because major changes to the training questions were introduced in 1998. See Booth and Bryan (2007) for discussion about the differences in the questionnaires and training responses before and after this change. Bryan (2005) analysed training changes over 1995–97, when no minimum wage was in place, finding no significant differential effect for workers who would have been covered by the minimum wage.

was defined as the total duration of the reported training events (up to 3) in each wave.[13]

The Wave 8 interviews of the BHPS took place between August 1998 and March 1999 and covered training received since 1 September 1997. The Wave 10 interviews were conducted between September 2000 and May 2001 and covered training experienced since 1 September 1999. The training reported in these two waves therefore fell unambiguously before and after the introduction of the national minimum wage. Training data were also collected in Wave 9 but could not be used in the analysis, since it was not known whether the reported events fell before or after the introduction of the national minimum wage. The analysis covered employees aged under 60 who were potentially covered by the national minimum wage, that is those aged 18 or over and who were not in the army or agriculture.

The national minimum wage was introduced at a main rate of £3.60, with a youth rate of £3.00 for 18–21 year olds and a development rate of £3.20 for some older trainees (although as already mentioned, there is scant evidence—including in the BHPS data used in the analysis—that the development rate has been widely used). The national minimum wage has been uprated annually since its introduction and the upratings have often exceeded the growth of average earnings. In principle, it would be possible to use the upratings as additional tests of minimum wage effects but, in practice, they have much less 'bite' than the original introduction of the national minimum wage into a labour market without any wage floor. The frequency of the upratings also makes it more difficult to isolate 'before' and 'after' observations corresponding to each national minimum wage increase and not affected by other increases. The analysis presented here is therefore restricted to the introduction of the national minimum wage and does not cover the upratings.

The methodology in Arulampalam, Booth, and Bryan (2004*a*) was similar to that of Stewart (2004). Stewart used the BHPS and two other datasets to analyse the employment effects for low-wage workers of the national minimum wage and found no significant evidence of employment effects. The idea in these studies is to compare the training of workers affected by the national minimum wage (a treatment group) with a similar group of unaffected workers (a control group).

To control for differences between the two groups which might affect the level of training received even in the absence of the national minimum wage, the analysis in Arulampalam, Booth, and Bryan (2004*a*) compares the change in training—rather than the level—for each group over the period of the introduction of the national minimum wage (1998–2000). The difference-in-differences estimate of the minimum wage effect is then

[13] The duration question is: 'Since September 1st [of the previous fieldwork year] how much time have you spent on this course or training in total?'

the difference (between the affected and unaffected groups) of the difference in training over time for each group.

It is important to define appropriate treatment and control groups. The treatment group needs to contain workers whose wages were increased by the national minimum wage, while the control group ideally needs to contain workers who are very similar to the treatment group but whose wages were unaffected by the minimum wage. To check the sensitivity of the results to the choice of groups, Arulampalam, Booth, and Bryan used two alternative treatment/control group definitions. The first (treatment/control group 1), was based on the hourly wage observed just prior to the national minimum wage in Wave 8, comparing workers whose wages would need to increase to comply with the national minimum wage with workers in a wage band just above this level. Treatment and control group 2 were defined using the answers to a question in Wave 9 in which respondents were specifically asked whether or not their wages had been raised up to the minimum wage.

The main results of the Arulampalam *et al.* (2004a) analysis are reproduced in Table 12.3. They show difference-in-differences estimates from a linear probability model (LPM) using the two different outcome variables: changes in training incidence, denoted by ΔT_{it}, and changes in training intensity, denoted by ΔT_{it}^*. The training intensity variable ΔT_{it}^* is identical to ΔT_{it} unless training incidence is positive in both periods; then $\Delta T_{it}^* = 1$ if intensity increases, $\Delta T_{it}^* = -1$ if intensity decreases and $\Delta T_{it}^* = 0$ if intensity remains the same. Thus the estimated equation represents a LPM in differences.

The left-hand panel of Table 12.3 presents the raw difference-in-differences estimates (without any added control variables), while the right-hand panel also controls for observable personal and job and characteristics. Considering first the raw difference-in-differences estimates, column [1] indicates that the training probability in treatment group 1 (based on the wage in Wave 8) increased by about 9 percentage points more than it did in control group 1, and the increase is statistically significant at the 5 per cent level. Using the treatment and control group 2, column [2] shows that training incidence also increased more in the treatment group (by 5.0 percentage points) than in the control group, although the estimate is not statistically significant at conventional levels. However looking at changes in training intensity, columns [3] and [4] report positive and significant estimates for both treatment/control group definitions. Affected workers appear to be 10 percentage points more likely to experience an increase in training intensity than workers in the control group. The increases are statistically significant.[14]

[14] We modelled the sign of changes in training intensity rather than the magnitude, since this relates directly to relevant theory. Modelling the exact change in training intensity would require us to address the issue that a change from 8 to 10 days is not necessarily the same as a change from 4 to 2 days or even a change from 2 to 0 days. Such analysis was beyond the scope of the current study.

Table 12.3 The effect of the national minimum wage on training

	Raw difference-in-differences				Regression adjusted			
	Change in training incidence Treatment/control group		Change in training intensity Treatment/control group		Change in training incidence Treatment/control group		Change in training intensity Treatment/control group	
	1	2	1	2	1	2	1	2
	[1]	[2]	[3]	[4]	[5]	[6]	[7]	[8]
Treatment group	0.0901**	0.0503	0.1004**	0.1046**	0.0785*	0.0422	0.0876*	0.0984**
	(1.98)	(1.18)	(1.97)	(2.19)	(1.72)	(1.00)	(1.71)	(2.02)
High-wage group	0.0343		0.0187		0.0392		0.0242	
	(0.98)		(0.47)		(1.12)		(0.61)	
Intercept	−0.0090	0.0204*	−0.0000†	0.0166	−0.0706	−0.0418	−0.0790	−0.0663
	(0.27)	(1.83)	(0.00)	(1.24)	(1.41)	(0.94)	(1.36)	(1.26)
Number of observations	3257	2504	3257	2504	3257	2504	3257	2504

Notes: † The estimated standard error for this coefficient is 0.04. Absolute robust T-statistics are shown in parentheses. * statistically significant at 10% level. ** statistically significant at 5% level. The regression-adjusted estimates used the following first-differences controls: age-squared, part-time status, whether the job is fixed-term or temporary, whether the worker changed employers, marital status, union-coverage, sector, firm size, 1-digit industry, local unemployment rate, and dummy variables for missing values.

Source: Arulampalam, Booth, and Bryan (2004*a*).

A similar pattern of results is evident in the right-hand panel of Table 12.3 (the regression-adjusted difference-in-differences estimates, controlling for individual and job characteristics), showing that the previous estimates were not caused by (observable) differences between the workers in the sample.[15] Overall, Arulampalam, Booth, and Bryan (2004*a*) concluded that there was no evidence that the minimum wage introduction reduced the training of affected workers, and some evidence that it increased it by around 8 to 11 percentage points. These findings provided little evidence supporting the perfectly competitive human capital model as it applies to training, and weak evidence of new theories based on imperfectly-competitive labour markets.

12.4 Conclusions

In this chapter, we have highlighted the relevance of work-related training to the minimum wage debate. We demonstrated that lower-paid workers are less likely than workers towards the top of the hourly wage distribution to receive work-related training. We then showed that work-related training is potentially important from a distributional standpoint, since it significantly increases individuals' longer-term earning prospects. We summarized our earlier empirical results indicating that the introduction of a national minimum wage in Britain had a small positive effect on subsequent training incidence for affected workers, and we argued that this provided some evidence in favour of new theories based on imperfectly-competitive labour markets.

A number of separate empirical studies have used British data to estimate the employment effects of the national minimum wage. These find that the introduction of the minimum wage has had no adverse effects on employment overall (Stewart 2004), although small employment losses have been detected in one heavily affected sector, care homes (Machin, Manning, and Rahman 2003). Moreover, while Draca, Machin, and Van Reenen (2006) find some evidence that firms' profits may have declined, they find no evidence that firms closed down because of this.

In summary, the available empirical evidence for Britain shows that minimum wages are associated with a small increase in work-related training for the low paid, and have not adversely affected the employment of British workers. Based on the UK's short experience of the national minimum wage it appears that, rather than shedding workers, firms have responded by trying to get more out of existing workers. Interesting questions for future research

[15] Separate effects were not estimated for men and women because of sample size limitations. In extensions to the main analysis, Arulampalam, Booth, and Bryan (2003*a*) and Bryan (2005) found no evidence for differential effects by gender. These studies also investigated the sensitivity of the estimates to changes in the definitions of treatment group 1 and its control group. The results were similar to those reported here.

that have not yet been addressed are: will the effects of the minimum wage continue to be so benign and will the minimum wage reduce wages inequality in the longer-term? The answers will depend partly on future increases in the minimum wage. We would suggest that the minimum wage will reduce wage inequality in the longer-term provided that it continues to be set at a level that does not threaten employment. This potential arises not just because of the direct and obvious effect of a minimum wage in increasing wages at the bottom of the distribution, but also through its more indirect effect on work-related training.

Ultimately, assessing the long-term effects of the minimum wage will require evidence about the progress of low-skilled workers over many years. There is a need for data which contain sufficient numbers of low-skilled individuals and which allow their trajectories—both in and out of the labour market—to be followed over substantial parts of the lifecycle. We hope that continuing developments in panel data resources will allow further investigation of these issues both for the UK and for a wider set of countries than those studied so far.

References

Acemoglu, D. and Pischke J.-S. (1999). 'The Structure of Wages and Investment in General Training'. *Journal of Political Economy*, 107: 539–72.

—— and —— (2003). 'Minimum Wages and On-the-job Training'. *Research in Labor Economics*, 22: 159–202.

Arulampalam, W., Booth, A. L., and Bryan, M. L. (2003*a*). 'Work-Related Training and the New Minimum Wage in Britain', ISER Working Paper 2003-5. Colchester: University of Essex.

——, ——,and —— (2003*b*). 'Training in Europe', Discussion Paper No. 933. Bonn: IZA.

——, ——,and —— (2004*a*). 'Training and the New Minimum Wage'. *The Economic Journal*, 114: C87–C94.

——, ——,and —— (2004*b*). 'Training in Europe'. *Journal of the European Economic Association*, 2: 346–60.

Bassanini, A., Booth, A. L., Brunello, G., De Paola, M., and Leuven, E. (2007). 'Workplace Training in Europe', in G. Brunello, P. Garibaldi, and E. Wasmer (eds), *Education and Training in Europe*. Oxford: Oxford University Press.

Blundell, R., Dearden, L., Meghir, C., and Sianesi B. (1999). 'Human Capital Investment: the Returns from Education and Training to the Individual, the Firm and the Economy'. *Fiscal Studies*, 20: 1–23.

Booth, A. L. and Bryan, M. L. (2007). 'Who Pays for General Training in Private Sector Britain?' *Research in Labor Economics*, 26: 85–123.

—— and —— (2005). 'Testing Some Predictions of Human Capital Theory: New Training Evidence from Britain'. *Review of Economics and Statistics*, 87: 391–4.

—— and Zoega, G. (2004). 'Is Wage Compression a Necessary Condition for Firm-financed General Training?' *Oxford Economic Papers*, 56: 88–97.

Brewer, M. and Shephard, A. (2004). *Has Labour Made Work Pay?* York: Joseph Rowntree Foundation.

Bryan, M. L. (2005). 'The Effect of the National Minimum Wage on Training', in M. L. Bryan, 'Essays in Labour Market Behaviour', unpublished PhD Thesis. Colchester: University of Essex.

—— and Taylor, M. P. (2004). 'An Analysis of the Household Characteristics of Minimum Wage Recipients'. Report to the Low Pay Commission. London: Low Pay Commission.

Chang, C. and Wang, Y. (1996). 'Human Capital Investment under Asymmetric Information: The Pigovian Conjecture Revisited'. *Journal of Labor Economics*, 14: 505–19.

Department for Work and Pensions (DWP) (2006). *Households Below Average Income. An Analysis of the Income Distribution 1994/5–2004/05.* Leeds: Corporate Document Services.

Draca, M., Machin S., and Van Reenen, J. (2006). 'Minimum Wages and Firm Profitability'. Unpublished paper. London: University College London.

Grossberg, A. J. and Sicilian, P. (1999). 'Minimum Wages, On-the-Job Training and Wage Growth'. *Southern Economic Journal*, 65: 539–56.

Hart R. A. and Ritchie F. (2002). 'Tenure-based Wage Setting'. Unpublished paper. Stirling: University of Stirling.

Hashimoto, M. (1982). 'Minimum Wage Effects on Training on the Job'. *American Economic Review*, 72: 1070–87.

HM Treasury (2006). *A Strong and Strengthening Economy: Investing in Britain's Future. Economic and Fiscal Strategy Report and Financial Statement and Budget Report March 2006.* London: The Stationery Office.

Leighton, L. and Mincer, J. (1981). 'The Effects of Minimum Wages on Human Capital Formation', in S. Rottenberg (ed.), *The Economics of Legal Minimum Wages*. Washington, DC: American Enterprise Institute, 155–73.

LPC (Low Pay Commission) (2001). *The National Minimum Wage: Making a Difference. Third Report of the Low Pay Commission, Volume One.* London: The Stationery Office.

—— (2005). *National Minimum Wage. Low Pay Commission Report 2005.* London: The Stationery Office.

Machin S., Manning A., and Rahman S. (2003). 'Where the Minimum Wage Bites Hard: The Introduction of the UK National Minimum Wage to a Low-Wage Sector'. *Journal of the European Economic Association*, 1: 154–80.

Melero, E. (2004). 'Evidence on Training and Career Paths: Human Capital, Information and Incentives'. Discussion Paper No. 1377. Bonn: IZA.

Neumark D. and Wascher W. (2001). 'Minimum Wages and Training Revisited'. *Journal of Labor Economics*, 19: 563–95.

Rosen, S. (1972). 'Learning and Experience in the Labor Market'. *Journal of Human Resources*, 7: 326–42.

Schiller, B. R. (1994). 'Moving Up: The Training and Wage Gains of Minimum Wage Entrants'. *Social Science Quarterly*, 75: 622–36.

Stevens, M. (1994). 'A Theoretical Model of On-the-Job Training with Imperfect Competition'. *Oxford Economic Papers*, 46: 537–62.

Stewart, M. B. (2002). 'Estimating the Impact of the Minimum Wage Using Geographical Wage Variation'. *Oxford Bulletin of Economics and Statistics*, 64: 583–605.

—— (2004). 'The Impact of the Introduction of the UK Minimum Wage on the Employment Probabilities of Low Wage Workers'. *Journal of the European Economic Association*, 2: 67–97.

Sutherland, H. E. (2001). 'The National Minimum Wage and In-Work Poverty'. DAE Working Paper, Amalgamated Series No. 0111. Cambridge: Faculty of Economics, University of Cambridge.

13

Government debt and the portfolios of the rich

Bernd Süssmuth and Robert K. von Weizsäcker

Differences in attitudes to risk between the wealthiest individuals and the least wealthy individuals have a potentially important effect on the evolution of the economy, and on the public finances in particular. The aim of this chapter is to investigate heterogeneity in risk aversion, its relationship to wealth levels, and government debt policies.

Most measures of the average realized rate of return on government debt for major OECD economies over the last three decades have been smaller than the real rate of economic growth. A series of studies has considered whether this stylized fact implies that governments can play a so-called 'Ponzi debt game', rolling over their debt and interest without ever increasing taxes. In such a scenario, the government issues bonds and rolls over interest and principal from period to period by perpetually issuing new bonds to render debt service. Whether such strategies are feasible and lead to a potential Pareto improvement has been analysed in numerous different settings. The major findings of the research are the irrelevance of the actual value of the average riskless rate of return for Pareto optimality and the crucial role of Ponzi debt games in providing intergenerational insurance. For the latter result the term 'sophisticated' Ponzi game is frequently used. In this case a rollover scheme improves intergenerational risk sharing. A comprehensive survey of the literature is given by Blanchard and Weil (2002).

In a two-class model consisting of high wealth individuals (class H) and low wealth individuals (L), Bohn (1999) showed that Ponzi debt games were suboptimal, using particular assumptions about the distribution of risk aversion (lower for H than L), combined with assumptions about class demography (whether H and/or L were dynastic or short-lived). By using alternative assumptions, in particular a relatively high degree of risk aversion for class H, we show that it is possible—but not very probable—to identify a scenario in which a perpetual rollover of public debt improves intergenerational risk sharing.

Our study proceeds in two stages. First, we make the case for alternative assumptions about the differences in risk aversion between wealth classes, in particular that risk aversion may be higher for class H individuals. Secondly, we embed these assumptions in an intertemporal model in order to check for optimality and derive our key conclusions about public debt policy. Finally, in the concluding section, we highlight two important tasks for future research: a move from basic two-class models to more sophisticated models, and the generation of further evidence about inequalities in risk aversion and their correlation with the inequality of wealth.

13.1 Bond holdings and wealth

Detailed data, especially in the form of time series, on government bond holding and the wealth distribution are scarce, though there has been some recent progress. For some European and North American countries, however, there is information on household portfolio shares held in government bonds by wealth percentile. For example, Guiso, Halliassos, and Jappelli (2002) provide detailed information about household portfolio composition for the United States, the United Kingdom, Italy, and Germany. (Their data about the Netherlands are largely incomplete or inadequate for our purposes.)

It is common knowledge that some European governments issue safe debt on a large scale. A lesser known fact is that, for some countries, this public debt forms a large portfolio share particularly for high wealth individuals. Evidence for German and Italian households can be derived from the data reported in Guiso, Halliassos, and Jappelli (2002), reproduced in Figure 13.1.[1] In Germany, the wealthiest 5 per cent of households held about an approximately equal share of their assets in safe and risky assets, significantly more than half of their portfolio (57%) was made up of 'fairly safe' assets, and only 7.6 per cent was made up of 'fairly risky' assets.[2] By contrast, the poorest 95 per cent of wealth holders held 52.5 per cent in fairly safe assets and 6.0 per cent in fairly risky assets.

[1] Asset shares for West Germany are based on the Income and Expenditure Survey (Einkommens- und Verbrauchsstichprobe) of the German Federal Statistics Office (Statistisches Bundesamt). They refer to the year 1993. Italian portfolio shares are computed from data from the 1995 Bank of Italy Survey of Household Income and Wealth.

[2] 'Fairly safe' includes the cash value of endowment life insurance, assets accumulated in building society savings contracts (Bausparverträge), municipal bonds, saving certificates, and government bonds. 'Fairly risky' includes other bonds and mutual funds invested in stocks or bonds.

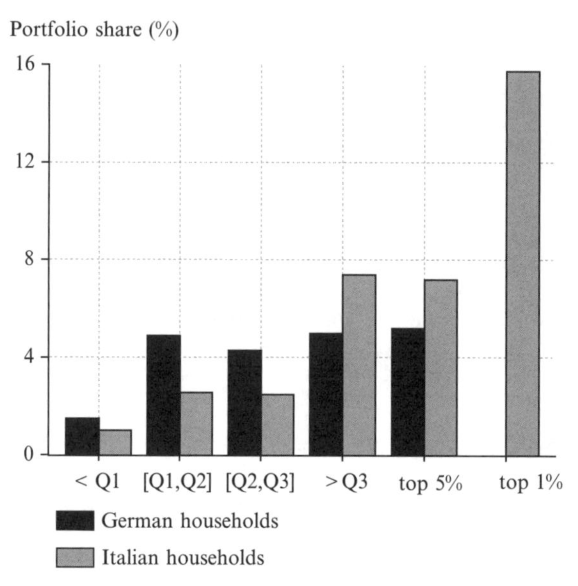

Figure 13.1 Share of total wealth held in government bonds, by wealth quartile: West Germany 1993 and Italy 1995

Notes: < Q1: below first net worth quartile. [Q1,Q2]: between first and second net worth quartile. [Q2,Q3]: between second and third net worth quartile. > Q3: above third net worth quartile.

Sources: Guiso and Japelli (2001); Eymann and Börsch-Supan (2002).

These patterns do not describe the situation in the UK or in the USA: see Carroll (2002) and the country chapters in Guiso, Halliassos, and Jappelli (2002). The cross-country contrasts may stem from cultural, sociological, and political factors (cf. Alesina, Glaeser, and Sacerdote 2001). However, since no comparable data on government bond holding by wealth percentile for other economies currently exist that would allow a thorough cross-national comparison, empirical research in this area remains a task for the future.

A straightforward explanation of what makes Italy and Germany distinct is the regional disparity in the distribution of wealth in each country. One way of looking at the type of inequality focused on in this chapter—differences in risk aversion by wealth level—is to look at countries for which regions correspond to the two wealth classes H and L. Due to the notable differences in the distribution of wealth between the East and the West in Germany, and between the South and the North in Italy, these two countries provide examples of a two-class situation. We return to this point in greater detail in the next section.

Before analysing public debt policies and risk sharing in a two-class model, where class H shows a higher risk aversion than class L, we first discuss how such an assumption can be reconciled with existing theories about the relationship between wealth and attitudes to risk.

13.2 Relative wealth, inequality, and societal risk profile

The argument of this section develops in two stages. First, drawing on a model originally proposed by Gregory (1980), we provide a theoretical rationale for risk aversion being higher for members of H than for members of L. Second, we examine German and Italian data in the light of these theoretical considerations.

In order to investigate the theoretical implications of the observations reported in the preceding section, we take up the idea that having higher wealth may raise one's marginal utility of wealth. Our argument is based on the idea that an individual's attitude to risk is determined by the relative position of that individual in the wealth distribution of a society rather than by her absolute net worth. Attainment and assurance of a particular position generate an additional gain in utility through status. Relative wealth should arguably belong in the utility function because of its role in conveying information and organizing market behaviour through status. In a 'pecking order' sense, relative wealth can influence marriage choices, hiring, promotion, access to clubs, and so forth, because those higher up the wealth 'pecking order' get access to clubs, friends, and other goods that are not available to those further down the pecking order (Becker, Murphy and Werning 2005), and so it is plausible to assume relative rather than absolute wealth to be maximized by rational individuals. This type of utility assumption dates back to two pioneering articles about a half century ago by Friedman and Savage (1948) and Friedman (1953).[3] The assumption has also been advanced by Gregory (1980) and, following him, we argue that inequality in the distribution of wealth causes attitudes toward risk.

The implication is a distribution of risk aversion, one that is a J-shaped function of wealth level. That is to say, preferences display more risk acceptance and a declining risk aversion for middle classes (Rosenthal 2004), and an increasing risk aversion for high worth individuals. Given the J-shape, the very poorest have higher risk aversion than part of the middle classes. In order to define our two wealth classes, we define class H to be those individuals that are more risk averse than the very poor.

To illustrate the basic idea, consider a utility function which is linear in wealth, thus being neutral with regard to its cardinal properties. Additionally, assume that there is a separable gain in utility u^* that an individual owning an amount of wealth W would obtain by belonging to a specific, more or less closed, group of society. Total expected utility can then be written as

$$U(W) = W + p(u^*|W)u^*,$$

[3] Recently, the Friedman-Savage preference for risk structure has been supported by both experimental evidence (Bosch-Domènech and Silvestre 1999) and survey-based econometric results (Guiso and Paiella 1999).

where $p(u^*|W)$ is the probability of attaining a position in society that is associated with the realization of a certain gain in status. Because competition for membership is based on a comparison of candidates' wealth, that probability is an increasing function of W. It should be noted, however, that by how much p is increasing in W crucially depends on the individual's position in the wealth distribution. If an individual has relatively high wealth, the increase in the probability of gaining u^* from a marginal increase in W is comparatively low. However, if an individual is on the borderline of getting access to a country-club or to appear on the Forbes List, and might do so with a marginal increase in W (thereby increasing his/her relative success), the increase in p is relatively high.

Now suppose that such an individual faces a one shot investment opportunity by which she can either win or lose a net amount w of wealth. Each outcome has a probability of 0.5. The appropriate decision rule is to invest if

$$0.5U(W+w)+0.5U(W-w)>U(W).$$

According to our utility function this is equivalent to investing if

$$0.5\ p(u^*|W+w)+0.5\ p(u^*|W-w)>p(u^*|W).$$

In our simple model, we suppose that every individual is born into one of two regions, either the South (denoted S) or the North (N). Each region is assumed to have the same population size, and there is no mobility or migration between regions. Hence, apart from the market for status, there is no opportunity to move up or down the economic scale. Prior to the investment opportunity, a status-seeker's *a priori* probability of a utility gain is given by

$$p(u^*|W)=0.5\ F_S(W)+0.5\ F_N(W),$$

where $F_S(W)$ and $F_N(W)$ denote the cumulative wealth distributions in the South and the North. This means that, although an individual is born into one of two regions with a probability of one half, and cannot move regions, her $p(u^*|W)$ depends on the wealth distributions in both regions. For illustration, suppose an extremely successful entrepreneur who happens to have been born in the poor region of the economy and run her business there. Her chances of being among the top ten millionaires of the nation as a whole clearly depend on the wealth distributions of both regions of the country.

It can be shown (Gregory 1980) that in this framework an agent is risk tolerant and participates in the investment game if

$$F_S''(W)+F_N''(W)>0,$$

where $F_S''(W)$ and $F_N''(W)$ denote the second derivatives of the regional cumulative distribution functions with respect to W, that is, the slope of the probability density function of wealth for South and North.

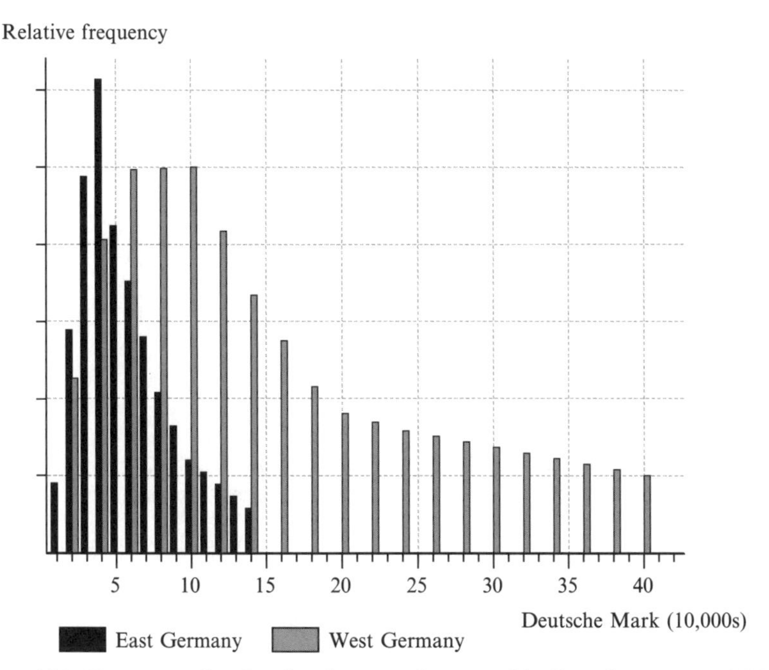

Figure 13.2 Histograms for the distribution of net wealth: East Germany and West Germany, 1998

Note: Derived from seven-category histogram for household net wealth using linear interpolation.

Source: Hauser and Stein (2001), own calculations.

Germany is an example of an economy characterized by a two-tiered regional structure and an inequality in disposable wealth that has remained stable over the last two decades, with a Gini coefficient of about 60 per cent (Hauser and Stein 2006). What is the implication for the societal risk profile of such an economy according to the argument made earlier?

Histograms (approximations to probability density functions) for wealth are shown for East and West Germany in Figure 13.2. Note, first, that the histograms are skewed to the right. Secondly, the shapes of the densities suggest that the condition that $F_S''(W) + F_N''(W) > 0$ holds up to a net wealth value of approximately 120,000 DM (61,000 Euro) at most. At this value, the sum of the slopes of the two approximated probability density functions is clearly negative, as both histograms begin to decrease as wealth rises, that is, $F_S''(W) + F_N''(W) < 0$. Our relative wealth argument suggests that values above this threshold are associated with a rather risk averse attitude.

This pattern broadly corresponds to the situation in Italy. Evidence about this can be derived from the 1995 wave of the Bank of Italy's Survey of Household Income and Wealth, which contained questions intended to elicit

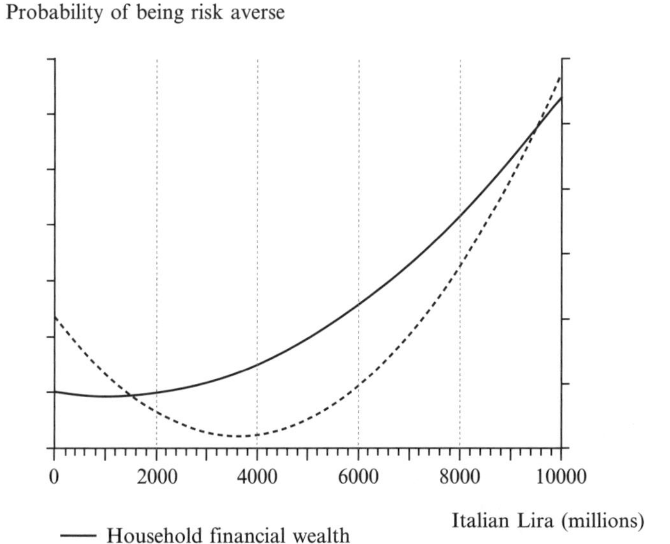

Figure 13.3 Risk aversion and household wealth: evidence from the Bank of Italy's 1995 Survey of Household Income and Wealth

Source: Guiso and Paiella (1999), and authors' calculations.

attitudes of Italian households towards risk. In order to assess the determinants of these attitudes, Guiso and Paiella (1999) classified households according to whether they were risk averse or not. Controlling for characteristics such as sex, age, number of siblings, and so forth, the relationship between the probability of being risk averse and a measure of household wealth endowments was found to be approximated well by a second-order polynomial function. This quadratic function of wealth allows us to identify the wealth level at which the impact of wealth changes. Figure 13.3 plots the relationship.[4] For financial wealth exceeding approximately one billion Italian Lira, or for net worth exceeding about four billion Italian Lira (i.e. about 500,000 and two million Euro, respectively), the probability of an Italian household of being risk averse increases.

Relative wealth considerations were introduced earlier with reference to regional disparities. To illustrate the role of regional differences in establishing the two classes H and L and a distribution of risk aversion (higher for class H than for class L), consider a top wealth household in East and in West

[4] Since Figure 13.3 shows *ceteris paribus* effects, showing the impact of wealth variables abstracting from other potential determinants of the probability of being risk averse (including the constant), we concentrate on the qualitative shape of the two functions and do not use value labels on the vertical axis.

Germany. If an individual is among the top five millionaires in East Germany, there might be a reasonable chance that, by realizing a return of w in a fair game, she may enter the national top ten list of wealthiest individuals, which would result in an additional gain in utility (u^*). It is rational for such an individual to be relatively risk loving. If, by contrast, an individual were to be among the top five millionaires in West Germany, she most probably already ranks among the national top ten. There is no prospect of an additional gain in utility to be had from accepting a fair game. Such an individual is likely to be relatively risk averse.

This example shows that our argument does not use regions as proxies for H and L *per se*, but uses them to represent aspects of relative wealth. Since agents can lose an amount w in the fair game, assuming a relatively high base level of risk aversion for the very poor is plausible. It marks the starting point of the J-shaped profile of risk aversion by wealth class (see Fig. 13.4). Risk aversion first falls as the probability density functions of wealth for both regions increases with increasing wealth levels. Then risk aversion starts to increase again at the point at which the sum of the slopes of the probability density functions becomes negative. However, as long as the implied risk aversion falls below the base level, we cannot speak about a class characterized by high worth individuals with comparatively high risk aversion. Therefore, we define the H class to be made up of those individuals who are more risk averse than the very poorest.

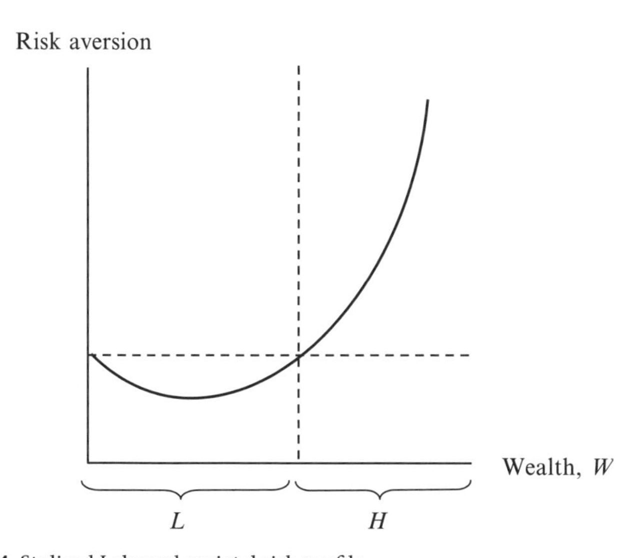

Figure 13.4 Stylized J-shaped societal risk profile

13.3 Public debt policies and optimal risk sharing in a two-class model

It is a stylized fact that, on average, the real return on government bonds has historically been below the average return on equities and generally below the rate of economic growth (see for example, Dimson, Marsh, and Staunton 2005). According to Bohn (1999: 1), the central implication of this is that '[if] the interest rate is below the average growth rate, a government may roll over its debt with interest—that is, run a primary deficit and not provide debt service—and still expect a declining ratio of debt to GDP.' In the literature, the practice of sustaining primary deficits by low-interest debt is sometimes referred to as a policy of 'exploiting safe debt'.

In the case of less wealthy and bequest-constrained agents being more risk averse than long-lived dynasties made of high worth households, Bohn (1999) has shown that a perpetual rollover is suboptimal with regard to an optimal allocation of risk. It should be noted that in this context optimality refers to the standard notion of Pareto efficiency which defines an allocation for which no Pareto improvements can be made. A Pareto improvement is a movement from one allocation to another, making at least one individual better off, without making any other individual worse off. In this sense, a sophisticated Ponzi game does not exist in Bohn's setting.

Here, we raise the question whether persistent budget deficits are unproblematic for the opposite constellation of risk attitudes of such a stylized society. In other words, we analyse a case characterized by two particular assumptions about the distribution of risk aversion and about class demography. With regard to the former, we let risk aversion be lower for class L compared to class H households. As argued in the preceding sections, there are some empirical indications for such a societal risk profile which can be explained by interregional and intraregional inequalities in wealth, in particular for Germany and Italy, the largest and third largest economies in the Euro-area. With regard to class demography, we follow Bohn (1999) and assume that class H individuals are dynastic and that class L agents live for one period only (a new generation of equal measure being born every period).

We suppose the structure of preferences for classes L and H, respectively, is summarized by the following expected utility functions for consumption over the lifetime (N periods in each case):

$$U^L = E\left[\sum\nolimits_{t\geq 0}^{N} \beta^t \frac{\left(c_t^L\right)^{1-\alpha^L}}{1-\alpha^L}\right]$$

$$U^H = E\left[\sum\nolimits_{t\geq 0}^{N} \beta^t \frac{\left(c_t^H\right)^{1-\alpha^H}}{1-\alpha^H}\right].$$

The key difference between the two utility functions is the degree of risk aversion α^L and α^H, for which we assume $\alpha^L < \alpha^H$. The summation is over time periods, c_t^L and c_t^H denote uncertain consumption in period t for each class, and β is the discount rate. These two functions are of the standard constant relative risk aversion type. In our two-class scenario, this means that, for any given state of the world, there is an intra-group marginal willingness to accept an increase in relative risk as the income of the wealth class increases. It should be noted, that in contrast to the Arrow-Pratt measure of absolute risk, this measure has the advantage that it remains valid, even if this relationship is not strictly convex or strictly concave over all income. An increased willingness to accept relative risk among agents of the same class would imply a smaller coefficient of relative risk aversion. The case under investigation here is a higher willingness to accept relative risk by class L, i.e. $\alpha^L < \alpha^H$.

In order to study issues of optimal government debt policies against the background of optimal risk sharing in a society of heterogeneous agents, we rely on a contingent claims price model. See Bohn (1999) in the context of fiscal policy and Ljungqvist and Sargent (2000) in general. These models include Euler equations according to which the distribution of returns of each type of asset equals the intertemporal marginal rate of substitution of class H evaluated at the equilibrium allocation, at which consumption equals income produced from a production sector that runs all technologies. Therefore, all differences in expected returns across securities arise from risk aversion. See the Appendix for further details of the model and the Euler equations.

To express this relationship in terms of marginal rates of substitution rather than interest rates is a key difference of the stochastic model with risk aversion in comparison to deterministic and certainty-equivalence models. In general, the Euler equation links marginal rates of substitution, state-contingent claims prices (that we abstracted from hitherto for reasons of simplicity), and distributions of assets returns (Bohn 1995). Here it also ensures that a low interest rate of government securities is due to the fact that governments tend to issue (nearly) safe debt.

Apart from the addition of a production sector, there is another central deviation from the standard model. Our assumption regarding the agents' planning horizons implies that asset returns depend on the preferences of type H agents only. However, type L agents are not independent of government policies. They will be affected by changes in the distribution of the tax burden.

Let the government impose equal taxes T_t on both the very wealthy households H and the less wealthy households L. Taxes are used to finance public expenditures which are supposed to be proportional to income $G_t = gY_t$. Like the class H households, the government can shift resources across time and states of nature. Its instrument to do so is the issuance of debt.

Furthermore, we suppose that debt consists of safe securities and/or of state-contingent liabilities. Let R_t denote the return on period $t-1$ debt. Government end-of-period debt D_t and taxes T_t must satisfy the following budget equation

$$D_t = (1 + R_t)D_{t-1} - (T_t - G_t) = (1 + R_t)D_{t-1} - Z_t,$$

and an intertemporal budget constraint of the form

$$(1 + R_t)D_{t-1} = E_t\left(\sum_{n \geq 0} MRS^H_{t,t+1} Z_{t+n}\right),$$

where $E_t(.)$ denotes the expectation conditional on some history of states of the economy at date t. The intuition for the latter constraint is that a positive initial public debt must be backed by future primary surpluses Z_{t+n}. This constraint looks similar to the discounted expected value constraints familiar from the literature, except that surpluses are not weighted by some fixed discount factors but by a marginal rate of substitution. Since the fiscal variables contained in the government surpluses may be correlated with the marginal rates of substitution, it is not generally possible to write these constraints in terms of fixed discount factors. To see why safe public debt is not a sufficient condition for using rates of return in the constraint, note that the marginal rate of substitution is related to the n-period return $R_t(n)$ on a default-free discount bond by $E_t\left(MRS^H_{t,t+1}\right) = [1 + R_t(n)]^{-n}$. Therefore, the intertemporal budget constraint can also be written as:

$$D_t = \sum_{n \geq 0}\left(E_t(Z_{t+n})[1 + R_t(n)]^{-n} + \text{cov}\left[MRS^H_{t,t+1}, Z_{t+n}\right]\right),$$

where cov(.) denotes covariance.

If the economy evolves deterministically or if individuals are risk neutral, the covariance terms of this expression drop out. However, in the presence of risk aversion, the covariances will vanish only if future primary surpluses are uncorrelated with future marginal utility (Sargent 1987: 118). In this context, Bohn (1995: 268) notes: 'In practice, such uncorrelatedness will probably be rare, since it is difficult to imagine a tax and spending policy that is uncorrelated with government spending (itself) and with aggregate income, which are the variables determining the marginal utility of consumption.'

From a model of the kind above, a central implication can be derived. Given an initial public debt and the present value of government spending, alternative tax and debt policies do not affect the consumption behaviour of type H households. See Süssmuth and von Weizsäcker (2006) and Bohn (1999) for details. Underpinning this key finding is the assumption according to which group H agents are dynastic, whereas group L agents are short-lived. It maintains Ricardian neutrality for type H agents. Additionally, it is the production sector assumption in combination with the proportionality of public spending to income that makes the consumption of class H independent of alternative policies. To see this, it is straightforward to write down the optimization problem for a representative agent from class H, confirming that changes in taxes and public debt leave optimal consumption unchanged.

Keeping this finding in mind, let us turn to the social planner's problem in order to study whether sustaining primary deficits through low-interest debt is Pareto optimal for $\alpha^L < \alpha^H$. Since class H households are unaffected by debt policies, they can be ignored in the welfare function. In other words, because a benevolent planner cannot influence c_t^H, the weights of utilities of class H individuals in a social welfare function are implicitly equal to zero. Therefore, any Pareto optimal allocation can be obtained as a solution to the following social planning problem applying some set of positive welfare weights $\omega_t > 0$:

$$\max_{c_t^L} E_0 \left[\sum_{t \geq 0} \omega_t \frac{(c_t^L)^{1-\alpha^L}}{1-\alpha^L} \right]$$

subject to

$$E_0 \left[\sum_{t \geq 0} \beta^t \left(\frac{Y_t}{Y_0} \right)^{-\alpha^H} (Y_t - gY_t - c_t^L) \right] = E_0 \left(\sum_{t \geq 0} MRS_{0,t}^H Z_t \right) = D_0^*.$$

It is straightforward to derive the optimal state-dependent consumption path of the less wealthy agents as

$$c_t^L(s) = \left(\frac{\omega_t \beta^{-t}}{\lambda} \right)^{1/\alpha^L} \left[\frac{Y_t(s)}{Y_0} \right]^{\alpha^H/\alpha^L},$$

where λ denotes the Lagrange multiplier. This expression is a monotone function of the state's income level with elasticity $\phi = \alpha^H/\alpha^L$. To allow for this optimal consumption stream of agents L, the government has to generate state-contingent surpluses since this stream determines $Z_t(s) = (1-g)Y_t(s) - c_t^L(s)$. (This optimal consumption stream is more volatile than income because it is proportional to $[Y_t(s)]^{\alpha^H/\alpha^L}$.) The optimal debt policy, therefore, is a linear combination of a security indexed to the first state-dependent component, that is, the growth rate of income $1 + x_t(s)$, and a security indexed to $[1 + x_t(s)]^{\phi}$.

In practical terms, this implies that the public debt portfolio optimally consists of income-indexed debt plus a 'hedge fund' that has a zero present value and pays returns proportional to a specific hedge position (dependent on ϕ). For $\phi > 0$, this hedge position obliges the government to make payments when income growth is low. The government, however, receives payments in states of high income growth. Thus by recognizing and treating less wealthy households as more risk tolerant, the government uses them to insure the more wealthy and more risk averse public debt holders.

Since type L agents may not require a full compensation for taking income risk (due to their relatively more risk acceptant attitude), the return on public debt can be below the growth rate of total income in this welfare maximizing optimum. See Süssmuth and von Weizsäcker (2006) for a rigorous mathematical derivation of this finding. This result implies that financial markets do not actually absorb risk. Additionally, it does not hold for any degree of risk aversion, making it decisively different from the case analysed by Bohn (1999), in which the relatively less risk acceptant group of agents is the one comprising the short-sighted poor agents. See Süssmuth and von Weizsäcker (2006) for details. In particular, it requires $\alpha^L > 1$. Since empirical parameter estimates are most often referred to lie in the 0.5 to 3 interval (Carlsson, Darvala, and Johansson-Stenmann 2005), this is a possible case. However, if there is no *a priori* reason why the more risk-averse agents should have a longer planning horizon than the more risk accepting ones, the case of debt policies exploiting low-interest debt being suboptimal is more probable. In fact, the observation that the top 5 per cent wealthy households hold 10 per cent more in fairly safe and only 2 per cent more in fairly risky assets (such as stocks) compared to the bottom 95 per cent of households, may be interpreted differently. It may support the case in which less risk averse agents (that is the very rich class H in Bohn's set up) plan and live longer (Bohn 1999), since holding equity is generally considered a comparatively long-term strategy. In our scenario motivated by German and Italian data this suggests that less risk-averse agents of class L plan and live longer.

13.4 Conclusions

Taking recent insights on risk attitudes by wealth class from the portfolios of the rich into account, our analysis does not unequivocally yield negative conclusions about government policies that sustain primary deficits through low-interest debt (according to the Pareto Criterion for optimal intergenerational risk sharing). However, the probability of a sophisticated Ponzi game being justified is very small, for two reasons. First, a high risk aversion parameter of the less wealthy is required ($\alpha^L > 1$). Secondly, a particular demographic scenario for the two classes, in which the comparatively risk averse rich (class H) are dynastic and the rest of the society is short-lived, needs to hold. Although both of these requirements are not fully implausible, in particular the demographic scenario seems not unambiguously justified given recent data on household portfolio composition.

It remains for future work to investigate more thoroughly different constellations of risk aversion by wealth classes and demographic scenarios in a framework with heterogeneous agents. A computable general equilibrium model may be a suitable way to capture different and more realistic compositions of planning horizons and risk attitudes of a population. Such a model would also allow us to extend the study by simulating and identifying feedback effects of public debt policies on the wealth distribution, the starting point of the present study. Thereby, the interaction of inequality in risk aversion, wealth levels, and government debt policies would be captured more realistically. Another future task is the extension of the assessment of Ponzi debt games in the light of distributional aspects by numerical exercises. See, for example, Heer and Süssmuth (2007) who assess monetary policies in a realistic demographic scenario with heterogeneous agents.

However, a sound base of comparable data is indispensable for the deeper understanding of the interplay of inequality in risk aversion, wealth levels, and government debt. Recent 'high income and wealth' studies have constructed and analysed shares of income and wealth for various upper-income and upper-wealth groups within the richest tenth and even within the richest 1 per cent of the respective distribution over several decades. New work on the 'top income' agenda is documented by Atkinson and Piketty (2007) and in the 2004 conference issue of the *Journal of the European Economic Association*. More than twenty countries are covered. Unfortunately, the constructed series are (not yet) sufficiently detailed with respect to wealth composition for the wealth and income groups within the top tenth or the top 1 per cent.

A first step in this direction can be seen in a representative sample of roughly 22,000 individuals living in Germany who were asked a novel set of survey questions on risk attitudes. It has recently been made available (Dohmen *et al.* 2005) and may help to understand the interplay at the national level. However, whether observed differences in the portfolio composition and risk attitudes of the very wealthy across the G-8 economies are due to cultural differences, or caused by other factors such as regional disparities, still remains an issue for the future. To assess this will require comparable data on government bond holding by wealth percentile. The recently-initiated Luxembourg Wealth Study aims to produce internationally comparable micro-data on household net worth on which a rigorous empirical analysis and the assessment of economic policies can be based. We expect that the most promising progress in terms of data for analysis of the issues addressed in this chapter will stem from the 'top income and wealth' research programme led by Atkinson and Piketty (2007).

Appendix

We assume type L agents to be endowed with Y_t in each period t, which is an exogenous stochastic income stream with growth rate x_t. In addition, we suppose that productivities are such that for all dates t and states s, the condition

$[\beta\pi_t(s) \;/p_t(s)]^{1/\alpha^H} = 1 + x_{t+1}(s)$ holds. Furthermore, we assume class H to have an endowed wealth in period zero equal to the present value of the sequence $\{Y_t\}$. Without government activity, group H agents would then choose to consume just the same amount $c_t^H = Y_t$ as class L agents. Thus, an exchange economy is nested within our set-up.

The Euler equations of the model are characterized as follows. At each date t, let the states of nature be s_t where s_t takes values in a set S_t. The history of the economy up to date t is assumed to be $h_t = (s_t, s_{t-1}, \ldots, s_0)$, where h_t takes values in a set H_t. Let prices in period t of securities that pay one unit of the consumption good in period $t+1$ in state s_{t+1} be given by $p_t(s_{t+1}|h_t)$. Then the Euler equations are

$$E_t\left[MRS_{t,t+1}^H(1+R_{t+1})\right] = \sum\nolimits_{s_{t+1}\in S_{t+1}} p_t(s_{t+1}|h_t)[1+R(s_{t+1}|h_t)] = 1$$

where $R_{t+1} = R(s_{t+1}|h_t)$ denotes the return on a financial asset in period $t+1$ when state s_t is realized. Note that the product $MRS_{t,t+1}^H(1+R_{t+1})$ does not have to be equal to one in every state of nature. Therefore, throughout the model the marginal rates of substitution $MRS_{t,t+1}^H$ in central equations such as the transversality conditions and intertemporal budget constraints cannot generally be replaced by present value factors. In particular, they cannot be replaced by discount factors involving realized returns on government debt or by safe interest rates, even if all government debt is perfectly safe. See Bohn (1995: 259–67) for further details.

Given our assumptions about preferences, the marginal rate of substitution for a representative individual from class H can be straightforwardly shown to be equal to

$$MRS_{t,t+1}^H = \beta(c_{t+1}/c_t)^{-\alpha^H}.$$

References

Atkinson, A. B. and Piketty, T. (eds) (2007). *Top Incomes over the Twentieth Century.* Oxford: Oxford University Press.

Alesina, A., Glaeser, E. L., and Sacerdote, B. (2001). 'Why Doesn't the U.S. Have a European-Style Welfare State?' *Brookings Papers on Economic Activity,* 2: 187–278.

Becker, G. S., Murphy, K. M., and Werning, I. (2005). 'The Equilibrium Distribution of Income and the Market for Status'. *Journal of Political Economy,* 113: 282–310.

Blanchard, O. J. and Weil, P. (2002). 'Dynamic Efficiency, the Riskless Rate and Debt Ponzi Games Under Uncertainty'. *Advances in Macroeconomics,* 1: 1–21.

Bohn, H. (1995). 'The Sustainability of Budget Deficits in a Stochastic Economy'. *Journal of Money, Credit, and Banking,* 27: 257–71.

—— (1999). 'Fiscal Policy and the Mehra-Prescott Puzzle: On the Welfare Implications of Budget Deficits when Real Interest Rates are Low'. *Journal of Money, Credit, and Banking,* 31: 1–13.

Bosch-Domènech, A. and Silvestre, J. (1999). 'Does Risk Aversion or Attraction Depend on Income? An Experiment'. *Economics Letters,* 65: 265–73.

Carlsson, F., Daruvala, D., and Johansson-Stenman, O. (2005). 'Are People Inequality-Averse or Just Risk-Averse?' *Economica,* 72: 375–96.

Carroll, C. D. (2002). 'Portfolios of the Rich', in L. Guiso, M. Haliassos, and T. Japelli (eds), *Household Portfolios*. Cambridge, MA: MIT Press, 389–429.
Dimson, E., Marsh, P., and Staunton, M. (2005). *The Global Investment Returns Yearbook*. London: ABN Amro and London Business School.
Dohmen, T., Falk, A., Huffman, D., Sunde, U., Schupp, J., and Wagner, G. G. (2005). 'Individual Risk Attitudes: New Evidence from a Large, Representative, Experimentally-Validated Survey'. Discussion Paper No. 1730. Bonn: IZA.
Eymann, A. and Börsch-Supan, A. (2002). 'Household Portfolios in Germany' in L. Guiso, M. Haliassos and T. Japelli (eds), *Household Portfolios*. Cambridge, MA: MIT Press, 291–340.
Friedman, M. (1953). 'Choice, Chance, and the Personal Distribution of Income'. *Journal of Political Economy*, 61: 277–90.
—— and Savage, L. J. (1948). 'The Utility Analysis of Choices Involving Risk'. *Journal of Political Economy*, 56: 279–304.
Gregory, N. (1980). 'Relative Wealth and Risk Taking: A Short Note on the Friedman-Savage Utility Function'. *Journal of Political Economy*, 88: 1226–30.
Guiso, L., Haliassos, M., and Jappelli, T. (eds) (2002). *Household Portfolios*. Cambridge, MA: MIT Press.
—— and Jappelli, T. (2001). 'Household Portfolios in Italy'. Unpublished paper. Sassari: University of Sassari.
—— and Paiella, M. (1999). 'Risk Aversion, Wealth and Background Risk'. Discussion Paper 2728. London: Centre for Economic Policy Research.
Hauser, R. and Stein, H. (2001). *Die Vermögensverteilung im vereinigten Deutschland*. Frankfurt/Main: Campus.
—— and —— (2006). 'Inequality of the Distribution of Personal Wealth in Germany 1973–1998', in E. Wolff (ed.), *International Perspectives on Household Wealth*. Cheltenham: Edward Elgar, 195–224.
Heer, B. and Süssmuth, B. (2007). 'Effects of Inflation on Wealth Distribution: Do Stock Market Participation Fees and Capital Income Taxation Matter?' *Journal of Economic Dynamics and Control, 31: 277–303.*
Ljungqvist, L. and Sargent, T. J. (2000). *Recursive Macroeconomic Theory*. Cambridge, MA: MIT Press.
Rosenthal, H. (2004). 'Politics, Public Policy, and Inequality: A Look Back at the Twentieth Century', in K. Neckerman (ed.), *Social Inequality*. New York: Russell Sage Foundation, 861–92.
Sargent, T. (1987). *Dynamic Macroeconomic Theory*. Cambridge, MA: Harvard University Press.
Süssmuth, B. and von Weizsäcker, R. K. (2006). 'Relative Wealth, Risk Taking, and Ponzi Games'. Unpublished paper. Munich: Munich University of Technology.

Subject Index

Note: page numbers in *italics* refer to Figures and Tables.

Author Index